The Doubled Life of Dietrich Bonhoeffer

The Doubled Life of
Dietrich Bonhoeffer

Women, Sexuality, and Nazi Germany

Diane Reynolds

CASCADE Books • Eugene, Oregon

THE DOUBLED LIFE OF DIETRICH BONHOEFFER
Women, Sexuality, and Nazi Germany

Copyright © 2016 Diane Reynolds. All rights reserved. Except for brief quotations in critical publications or reviews, no part of this book may be reproduced in any manner without prior written permission from the publisher. Write: Permissions. Wipf and Stock Publishers, 199 W. 8th Ave., Suite 3, Eugene, OR 97401.

Cascade Books
An Imprint of Wipf and Stock Publishers
199 W. 8th Ave., Suite 3
Eugene, OR 97401

www.wipfandstock.com

PAPERBACK ISBN: 978-1-4982-0656-3
HARDCOVER ISBN: 978-1-4982-0658-7

Cataloguing-in-Publication Data

Reynolds, Diane.

    The doubled life of Dietrich Bonhoeffer : women, sexuality, and Nazi Germany / Diane Reynolds.

    xvi + 444 p. ; 23 cm. Includes bibliographical references and index.

    ISBN 978-1-4982-0656-3 (paperback) | ISBN 978-1-4982-0658-7 (hardback)

    1. Bonhoeffer, Dietrich, 1906–1945. 2. Women—Bonhoeffer. 3. Biography Religious. I. Title.

BX4827.B57 R46 2016.

Manufactured in the U.S.A.   03/04/2016

Thanks to the von Kliest family for permission to use the wedding photo of Ruth von Kleist-Retzow.

Thanks to Aleida Assmann for use of the photograph of Elisabeth Zinn.

For Roger and Richard

> "Do you still . . . me a bit? I still . . . you a little, but only a little—hardly at all! I think this is quite a nice letter all the same!!!"
>
> —LETTER FROM MARIA VON WEDEMEYER TO
> DIETRICH BONHOEFFER, MAY 6, 1944

Contents

List of Illustrations | xi
Acknowledgments | xiii
List of Abbreviations | xv

Introduction | 1
Prelude | 21

PART I–Pleasure and Pain (tob and ra)

1. "Sacred Space" | 25
2. Ruptures | 34
3. Life Amid the Ruins | 39
4. Happy Times | 46
5. Weddings | 52

PART II–Seeking Ground

6. Wanderings and Worries | 61
7. Manhattan | 65
8. Nazis | 69
9. London | 76
10. Battles and Choices | 84

PART III–The Incomparable Year

11. New Ground | 93
12. New Arrival | 97
13. Finkenwalde | 101
14. Murmurs of War | 107
15. First Encounter | 110
16. Ruth | 112
17. Collision Courses | 117

PART IV—Reconfigurations

18 New World | 125
19 Days of Love and Hope | 130
20 Squaring Off against the Führer | 134
21 Friendship | 139
22 "Convents" and Concentration Camps | 145
23 What Will It Be? | 149

PART V—Decisions

24 Troubles | 159
25 Escape | 165
26 Changes | 171
27 War Worries: 1939 | 176
28 London Redux | 179
29 Sailing Away | 185
30 Agony | 189
31 Do You Want Me? | 193

PART VI—War and Conspiracies

32 Homecoming | 201
33 Cold Idyll, Dark Nights | 206
34 Winter, War, Wonder, Woe | 210
35 Gert Gone | 214
36 Darker Hours | 219
37 Exile in Ettal | 226
38 The Foretaste of Paradise | 233
39 Human Hearts in 1941 | 237
40 Conspiracies | 241
41 City Life, Country Life | 247
42 Horrors and Joys | 254
43 Shadows | 260

PART VII—Cornered: 1942–43

44 Risks | 269
45 Ruth and Maria | 275
46 Sweden, Krössin, Berlin | 280
47 Maria | 288

48 Pursuit | 294
49 The Noose Tightens | 300
50 Trapped | 304
51 White Nurse | 307

PART VIII–Alone

52 Locked In | 313
53 Care and Feeding | 317
54 The Wedding Sermon | 322
55 Don't You Like Being Romantic? | 328
56 Writing and Dissatisfaction | 333
57 Doubts and Delights | 341

PART IX–Eberhard and Maria

58 Joy | 349
59 Christmas | 354
60 Berlin Falling | 362
61 Birth and Ruin | 368
62 Seesaw | 373
63 Maria, Eberhard | 377
64 Unraveled | 380

PART X–Saints

65 Catastrophe | 389
66 Endings | 392
67 Revenge | 396
68 Arrest | 400
69 Escape | 403
70 Threads | 407
71 Over | 411
72 More Threads | 414

Epilogue | 419

Appendix I: Maria von Wedemeyer Timeline: 1935–45 | 421
Appendix II: Orientation and Celibacy Questions | 428

Bibliography | 435
Index | 443

Illustrations

PART I

Figure 1: Frontispiece: Dietrich and Sabine as children | 23
Figure 2 Tübingen | 29
Figure 3: The Bonhoeffer's Friedrichsbrunn summer house | 40
Figure 4: Tübingen alley | 47
Figure 5: Tübingen, university library | 48
Figure 6: Elisabeth Zinn | 56

PART II

Figure 7: Frontispiece: 1920s Barcelona | 59
Figure 8: The Bonhoeffer manse in London | 77

PART III

Figure 9: Frontispiece: Ruth von Kleist-Retzow wedding photo | 91
Figure 10: Finkenwalde site | 103

PART IV

Figure 11: Frontispiece: Swastika-covered church, Berlin. | 123

PART V

Figure 12: Frontispiece: Sabine and Dietrich in London garden, 1939 | 157

PART VI

Figure 13: Frontispiece: Bethge and Bonhoeffer | 199
Figure 14: Backyard of Schleicher house | 242
Figure 15: Bonhoeffer's clavichord | 244
Figure 16: Woods of Friedrichsbrunn | 249

PART VII

Figure 17: Frontispiece: Maria von Wedemeyer | 267
Figure 18: Ruth von Kleist-Retzow | 282

PART VIII

Figure 19: Frontispiece: Tegel prison building | 311

PART IX

Figure 20: Frontispiece: Bethge and Bonhoeffer | 347
Figure 21: Frontispiece: Maria | 347

PART X

Figure 22: Frontispiece: Crucifix sculpture from Friedrichsbrunn church | 387
Figure 23: Pillar saint | 409

Acknowledgments

MANY THANKS TO EARLY readers Susan Yanos and Jennie Kiffmeyer, who helped steer the direction of this book. Earlham School of Religion provided a travel grant that allowed me to visit Bonhoeffer sites in Germany and Poland. Marcia Nelson, always kind and generous, helped connect the book with a publisher. Internet friends, including Elissa Schiff, Elaine Pigeon, Ellen Moody, Arnie Perlstein, and Diana Birchall, have offered ongoing intellectual stimulation as well as enthusiastic support for the project. Thanks too go to friend Jane Tipton for being an ever-faithful cheerleader and Bonhoeffer fan. Donna Cappuzzetto and Brad Cecil, librarians at Ohio University Eastern, processed a great number of interlibrary loans about Bonhoeffer. Jean Westerman, also at Ohio University Eastern, has offered welcome support. Great thanks go to Internet friend Fran Zichanowicz in Germany, who scoured her country trying to find a photo of Elisabeth Zinn, and when that failed, put me in touch with Zinn's daughter, Aleida Assmann. Scholar Aleida Assmann took time out of a busy schedule to provide a photo of her mother, Elisabeth Zinn Bornkamm, for which I thank her. I also extend thanks to the von Kleist family for allowing me to use their wedding photo of Ruth von Kleist, and to Jane Pejsa for putting me in touch with the von Kleist family. Nils Bechtel checked my German translations for accuracy. Julie Marsh of The Gentle Reader offered helpful direction on a later draft of the book. I can't say enough about my own family, who have long put up with piles of Bonhoeffer books everywhere and my new penchant for watching documentaries about Nazi Germany. Special thanks go to Bonhoeffer scholar Scott Holland.

List of Abbreviations

DB: *A Biography*: *Dietrich Bonhoeffer: A Biography* (Fortress Press, rev. ed., 2000).

DBWE: *Dietrich Bonhoeffer Works*, English edition. The number following *DBWE* indicates the volume number of the work. For example, *DBWE 8* is *Dietrich Bonhoeffer Works*, English edition, volume 8. The full list follows:

DBWE 1: *Sanctorum Communio: A Theological Study of the Sociology of the Church*
DBWE 2: *Act and Being*
DBWE 3: *Creation and Fall*
DBWE 4: *Discipleship*
DBWE 5: *Life Together and Prayerbook of the Bible*
DBWE 6: *Ethics*
DBWE 7: *Fiction from Tegel Prison*
DBWE 8: *Letters and Papers from Prison*
DBWE 9: *The Young Bonhoeffer: 1918-1927*
DBWE 10: *Barcelona, Berlin, New York: 1928-1931*
DBWE 11: *Ecumenical, Academic, and Pastoral Work, 1931-1932*
DBWE 12: *Berlin: 1932-1933*
DBWE 13: *London: 1933-1935*
DBWE 14: *Theological Education at Finkenwalde: 1935-1937*
DBWE 15: *Theological Education Underground, 1937-1940*
DBWE 16: *Conspiracy and Imprisonment, 1940-1945*

I Knew: *I Knew Dietrich Bonhoeffer*

LPP: *Letters and Papers from Prison*

Introduction

ONCE, DURING GERMANY'S DARKEST days, a twin brother and sister, closer than close, found themselves venturing in different directions. One was cast from a privileged life into one of fear and exile. The other fell in love and found the ground he had long sought in the heart of Nazi Germany.

In the "magical" spring of 1939, the brother, Dietrich Bonhoeffer, enjoyed London's sights and cinemas with his beloved twin, Sabine, and his best friend Eberhard Bethge. War loomed, and during idle moments in Sabine's garden amid the forsythia and dark mauve lilacs, Dietrich wondered if he should stay in England with the two people in the world with whom, "in contrast to . . . other people" he felt "a remarkable sense of closeness."[1] Instead, he returned to Germany.

Nazi Germany changed both twins' lives. One would die young at Nazi hands and become an international superstar, his life the subjects of books, music, and films, because he lived out his faith in struggling against the Nazis, and wrote with raw candor about his faith's place in a secular world. Yet when I went looking for a book on Dietrich Bonhoeffer and women—certainly, I reasoned, such a famous and influential man with a twin sister had spawned at least half a dozen?—I was stunned to find nothing but two brief articles. Where in all his story were his sisters, I wondered . . . and all the other women—mother, grandmother, friends, fiancée—who were part of his life? Why were they pushed to the margins or off the screen? This book, though in ways I never expected, attempts to address that question. And in doing so, it becomes more than a book about the women.

I discovered during my research that the Bonhoeffer we think we "know" differs from the Bonhoeffer hiding in plain sight. To a large extent, Bonhoeffer's saga has become what filmmaker Laura Poitras calls a "locked narrative," a single version of a story that has been told so many times that it gains a truth of its own. According to the locked narrative, Bonhoeffer,

1. Bonhoeffer, *DBWE 16*, 78.

pastor and martyr, functioned as the courageous man's man who nobly kept the female sex at bay in order to fight the Nazis. He alone was responsible for the "remarkable achievement" of writing two dissertations before age twenty-five. He alone—or with a handful of other men—fought the Nazi church. Only at the end of his life did he suddenly fall in love with a much younger woman. Bonhoeffer himself participated, if unwittingly, in creating this male-centered narrative, and it continued after his death, propelled along by his biographer Eberhard Bethge.

Why so marginalize the women who, as it happens, were highly important in his life? Klaus Theweleit's *Male Fantasies* offers one explanation:

> A further word about biographical tradition. To Ernst Bluher, one of the founders of the wandervogel, that tradition [biography] was anything but naive convention. Quite the contrary: commenting on the autobiography of Carl Peters, a German colonial in Africa, Bluher noted . . . "The book is very personal, more than one would expect; and women play almost no role in that personal content. Even mothers are given short shrift. . . . We see before us one of those indefatigable conquerors and organizers; one of those men of action and politicians who has nothing to do with women; one who needs male society, the constant company of men, an endless cycle of making and breaking friendships with them . . ."
>
> It seems to be the way of men to keep silent about their (private) women in their (public) biographies. . . . Should our analysis not then take into account cultural norms? Indeed, it must.[2]

It no doubt has been, in part, biographical convention that has obscured the women, and this erasure has dogged Bonhoeffer scholarship to this day. For example, Charles Marsh, in his recent Bonhoeffer biography, writes that Ruth von Kleist-Retzow regarded Bonhoeffer's engagement with her granddaughter with "displeasure." Nothing could be further from the truth, but Marsh does not focus on the women.[3]

In fact, the women's real stories have not been erased: the women have released portions of them, then tactfully receded. Women played a vitally important role in Bonhoeffer's life, but often they flit across the texts as disembodied shadows, easily missed, even when they speak. The gaps in the conventional narrative can be surprising: in one striking instance that becomes a metaphor for how biographers have literally *not seen* a woman

---

2. Theweleit, *Male Fantasies*, vol. 1, 27 and 26.
3. See Marsh, *Strange Glory*.

purportedly significant in Bonhoeffer's life—no photo of Elisabeth Zinn, proposed by Eric Metxas in his best-selling biography as Bonhoeffer's first fiancée, has ever been published. This surprised me—and I was grateful when Zinn's daughter provided me with the picture I include in this book. Yet perhaps I should have expected this, for no book until now has given an accurate account of the women in Bonhoeffer's life.

Shining a spotlight on the women reveals how much they mattered to Bonhoeffer, even if he often took them for granted. Although most often understood as a operating in a masculine arena, Bonhoeffer, in his last decade, had an inner circle consisting of two, and then three *women*: his twin sister Sabine, Ruth von Kleist Retzow, and in the last years, his fiancée Maria—and one man, Eberhard Bethge. This completely turns on its head the male-centered German biographical tradition. And the real story of these women—especially of Ruth and Maria—has been missed.

As Stephan Haynes aptly outlines in *The Bonhoeffer Phenomenon*, a wide range of religious groups from evangelical to liberal to radical have appropriated Bonhoeffer as one of their own. This becomes possible because Bonhoeffer reflects a prewar—what we might call a pre-postmodern—consciousness, a consciousness that no longer fully exists. We view him anachronistically, through our different set of lenses, and thus he shatters or refracts, like an abstract painting, into a dozen disparate images because he doesn't fit conventional postwar paradigms. He remains, in some sense, untranslatable. His death, shortly before the end of World War II, freezes him forever in a lost time, like the Grecian figures on Keats's urn. His world couldn't fully be laid to rest until it faced the Holocaust, the atom bomb, and the enormity of the costs of racism, colonialism, war, and the unbridled will to power. As Leo Damrosch writes in his biography of Swift, quoting Yeats: "We should see certain men and women as if at the edge of a cliff, time broken away from their feet."[4]

Being on the cusp of a new time can also explain Bonhoeffer's treatment of women. A patriarchal culture that routinely devalued the female produced him. In Weimar and Nazi Germany, this culture sometimes went so far as to valorize a male-only cult of hypermasculinity. In taking women for granted, Bonhoeffer behaved normally for his time and place. We need both to acknowledge this and be willing to interrogate this mind-set.

During his life, Bonhoeffer kept glancing backward, then forward. Modernity, which he experienced in the form of National Socialism, meant the destruction of Christianity, civilization, morality, decency, and humanity.

---

4. Damrosch, *Jonathan Swift*, 4.

As time went on, Bonhoeffer began to hope for a restoration of monarchy, rejected women leaving the home, and may have been celibate because of a deep, Victorian aversion to sex. He moved comfortably in a world of top hats and tails, princes and clicking heels, countesses and chauffeurs. His young fiancée would criticize his embrace of yesteryear's forms, such as his appreciation of the old aristocratic women who put on gloves to touch their shoes.

Yet Bonhoeffer recognized too that the backward gaze boxed him in: this, arguably, explains why he dropped his prison fiction projects. Instead, he took his theology as far out as it could go forward in his letters to best friend Eberhard Bethge, paving the way for the postwar world. In many ways, Galileo is an apt cognate, a man who recognized that the earth revolved around the sun, but who lacked the theoretical apparatus to prove it—stunningly, the man could drop objects of different weights from a tower and measure their rate of fall, yet lived in a world that had not conceived of gravity. Galileo died the year of Newton's birth, a hairsbreadth before gravity would have made sense of his observations. Bonhoeffer died the year a new world started to come into being.

A Doubled Life

Living in Nazi Germany forced Bonhoeffer to pretend to be what he was not, to lead a double life. As Iranian literary critic Azar Nafisi notes, "the worst crime committed by totalitarian mindsets is that they force their citizens, including their victims, to become complicit in their crimes."[5] From habitual lying as he pretended to be a loyal citizen of the Reich to getting involved in an assassination plot, survival meant appearing to become a mirror of what Bonhoeffer hated, as all the while he struggled to maintain his integrity. Nafisi writes that it's easy to undervalue the immense import of the small gesture in a totalitarian setting: a loose lock of hair escaping the veil in 1980s Tehran or a psalm reading (considered "Jewish") at Bonhoeffer's Finkenwalde seminary in Nazi Germany both became subversive gestures.

The world of his childhood home stuck deeply with Bonhoeffer, and he called it "a refuge, even a sacred space." He sought to replicate it all his adult life, especially as a defense against the National Socialist state. As many have mentioned, it permeated his vision of his various seminaries. As he himself repeatedly noted, he did not find people fungible: he couldn't simply randomly replace one person with another, and the very idea repulsed him. Yet

---

5. Nafisi, *Reading Lolita in Tehran*, 76.

at the same time, he did replicate or double in his adult life the *patterns* of his childhood.

Bonhoeffer's personality also could be double-sided. Like the fictional Mr. Darcy in *Pride and Prejudice,* he could be cold to outsiders, shunning those he disliked or who didn't interest him, and yet filled with warmth and generosity to those who made it into his inner sanctum—or to those more peripheral figures on whom he freely bestowed his charm.

Silences

In the inverted world of Nazi Germany, gaps and absences become presences or clues. People in Nazi Germany routinely wrote and spoke in what Leo Strauss called esoteric language, language with one meaning in ordinary discourse and another to those in the know. When the Bonhoeffer family would otherwise look bad in primary source documents, footnotes often explain a statement as code, but in some cases, the meaning of what one suspects might be code—such as late in his prison experience Bonhoeffer asking his fiancé Maria to fix his underwear—is lost.

As Bethge himself points out, silences speak—missing diary pages, for example, in his opinion, indicate Bonhoeffer's involvement in the anti-Hitler conspiracy. Bethge, naturally, does not point to his own silences or evasions—nor do the women around Bonhoeffer, who are so careful in their wording. Yet patterns emerge as these habits of silence and double entendre extend beyond the war and become texts through which we can read a different story from the locked narrative.

The rich, complex density of Bonhoeffer's life also complicates writing his story. Bethge's biography reflects this complexity: it extends to more than 900 pages, and yet it leaves out almost everything about the women—Bonhoeffer's extraordinary relationship to Maria, for example, covers a scant three pages. (The Bonhoeffer world cries out for an exhaustive, multivolume biography.)

Given that I added the stories of important women in his life to an already complex narrative, writing a manageable account inevitably became for me an exercise in compression. Thus, this biography is not an account of the Confessing Church struggle nor is it an account of the anti-Hitler conspiracy. Instead, it goes *behind* the church struggle and the plot against Hitler to the people, like Sabine, who motivated Bonhoeffer's actions and brought life to his theology. For Bonhoeffer, this personal experience was crucial: he found the personal in the theological and the theological in the personal. As Robin Lovin and Jonathan Gosser note, coming to grips with

Bonhoeffer's life becomes not an interesting add-on but "a necessary project." They write, "it is only as the man emerges for us from his work [or, I would say, as that work emerges from the man] that we are restrained from appropriating his suggestive, enigmatic and fragmentary words and twisting them entirely to our own purposes."[6]

I don't dwell unduly on Bonhoeffer's theology, but my understanding of it deeply informs my understanding of Bonhoeffer himself. A few basic principles or premises about his theology underlie this book and can be summed up as follows:

As mentioned above, the theological is always the personal for Bonhoeffer. He could be reticent about his personal life, but his theology is always shaped by his dialogue with his circumstances.

Bonhoeffer's theology is deeply this-worldly. He finds his grounding for this in what he calls the Old Testament and what we might call the Hebrew bible. He deeply appreciates prayer, but as a complement to, not a substitute for, action. He values the sensual joys of this life—but sacrifices them too.

His theology is also deeply communitarian. He rejects a theology that runs as followed: I—an individual—am "saved" because I have verbally accepted Jesus Christ, am baptized, go to church, pray, and take communion. He rejects a notion of personal salvation that allows people to bury their heads in the sand and ignore injustice as long as they themselves are "churched." He rejects a theology that says we don't have to worry about worldly suffering because this will get worked out in heaven after we die.

In tandem with the above, Bonhoeffer rejects piousness and religiosity focused on personal purity. He is willing to risk sin—and sin boldly—to save others.

Bonhoeffer's theology is radically centered in Christ. Christ for him is the Jesus of the Sermon of the Mount who preached peace and forgiveness. He rejects attempts to fashion less demanding substitutes for this theology: worship of nation, custom, or institutions, even the church.

While I initially tried to include every woman who crossed Bonhoeffer's path in my book, I had to cut deeply or end up with a biography of multivolume proportions. I have instead offered a few examples of women who flitted peripherally across his life, alongside the women most important to him. I have also, with regret, compressed Bonhoeffer's rich time in Barcelona, Manhattan, and Berlin before the Nazi takeover, because these periods

---

6. Lovin and Gosser, "Dietrich Bonhoeffer," 148.

brushed only glancingly against the relationships on which I focus. Compression also inevitably meant losing some of the movement that characterized Bonhoeffer and others of his class, who crisscrossed their country with dizzying frequency, travelling around Germany so often, even during the height of the World War II, that our own "on the road" Americans begin to look pedestrian.

Life doesn't rhyme, and although I initially meant to write book reframing Bonhoeffer through the lens of women, I very quickly found that impossible without highlighting the central role of Bethge, whose arrival on the scene almost exactly ten years before Dietrich's death was the seismic event of Bonhoeffer's last decade—and arguably of his life. Without acknowledging this, no sense could be made of the configuration of his relationships with women.

If women have been routinely downplayed in Bonhoeffer's story, Bethge, the all-important best friend, has not. As early as the 1950s, the intimacy of the prison letters raised questions about the nature of his relationship with Bonhoeffer: were the two more than close friends? John de Gruchy, in his Bethge biography *Daring, Trusting Spirit*, all but connects the dots about the "special friendship" between the two men—but never does. In his recent biography, Charles Marsh, while hovering suggestively around the issue of Bonhoeffer's sexuality, also doesn't take a definitive stand, beyond opining that Bonhoeffer was celibate. My book explores this issue, while making a distinction between being same-sex attracted and *acting* on the orientation—to be same-sex attracted doesn't imply "crossing a line," whatever that means. I will openly argue, however, that Bonhoeffer went beyond emotional friendship with Bethge and was *in love* with him—and that Bonhoeffer's fiancée knew it. And while the *physicality*, though not the orientation of the Bethge/Bonhoeffer relationship is largely irrelevant to my project, the book will weigh the evidence as to celibacy. It will, as well, explore the seeds of a nascent queer theology in Bonhoeffer's writing.

Truth-telling is essential, no more so than when uncomfortable, and I hope an exploration of the sexuality of one of the Christian martyrs of the twentieth century might, like the Catholic Church's openness in revealing the faith struggles of Mother Teresa, help others who struggle. Paraphrasing Christian blogger Justin Lee, if we can accept that someone of Bonhoeffer's stature might have struggled with his sexual feelings, "maybe your nephew or best friend will have someone to look to as a role model, to know that he doesn't have to leave his faith behind because of what he's experiencing."[7] And as is so often the case with Bonhoeffer, either side can have it their own way.

---

7. Lee, "Questions from Christians #4."

The first pages of this book outline in quick strokes the early years of Bonhoeffer's life, with an emphasis on his close relationship with his sister Sabine. These years formed him, led him to become a theologian, and sent him into lonely wandering in search of "a ground to stand on." These years also included times of great foreboding, perhaps best illustrated through Sabine, in her younger days possibly the most polished of the four daughters (though she would deny it), the one who made the wealthiest match, a woman artistic, musical, nurturing, and witty, but so distressed by the Nazis that her life was thrown into upheaval.

Because Bonhoeffer met two of the most important women in his life, Ruth von Kleist-Retzlow and Maria von Wedermeyer, as well as Eberhard Bethge, in his last decade, I chose to concentrate on that period—the time, from the start of the Finkenwalde seminary, that Dietrich repeatedly called "the incomparable years." For from 1935, no matter how dark the outer world, Dietrich had found his long-sought "ground to stand on."

I tell the stories of three women in his inner circle: Sabine, Ruth, and the young woman dragged there unwittingly, Maria von Wedemeyer. Some have asked, why not concentrate more fully on Bonhoeffer's mother Paula? Paula clearly had an enormous influence on her son's life: she established the pattern of domestic living he loved and recreated in his seminaries, fostered his love of music, took an intense interest in his theology and the church struggle, and stayed in touch with him on almost daily basis: her importance can hardly be overstated. Yet Bonhoeffer did not include her in his innermost circle, did not make her privy to his innermost dramas. While highly involved in their lives, she kept her children at a distance, insisting on the prerogatives of rank: parents above children. Dietrich turned early to other women to meet his deeper intimacy needs: Sabine, his governess, his grandmother. Paula does sometimes joke with Dietrich, but with her, he is more reticent, more respectful, more careful in presentation, less likely to take on the casual and sometimes demanding tone he adopts in letters to his inner circle. Paula, though ever-present in this volume, as she was in her son's life, thus remains an outsider. And while the book focuses on the inner circle women, many others appear in the text: Bonhoeffer's sisters, including forthright Christel, who could intimidate Bethge (and reminded him of Paula), nurturing Ursel, whose self-starvation during the war years was possibly loving with a vengeance, and the outgoing but ever awkward Susi, as the youngest, always racing to keep up. The book also includes the scholar Berta Schulze, as well as dissident Elisabeth von Thadden, who signaled her contempt for Hitler by heiling with a limp wrist, along with aunts and governesses, friends and supporters, the indefatigable seminary housekeeper Mrs. Struwe—and Elisabeth Zinn—and because life does not rhyme, periods when the women (seemingly) fade away and Bethge and the "brethren" necessarily take center stage.

The book attempts to include some of the look and feel of Germany during Bonhoeffer's life. It helps, for instance, to understand that the freezing temperatures Bonhoeffer repeatedly writes about from remote Sigurdshof in 1939–40 refer to the coldest winter in Europe in one hundred years. We can understand the heroic lengths Bonhoeffer's mother must have gone to when he sent her his laundry if we understand that during World War II, rationing meant every German got a single matchbox size bar of soap once a month for washing both body and clothes. It adds to our appreciation of his fiancée Maria's dedication to acknowledge the filthy train cars in which she travelled to visit him or the way Berlin's devastation confronted her every time she rode the trolley to his prison. In a similar way, I have tried to capture what to the modern mind is a startling aspect of the German church struggle: both the openness of the Nazi reaction against Christianity and the extent to which most of the clergy, though not Bonhoeffer, were willfully blind to the hostility.

Bonhoeffer and Hitler

It's almost impossible to write a book set in 1930s Germany without bumping up against Hitler.[8] Much as I wished the story we have of that period had taken a different turn, I had to accept that it didn't. I found myself, instead, desperately looking for redemptive moments in Hitler's life, as if by finding one, I could somehow make sense of the suffering he inflicted. I faced instead that Hitler never transcended his lowest instincts. His character comes across as, if opportunistic, also fundamentally rigid, unchanging, mechanistic, and frozen in outlook, lending credence to writers such as Lucy Dawidowicz, who insists Hitler knew what his goals were in 1919 and never deviated from them.

In contrast, people like Bonhoeffer, Maria, and Ruth, among many others in his circle, emerge as fully human, capable of growth, change, humility, empathy, and self-transcendence. The forceful Ruth, indomitable, dominating, self-willed, not one to second-guess her decisions, experienced moments of uncertainty and self doubt. Bonhoeffer had a deep experience of transformation after the failed Hitler assassination attempt of July 20,

---

8. To avoid entering the many lively debates on whether we should interpret history through the lens of the so-called great man or through impersonal socioeconomic forces, I use "Hitler" to represent both a distinct individual and the larger mind-set of National Socialist ideology.

1944—there's a reason beyond the obvious that Bethge kept his poem "The Friend" in his wallet for the rest of his life. And who can forget Maria, trekking with a rucksack (not a suitcase!) miles across a cold terrain in February 1945, trying to bring supplies to Bonhoeffer at Flossenbürg long before he had arrived?

Albert Speer, Hitler's architect and armaments minster, became for me a counterpoint to Bonhoeffer. Born just eleven months earlier than Bonhoeffer, he grew up in the same privileged milieu. Yet his choices could not have been more different. By throwing in his lot with Hitler, he earned unparalleled privilege and prestige at the same time that Bonhoeffer courted risk and reprisal. Yet amid his splendor, Speer recounts his torment at long afternoons spent with Hitler's entourage, almost entirely with people he despised as uneducated petit bourgeoisie. He sat through many a social weekend of excruciating monotony and boredom, the life sapped from him, years later almost snarling with resentment at the memory of what he endured for ambition's sake. In contrast, during this same period, Bonhoeffer experienced what he would call "a foretaste of paradise," surrounded with people he loved, and working to build Christian communities he hoped would redeem Germany.

It can seem as if ethical individuals like Bonhoeffer, Sabine, Ruth, and Maria sprang out of nowhere, but nothing could be less true. While reticent in talking about the depth of their faith lives, all those in Bonhoeffer's inner circle, including, of course, Bonhoeffer himself, were deeply religious in the purest sense, though Bonhoeffer vehemently came to reject the word *religious* as hypocritical and self-righteous. All the same, a deep-seated felt *experience* of the living Christ (not based on lip service nor mere intellectualism, though Bonhoeffer would consistently try to distance himself from "enthusiasm") animated the lives of Bonhoeffer's inner circle and made their moral discernment easy if anguished—they had no trouble telling barbarity from faith, cruelty from kindness, cowardice from courage, living spirit from intellectual abstraction or rationalization. This real faith—so difficult to write about as it only manifested in actions that are too easily divorced from their roots, as if the actions stand alone or come from rationality alone—defined the heart of this group. Yet it could also frustrate: If Bonhoeffer and his friends "got it," so many did not, notably the arid intellectuals in Manhattan espousing a philosophical/political social justice gospel cultivated parallel to rather than from faith, and fellow pastors in Germany who didn't see that the Christ spirit could never tolerate anti-Semitism. Bonhoeffer drew close to others who "understood"—among them, spirit-filled blacks in Harlem in whom he saw the face of Christ as well as his dissident church cohort in Germany. His inner circle—Sabine, Bethge, Ruth, Maria, and others in his life—based their lives on this faith. These people all happened to be Christians, but Bonhoeffer also developed an extraordinary sensitivity to like-minded people whatever their faith backgrounds, whether Jewish, atheist, or something else—and touchingly, even on his last full day of life, rather than force his Christianity on another, he demurred from giving a sermon because an atheist prisoner might be offended. Only when the prisoner urged him to speak would Bonhoeffer proceed. An elite of such decency as he had known and been, which he understood cut across class and faith lines, he hoped, would one day run Germany.

As I sought to place myself in the world that Bonhoeffer and the women around him would have experienced, the German people also became a character in the story. I grew up with a post-war US narrative of Germans as the Other, but my immersion in their culture changed my views. Yes, as Theweleit argues in *Male Fantasies,* a group that became a nucleus of Nazism enjoyed violence for violence's sakes, reveling in blood spurting, people dismembered, screaming, dying, and smashed to pulp, just as some people today enjoy beheadings and live burnings, but these were and are a minority. One of National Socialism's chief challenges—and defeats—lay in its inability to change the way many ordinary Germans clung to human decency: imposing the death penalty for giving a loaf of bread to a foreign worker only reveals the desperation of a regime unable to stem small acts of kindness and mercy. I read over and over too from foreign travelers in Germany in the 1930s expressions of love for the German people and their awareness of how many suffered anguish over the actions of its leaders. This is not in any way to discount or excuse the atrocities committed by ordinary Germans or the inaction that Bonhoeffer so roundly condemns, or to equate qualms of conscience experienced amid ease and comfort with the immense bodily and mental sufferings of Jews and others, but to add gray areas to the story. Important to this book, though necessarily silent in their writing, is what people like Maria and Dietrich saw as they constantly crisscrossed Berlin and Germany. We know Maria witnessed the abused prisoners working on her family estate under the jurisdiction of the SS—she even obliquely comments on it once. This brings us back to both anachronism and silence—what people of the era knew and could not say, under fear of being accused of treason, is in many ways outside of our own everyday experience—and yet ever-present behind what the players write.

While it could be troubling at times to read accounts of Germans traumatized and outraged by being ousted from a house by a Pole at war's end, as if this somehow ranked worse than the immense slaughter, torture, and suffering of Jews, Poles, Russians, and others (and showing an all too human propensity to highlight our own sufferings and discount those of others), I also found it refreshing to read the accounts of those who took responsibility, as Bonhoeffer had hoped to do. One of many that stands out is Anonyma,[9] who in *A Woman in Berlin,* while writing wrenchingly of the repeated and incessant rape she and other women suffered at the hands of the sitting Russian army, also acknowledges, as other Germans do, that whatever was done to them was more merciful than what their people had done. In this awareness of human moral responsibility, in this empathy, as Bonhoeffer (and Sabine and Ruth and Maria) so well understood, was the beginning of redemption and renewal.

The Phases

Bonhoeffer's life falls into six phases:

I. **Security:** Birth to age twenty (1906–1926). Sabine's marriage marks the first great rupture in his life. But 1918, when World War I hit home, also marks a division.

II. **Wandering:** Age twenty to twenty-nine (1926–1935). Bonhoeffer wanders and achieves, writing two dissertations, each published as a scholarly book, and a third book on Genesis 1–3. During this time he lives in Barcelona, Manhattan, and London. Manhattan marks a watershed: his whole view of the world changes during his year at Union Theological Seminary.

III. **Joy:** Age twenty-nine to thirty-six (1935–October 1, 1942). Bonhoeffer's incomparable years: He finds fulfilling work in running seminaries and meets crucially important people. He publishes *Discipleship* and *Life Together* and works on *Ethics*.

IV. **Change:** Age thirty-and-a-half to early thirty-seven (October 1, 1942–April 5, 1943): A liminal period during which it becomes clear he can't evade arrest and other changes.

V. **Imprisonment:** Age thirty-seven to early thirty-eight (April 5, 1943–July 20, 1944): First phase of imprisonment.

VI. **Sainthood:** Age thirty-eight-and-a-third to thirty-nine (July 21, 1944–April 9, 1945): Second phase of imprisonment.

---

9. Another is writer Christa Wolf.

INTRODUCTION

How do we unearth some of the reality of Dietrich Bonhoeffer, this man for whom the personal was always the theological and the theological always the personal?

Beyond his own writings, we look inevitably—necessarily—to the fragmented and elusive, often frustrating, memories of those who knew him, to letters and memoirs.

Bonhoeffer and his cohort spent so much time on the phone I'm amazed we have any letters at all. I'm also surprised that nobody has yet stumbled on Gestapo tapes of phone conversations—the Gestapo were tapping Bonhoeffer and his brother-in-law's phone lines at least as of late 1942 and probably earlier. In writing or reading about Bonhoeffer, however, we necessarily fall back on the letters we have, keeping in mind that they represent the tip of the communication flow between people in almost constant phone contact: even before World War I, the parents had installed a phone line in their summer home in the Harz mountains, and friends over and over marveled during his life at the frequency of Bonhoeffer's calls to and from home. Ruth, a consummate networker, also seems to have been almost continuously on the phone.

I puzzled over why they wrote letters when they were always talking on the phone and recognized that the letters fall into several categories: Bonhoeffer routinely exchanged birthday letters with those closest to him, particularly, of course, Sabine, Ruth, and Bethge. Friends also commonly exchanged Christmas letters (falling in time anywhere from Advent to New Year's). People wrote personal thank you letters as well. Bonhoeffer often shoots off brief letters with packages home to his mother or postcards when in transit, for example, while "laid over" in Amsterdam on a flight from Berlin to London. In Manhattan in 1930, while he telegraphed home frequently, telephoning Berlin was so difficult and so expensive (the equivalent of $60 a minute in our money) that even the Bonhoeffers eschewed it, so Bonhoeffer wrote letters. At other times, letters clearly express emotions or ideas that can't be verbalized easily, put plans in writing, or continue conversations already begun. And "over and beyond all that" as Bonhoeffer might have said, moments simply occurred when people wanted to write to one another. Finally, we get to the prison years, where Bonhoeffer was without phone access most of the time. Here letters became a lifeline. But the letters don't reflect the fullness of the dense, close, entwined relationships.

I sometimes met with surprises during my research: for instance, while I expected them to be close, I was startled at how very close Dietrich felt to Sabine for his entire life. This became difficult to document, especially after World War II began. During the war, Sabine increasingly became a shadow in terms of texts: we have nothing like the robust interchange between

Bonhoeffer and Bethge or Bonhoeffer and von Wedemeyer. Yet, even without a detailed correspondence, we can trace that Sabine was never far from Bonhoeffer's thoughts—and at times his emotions burst out with surprising clarity, such as when he wrote in frustration to Bethge from prison that he kept asking his family over and over about Sabine and not getting a response. At other times, we find out how much she occupied his thoughts in more oblique ways. Bethge's biography also corroborates how close Dietrich felt to Sabine, but he does so with such understatement that it can be easy to overlook. In addition, as Bonhoeffer's niece Renate Bethge writes, Bonhoeffer himself stuck to a code of "reserve and keeping silent . . . above all, about things that affect one most deeply."[10]

Bonhoeffer's relationship with Ruth can seem confusing. His deep attachment to her becomes clear especially in his prison correspondence with Maria, but Ruth often felt neglected and frustrated by his absences. He was busy; she was demanding; he was a younger person in better health and hence with greater mobility—the older Ruth often could do little but invite and wait, saying she would not beg him visit, and he was the man, sometimes oblivious to how he was treating the woman—yet to him she was a muse, kindred spirit, and comfort, the dearly loved woman whose home, where he so often ended up, soothed his soul.

Sources

A helpful source for the layout of the church struggle and the extent to which women participated is Victoria Barnett's *For the Soul of the People*. Sabine Dramm's *Dietrich Bonhoeffer and the Resistance* offers a fine analysis of the various plots to kill Hitler. Ferdinand Schlingensiepen's lively biography of Bonhoeffer came out as I began working and I found it helpful as well. Renate Wind's short biography, *A Spoke in the Wheel*, offered useful snippets: for example, she contacted Elisabeth Zinn while Zinn was still alive. I discovered Lisa Dahill's feminist work on Bonhoeffer's theology early on and have found it lucid and validating. My understanding of Bonhoeffer has been informed and enriched as well by a host of Bonhoeffer scholars such as Ruth Zellner, John de Gruchy, and Clifford Green, just to name a few.

Despite being often largely overlooked, many of the women themselves wrote their stories: Sabine published a memoir, while Ruth von Kleist-Retzow left an unpublished draft of her life which became a main source for Jane Pejsa's *Matriarch of Conspiracy*. An anecdotal and helpful first-person source, *I Knew Dietrich Bonhoeffer*, includes accounts of various friends and

---

10. Bonhoeffer, *DBWE* 7, 202.

family, including women. Mary Bosanquat's *The Life and Death of Dietrich Bonhoeffer*, the first Bonhoeffer biography, functions almost as a primary source, as it relies heavily on interviews with Bethge and Sabine, who Bosanquat became friends with in 1948, and even includes a smidgen of correspondence from Bonhoeffer's aged governesses. Fiancée Maria left her love letters and an essay about Bonhoeffer, some published diary entries, and a brief but telling 1974 television interview. Bonhoeffer's sister Susi wrote recollections that Schlingensiepen used. She also gave a filmed interview, as did sister-in-law Emmi Delbrück, and Maria's older sister, Ruth-Alice von Bismarck. Along with these sources, Fortress's sixteen-volume *Dietrich Bonhoeffer Works*, now completely translated into English, includes letters by women. The context, introductions, notes, and appendices in these volumes have been very helpful.

Working with primary sources, while a gift, presents challenges and these must be treated with care—these accounts are subjective, inherently unreliable if invaluable, often leave out precisely what one wants to know, and sometimes are frustratingly vague as to dates, though they often present consistent and comprehensible emotional landscapes. As far as possible, I have tried to cross-reference or find logical reference points for dating and for corroborating information.

Remarkably few have consulted Maria von Wedemeyer's letters as a source of information. When in doubt, I have used them to place Dietrich and Maria, assuming he—or she—would know better than anyone else where they were at significant points in life, especially shortly after the fact. I have tried to correlate Maria's letters with the prison correspondence to Bethge as well as to the prison fiction, since Bonhoeffer did all this writing at the same time. Often, not surprisingly, Bonhoeffer would repeat himself in letters to Maria and Bethge, in which case what he omits in a letter to one or another becomes telling. If nothing else, I hope this book succeeds in beginning the recovery of Maria as the full and extraordinary—and too often misused—human being she was. In addition, since she has so often functioned as a stick figure in texts and hence not received full attention, I have included my own Maria timeline in the appendix, knowing that more will be revealed should her journals be made more fully available, as I hope they will. Maria's later memories of the events of her courtship have to be used with care, however, as her recollection of events grew hazier over time.

If we want to gain a sense of an embodied Bonhoeffer, the television interviews with the women, especially his sister Susi and sister-in-law Emmi, who grew up in the same neighborhood with him from the time he was ten, help flesh him out. We have no audio recordings of Bonhoeffer and only a one- or two-second snippet of film in which he tosses a ball. Bonhoeffer's

English might have had more of an American accent than his sister's and sister-in-law's, but from Susi and Emmi we can get a sense of the commanding (to American ears almost stereotypically "Nazi") cadence he must have had. Susi and Emmi speak decisively, assuredly, with self-possession and without hesitation. Since contemporary accounts emphasize Bonhoeffer's assurance, we can imagine he sounded, with a deeper voice, very much like these sisters. As I listened to them and watched them, I saw women used to being in charge, sure of their privilege, and completely unintimidated by the camera. This, I thought, was Bonhoeffer.

Bethge, the gatekeeper to Bonhoeffer, both eyewitness to many of the events in the last decade of Bonhoeffer's life as well as author of a monumental biography, pours out floods information—and yet withholds. His biography is labyrinthine, winding up and down and back and forth and sideways and all around—woe to the poor researcher who fails to note a page numbers. To some extent, this reproduces the labyrinthine, ever-moving quality of Bonhoeffer's life—but Bethge's method frustrates a straightforward narrative. I toyed with the idea of writing a non-chronological narrative, so that I could laser focus on the women and skip everything else, but feared leaving the reader entirely confused. Also, I had spent so much time unraveling chronology (the timelines in the Dietrich Bonhoeffer *Works* series were helpful starting points), that I felt I should preserve this part of the research.

As noted above, Bethge's monumental biography marginalizes women. Bethge had choices and his choice as late as the 1960s to write within an anachronistic tradition that downplayed females might say something to us about the Bonhoeffer he hoped to construct.

Bethge's *opinions* often function, in practice, as fact. One must be careful or what Bethge *believes* can come to carry the de facto weight of truth. I believe that Bethge deliberately obfuscates the nature of his relationship with Bonhoeffer, going so far, at least once, to quote from a letter and then supply an explanation of what Bonhoeffer meant that is badly out of context. He also evades issues by veering away from them (his weaving narrative adds to this), and by using understatement or esoteric language. Even the title of his biography: *Dietrich Bonhoeffer, A Biography,* implies an agenda-lessness, a dealing in objective fact, that no biography can reasonably assert. His story also sometimes simply varies from the other primary sources, especially for figures such as Maria von Wedemeyer. All the same, his book provides a valuable, often first-person account of a life, much as he tried to distance himself from that stance by using the third-person voice.

The periods of Bonhoeffer and Bethge's separation led to spikes in letter writing, and thus offer incomparable windows into their relationship—these times include in the summer of 1936, June of 1939, the winter of 1940–41, and of course, the prison correspondence.

Charles Marsh's biography came out after my manuscript was almost complete. I have found it both well written and informative, and at first my heart beat happily—sometimes wildly—as certain statements seemed to confirm a suspicion I held or to point to a passage of lyrical beauty I'd missed in the primary source material. My heart thumped, for example, when I read in Marsh that Elisabeth Zinn bore a striking resemblance to Sabine—I had only read, previously, accounts that she bore a vague, indefinable resemblance to his twin. As one of my working theses was, that in a gentle and humane way, Bonhoeffer replaced people in his life with people who reminded him of people he liked, I was excited, but I couldn't source this tidbit, and so had to drop it. In another instance, I thought I had missed a particularly colorful passage from a childhood trip to the beach in which, one night, "the wind caused an unfastened shutter to beat against the side of the house in loud, startling claps,"[11] but couldn't find that particular detail in the source: this is not necessarily to criticize a method that seeks to capture the lyrical essence of a moment but to note that our approaches differ. In the end, Marsh's primary interest is not the women, and so the old distortions remain.

Marsh's effete Bonhoeffer is not my Bonhoeffer—I agree, for example, that Bonhoeffer liked to dress well, but primarily from pride in his appearance rather than a "flamboyant abbot" quality. My Bonhoeffer is primarily masculine in dress, performance, and outlook. And while I don't miss the privilege Marsh notes, especially Bonhoeffer's blindness to his gender privilege, what most strikes me is the man struggling, if often failing, to transcend his circumstances.

In addition to privilege, upheaval also formed him: Bonhoeffer truly led a doubled life. Despite privilege, he went hungry during World War I, an experience unknown to most modern Westerners. He worked, albeit briefly, on a farm as child: he gratefully gleaned wheat as if he were a biblical Ruth or Naomi. When he saw hungry people on the streets or on a train, wealthy as he was, their experience could not be abstract to him. If few of us can brag of living at the level of privilege that Bonhoeffer enjoyed—maids, chauffeurs, brilliant parties, grand pianos, first-class travel, summer homes, and access to palaces—most of us also haven't lived with bombings, raids, hunger, imprisonment, and finally, in a Nazi concentration camp.

Since laughter and lightheartedness don't predominate in Hitler's Germany, what can get lost in this grim period—one of deep threat—is the sense of humor Bonhoeffer and many of his cohort shared. I have tried to capture

---

11. Marsh, *Strange Glory*, 18.

some of the wry wit that shines forth from Sabine's memoir, and I have snagged some fleeting glimpses of Bonhoeffer's humor in his correspondence. Bethge shows flashes, as does Maria, who had a deeply sardonic outlook. These individuals' humanity perhaps emerges most deeply in their ability to joke through the dark moments.

We've tended to sanctify Dietrich Bonhoeffer, but by his late thirties, he himself had learned not to seek perfection. "A bit more selfishness would make one truly selfless," he wrote from Tegel prison on March 19, 1944, regarding his fiancée's mother, who was "always wanting to do 'good.'"[12] To him, too much self-sacrifice became a form of egotism—yet he laid down his life for his beliefs.

He did his best, however, not to die at Nazi hands and that reflected his theology. For him, one lived the religious life in the midst of the world's joys and struggles, in the center, as he put it, of the village. This reflected Old Testament—Jewish, hence in Nazi Germany, subversive if not illegal—theology. He never, like his mentor Harnack, advocated stripping the Jewish Scripture from the Christian Bible.

Against the backdrop of National Socialism, Bonhoeffer's struggle to be human and decent stands out sharply. I have tried to depict him as a full person, which I think makes him more admirable, not less. He himself resisted being cast as a "pillar saint," though ironically he became one. In life, he could be short-tempered, arrogant, demanding, and excluding—but he could also be a person who loved deeply and cared deeply, a person of extraordinary perception, groundedness, and gentleness, a person of deep loyalty, deep faith and deep conviction, a person largely able to maintain integrity in a extraordinarily dark period. He is worth reading about. Most of all, both he and the women around him have lives worth seeing—if that is ever possible—as they really were.

A Note on Usage: Dietrich, not Bonhoeffer

A problem emerged for me in writing as I strove for gender equity. How could I call Bonhoeffer "Bonhoeffer," while calling Maria von Wedemeyer "Maria" or Sabine Bonhoeffer-Leibholz "Sabine"? Yet a constant run of Leibholzes and von Wedemeyers became too clunky. I chose, therefore, to use first names, a move which underscores the intimacy of these relationships. Hence Bonhoeffer is Dietrich, a first name he was proud of. Exceptions include Hans von Dohnanyi and Franz Hildebrandt—their first names are so common that it made better sense to reference them by surname. I do refer

---

12. Bonhoeffer, *DBWE 8*, 325.

to Dietrich's grandmother sometimes as Tafel, her maiden surname, and I refer to Eberhard as Bethge when I want to indicate his role as biographer or chronicler rather than player in the action. The Bonhoeffer sisters I refer to by their more personal names: Susi instead of Susanne, Ursel instead of Ursula, and Christel instead of Christine, mostly to emphasize the closeness of this family. This underscores the extent to which I felt that I got to know the family—the dirt between Susi's toes as she throws herself into play in Friedrichsbrunn, the sweat I imagined pooling under Christel's arms as she ironed her brother's shirts in Tübingen. In other cases, I use names in the way I hope lends the greatest clarity to understanding.

This book uses both the 1971 *Letters and Papers in Prison* and the later translation of that work released by Fortress as *DWBE 8*. In some cases, the earlier translation of certain letters, such as Bonhoeffer's description of being formed by the Harz mountains, had become so familiar to me that it seemed odd to use the later translation, in the same way that non-King James versions of the Lord's Prayer can seem alien. In other cases, *DBWE 8* included information left out of the earlier version, so I also relied on it.

Prelude

THE BRESLAU HOUSE OF Dietrich's birth, with its parlor maids and governesses, nurses, chambermaids, gardeners, and cooks, Piranesis in the dining room and an acre of garden, could have been the setting for a novel. The parents were firm and distant. The father, a prominent psychiatrist who never subscribed to the seemingly outlandish theories of his colleague, Sigmund Freud, functioned as the undisputed patriarch or "ultimate authority" in the household—though his wife ran the home.

This family of origin became the template that Dietrich Bonhoeffer would repeatedly try to reclaim in later life: the best friend closer than close, the mentoring grandmother figure, the brothers and sisters morphing into "brethren," until, in the end, these patterns and repetitions led to a final dramatic clash.

Dietrich came from a patrician world of wealth, status, and privilege. He referred to his family as "middle class," but this presupposed a level of comfort, education, and status that most of us would describe as wealthy. His contemporaries knew him as part of a trans-European elite marked by striking similarities in taste, education, and breeding. His aunts were countesses in Munich and the Netherlands, while friends owned large landed estates or held prominent government posts. Some, like the labor-minded Bishop of Chichester, lived in palaces, while his aristocratic Prussian friends lived in manor houses. In one of the many bizarre tableaux that marked the end of the Nazi era, Bonhoeffer's aristocratic fiancée stayed in her cousin's turreted medieval castle, where the women gathered after dinner as in a fairy tale, spinning thread at their wheels as Allied troops drew closer.

While Bonhoeffer was not a member of the aristocracy (he had no telltale "von" in his name) his mother came from an aristocratic lineage. Her father had served as court preacher to Emperor Wilhelm II. Bonhoeffer floated on a sea of money—albeit at strained times during the inflation of the early 1920s—in sharp contrast to most of his fellow Berliners. "Our families lived, at that time, the broad and comfortable life of the well-to-do" remembered his friend Gerhard von Rad. "If we wish to understand Dietrich Bonhoeffer, such as his great candour and the worldly assurance he retained in all situations, we must know that he came from a splendid home."[1]

Thus, while Bonhoeffer's life story is more complicated than an account of privilege suggests, his drama plays out against the backdrop of privilege. Yet we do Bonhoeffer a disservice if we forget that his privilege meant he could have—and chose not to—escape suffering in a way only dreamed about by ordinary people.

Because of love, that greatest leveler, he left safety when he could have had it and stepped back into Nazi Germany.

---

1. Zimmermann and Smith, eds., *I Knew Dietrich Bonhoeffer*, 176. Others attest to his aristocratic and wealthy qualities: e.g., Paul Lehman, a friend from Union Theological Seminary in 1930, noted in a BBC radio talk after the war that "his [aura of] aristocracy was unmistakable, yet not obtrusive" (ibid., 50). Theologian Robin Lovin, after studying his life, wrote of Bonhoeffer's "aristocratic reserve" (ibid., 147). Josiah Young, in *No Difference in the Fare*, was one of the first secondary sources to draw attention to Bonhoeffer's high status.

PART I

Pleasure and Pain
(*tob* and *ra*)

— 1 —
"Sacred Space"

When Dietrich was born, along with twin sister Sabine, on February 4, 1906 in Breslau, the sixth and seventh of eight children in a seemingly idyllic family, few could imagine the upheavals that would later mark, scar, and form him.

Dietrich's father, Karl, held a position as professor of psychiatry and director of the Breslau University Hospital of Nervous Diseases. In 1906, while servants and the prominent pediatrician A. Czerny[1] fussed over the new Bonhoeffer twins, Adolf Hitler, a lackluster teenager with a drooping face, drifted around Vienna on an orphan's pension, hoping to become a painter. Hitler was the last person anyone from Bonhoeffer's cohort could have imagined gaining the power to wreak havoc on the Western world. World War I remained blissfully unanticipated, at least by the Bonhoeffers.

If Sabine had been able to revisit Breslau after her return to Germany in 1947, she would have seen the city of her early childhood virtually obliterated. As in Berlin, long blocks of bombed-out buildings stood still and ash white like crumbling bones against the sky, while great, desolate hills of rubble filled the empty lots. The Holocaust had hollowed out this Jewish cultural center, once numbering 5 percent of Breslau's population in a country less than 1 percent Jewish. Now called Wroclaw, part of Poland, the city worked to eradicate any vestige of a German past. Most Germans had been forcibly expelled, and what had not been destroyed, either by the Nazis or the Russians, faced an uncertain future.

Sabine, who as a German would no longer have been allowed in the ghostly ruins of her birthplace, had with Dietrich spent her earliest childhood in a house there at Birkenwäldchen 7, among a sea of siblings and servants. The family lived near Scheitinger Park, where broad walkways circled a placid lake, and one could stroll amid Japanese-style gardens across humped bridges, seeing in the distance park buildings topped with pagoda-like towers. Birch trees surrounded their family home, while a balcony overlooked

---

1. Bethge, *DB: A Biography*, 18.

the vast backyard. Older family members played tennis on the court next door. In this household, Sabine would later write, she and her siblings grew up in "an order that seemed firmly enough established to last forever."[2]

In 1909, the younger Bonhoeffer generation swelled to eight, with the birth of Dietrich's sister, Susanne, called Susi, the final child in the family. His parents grouped Dietrich with the two youngest daughters as the "little ones," though in reality Susi was the odd one out in this trio. One idyllic photo shows the family circled harmoniously around infant Susi. Sabine and Dietrich, on either side of the sleeping bundle, glare at their new rival with intense and deadly concentration.

Dietrich and Sabine, he flaxen-haired liked an angel, she with a thick brown mane, grew up closer than close. "We were always united," Sabine remembered, with a "special unity" they did not share with their other siblings.[3] In contrast, Dietrich would later refer to his three older brothers as of a different "generation." They, in turn, dismissed him for having "no interests" because he did not share theirs.[4]

In 1910, Sabine sat by four-year-old Dietrich in his party frock, the white dress little boys wore, watching him stroke his blue silk underskirt with a small hand. Later, she remembered, he watched baby Susi as she sat on their grandfather's knee, golden sunlight pouring in on them.

In quiet moments, their mother, Paula, told the tiny Sabine and Dietrich Bible stories. The children couldn't yet read, so, to their delight, Paula, her hair wound in plaits, showed them illustrations from a big picture Bible.[5] Dietrich addressed his first theological questions to his mother, early on showing his penchant for placing God in "this world," asking her if the "good God" loved the chimney sweep, and if God ate lunch.[6]

Paula, though a countess's daughter, had trained as a teacher and passed the state teaching exams, so she taught her children herself in their early years. She also made sure her children grew up in an intellectually rich environment: her homes had classrooms with desks, books, a zoology room with live snakes and lizards, a carpentry room for the boys and a doll's room for the girls, musical instruments, and a box of costumes for performances.

---

2. Leibholz, *The Bonhoeffers*, 4.

3. Ibid., 32.

4. Bethge, *Dietrich Bonhoeffer*, 10; also Bosanquet, *The Life and Death of Dietrich Bonhoeffer*, 41.

5. Leibholz, *The Bonhoeffers*, 20.

6. Ibid., 37.

In these early days, the twins played together in the sandbox behind their big brick house.[7] They built castles and volcanoes, created marble courses and magic fountains and galloped together on hobbyhorses. Sabine remembered Dietrich playing intensely, heedless of thirst, "a mass of ash blond hair around his sunburnt face."[8] They visited with the animals in a carriage house converted to a barn and baptized baby dolls, but Dietrich soon turned his attention to horses and a knight's castle.[9] Later, amid World War II's bombings destruction, fear, and food shortages, Paula would recall the "many happy children's birthdays with cakes, whipped cream, Punch and Judy shows and masquerades."[10]

At Christmas, the twins joined the family in festivities fit for *The Nutcracker*. As the youngest, Dietrich, Sabine, and little Susi walked in first on Christmas Eve to view the lighted tree. Holding hands and looking up in wonder at the flickering candles and shining ornaments, breathing in the scent of pine, the three would sing, in their childish voices, "Christmas tree, loveliest of trees." Dietrich's hair, almost white, was like a halo. As they sang, the older siblings, parents, and servants filed in and joined them.

Paula had been "a mystical vision" when her husband-to-be first saw her in all her blond-haired, blue-eyed beauty. Now, in a lace-collared black velvet dress, her fair skin flushed with pleasure, she read aloud the Christmas story, as everyone, including the "maids in their white aprons" sat in a circle around her in the parlor. Paula's eyes filled with tears as she spoke of Mary pondering the words of the Holy Spirit. This show of emotion distressed young Sabine and Dietrich, whose hearts lifted in relief when their mother's face once again cleared, and the joyous Christmas carols began.[11]

Highest in hierarchy amongst the small army of household help were the governesses Maria (called Horchen) and Käthe Horn. These sisters belonged to the Hernhuter branch of the Moravian Brethren. Paula herself had attended a Moravian boarding school in Gnadau. In the 1700s, this sect had been saved from persecution by the German Count Zinzendorf, who as a child had sent letters to Jesus fluttering from tower windows of his family castle.

Dietrich yearned to protect Käthe Horn. "When I am big, I shall marry you, then you will stay with us always," he told her.[12] During the Christmas

---

7. Bethge, ed., *Last Letters of the Resistance*, 95.
8. Bosanquet, *The Life and Death of Dietrich Bonhoeffer*, 24.
9. Zimmermann and Smith, eds., *I Knew*, 19.
10. Bonhoeffer, *LPP*, 196.
11. Bosanquet, *The Life and Death of Dietrich Bonhoeffer*, 32–33.
12. Ibid., 29.

holidays in 1930 when he was studying in New York, he may have visited Käthe in Cuba,[13] amid palm trees and clusters of vultures on the roofs. The Horn sisters' Moravian teachings, hymns, and prayers would stay with him all his life, and it is tempting to imagine that the first seeds of his ecumenicalism were planted by these heirs to Zinzendorf, who had promoted ties between Moravian, Lutheran, and Reformed churches.

Around Easter of 1912, the Bonhoeffer family moved to Berlin, to a home near the royal palace and next to Bellevue Park where the royal children played. In a perhaps uncanny foreshadowing of so many of his children's futures, their father, in his memoir, described the new house as having "something of the character of a dungeon."[14] All of the large rooms, lined up in a row, communicated with a narrow corridor that ran the length of the home. Before school, the children, wearing the old-fashioned, hand-sewn clothes that their mother preferred, breakfasted on the verandah, eating rye bread, butter, jam, and hot milk—the hated milk often ending up poured in window boxes until Paula ordered it replaced with hot cocoa.

Berlin boomed in these prewar years, but remained a city of extraordinary cleanliness and order, despite its rapid growth. Foreign visitors linked the city's safety to the German respect for authority—perhaps too much respect in the eyes of some Americans, who noticed "verboten" signs everywhere.[15] Even so, in 1913, seven-year-old Dietrich was frightened when, separated from his twin, he had to head by himself to school at Friedrichs-Werder Gymnasium. Paula had a servant walk with him, but on the other side of the street, so that Dietrich would not be embarrassed.[16]

Dietrich was proud of having been born minutes before Sabine. Both sisters in the youthful trio dubbed him "their knight in shining armor who protected them." They were "happy to let him play the role of older brother." Dietrich would hold up his arm and make a fist to show off to Sabine his "splendid biceps."[17]

Between school terms the children sometimes holidayed in Tübingen near the Black Forest, home of their grandmother, Julie Tafel Bonhoeffer.

---

13. Bethge does not have him visiting Käthe in Cuba (see *DB: A Biography*, 151), but Bosanquet, who corresponded with the Horn sisters, does. See *The Life and Death of Dietrich Bonhoeffer*, 87.

14. Bosanquet, *The Life and Death of Dietrich Bonhoeffer*, 25.

15. Blackbourn, *History of Germany: 1780-1918*, 283. In 1900, Jerome K. Jerome wrote a satire on the German submission to authority, while in 1914 Thomas Mann finished *The Loyal Subject*, a novel about middle-class German "self-abasement" that became popular when published after the war.

16. Leibholz, *The Bonhoeffers*, 33.

17. Ibid., 31.

In Tübingen, church steeples mingled with red-tiled-roof buildings and crooked streets opened into cobbled plazas. Tall, half-timbered shops in the town squares evoked a German fairy-tale world—or perhaps a Disney World to modern eyes. From their grandmother's balcony, the twins gazed down on Neckar River, which wended its quiet way, sparkling in the sunshine and reflecting the patterns of the leaves of the plane trees that lined its shores. Strolls through the town led to a castle, perched on hill, or past the Tübingen synagogue, which would burn during the Nazi Kristallnacht in 1938.

"Tall, half-timbered shops . . . evoked a German fairy-tale world." Tübingen retains much of the character of a pre-war German city. The house overlooking the Neckar where Julie Tafel lived no longer stands.

On other holidays, the Horn governesses and the Bonhoeffer children took off in grand style in two reserved train compartments for the family vacation home in Friedrichsbrunn. The train chugged west, towards the Harz Mountains, usually during the Easter school holidays or summer break.

The children were, in birth order, the three older boys, Karl-Friedrich, Walter, and Klaus—Klaus, the youngest of these boys, five years older than Dietrich—and then sisters Ursel and Christel, twins Sabine and Dietrich, and finally, little Susi. The train would take them to the town of Thale with its steep hills, legends of dancing witches and Teutonic gods, and a grand stone Gothic church in the town square. The boys hiked the roughly four miles[18] through the mountain woods, where mosses and mushrooms grew, to the unelectrified brick Friedrichsbrunn summerhouse, while the girls, governesses, and trunks arrived in horse-drawn carts.[19]

Both Sabine and Dietrich adored their time in these mountains. "Some of my happiest childhood memories are of the holidays we spent there,"[20] wrote Sabine. Dietrich would later muse that the hills and forests of the Harz had formed him.

During these holidays, big brother Walter showed the younger children where to find strawberries, raspberries, and little lobsters amid the hills and trees. He built a raft for sailing on the mountain lakes. Once he killed a falcon with one shot, but when he saw the dead bird, he burst into tears.[21]

By day, the twins explored the nearby village, which stretched along a rambling dirt road with a small stone church near one end. They swam and gathered berries or crawled around on the ground to find mushrooms in the woods. Novels, including *Uncle Tom's Cabin*, absorbed Dietrich as he sat under the rowan trees in the meadow by the house. In the evening, he and his siblings played games or sang songs, and watched the mists rise and wrap themselves around the tall fir trees.[22] Sometimes, the parents joined the children and their governesses.[23] One photo shows a governess surrounded by the Bonhoeffer brood, little Susi with her arms raised exuberantly in the air, while the parents watch benignly from the fringes of the scene. The children talked frequently with their often absent parents: the summerhouse might have no heat or electricity, but the parents did install a telephone.

On July 28, 1914, as eight-year-old Dietrich and Sabine enjoyed the horse-drawn merry-go-round and "pretty stalls" at the Friedrichsbrunn village shooting festival, cries went up: war had started. Miss Horn, her face pale and drawn, tore the children away to pack for Berlin, while the excited

---

18. Six kilometers.
19. Leibholz, *The Bonhoeffers*, 7.
20. Ibid., 6.
21. Ibid., 16–17.
22. Zimmermann and Smith, eds., *I Knew*, 26.
23. Leibholz, *The Bonhoeffers*, 26.

villagers dismantled the fair. Later that night the children heard the shouts and songs of the jubilant soldiers, ready for battle.[24]

The Kaiser and the German high command counted on a quick war, but instead, the fighting bogged down.

A few months into the war, their cousin Lothar arrived back in Berlin "half blinded and limping on crutches, head and legs swathed in bandages . . . [but] quite unbroken in spirit,"[25] a source of fascination to the twins. Another cousin, Hans von der Goltz, wearing a blue uniform, visited the family en route to the front. Delicate, fair haired, and blue eyed, he seemed too ethereal for war—and soon enough was killed.[26]

As the death tolls mounted, the twins would lie awake in their beds at night talking in their high-ceiling bedroom. "We had very serious discussions about death and eternal life," Sabine remembered. For months, they concentrated on the word *eternity*, trying to clear themselves of all other thoughts. They tried to imagine the nothingness, or perhaps transcendence, of death, comforted by the phosphorescent gleam of the glowing crosses above their beds. They said the word *eternity* over and over again. "We often felt dizzy," Sabine recalled. They shared intense conversations about theology and developed rituals to ward off evil, each vying to be the last to say "good night" to the other. By doing this, Sabine believed, she was saving Dietrich from being "'devoured' by Satan." These rituals remained "an absolute secret between us twins," Sabine said. There was, as well, "a secret language between us."[27]

At eight, Dietrich began piano lessons and soon his talent shone forth, even amid a musical family. He showed sensitivity as an accompanist, often playing for Paula as she sang. The two grew closer over music.

Paula cried when nine-year-old Dietrich broke a front tooth and had to have it replaced with a false one. Sabine "was quite dismayed at Mama's tears."[28] During this period, Dietrich had a hard time writing school essays, and Sabine often helped him.[29]

Paula, with a long, slim face, her hair still often plaited and wrapped around her head, was "intelligent, warm-hearted and unaffected,"[30] but also emotional, with a temper. "If we were disrespectful to others she did not

24. Ibid., 4, and Bosanquet, *The Life and Death of Dietrich Bonhoeffer*, 34.
25. Leibholz, *The Bonhoeffers*, 4.
26. Ibid.
27. Ibid., 33, also, Zimmermann and Smith, eds., *I Knew*, 24–25.
28. Since Bonhoeffer seldom opens his lips for a photo, it is impossible to see how the false tooth looked. As no one mentions it, it no doubt passed muster.
29. Bosanquet, *The Life and Death of Dietrich Bonhoeffer*, 31.
30. Zimmermann and Smith, eds., *I Knew*, 19–20.

hesitate to box our ears,"³¹ Sabine remembered. Sabine also noted, with some of her characteristic wryness, the double standard that prevailed in the house. Their father chided the children if they forgot to run an errand for their grandmother—"We were even then made to realize that such forgetfulness in the young was egoism and inexcusable thoughtlessness." However, "if my mother forgot something it was because it was too much to demand and because she lacked the strength."³²

In 1916, hunger hit even this wealthy and privileged family. The German government, bent on a speedy war, had not worried as farm workers flocked to the front. But now, between the war dragging on and a British blockade, food disappeared. People, eating turnips, subsisted on starvation diets of 1,000 calories a day, not even enough for children.³³ More than 700,000 Germans starved during the war,³⁴ and many more feared they might.

In response, the Bonhoeffers moved to the Grunewald neighborhood on the western edge of Berlin, to a house at 14 Wangenheimstrasse. Their acre of grounds allowed them to keep a goat and poultry. Dietrich saved money for a hen, and became expert at learning to find black market sausage, milk, and butter.³⁵

Like their other homes, this grand house held antiques, German mountain landscapes painted by relatives, and in their father's study, great tiers of books that ran up the twelve-foot walls. A broad staircase swept to the upper floors. In the huge parlor, the obligatory grand piano "formed no more than an agreeable incident," while in the dining room, the table that seated twelve stood like an island in "a lake of shining parquet." Velvet curtains separated a smoking room from the dining room. Upstairs, the children found more rooms than they had ever before counted. Despite a family of ten, plus a staff of servants, the family easily absorbed frequent houseguests and sometimes soldiers.³⁶

In these days of scarce food, Dietrich, a fast-growing boy, often complained to Sabine of his gnawing hunger. In January 1918, the eleven-year-old described to his grandmother a dinner at the next door neighbor's house in Grunewald: sausage soup from a newly slaughtered pig, with "vegetables,

---

31. Leibholz, *The Bonhoeffers*, 6.

32. Ibid., 12.

33. "Starvation and Disease."

34. Ibid. There's debate about how many starved, versus dying of opportunistic diseases such as influenza, brought on by hunger, but the important point is many people died.

35. Bosanquet, *The Life and Death of Dietrich Bonhoeffer*, 35.

36. Ibid., 26–27.

asparagus and carrots," followed by coffee and preserves, tea, and cheesecake, a simple enough meal in ordinary times, but a feast to a hungry boy. The youngster also drank a "very good wine, of which everyone was served quite a lot."[37]

Yet as 1918 moved onward, the Bonhoeffers remained insulated from the war's cruelest effects. Karl-Friedrich, who took physics books to the front with him in his knapsack, and Walter, who loved the outdoors, sallied off cheerfully to the Western front.

Now Paula moved Dietrich to a bedroom of his own, and Susi shared with Sabine. A wall separated him from his twin, his other half; he would knock on it so the two could continue their nightly meditations. Did he feel like a paper doll torn in half, alone for the first time in a dark, high-ceiling chamber, a thick, hushing layer of plaster separating him from Sabine? Susi remembered that he would knock on the wall three times to alert them each time he thought of God.

Games and school days continued. When choosing teams, Dietrich picked Sabine first, even over stronger players, so they could be together—even though he liked to win. "Inevitably we were a team," Sabine recalled. Each invited the other along when "some new adventure...presented itself."[38] One adventure involved digging "underground passages" in the backyard and plotting warlike stratagems against their enemies, brother Klaus among others, with the goal of trapping them in "a deep hole."[39] Other children often joined them, but Sabine and Dietrich needed only each other. They were, Sabine remembered, "self-contained with their own relationship."[40]

---

37. Bonhoeffer, *DBWE 9*, 19–20.
38. Leibholz, *The Bonhoeffers*, 32.
39. Bonhoeffer, *DBWE 9*, 23.
40. Bosanquet, *The Life and Death of Dietrich Bonhoeffer*, 30.

— 2 —

Ruptures

One bright early May morning in 1918, while twelve-year-old Sabine prepared to head for school, two telegrams arrived. Her father read them. He turned pale, walked into his study, sat at his desk, and put his face in his hands.[1] Sabine, standing in the hallway, would have seen her father's silver-handled walking stick gleaming in the sun, jackets and shawls lined neatly on their hooks, as the day turned dark.

Paula, "deathly pale," wore a heavy black mourning veil to Walter's funeral as horses slowly pulled the hearse to the Berlin chapel. Black-clad mourners entered silently. Dietrich, sitting beside Sabine, joined in singing the somber funeral hymns. Uncle Hans von Hase preached the service. As friends carried the casket from the church, trumpeters played a hymn chosen by Paula: "What God has done, that is well done."

Walter, eighteen, had died of an infection when splinters from an exploded shell pierced his leg. He had been in France two weeks.[2] Death had danced around the edges of Dietrich's consciousness since his earliest days in Breslau watching the black plumes on the horses who pulled the hearses headed for a nearby cemetery, and in memories of a child drowning near their summer home—and the near miss when Maria Horn heroically saved a drowning kindergarten teacher. Now death had fully arrived at the Bonhoeffer doorstep, an experience Dietrich would never forget. "This drew the first line across the children's lives,"[3] wrote his biographer Bosanquet. Paula took to her bed, unable to cope.

That June, to allow their mother time to convalesce, Dietrich and Sabine arrived at the Baltic resort town of Boltenhagen. They had hoped to enjoy the sand dunes and cool sea breezes with Susi and Maria Horn, and their cousin Hans-Christoph von Hase. Instead, they met with a malevolent seascape of turbulent, crashing waves. They tossed washed-up jellyfish back

---

1. Leibholz, *The Bonhoeffers*, 17. Walter actually died on April 28.
2. Ibid., 18–19.
3. Bosanquet, *The Life and Death of Dietrich Bonhoeffer*, 35.

into the water, and eagerly bought shovels and a flag from a kiosk. Dietrich, aching because of Walter's death (and, no doubt, his mother's withdrawal, for he would never forget her "wild suffering"), was rude, at least to Susi.[4]

The children built fortresses and ramparts, dug canals, and ate food still scarce at home: eggs, sausage, ham, butter, and milk. They sunburned sleeping in a sandcastle and hiked three miles up the beach to a town where they had a hard time trading their ration coupons for bread. In the evenings, they played music. One day, when a storm "suddenly raged very violently," covering their wicker beach chairs with sand, Dietrich, housebound with the rest, wrote to his grandmother: he had seen two planes crash, killing a pilot. When the surviving pilot flung himself into the sea, trying to drown himself, Maria Horn discussed the incident fully with the curious children.[5] Acts of nature, acts of war: both seemed of a piece with the whirlwind the world was becoming.

Back at home that summer, Dietrich and Sabine dug out an underground cave in their yard for war games. Dietrich rode horses with his cousin Klara, and in the fall, food still scarce, went for a holiday to his cousin von Hase's farm in Waldau. He eagerly immersed himself in rural life, gleaning wheat, reporting knowingly on the yields of beets, wheat, grapes, and apricots, steering livestock to hay bales, and even driving a wagon.[6]

In November 1918, to the great shock of the nation, Germany surrendered amid domestic upheaval. Wilhelm II abdicated and fled the country. Karl Bonhoeffer remembered the day of the Republic's formation, which forestalled a communist revolution, writing of "pale starved figures covered in sweat . . . addressing the soldiers with excited gesticulations and dragging the guns from their hands . . . [while] others . . . perhaps hurried more quickly to their places of business."[7] As part of their bifurcated lives, the privileged Bonhoeffer children passed through this "curious sub-revolutionary atmosphere"[8] on their way to school.

Maria Horn wept at the abdication of the Kaiser, but none of the Bonhoeffers joined her. The Bonhoeffer parents rejected the Horn sisters' fascination with royalty, veered to the urbane left of the governesses' provincial conservatism, and frowned at their raptures over royal sightings in Berlin.[9]

4. Schlingensiepen, *Dietrich Bonhoeffer 1906–45*, 13.
5. Ibid., 14
6. Bonhoeffer, *DBWE* 9, 24.
7. Bosanquet, *The Life and Death of Dietrich Bonhoeffer*, 39.
8. Ibid., 39.
9. Leibholz, *The Bonhoeffers*, 4.

For if wit, artistic talent, and imagination flourished in the family, so too did a rigid belief in their own ways. The Bonhoeffer aversion to "mannerism and affectation of thought" sharpened their intellects, and yet "made them intolerant, even unjust,"[10] remembered Emmi Delbrück, later wife of Dietrich's brother Klaus. Karl Bonhoeffer could be withering in response to what he considered banal questions or comments. Emmi contrasted him to her own father, who "took even the silliest questions of us children quite seriously . . . so that we were encouraged to ask. In the Bonhoeffer family one learned to think before asking a question or making a remark." A cold or sarcastic response from a parent was "embarrassing" or "absolutely devastating." In addition, rigidity in small matters prevailed: "In theory, one was liberal in tolerating other styles of living, but in practice the English 'that's not done' played so great a part that you felt it as soon as you were inside the porch."[11] Sabine remembered she and her siblings being encouraged to play with the local Friedrichsbrunn children at their summer home, but also that the local children were lined up and made to wash their hands with soap and water before receiving snacks from the Bonhoeffers.

"It was only on very special occasions that we received kisses from our parents," Sabine recalled. "I can positively count the number of times this happened."[12] Susi envied the attention her father paid to the children who came to him as patients, wishing it were for her.[13] Dietrich and Sabine turned to each other early for the intimacy and warmth that their parents did not provide.[14]

"We were," Sabine wrote, "very dependent upon one another."[15]

Dietrich also depended on his grandmother Tafel, who, with her white hair pulled into a tight bun behind her slender, ruddy face, became comforter and counselor, dispenser of wisdom and welcome, a figure more approachable than his parents. Tafel, in turn, lavished attention on her grandson, as

---

10. Zimmermann and Smith, eds., *I Knew*, 36.
11. Ibid., 36–37.
12. Leibholz, *The Bonhoeffers*, 58.
13. Wind, *A Spoke in the Wheel*, 5.
14. In his biography of Albert Speer, Hitler's architect and armaments minister, and a contemporary of Bonhoeffer from the same social class, Van Der Vat notes that "displays of emotion were discouraged" in what he calls the German "grande bourgeoisie," who were "more Victorian than the Victorians" (*The Good Nazi*, 12). What perhaps set the Bonhoeffer parents apart is the extent to which they tried to provide a compassionate and child-centered upbringing for their children.
15. Leibholz, *The Bonhoeffers*, 33.

she did on both children and grandchildren.[16] She was a forthright, unsentimental caretaker, treating aid to others as a civic duty that extended beyond the bounds of family. She noticed the plight of marginalized women and helped found both a home for elderly women and a domestic school for poor girls. At the same time, she never opened herself to what the family considered the "ridicule" of becoming a feminist and never stepped out of the conventional role of wife and mother.[17]

Embracing that role, she threw herself into activities. She was "wearing herself out with Christmas preparations," Dietrich wrote to his parents. "She always says you are best able to develop a resistance to an illness if you participate in everything."[18]

Paula remained convalescing at a neighbor's home during the fall of 1918, still in shock from Walter's death, but slowly improving. "In the morning, she still feels quite weak, but in the afternoon she feels steady again," Dietrich wrote to Tafel on December 8. "Sadly, she still eats hardly anything." The doctor thought that in "eight days," she could "get up for an hour at a time."[19] Dietrich hoped she would return home for Christmas Day.

Christmas 1918 dawned dismally, the snow of a few days before turning to slush, but Dietrich's letter to his grandmother radiated cheer as he thanked her for the postcards and stationery he had asked her for. "All of us received a tremendous number of things," he wrote, for him books and a war game among other gifts, and a plate of "goodies."[20]

In early January, Paula returned. She was not yet well, but mending. Outside, the political situation remained in turmoil. A revolt and a general strike lasted until January 12. Dietrich wrote to his grandmother that the communists had attacked the Halensee train station, just half a mile from the Bonhoeffer home, but "they only got bloody heads." Meanwhile, schools extended their winter breaks due to a coal shortage.[21]

Amid the turmoil, the twins took dance lessons together, the muscular Dietrich, "still in shorts," initially treating dance as a "form of

---

16. Bosanquet, *The Life and Death of Dietrich Bonhoeffer*, 21.

17. Ibid., 21, 50.

18. Bonhoeffer, *DBWE* 9, 77. This may be a criticism of Paula's withdrawal and illness after Walter's death.

19. Ibid., 25.

20. Ibid., 27.

21. Ibid., 27. (See note 2 for attack on Halensee. The "800 meters" the editors speak of would be almost exactly one-half mile.)

physical training." Eventually, he became good at it, gracefully enjoying the open waltz, the quadrille, and the francaise, Sabine, his dance partner, remembered.[22]

In May 1919, Germany, still destabilized and still fearing a communist takeover, signed the Treaty of Versailles after Britain reblockaded its ports, threatening the country with another bout of starvation. Dietrich commented on the victors' demands in a letter to his parents, noting the harshness of the terms, "but to be sure," he wrote, remembering the hunger, "one has to keep in mind that our enemies might eventually halt food shipments until we accept."[23] The Bonhoeffers, along with other Germans, felt the humiliating sting of the defeat, but the family wholeheartedly supported the new Weimar Republic and the possibilities inherent in democracy.

In contrast, Albert Speer, Hitler's architect, designer of the staging of the Nuremburg Rallies, drew different lessons from the crisis. In his tersely worded opening chapter about his childhood in *Inside the Third Reich*, Speer, just a year older than Dietrich, reflected on his own class privilege. He had spent his childhood in a lavish fourteen-room apartment with a staff of servants and a spectacular crystal chandelier. He noted that only twenty or thirty families in his town, Mannheim, a booming industrial center, lived at the level of luxury enjoyed by his family.[24] Yet he also suffered the privations of the war, including the hunger and the "turnip days"—periods when only turnips were available—before his family, too, like the Bonhoeffers, moved to a home where they could grow food.[25] For Speer, the answer to Germany's crisis would be offered not by democracy but by a seemingly messianic dictator who promised to restore the shattered German psyche: not only offering a scapegoat to explain the defeat, but a plan for world domination.

---

22. Zimmermann and Smith, eds., *I Knew*, 27.
23. Bonhoeffer, *DBWE*, 9, 29.
24. Speer, *Inside the Third Reich*, 4.
25. Ibid., 7.

— 3 —
Life Amid the Ruins

ON NEW YEAR'S EVE of 1920, thirteen-year-old Dietrich and Sabine were allowed for the first time to stay up for the New Year's celebrations. Finally, they could join in high-spirited family traditions that included a card game predicting the future, drinking hot New Year's punch, and helping to relight the Christmas tree candles—and listen as their mother read the 90th psalm.[1] Near the stroke of midnight, they all joined in Gerhardt's New Year hymn —"To God who to this hour/Has given us life and power"—and "when the sounds of the last verse had died away, the bells were already ringing in the New Year."[2]

For their fourteenth birthday in February, young Dietrich and Sabine hosted a party. The warm weather enticed the twins and their guests outside to play, where they "even danced a little" under a bright sun that made the frost sparkle. The family gave Dietrich, pegged as a future musician, sheet music and a Beethoven biography. Since food shortages continued, Dietrich also received coveted bread ration coupons and sausage.[3]

February 24, 1920, marked the official birth of the Nazi Party. The twins continued their bifurcated existence, living in comfort while outside their sheltered environs problems brewed and people went hungry. Dietrich, now fourteen, maintained a full schedule of piano, swimming, rowing, and dance lessons in addition to school. He joined the Boy Scouts and found their exercises and war games "very nice." Rowing lessons kept him from Susie's August birthday party. Sabine studied art, dancing, and violin. In the fall, Christel, who had a "highly sensitive brain which might have served a man better,"[4] began to attend Dietrich's Grunewald gymnasium. Dietrich wrote to his grandmother that his school now had "quite a few girls."[5]

1. Zimmermann and Smith, eds., *I Knew*, 28–29.
2. Bosanquet, *The Life and Death of Dietrich Bonhoeffer*, 33.
3. Bonhoeffer, *DBWE* 9, 32. Rationing continued after the war had ended.
4. Bosanquet, *The Life and Death of Dietrich Bonhoeffer*, 30.
5. Bonhoeffer, *DBWE* 9, 30.

In April and again in July, Dietrich vacationed in Friedrichsbrunn, writing to Klaus in July of sunny weather and "unbelievably many mushrooms." He wondered if their grandmother would like some, dried, for her birthday.[6]

Though a café has been added to one end and more buildings have sprung up around it, the Friedrichsbrunn house appears largely the same as in photos from years past.

Dietrich visited Nordhausen, "an extremely beautiful old town with a magnificent Romanesque cathedral. We were in it. . . . It is obviously still used as a Catholic church," he wrote to his parents. It marked his first time inside

6. Ibid., 34.

a Roman Catholic sanctuary, where he "was completely surprised by the splendor" of the gold-covered altar and richly colored paintings of saints and the Virgin Mary. "One can understand how something like it could attract simple people," he wrote.[7]

December brought Boy Scout piano recitals and another visit from the disabled but ever fascinating cousin Lothar. Paula's steadily improving health meant a livelier Christmas too, with guests and dancing, not to mention a new sled for Dietrich.[8]

"The decisive influence [on Bonhoeffer]" wrote his biographer Bethge, "was Berlin and its complex diversity . . . the conservative and cosmopolitan Berlin, with its academic and working class sectors, its concert halls and museums; the Berlin of street brawls and political plots."[9]

As Dietrich traversed Berlin, he would have seen what outsiders did just after the Great War: pock-marked, crumbling buildings, shabby facades in need of paint, old newspapers fluttering or smashed in gutters, all a mirror of morale in tatters. Berliners looked half starved and ragged. Former soldiers milled around the streets and sometimes begged, often leaning on crutches, often missing limbs.

Kay Smith, lively and twenty-two, the wife of US assistant military attache Truman Smith, arrived in Berlin to be startled by children with rickets, and bullet holes marring the façade of the posh Adlon Hotel, a gracious beacon of the old international order with its lobby encased in fin-de-siècle gold, bronze, marble, mosaic, and glass. It shocked her when her maid asked if she could eat the remains of her husband's runny breakfast egg. "'Eat that cold, smeared egg! . . . Why?'" The maid explained she had not tasted an egg since before the war. When Kay told her to eat all the eggs she wanted, the maid, in turn, was shocked—in German households food would be kept under lock and key.[10] Dietrich himself remarks in a 1920 letter of having his first "whipped cream" since the end of the war.[11]

Berlin had ballooned from 172,000 people in 1800 to nearly 2,000,000 by 1900, its enormous growth fueled by German unification. Mark Twain likened it to vibrant Chicago with its sprawling 900 square kilometers of

---

7. Ibid., 35–36.
8. Ibid., 32.
9. Bethge, *DB: A Biography*, 23.
10. Nagorski, *Hitlerland*, 13–14. Speer, too, spoke of his grandmother counting sugar cubes and keeping them in a locked container.
11. Bonhoeffer, *DBWE* 9, 40.

space.¹² Yet unlike Chicago, Berlin would never become a city of skyscrapers, instead remaining a spreading land of parks and gardens, a city Dietrich traversed with remarkable frequency and freedom from his early teens on.

Like other observers, playwright Carl Zuckerman witnessed the desperation. Berliners, lacking other alternative, increasingly turned to selling their bodies. At one Berlin club party, the waitresses, who could be "freely handled," wore nothing but "transparent panties" embroidered with a silver fig leaf. A sign on the wall called "Love . . . the foolish overestimation of the minimal difference between one sexual object and another."¹³ Back in Berlin while his parents travelled, Dietrich wrote to them of letting "all the blinds down in the evening" for fear of crime. "Isn't that unbelievable?" he commented about the desperation, *unbelievable* a term of concern. "Even women have now become robbers."¹⁴

Hitler had his own ideas about the situation, and wrote that the problem was the Jew: "Jewry is without question a race and not a religious fellowship . . . . Rational anti-Semitism['s] . . . final objective must unswervingly be the removal of the Jews altogether."¹⁵ The Bonhoeffers had no idea where this would lead.

Even this early, however, Karl Bonhoeffer worried about the possibility of sociopaths seizing power. He worried that the war, which had killed a million German youth, had reduced the stock of "socially and biologically valuable men," leaving the "inferior" types more prevalent.¹⁶

Behind the lowered blinds, the family, like most of their class, kept up a rich musical tradition. Saturday musical evenings included Bach, Haydn, Mozart, Brahms, and Strauss. Sabine played the violin, as Dietrich did the piano, and joined by Klaus or another on the cello, they performed trios in the large Grunewald living room. At fourteen, Dietrich wrote a setting for a psalm and attempted to compose a trio version of Schubert's song "Gute Ruh."¹⁷ When older brother Karl-Friedrich criticized their father for spending on music lessons while people went hungry, his father responded sharply. The tension unsettled Dietrich, who also worried about the poor.¹⁸

---

12. Ibid., 184.
13. Nagorski, *Hitlerland*, 10.
14. Bonhoeffer, *DBWE* 9, 37.
15. Dawidowicz, *The War Against the Jews*, 16–17.
16. Stern and Sifton, *No Ordinary Men*, 12.
17. Leibholz, *The Bonhoeffers*, 34.
18. Bonhoeffer, *DBWE* 7, 81. This comes from the autobiographical fiction, which in the judgment of Dietrich's niece, Renate Bethge, reflected real-life experiences.

Though his family still expected him to pursue music, Dietrich felt a different pull: theology. His brothers derided him, and his father feared he was throwing his talents away, but the women in the family supported him. Paula's father, Karl Alfred von Hase, had, for a time, been court preacher to the ill-fated Kaiser Wilhelm II, so there were family precedents, and Paula herself had an active interest in theology.

Dietrich and Sabine attended church services together. They discussed the sermons,[19] and at 14, began sex-segregated confirmation classes at the Grunewald Church. On Palm Sunday, March 15, 1921, the twins, now fifteen, woke up to the sweet cadences of the family singing hymns to celebrate their confirmation day. Dietrich expressed his pleasure that the girls and boys were confirmed as a group, as he found that "more natural than . . . to be with the other boys."[20]

That August, both Dietrich and Sabine got sick. As Sabine recovered from a stomach ache and vomiting, she offered Dietrich good company. She's "lively . . . and tells jokes," he wrote to his parents from Berlin. The following spring, sixteen-year-old Dietrich yearned to be with his twin in Tübingen. "In two weeks I will be with you," Dietrich wrote to her in June. "I'll probably see you on the 7th, dear Sabine."[21] He assured Sabine, who apparently hoped to go riding with him, that "Mama will treat me to riding lessons if you can be patient. I will bring a whip along as well."[22] Music, as ever, bound them and Dietrich encouraged, as always, his sister's violin: "It is very nice that you are now playing in a string orchestra there," he wrote. He himself, still not entirely abandoning the idea of a musical career, confided to her that he done a piano audition with the famous Leonard Kreutzer, teacher at the Berlin Academy. Kreutzer, Dietrich told Sabine, urged him to enter the academy after high school and study with him there.[23]

One day, back in class at school, Dietrich wrote to Sabine that he'd heard gunshots. They came from the assassination of the German foreign minister, Walther Rathenau, a Jewish man killed less than a quarter mile from Dietrich's school by right-wing activists because he had signed a treaty with communist Russia. Dietrich wrote to Sabine, who was in Tübingen, of a Berlin "crazed with excitement and rage." Fistfights had broken out in the Reichstag.[24]

---

19. Leibholz, *The Bonhoeffers*, 30.
20. Ibid., 31.
21. Ibid., 49–50.
22. Bonhoeffer, *DBWE 9*, 45.
23. Ibid., 46. Sabine notes Dietrich had "the good judgment" to realize "he would not be good enough at the piano" to pursue it professionally (*The Bonhoeffers*, 34).
24. Ibid., 49.

More hints of Germany's postwar turmoil weaved through Dietrich's letters. Writing to his parents of arriving safely in Tübingen, though he'd forgotten to bring his toiletries, he mentioned sharing a train compartment with a man "very narrow mindedly right wing . . . . The only thing he had forgotten was his swastika." He also wrote of a hungry train conductor who asked the well-heeled lad to share a roll: the man was delighted when Dietrich offered him "some chocolate and two rolls."[25]

In Tübingen, Sabine left the newly arrived Dietrich at their grandmother's to enjoy the romantic whirl of a sixteen-year-old, attending a dance at family friend Gerhard von Rad's fraternity, the Stuttgartia. Although her twin might have liked her company at home, Sabine couldn't, Dietrich informed his parents, cancel her party plans at the very last minute. Sabine was also "terribly excited" about their upcoming trip with other siblings and friends to Lake Constance.[26]

Later in Berlin, Sabine, at Dietrich's request, painted him a verse for his seventeenth birthday. It included the lines, "Oh sweetness of eternity, May my heart grow to love thee."[27] For the twins, the verse, which hung above Dietrich's bed, held meanings that only the two shared, a reminder of their old nighttime rituals. More than twenty years later this verse became part of the Christmas prayers Dietrich compiled in Tegel prison. Religion would always have a domestic face for Dietrich, and for him the personal would always be the theological.

By now, 1923, Paula had recovered from the shock of Walter's death, and her legendary entertainments began again. Family life by this time "once more burst out into a cheerful blaze,"[28] the family entertainments "a mobile pattern of music and laughter . . . gathered into one with a web of conversation which was as light as it was brilliant."[29] At one of their costume balls, Karl and Paula appeared dressed as the pagan gods Freya and Wotan.[30] At another, Dietrich came dressed as Cupid and enthusiastically shot blunt arrows.[31]

Dietrich and Sabine acted in the family's theatrical evenings. Dietrich adapted Hauff's fairy tales for staging and played Argan, the lead role, in

---

25. Ibid., 55
26. Ibid., 50. Gert Leibholz, her future husband, may have gone on this trip.
27. Leibholz, *The Bonhoeffers*, 34
28. Bosanquet, *The Life and Death of Dietrich Bonhoeffer*, 46.
29. Ibid., 60.
30. Ibid., 46.
31. Zimmermann and Smith, eds., *I Knew*, 30.

Moliere's *Imaginary Invalid*. He and Sabine enjoyed play going, seeing, for instance, a "truly distinguished" *Antigone* at the People's Theater,[32] an affordable socialist venue.[33] In order to have Sabine's company, Dietrich would exchange his better seat at the state opera for two cheaper balcony tickets. Once they saw *Carmen* in the standing room section. Young and high-spirited, they loved the show.[34]

---

32. Bonhoeffer, *DBWE* 9, 43.

33. Pachter, *The Weimar Etudes*, 123.

34. Bethge, ed., *Last Letters of the Resistance*, 99. Bonhoeffer would retain a special affection for *Carmen*, seeing it often, and Bethge would see it on his honeymoon.

4

Happy Times

One can imagine Dietrich bursting in on Sabine, or Bina[1], as he sometimes called her, in the Grunewald parlor shortly after graduating the gymnasium in March 1923, cheeks flushed and blue eyes bright, flinging himself into the chair beside her. Or perhaps she sat at a table on the back terrace, touching up one of her paintings.

Dietrich asked that she share his walking tour, financed by graduation money, through the Thuringen forest.

The two, bearing heavy backpacks and walking sticks, set out eagerly in the beautiful early spring weather, singing as they hiked, two carefree, wandering youths. Heading deeper and higher up into the forest, the shadows growing longer, they discussed their lives, family, friends, and their bright, bright hopes for the future. As they climbed, the terrain suddenly turned wintry. Unprepared, they found themselves plowing through deep snow. Then an ice storm hit. "My long skirt was flapping around my ankles with encrusted ice, and we sank to our knees in the snow," Sabine remembered. Dietrich, strong and muscular, carried her backpack with his own, and forged a trail for her. Over and over, while fighting his way forward up the mountain, he turned back to knock frost from the hem of her dress as he tried, with his body, to shield her from the worst of the storm.[2]

Later, when they reached the summit, all was calm. They looked down in the silence over the treetops to Nicholas Church and Bach's house, the wintry landscape "glittering in the sun." Dietrich was thrilled.[3]

In April, he began the traditional year at the university in Tübingen that his father and older brothers had completed. Christel, with her "male brain," came too, to study biology. Initially, Dietrich took up lodgings with a

---

1. Bonhoeffer, *DBWE* 9, 15.
2. Bethge, ed., *Last Letters of the Resistance*, 98-99 and Zimmermann and Smith, eds., *I Knew*, 31.
3. Zimmermann and Smith, eds., *I Knew*, 31.

Mrs. Koken, and by May moved to another house, renting a room that cost 6,000 marks a month for four "naked" walls, a bed, a table, and two chairs.[4]

A Tübingen alley.

Dietrich's "line" during these teen years, according to future sister-in-law Emmi, "was to be interested without curiosity," to be detached without being cold. He wore a bowler hat, which he lifted "neither ostentatiously nor sloppily. His straight-kneed walk made his gait look taut, almost rigid."[5] He bowed and clicked his heels together in the German manner.[6] He had already, wrote Sabine, "the gift of perfect assurance of manners."[7]

4. Bonhoeffer, *DBWE 9*, 58.
5. Zimmermann and Smith, eds., *I Knew*, 35.
6. Ibid., 42.
7. Ibid., 33.

Dietrich joined the Igel, or Hedgehog, fraternity, which his father had belonged to as a student.[8] In the short vitae Dietrich provided the Hedgehogs, he slipped in Sabine: "I, with my twin sister, saw the light of day" on February 4, 1906, and added that from age thirteen "it was clear to me that I would study theology. Only music caused me to waver during the past two years."[9]

Now, most of his attention focused on Tübingen's Eberhard Karls University, founded in 1477. Long known for its theological studies, its church had been one of the first to convert to Lutheranism. In the nineteenth century, it became a center for the historical analysis of biblical texts under Ferdinand Christian Baur.

The library at the neoclassical Eberhard Karls University.

8. The Hedgehog society had been formed as a protest to dueling societies. The members, rather than sporting the brightly colored outfits and crisscrossed facial scars of fencing duelers, chose to wear hats made of hedgehog skins along with gray-toned clothes. Dietrich, however, took fencing lessons in Tübingen (Bonhoeffer, *DBWE* 9, 60).

9. Ibid., 60. Other iterations of his vitae in Bonhoeffer, *DBWE* 9 showed that Dietrich hardly changed it—but he did drop the reference to Sabine.

During his time there, runaway inflation hit Germany: in April, when Dietrich and Christine arrived, a textbook jumped from 55,000 to 70,000 marks in a day and a pound of sausage leaped to 14,000 marks. By July, a dollar was worth 353,581 marks, by October 25 billion marks.[10] Dietrich noted the "unease" among the workers he heard on a train trip when the dollar shot up to 7 million marks.[11] Yet because foreign clients often paid Karl Bonhoeffer in their own currencies, the Bonhoeffer family rode out the worst of the troubles.[12] Meanwhile, Sabine took art lessons—until her art teacher told her: "Fräulein Bonhoeffer, you must live more intensely." To "live more intensely" became a derided phrase in the family. The parents withdrew Sabine from the art school.[13]

In August, the twins vacationed together in Friedrichsbrunn, visiting the Witches' Dancing Place at night with an old servant and having a "wonderful trip" to two "old cities" in the area.[14] These may have been Halberstadt or Quedlinburg, where, Sabine wrote, Dietrich liked to "look at the large churches."[15]

To save money during their second term in Tübingen, Christel and Dietrich moved in with their grandmother. Strong-willed Christel, although also a busy student, now had to do Dietrich's laundry and iron his shirts, tasks she resented.[16] Meanwhile, Dietrich, mustering up all his youthful arrogance, confronted the landlord who tried to evict his grandmother. He wrote to his parents, asking them to invite Tafel to live in their in Berlin home.[17]

"I think it is crazy and silly of you not to play the violin at all anymore. . . . You could surely find a half hour a day to practice," Dietrich chided Sabine that November. "At the very least, practice a trio for Christmas so that we can play one together."[18] In December, he wrote to her in alarm again about her lapsed music practice: "Can it be true you haven't planned anything for Klaus's . . . teacher trainee? Tell me! I would really like to know! I won't be able to play anything alone, because I am terribly out of practice. . . . If

---

10. Ibid., 56.
11. Bonhoeffer, *DBWE 9*, 63.
12. There is, however, the famous story of Karl Bonhoeffer's life insurance policy becoming worth a pint of strawberries.
13. Renate Bethge, in Bonhoeffer, *DBWE 7*, 141.
14. Bonhoeffer, *DBWE 9*, 64.
15. Leibholz, *The Bonhoeffers*, 34.
16. Schlingensiepen, *Dietrich Bonhoeffer 1906-1945*, 18.
17. Bonhoeffer, *DBWE 9*, 65–66
18. Ibid., 72.

possible, ask Mama to give us tickets to the Christmas Oratorio," he told her, "then go and pick them up. I really would like to listen to a beautiful concert; there is nothing at all like that here." He also sought Sabine's advice for Christmas gifts: "I don't know what I should give Mama at all, or Papa. Write me if you can think of anything."[19]

His 1924 birthday letter to Sabine overflowed with exuberance: "I received all sorts of fabulous and magnificent things for my birthday, including a splendid guitar. I am sure you will be jealous because it has a wonderful tone. I . . . am very happy about it."

He then poured out his heart: "And just so you won't get over your astonishment, I'll tell you about the next completely unbelievable occurrence. Just think, it is just possible that next semester—I will be studying in Rome!! Of course, nothing is at all certain yet, but it would be absolutely the most fabulous thing that could happen to me. I can't even begin to imagine how great that would be! . . . I want to do it so much that I can't imagine ever wanting to do it more than I do now. . . . Talk about it a lot at home; it can only help things. Keep your ears open as well . . . please give everyone my love, because I can't possibly write anyone else today."[20]

Finances, however, still cast a pall, and in his letter to his parents a few days later, Dietrich adopted a more measured tone about the trip: "fees less expensive. . . . Food and lodgings both very inexpensive and easy to find . . . many Germans live there."[21]

Drenched in art and atmosphere, Rome made a lasting and haunting impression on Dietrich that spring. "You are under her spell and can hardly escape,"[22] he wrote Sabine. He thrilled at the Laocoon, that twisting statue of muscular nudes with serpents coiled around them. "When I saw the Laocoon for the first time, a tremor ran right through me. It is unbelievable," he wrote. After hearing an "angelic, a supernaturally beautiful" *Te deum* at St. Peter's, he "saw what Catholicism is." "You really must come to Rome,"[23] he told Sabine. He and Klaus, on a tight budget, "consumed vast quantities of . . . cassatas,"[24] a Neapolitan ice cream containing fruits and nuts.

---

19. Ibid., 76.
20. Ibid., 78.
21. Ibid., 80.
22. Ibid., 110.
23. Ibid., 121. Years later, in fake diary accounts left for the Gestapo, Dietrich feigned indifference about the Laocoon.
24. Bonhoeffer, *LPP,* 340.

One day, filled with the heady, sensual beauty of Rome, Dietrich saw forty young female novices file into the Trinita dei Monti, a church poised above Rome's Spanish steps, in habits with blue and green sashes, their faces open and alive with faith. Overwhelmed, he again felt full force "the reality of Catholicism." The simplicity, grace, and earnestness of the young girls as they knelt and prayed was not ritual, but true worship. Dietrich's sense of their faith was enhanced by the intoxicating view of the setting sun, yellow and red flames, melting into the domes of Rome.[25]

His letters to Sabine ran over with both enthusiasm and complaints—especially about his lack of money and his annoyance at Klaus, who insisted on being in charge. "Can you lend me a little money?" he asked her in April, while instructing her to find and send a photo of him for a museum identification card.[26] In May, he thanked her for sending funds and urged her to ask Grete, his future sister-in-law, to lend him some cash. "Think about it," he wrote.[27]

He searched for a guitar for Sabine and found "a beautiful [one] with an adjustable bass string," but didn't buy it.[28] On May 22, he told her, "I've looked for a guitar for you every day." A day later, he hit the jackpot, finding "an incredibly fabulous one with a bass string that is in good condition.... I envy you unbelievably!"[29]

Back in Berlin, laden with the guitar for Sabine that she had paid for, he greeted her with that rarest of commodities in the Bonhoeffer family: a kiss, meant to celebrate her marriage engagement.[30]

---

25. Bonhoeffer, *DBWE* 9, 89.
26. Ibid., 110.
27. Ibid., 121.
28. Ibid., 110.
29. Ibid., 123

30. Bosanquet, *The Life and Death of Dietrich Bonhoeffer*, 55. None of his letters to her from this period, however, mention her engagement.

5

Weddings

If lovestruck Sabine ran lighthearted into the grand house in Grunewald hoping her engagement to Gerhard Leibholz would be greeted with joy and enthusiasm, she was disappointed. "Now things will be difficult for you," Paula said.[1] Her parents worried that Gert's Jewish ancestry—even in the liberal 1920s—would hurt his academic career.

Family tradition dictated that Sabine, now eighteen, wait until twenty to wed. Dietrich thus had a two-year reprieve before the ground was pulled out from under him and, meanwhile, pursued a "regular routine" of swimming, academic work, and a weekly musical evening "which gives us all great pleasure."[2] He wrote to Paula of going hiking, joking drily that it would help him lose weight and "conform to my sisters' perception of beauty."[3] The weather was cool and rainy.

Susi remained the outsider. Earlier, Dietrich had hinted at the difficulties in finding a place for her to go for holidays.[4] Now, Dietrich apologized for being so swamped with work that he couldn't accompany Sabine to Friedrichsbrunn: "You don't seem to want to go up there with Susi and her friend."[5] Because Susi didn't share their musical bent, they thought of taking her to Peacock Island for her fifteenth birthday, a tourist destination that boasted free roaming peacocks and a turreted white palace.[6] In contrast to Susi's lack of musicality, Sabine, to Dietrich's delight, had taken up her violin again, amid drawing and reading. So they carried on. Dietrich studied theology, walked, and practiced the piano, took hiking tours and vacations, and attended parties, weddings, and outings. He sliced perfect figure eights

---

1. Leibholz, *The Bonhoeffers*, 56.
2. Bonhoeffer, *DBWE* 9, 133.
3. Ibid., 133.
4. Ibid., 45. (This would be the April holidays.)
5. Ibid., 129. Sabine apparently did go with Susi.
6. Bonhoeffer, *DBWE* 9, 136.

through the ice during nighttime skating parties, despite earlier having suffered a concussion ice-skating in Tübingen.

In 1926, Sabine married Gert. Opulence marked the three days of festivities. Guests decked out in ball gowns, jewels, and evening dress arrived at the party on the wedding's eve. Amid the laughter and rising excitement, Dietrich, paired with Susi, performed Max Bierbaum's "Ring-row-rosary: I dance with my wife," just as he and Sabine had done for sister Ursel's wedding three years past. It "earned great applause," and no doubt laughter and shouts. Then the bridesmaids entered with a bridal garland of purple and blue ribbons, singing "we bind for you the maiden's crown" and danced circles around the bride and groom, who sat on golden chairs.[7]

At this pre-wedding party, high spirits mingled with the flowers and ribbons, music and wedding poems, free flow of food and drink, and the traditional crockery breaking to bring good luck. One relative, General Rüdiger von der Goltz, refused to attend the celebrations as he could not countenance a Jew in the family, but this didn't mar the excitement. Christel called him an "ass."[8]

For the wedding itself, the couple rode in a fairy-tale wedding coach, "decked out with white silk and . . . drawn by two pretty white horses,"[9] to the Grunewald church. Sabine, as her sisters had, wore her mother's wedding gown.

After the guests left, Sabine headed off with her new husband, and the maids swept up the last of broken china, wedding crumbs, and faded garlands. Silence fell. Now Dietrich faced the crisis of the loss of his beloved twin, his other half. As his biographer Bosanquet writes of the aftermath of the wedding, "But now, though their mutual affection was never to wane, he must . . . part with Sabine, and the sense of ultimate isolation which had begun to take hold of him as he grew up . . . was deepened and intensified."[10] Other siblings would visit him in his travels to Barcelona, London, Finkenwalde, and Ettal—but not Sabine and Gert. From now on, they would meet at their parents' home or Dietrich would come to her.

If only unconsciously, Dietrich a few years later encoded this rupture in *Creation and Fall*, his meditation on Genesis 1–3. For Dietrich, the childhood homes in Breslau and Berlin represented, if imperfectly, the garden of Eden, and Sabine's marriage marked the fall. In Dietrich's envisioned Eden, Adam and Eve behaved like the other animals in the garden, roaming naked

---

7. Leibholz, *The Bonhoeffers*, 56.
8. Stern and Sifton, *No Ordinary Men*, 18.
9. Leibholz, *The Bonhoeffers*, 59.
10. Bosanquet, *The Life and Death of Dietrich Bonhoeffer*, 55.

and yet innocent. Adam and Eve, like Dietrich and Sabine, were "one and yet two."[11]

If joyful and chaste companionship with an opposite-sex partner represented paradise, sexuality in Dietrich's reading became the sign of the fall. Lust severed the relationship between Adam and Eve, who earlier, in Dietrich's words, had been like "siblings" in the garden. For Bonhoeffer, sex marked the "sundering of the original unity between man and woman . . . the innermost rupture in the community between them."[12] It was "knowledge of duality, of the whole as torn apart." It was *tob* and *ra*, pleasure and pain. Sex, for Adam—and for Dietrich—was no less than "god's wrath."[13] Marriage, whose festivities Dietrich had participated in with outward cheer, showed "a reaching out to grasp the strength and glory of the Creator for oneself."[14] *Creation and Fall*, as two decades later a wedding sermon would, expressed Dietrich's cry of pain at the loss of the beloved. Yet within the rigid confines of the Bonhoeffer family, which even in the relatively liberal 1920s ridiculed the "New Woman" who sought a career, Sabine had little choice but to marry, and evidently, every desire to do so.

For nine years after this rupture, Dietrich would drift alone, "between curse and promise,"[15] throwing himself into work that "express[ed] an obsessive nostalgia for the original unity." Work, for Dietrich, would function as a promise that humankind "is still allowed to live alongside nature, from which it was taken and to which it belongs as a sibling."[16] Working obsessively, and then wandering, he sought to find a place to stand.

Among the Bonhoeffer set, young people married the children of their parents' friends, a common pattern in Germany.[17] Within a world of Shakespeare readings, theater outings, dinners, and late night ice-skating parties under cold, star-studded winter skies, Karl-Friedrich Bonhoeffer married Grete von Dohnanyi, while Christel married Grete's brother Hans von

---

11. Bonhoeffer, *DBWE* 3, 97.

12. Ibid., 133. None of this is to say that *Creation and Fall* can't be read purely as a theological treatise. However, Marsh notes rightly that *Creation and Fall*, without footnotes, marks a change from the earlier, more scholarly texts, calling it "expressionistic and poetical, meditative and devotional . . . a dazzling, cyclonic utterance . . ." (*Strange Glory*, 155).

13. Ibid., 121–22.

14. Ibid., 101.

15. Ibid., 131.

16. Ibid., 134.

17. Theweleit, *Male Fantasies*, vol. 1, 124.

Dohnanyi. Klaus Bonhoeffer married Emmi Delbrück, the sister of his close friend Justus. Dietrich's friend Walter Dress married little sister Susi.[18]

Dietrich had become close with at least three of his brothers-in-law—Walter, Hans, and Gert—before their weddings to his sisters. He wrote to Hans with details about plans for a hike in the Alps in 1922, three years before his friend's marriage to Christel, asking casually if "Leibholz" was coming too. Dietrich also became friends with Walter Dress, a fellow theology student, years before Dress married Susi and would write to him in tones of striking informality. In one letter, he joked and apologized for his parent's servants: "Naturally these pearls of maids didn't understand [that only Walter was to be let in while the parents napped]; and so the unhappy event happened that you were sent away." Dietrich then quoted Horace, a joke at Walter's expense: "I despise the uneducated throng and I keep them at distance."[19] Rüdiger Schleicher, eleven years older, later became close to Dietrich over music-making and conspiracy, especially once the Schleichers moved next door to Dietrich's parents. To a remarkable degree, Dietrich felt welcomed, close to, at ease, and in sympathy with all these brother-in-laws, each vetted as an appropriate member of the family.

This pattern of marriages perpetuated a largely closed caste system in which the children of the ruling class inherited society's spoils. The merriments that seemed innocent to the young people were the exclusive province of a handful of privileged youth, a social life orchestrated within a closed circle. So sharp were class divides that when Karl Bonhoeffer appeared at one of his wife's masquerade balls dressed as a servant he wasn't recognized.[20] The sons of professors married the daughters of professors and became professors themselves; the sons of diplomats and government officials married their own kind and took over their fathers' positions, power, and prestige.[21]

Until the Versailles treaty limited the size of the army to 100,000, Germany's military had provided an outlet for ambitious young men without class privilege. A career in the army offered a literal way up the ranks into a position of status, money, and security. A successful military career meant

18. Bonhoeffer, *DBWE 9*'s letters suggest how the Bonhoeffer family as a whole wooed an eligible suitor.

19. Bonhoeffer, *DBWE 9*, 161.

20. Bethge, *DB: A Biography*, 47.

21. Yet the Bonhoeffers also allowed their children to wed Grete and Hans von Dohnanyi, who came from more modest means. Hans's and Grete's parents, the Hungarian pianist Ernst von Dohnanyi and his pianist wife, Elisabeth Kunwald, had separated, and their father returned to Hungary. During the war, fourteen-year-old Hans tutored fellow students to supplement his mother's income from piano lessons (Stern and Sifton, *No Ordinary Men*, 32).

a man could marry, buy a small house, and support a family. Suddenly, that outlet contracted sharply, and many people, already convinced the army had been stabbed in the back, became increasingly disenchanted at a social order that seemed to offer them nothing.

A paradox remained: The upper classes recognized their privilege, yet, like most of the trans-European elite, registered the diminishment of their own lives from lavish prewar levels. The Bonhoeffers, like others of their class, were caught between having far more than most people and far less than before the war.[22]

In 1927, Sabine bore her first child, Marianne. Dietrich worked on his dissertation, *Communion of Saints*. When Sabine came over, slim, elegant, and good-humored, wheeling the baby carriage into her parents' garden, Dietrich gladly broke away from his standing desk for a visit.[23] He was delighted to be asked to be Marianne's godfather.

With his twin married, Dietrich now turned to Elisabeth Zinn, a third cousin who had grown up in Grunewald in a house opposite the Bonhoeffers', and who bore "a shadowy and indefinable resemblance to Sabine."[24] Zinn's father and Karl Bonhoeffer, both doctors, were friends and colleagues. The Bonhoeffer and Zinn children played together. According to her daughter, Aleida Assmann, Elisabeth was especially close to Sabine.[25] It's not hard to imagine Sabine doing some matchmaking.

---

22. Examples of this abound. A few follow: Dietrich was almost pulled home from his year in Tübingen, although "a family tradition" (Bethge, *DB: A Biography*, 47), for financial reasons, and he had to persuade his parents that his trip to Italy could be done economically. Sabine wrote of the strain her mother was under after the war providing her married daughters with the expected furniture and one servant, a comedown from her own full staff as a young bride. Dietrich wrote to his grandmother during this period of traveling fourth class on the train to save money.

23. Leibholz, *The Bonhoeffers*, 35.

24. Bosanquet, *The Life and Death of Dietrich Bonhoeffer*, 62.

25. E-mail correspondence from Aleida Assmann.

Elisabeth Zinn, a family friend, good friend of Sabine's, and sometimes purported first love of Dietrich's, was thought to bear a resemblance to Sabine.

Elisabeth, who loved music, played the piano and sang. Her "defining trait," however, was her intellect.[26] Like Dietrich, she pursued a doctorate in theology. And as Dietrich and Sabine had once done, Dietrich and Elisabeth explored theology together. Zinn wrote her doctoral dissertation on the theosophist Friedrich Christoph Oetinger, author of a favorite Bonhoeffer quote—"embodiment is the end of God's path." A scholar "who knew the old languages better than [her] teachers," Zinn would maintain a lifelong interest in religious studies.[27] In myriad ways, from intellectual and musical pursuits to being an upper-middle-class neighbor, Zinn fit the profile of the ideal wife for Dietrich. Yet the relationship, "awkward and unrewarding," floundered.[28]

By 1928, Dietrich had earned his doctorate in theology. Living at home, he often spent quiet evenings with his grandmother. As his siblings married and started their own families, he became lonelier, while beyond his home, the world was in flux. In the midst of it, he cast around, longing for a break with the past.

---

26. Ibid.
27. Ibid.
28. Bosanquet, *The Life and Death of Dietrich Bonhoeffer*, 62.

PART II
Seeking Ground

— 6 —
Wanderings and Worries

When Dietrich was handed his phone's black receiver to take a call, the voice on the other end[1] offered him the position of vicar of the German Evangelical Congregation in Barcelona for a year. He said yes. "This offer seemed to bring to fruition a wish . . . to stand on my own feet for a longer period completely outside of my previous circle of acquaintance," he wrote. Intuition rather than logic led him: "this clarity is not so much intellectual as it is instinctive. . . . I finally just wanted to do it . . . ."[2]

"Shivers" went up and down his spine as his Berlin congregation prayed for him on the eve of his February departure. "Where the church is, there is never loneliness," he wrote, as if to reassure himself.[3] It would be his first time living without at least one family member close at hand. In the fashion of those days, as they had done when he left for Rome, his brothers and sisters, after throwing him a bon voyage party, accompanied him gaily to the train station to cheer him off on his adventure.

Arriving in Barcelona to serve about 300 of the 6,000 German expatriates in the city, Dietrich threw himself into his activities. A misty mountain bordered the city on one side, purporting to be where the devil tempted Jesus, and, on the other side, palm trees waved in the sea breezes. The streets thronged with a mix of people, rich and poor, dancing the traditional jigs—and the Charleston. Dietrich mingled with beggars and watched people lingering at café tables nursing cups of coffee at the Plaza Cataluna. He jumped full-force into the life of his congregation, revitalizing and growing the youth program—and, at least by Dietrich's own account, igniting some sparks of jealously in the more pedantic senior pastor Fritz Olbricht. He reveled in Barcelona's sultry warmth on late winter days. In the summer, he would complain about the heat.

1. Max Diestel, superintendent of the Lutheran Church in Berlin.
2. Bonhoeffer, *DBWE 10*, 57.
3. Ibid., 58.

His boarding house room, large and unheated, had balcony windows looking out at whitewashed buildings. By mid-March, scarcely three weeks after he'd left, Sabine chided him for not writing.[4] By early November, the tables had turned, and he wrote plaintively to his grandmother that "Sabine has been cloaking herself in complete silence—I hope not with hurt feelings."[5] He noted that he had been sick for eight days with a "slight bout of gastric influenza,"[6] as if a break of little more than a week in correspondence required an explanation. He "tried to induce us to visit him there [in Spain] so he could show us all its beauties," Sabine remembered.[7] The Leibholzes did not go.

Loneliness dogged him, and he wrote to his grandmother wistfully about how long the languid Spanish evenings seemed. He poured out to Tafel a rush of sweetness and yearning—"During the evening now I often think, dear Grandmama, about the hours I so often sat with you in your room and which now often come to mind, in all their calm and peacefulness. Just eight more months and these hours will come again."[8] On July 17, he reminded her "how glad and grateful we are . . . that we have you completely [in their Berlin home]."[9] On her birthday, a month later, he mentioned his gratitude again to her for living with them in Berlin and continued: "A house in which a grandmother lives has a special bond and special stability. It's a way the past reaches into the present." Later he would write to her, "Where there is a grandmother, there is an ear for everyone, a place of true peace, and a word of advice for each individual; there one acquires a living understanding of the meaning of tradition and sees that everything is an ongoing continuum and that what even seems most new derives a large part of its energy from the past."[10]

He called home during the double baptisms of a niece and nephew: "I was very glad to hear grandmamma!" But first came the complaint: "I was enormously pleased to be wholly transported into the festive mood there by all your voices. But where were *Sabine,* Suse and Walter?"[11] (emphasis Bonhoeffer's).

---

4. Ibid., 78.
5. Ibid., 148.
6. Ibid.
7. Leibholz, *The Bonhoeffers,* 35.
8. Bonhoeffer, *DBWE 10,* 97.
9. Ibid., 118.
10. Bosanquet, *The Life and Death of Dietrich Bonhoeffer,* 132.
11. Bonhoeffer, *DBWE 10,* 149.

In late June, 1930, two months before he would sail for Manhattan for a year of study at Union Theological Seminary, Dietrich longingly remembered "those pleasant days"[12] he had recently spent with Sabine. Sabine now lived in Greifswald, a small town near the Baltic with bracing sea breezes where she enjoyed the local eel and where Gert had taken a university post. These balmy, breezy days of picking the wild poppies and blue cornflowers that grew amid the corn in "sun drenched fields" around Greifswald[13] would come back to Dietrich in prison, where he would liken friendship to a cornflower.

Restless and lonely, he sat by his open window in the Grunewald home, listening to dance music drifting in from a nearby house. "Solitary couples are walking in the garden —just as in the old days! —and I am longing for nothing more than to join in the dancing." Having escaped the noisy racket caused by his mother and sister Susi, he dreamed of the quiet he imagined in Greifswald: "How wonderful that is."[14] He yearned to have come to Greifswald to join in the birthday festivities for Sabine's tiny daughter, Marianne.

Dietrich submitted his second dissertation, *Act and Being*, in 1930, earning the right to teach at the university level. By the time he wrote to Sabine of noise and loneliness, he had also received confirmation of his Sloane fellowship at Union Theological Seminary in Manhattan.

If Sabine, on marrying, had expanded her circle of family and friends, Dietrich continued adrift. He had been restless since his return to Berlin, finding academic life stale and stifling. But Sabine was beginning to have troubles of her own.

One day, her father-in-law came to visit in Greifswald. A busy industrialist, he looked forward to an outing to nearby Strasland. His big car, driven by his chauffeur, moved slowly though Strasland's marketplace. A mob of Nazis appeared. Identifying Sabine's father-in-law as Jewish, they surrounded the slow-moving vehicle, smashing their faces against the windows. They began banging on the glass and shouting threats, then rocking the car. Sabine was frightened. "Very quickly, I took ... Marianne, who at that time was flaxen-haired and blue-eyed, from my lap and put her on her grandfather's knee," recalled Sabine. "That saved the situation.... But the shock remained."[15]

More shocks came. In the fall of 1930, a public weary of economic crisis voted 107 National Socialists into the Reichstag, up from twelve. Meanwhile, the pregnant Sabine saw "a man raking up the leaves who was dressed

12. Leibholz, *The Bonhoeffers*, 62.
13. Ibid.
14. Ibid.
15. Ibid., 66.

in a uniform that was unfamiliar to us and wearing jackboots." Sabine asked a young boy, the son of an acquaintance, "Who is this man? Isn't that a tropical uniform he's wearing?"[16] The friend told her he was an SA man, a Nazi brownshirt.

Sabine's observation about his "tropical" garb proved all too apt, for Hitler, seeing that other European powers had reaped the benefits of colonial exploitation, turned his eyes to Eastern Europe as Germany's rightful territory. Soon enough, the National Socialists would be treating non-Aryan groups in Europe with a violence usually reserved for darker skinned peoples in far-flung colonies. Uneasy at what the brownshirts might represent, Sabine nevertheless dismissed her forebodings.

---

16. Ibid.

— 7 —
Manhattan

DIETRICH WROTE TO HIS grandmother as he sailed across the Atlantic, noting the calm ocean, which reminded him of Berlin's Wannesee Lake. Perhaps of more interest to her was his cabin mate, Dr. Lucas, the president of a college in Lahore. He invited Dietrich to India, which since at least 1928 had been a dream of Tafel's for her grandson. India had cast its spell on Dietrich as well, and in Friedrichsbrunn that summer, he had mulled over with his siblings the idea of a trip.[1]

In Manhattan, Dietrich faced a city astonishingly vertical compared to flat Berlin, the Empire State Building going up before his eyes. His seminary home, however, harkened back to Europe. Built in 1910 on upper Broadway, near Harlem, just north of Columbia University, Union Theological took its inspiration from medieval—or Gothic revival—Europe. Here, four stone buildings, all connected and wrapped around a city block, made a fortress protecting a grassy central area dotted with benches, more lush with foliage then than now. Leaded windows lined the enclosed arched corridors that ran around the ground floor. The Gothic-style windows came to points, some decorated with trefoils, others with the quatrefoils that looked like four-leaf clovers. To step through the stone entranceway and into the corridor surrounding the courtyard was to enter a cloistered world, separate from Manhattan's blaring horns, crowds, and rush.

The rectory had a vaulted, half-timbered ceiling and floor of polished, brick-red tiles, the tall leaded windows letting in a diffused light. The cast-iron chandeliers evoked a medieval ethos, though electrified with light bulbs, and perhaps the seminarians thought of themselves as Robin Hood's men as they ate beneath them.

During this year abroad, thrust for the first time outside of the German or German expatriate community, Dietrich changed—a change he would later note as one of the most decisive in his life. He lived for the first time in

1. Bethge, *DB: A Biography*, 147–48.

a dormitory setting, surrounded by a buzz of people of all kinds. As he wrote to his grandmother, "one just blabs away so frightfully much time here."[2] Here he made friends with Jean Lasserre, a Frenchman, overcoming his German animosity towards the French. Under Lasserre's influence, he became a pacifist.

Both men shared a passion for living their faith. Through Lasserre, Dietrich came to view the Sermon on the Mount, with its message of radical forgiveness and nonviolence, as the blueprint for the Christian life. Riveted by the antiwar film *All Quiet on the Western Front*, which they saw together, each became more certain that peace stood at the center of the gospel. Here, too, in New York, Dietrich, formerly fascinated by *Uncle Tom's Cabin*, made friends with black seminarian Frank Fisher, immersed himself in Harlem's vibrant black community, and jumped into the life of the famed black Abyssinian Baptist Church, led by Clayton Powell Sr.

At Abyssinian, Dietrich heard a gospel message that stunned him, finding for the first time in the US a genuine proclamation of the Christian spirit.[3] Christian power and originality lived not in white, but black America. "Here one really could still hear someone talk in a Christian sense about sin and grace and the love of God and ultimate hope, albeit in a form different from that to which we are accustomed," he told a friend.[4] This was not the arid social justice of middle-class American theology students, but an embodied, deeply felt faith. Dietrich enjoyed the audible reaction of "amens" and "alleluias" when he himself preached in the black church. He taught—or was taught by—a group of black women. In black Christianity he found hope for the future and a theology that included a view of life from the bottom, looking up. Black theology—the view from below—would remain with him the rest of his life.

Amid these new experiences, Sabine's second pregnancy loomed, and Dietrich fretted about the upcoming delivery. On November 7, he wrote, "I am thinking of you several times a day from across the water with many good wishes. Of course you will let me know at once?"[5]

At Christiane's birth in early December, Sabine, after drinking a glass of champagne with her parents and Gert, as well as the doctor, midwife, and nurse attendant, sent a telegram "straightaway" to Dietrich in Manhattan. He, in turn, responded "surprisingly quickly" with congratulations, followed

---

2. Bonhoeffer, *DBWE 10*, 294.
3. Ibid., 266.
4. Ibid., 30.
5. Leibholz, *The Bonhoeffers*, 63.

by a long letter "full of kindness."[6] Later that month, he headed to Cuba with another new seminary friend, Erwin Sutz, a fellow German speaker from Switzerland. Dietrich wrote to Sabine from Florida: "I have travelled from the winter in New York right into the midst of summer. Today I have been lying in the sun for a few hours in a palm grove. It is fantastically beautiful. All best wishes." But he longed for her companionship: "What a pity that we cannot share this kind of experience together."[7]

Cuba captured Dietrich's imagination and his body reveled in the sun. He drank in the heady scent of flowers. And he continued lonely: "I have rarely had this much trouble getting into the Christmas spirit," Dietrich wrote to a friend from Cuba, and his Christmas sermon to the German congregation in Havana reflects that melancholy. In it, he spoke personally, a cry from the heart: "We know from our own, small daily lives what small unfulfilled hopes are. . . . Some of us may even be familiar with great unfulfilled hopes . . . like the hope we may overcome secret weaknesses or disavow concealed sins. How many despairing attempts we make, how fervently we pray in such distress, and how difficult it is when our hopes are not fulfilled . . . ."

Advent should be a "time of penitence, not joy." While he looked forward to a future when "no more lonely suffering is to suffocate or threaten us," he returned to melancholy: "Each of us approaches Christmas with different personal feelings. Some approach it with pure joy . . . . Still others approach Christmas with much trepidation . . . disturbing thoughts of separation awaken in them; it is precisely on this day that they become particularly aware of their personal misery, of their loneliness . . . ."[8]

Did he visit Käthe Horn, the governess he had once wished to marry? Bosanquet, who corresponded with the Horn sisters, states that "the beloved governess" was there in Havana, teaching in a German school.[9] Bethge says no, that Dietrich visited yet another sister of Käthe and Maria Horn.[10] Oddly, Dietrich makes no mention of any Horns in letters home, and his melancholy mood, which may well have been intensified by a meeting with Käthe and the remembrance of days gone by, does little to settle the question.

On January 2, on board a ship back to Manhattan, Dietrich wrote to Karl-Friedrich, describing Cuba's beauties: the silhouettes cast by the swaying

6. Ibid., 64.
7. Ibid.
8. Bonhoeffer, *DBWE 10*, 585–89.
9. Bosanquet, *The Life and Death of Dietrich Bonhoeffer*, 87.
10. Bethge, *DB: A Biography*, 151.

trees and the many birds, including the brilliant flamingoes, the fields of pineapple and sugar cane—but also the terrible roads and the poverty.[11]

A month later, writing on their 25th birthdays in February from chilly Manhattan, Dietrich contrasted Sabine's stable life with his continuing uncertainty, beginning with a telling insight: "It . . . is still always as a twenty-year-old that you figure in my subconscious thoughts, probably because since that age we have no longer lived together. And for all this I cannot really beguile myself into forgetting that you already have quite different achievements to look back to than I. If I had been married for five years, and had two children and a house of my own like you, then I would feel I was fully justified in being 25."[12]

In October 1931, after Dietrich's return from Manhattan, the Leibholzes and their fine furniture moved to the university town of Göttingen, where Gert became a professor of constitutional law. The family bought a comfortable house on a main thoroughfare. Intoxicating scents of cherry, apple, plum, and pear drifted in from the backyard orchard. The orchard "was enchanting," Sabine wrote, "especially when the white beds round the borders were etched out in sharp relief in the moonlight and also in blossom time when the morello cherries with their graceful branches were decked in white blossoms."[13] But the serpent had already arrived.

---

11. Ibid., 268–69.
12. Leibholz, *The Bonhoeffers*, 67.
13. Ibid., 70.

— 8 —
Nazis

BACK IN GERMANY THAT summer and fall of 1931, Dietrich feared what was coming politically, in more urgent if less poetic terms than Yeats glimpsing that the center would not hold. He wrote to Sutz: "Matters really look exceedingly serious. There is literally no one in Germany who is able to grasp the situation, even remotely. But one cannot escape the strong impression that we are facing a major turning point in world history."[1]

In the same letter, he worried about the coming winter and the plight of "the seven million unemployed, that is to say fifteen or twenty million hungry, I do not know how Germany or how individuals can survive this."[2] Sabine's Göttingen's home became a welcome refuge. "We had a pretty southern veranda where Dietrich liked to take the sun," Sabine wrote.[3]

In November 1931, Dietrich's mother, grandmother, and Sabine (but not his brothers or father) witnessed his ordination. Paula sometimes attended church services with him. At the urging of his grandmother and with the financial backing of Anneliese Schnurmann, an assimilated Jewish school friend of his, he helped establish a "youth room" in Charlottenburg for the unemployed. It opened in the fall of 1932. He gathered around him a coterie of students, including such women as Hilde Pffeiffer, Adele Hoffmann, Helga Zimmermann, and Urusla Weymann.

At the same time, Nazi students demanded the right to march in the University of Göttingen's opening ceremonies, waving their gold-fringed swastika flags. University officials—though many supported Hitler—refused.[4] Despite their growing fears, Sabine and Gert took comfort in this. For the couple, Nazi anti-Semitism posed a grave threat: Gert might have been raised and confirmed a Lutheran, but since the National Socialists

1. Bosanquet, *The Life and Death of Dietrich Bonhoeffer*, 94.
2. Ibid.
3. Leibholz, *The Bonhoeffers*, 70.
4. Ibid., 69.

considered the Jews a racial, not a religious, group, Gert's Christianity offered no protection.

In these days leading up to the Nazi takeover, Berlin threatened to boil over, full of people hungry, desperate, and in tatters. Dietrich taught at Berlin University, worked as a youth pastor in a poor neighborhood and, after hours, met with his theology students. One, the tall, blond pastor's son, Wolf-Dieter Zimmermann, had become disenchanted with the irrelevance of his theological education. Then he happened on Dietrich's lecture on the nature of the church. At first, dismayed at the small handful of students attending the lecture, he imagined it would be no good, but instead found himself riveted. "Every sentence went home," Zimmermann remembered, as Dietrich reframed the question "Do we still need the church?" to "God needs us. Will we serve?"

When Dietrich invited Wolf to be part of his small weekly discussion group, the enthusiastic student offered his room as the meeting place. For three hours, ten to fifteen students crowded into the small attic space, amid "a bed, a washstand, desk, armchair and bookshelf." While Bonhoeffer numbered women among his students, Zimmermann doesn't mention if they participated in these theological discussions, the air "thick with heavy smoking." From 10:30 PM on, the group moved to the crowded streets and then into a smoky Alexanderplatz beer cellar—and Dietrich always paid the tab.[5]

Zimmermann learned "with astonishment" that Dietrich was a "convinced socialist and a pacifist."[6] Paul Lehman, however, noted tactfully that because of his "aristocratic heritage and taste" and his "conservatism," Dietrich could not embrace "doctrinaire" socialism. Instead, "his revolutionary sensitivity to the injustices of a capitalist and colonial society" meant an openness to social change.[7]

Another student, Ferenc Lehel, a Hungarian, recalled that when he or others would try to turn down a dinner invitation to Paula's house out of fear of imposing, Dietrich would insist. "That is not just my bread, it is our bread" he would say, "and when it is jointly consumed, there will still be 12 baskets left over." When Lehel wanted to visit the Baltic island of Rugen, Dietrich not only helped him plan the holiday but lent him his bicycle.[8]

While Dietrich's lectures began to attract more students, his sermon preaching at Trinity Church fell flat. Zimmermann noted "sixty to seventy people sitting scattered and forlorn in the spacious church," and attributed

---

5. Zimmermann and Smith, eds., *I Knew,* 61–62.
6. Ibid., 67
7. Ibid., 44.
8. Zimmermann and Smith, eds., *I Knew,* 69.

the dismal attendance to Bonhoeffer's tendency to preach with "a certain rational coldness." If Dietrich had reveled in his popularity as a preacher in Barcelona, in Berlin neither fellow clergy nor his congregation were as impressed.[9]

Once, too, as they were walking across the busy Potsdammer Platz in the heart of Berlin, Wolf told Dietrich that he "often made [such] an impression of coldness, of distance, that sometimes one felt almost repulsed by him, or as if he wanted to withdraw from the other person." Dietrich stopped, looked straight at Wolf, and said, "Why can't you let somebody be as he is?"[10]

"He did," added Wolf cryptically, "have conflicts in his private life just as we had."[11]

On January 30, 1933, when Hitler became chancellor, the National Socialists exulted in their triumph. "Some of the uncanny feeling of that night remains with me even today," remembered one German woman, who as a teen thrilled to fascism's rise in "the crashing tread of the feet, the somber pomp of the red and black flags, the flickering light of the torches on the faces and the songs with melodies that were at once aggressive and sentimental. For hours the columns marched by."[12] Dietrich, though deeply alarmed by events, also used the word *uncanny* in a letter he wrote to a Reinhold Niebuhr a week after Hitler's ascent: "We . . . live in an uncannily interesting time and one would hardly want to exchange it for another . . . ."[13]

As for Nazism's ascent, wrote Dietrich's father, these were "events we regarded from the outset as disaster, and all members of the family were unanimous in this."[14] Karl Bonhoeffer despised Hitler's demagogic speeches, his strange colleagues, and his tendency to carry a whip. He feared what he heard from his psychiatric colleagues about Hitler's sociopathic tendencies.[15] But in 1933, "sensible people" were sure Hitler would soon be gone —a civilized culture, many thought, wouldn't long endure mass hysteria and terror as substitutes for governance and law.[16]

---

9. Ibid., 62.
10. Ibid., 65.
11. Ibid., 67.
12. Nicholas, *Cruel World*, 100.
13. Quoted from Stern and Sifton, *No Ordinary Men*, 33.
14. Leibholz, *The Bonhoeffers*, 81.
15. Ibid.
16. Dawidowicz, *The War Against the Jews*, 49.

In a 1933 photo, Sabine looks like a movie star, slim, young, and elegant in a slinky white satin evening gown. Her youngest daughter sits on her lap. The oldest stands beside her. The girls wear matching white organdy dresses with three flounces at the hem, printed with sprigs of flowers. What looks like a stuffed toy poodle—though it may be real—sits at Sabine's feet, which are shod in glamorous pointed white shoes. In all ways, the girls and Sabine project a veneer of wealth, confidence, and ease, looking as if they float on the lap of luxury, protected and pampered, without a care in the world. But already, this world was collapsing beneath them.[17]

In the wake of the National Socialist takeover, Gert found his Göttingen lectures boycotted, Nazi brownshirts folding their arms, planting their boots, and blocking the door to his classroom. On Sunday mornings, the family listened fearfully amid their fine Biedermeier furniture as the SA men marched up and down the family's broad street singing "hang the Jews, shoot the Jews."[18] Knives dripping blood appeared on posters, promising revenge to all who'd betrayed Germany, Jews topping the list. In most of the local villages near them, signs read, "Jews get out."[19]

Dietrich vehemently opposed any church compromise with the regime. Hitler wanted to remake Christianity conform to Aryan ideology, including banning Jewish converts from ministry positions and planning to ban Jews from the church. Zimmermann remembered that Dietrich "read in fury" a Lutheran manifesto calling for the church to be apolitical.[20] Yet Dietrich accepted the advice of his church superintendent that he shouldn't preach at the funeral of Gert's Jewish father, William Leibholz, the man who a few years earlier had been terrorized by brownshirts rocking his car.

In April's "The Church and the Jewish Question," Dietrich expressed both his distress over Nazi persecution of the Jews and his supersessionism, the idea that Christianity should supplant Judaism. Like others of his class and time, Bonhoeffer framed Judaism as a problem—one, in tandem with most of his coreligionists, he thought could be "solved" by Jewish conversion to Christianity.[21] Although often deplored for supersessionism, the

---

17. This photo appears in the hardcover version of Leibholz, *The Bonhoeffers*, but is replaced with a less glamorous photo in the paperback edition, perhaps part of a campaign to downplay the family wealth, showing a snapshot of Sabine and her two daughters in ordinary clothes (Sabine, however, wears her signature heirloom pearls).

18. Leibholz, *The Bonhoeffers*, 78.

19. Ibid., 75.

20. Zimmermann and Smith, eds., *I Knew*, 63.

21. Barnett, "The Church and the Jewish Question": "The history of the suffering of this people, loved and punished by God, stands under the sign of the final homecoming of the people of Israel to its God," wrote Bonhoeffer. "And this homecoming happens in

essay also calls out strongly for challenging state persecution of the Jews, helping the victims of persecution and, if necessary, actively sticking a spoke in the wheels of an unjust political system. In April, Dietrich, Klaus, and Union Theological friend Paul Lehman wrote a joint letter of support to Stephen Wise, an outspoken US critic of Nazi anti-Semitism.[22]

On the night of May 10, 1933, the Nazis burned books, lighting spectacular bonfires of banned volumes in another nighttime ceremony, another horror to the Bonhoeffers. Joseph Goebbels, Reich propaganda minister, saw it differently: "The soul of the German people can again express itself. These flames not only illuminate the final end of an old era; they also light up the new."[23] For true believers, the Nazi penchant for eerie nighttime rituals, amid fire, smoke, and mists, conjured a mythic, mystical past, Teutonic Knights sprung from the grave, purity restored to Germany. To one observer, the German people exhibited a "new hope and a new confidence and an astonishing faith in the future of their country," believing Hitler would erase the humiliations of the past.[24]

The new regime assaulted what it called decadent bourgeois culture. The government banned Mendelssohn's music because he was Jewish. Theaters could perform Goethe, Schiller, and Shakespeare—as long as cast and crew remained Aryan. George Bernard Shaw's plays dodged the Nazi axe as well, "perhaps . . . because his wit and left wing political views escaped the Nazi mind."[25] The Jewish Max Reinhardt, that most famous

---

the conversion of Israel to Christ."

The question of Bonhoeffer's relationship to unconverted Jews remains open. Those he helped were almost entirely "baptized" Jews—assimilated Jews, largely of his social class, who had converted to Christianity. However, the Nazis made no distinction between those of Jewish descent who were practicing Judaism and those who had converted. Privately, Bonhoeffer was unequivocal in his condemnation of anti-Jewish violence; some question, nonetheless, whether he spoke out publicly often enough in defense of the Jews. See e.g., Rubenstein, "Was Dietrich Bonhoeffer A Righteous Gentile?" and Paldiel, "The Poisonous Well of Anti-Jewish Rhetoric." The question is complicated—it took full knowledge of the Holocaust to shatter the prevalent Christian supersessionist attitudes towards Judaism. Bonhoeffer, as Karl Barth noted, was one of the first clergy to speak out in defense of the Jews and consistently held to that stance. We note that two brother-in-laws, a sister-in-law, and several close family friends were Jewish, so the question was personal for him.

22. Ibid.
23. Shirer, *The Rise and Fall of the Third Reich*, 241.
24. Ibid., 231.
25. Ibid., 242–43. Or perhaps because of Shaw's outward conformity to traditional realist dramatic norms.

director of Shakespeare in Berlin, whose stagings Dietrich had seen,[26] fled to Hollywood.

Dietrich's brother-in-law, Rüdiger Schleicher, a lawyer in what had now become Göring's Air Ministry, agonized and then joined the Nazi Party in May, 1933 so that he could keep his job, and the access it offered him to undermining the state.[27]

Fear grew. The Nazis imposed a level of regimentation that surprised even Germans. As early as 1923, the Nazis had planned concentration camps for "all persons dangerous to security and useless eaters,"[28] and by the end of 1933, fifty "wild" ones had sprung up. Several of Gert's cousins would in later years end up dying in the concentration camps that became regimented in chilling and deadly ways.[29]

"Jews not welcome" signs popped up in shops, hotels, beer gardens, and public entertainment centers, while brownshirts attacked Jews on the street and police refused to intervene. Meanwhile high-ranking Nazis put on spectacular displays for foreign guests, such as Arabian Nights dinners, and rode through Berlin in conspicuously large Mercedes.

Hans von Dohnanyi, Dietrich's brother-in-law, by this time a rising government official like Rüdiger, survived the regime change despite having been a fervent supporter of the Weimar Republic. But because his maternal grandfather was Jewish, Dohnanyi had more than a few worries.[30] That summer, Hitler summoned him for a meeting. Hitler, who liked Hans, disregarded his "racial origins," but he and his sister Grete did not receive the needed official word of their racial "purity" until 1940.[31]

In July 1933, the Lutheran church in Germany fell in line and transformed itself to conform to the new regime. In August, the government took its first steps to dissolve the Catholic Youth League. Many Catholic priests, nuns, and lay leaders found themselves arrested, often on such manufactured irregularities as "currency violations,"[32] a charge that would later plague Dietrich. By the end of 1933, Hitler was insisting Germany's youth

---

26. Bethge, *DB: A Biography*, 65.
27. Stern and Sifton, *No Ordinary Men*, 53.
28. Dawidowicz, *The War Against the Jews*, 99.
29. Leibholz, *The Bonhoeffers*, 73.
30. Stern and Sifton, *No Ordinary Men*, 45.

31. Ibid., 47. Hitler tended to assume even assimilated Jews were enemies of the state; his persecution of Jews tended to make this a self-fulfilling prophecy, as anybody in danger of being labeled a Jew, like von Dohnanyis, would likely have equivocal feelings about the regime.

32. Shirer, *The Rise and Fall of the Third Reich*, 235.

were his. "Your child belongs to us already. . . . You will pass on. . . . Your descendants . . . will know nothing else but this new community."³³

Journalist Dorothy Thompson, driving in the countryside in 1934, stumbled on a Hitler Youth camp. She saw thousands of singing children and a huge banner stating "You were born to die for Germany." Such propaganda aimed at children chilled her.³⁴

In 1933, as his old world crumbled, Dietrich applied for and was turned down for a Berlin pastorate. He had joined the Pastors' Emergency League, hastily formed to oppose the Nazi redefinition of Christianity into Aryanism. The League's weak response to the Nazi quest to expel Jews from the church distressed him. He abandoned theological avenues he'd been exploring to pour his energy into the struggle to save the church from Nazi reinvention. By October, wearied, shaken, and feeling thwarted on all sides, Dietrich left for London to pastor two expatriate congregations. London was his crossroads, the last time everything could have gone one way or another.

---

33. Ibid., 249.
34. Nicholas, *Cruel World*, 106.

9

London

"I FIND MYSELF IN radical opposition to all my friends," Dietrich wrote to theologian Karl Barth, justifying his exile shortly after his October arrival in damp, dismal London. "[I was] increasingly isolated .. . . All this has frightened me and shook [sic] my confidence . . . ."[1]

In England, Dietrich moved to 23 Manor Mount in Forest Hills, the neighborhood of the wealthier of his two London congregations, a comfortable suburb on the opposite side of the Thames from downtown London. His church, a brick neo-Gothic structure, had a tall, narrow steeple on one side pointing like a rocket toward the heavens. He lived near the 1854 Crystal Palace, a huge glass building that had been a technological marvel in its time. It had been moved across the Thames long ago and was undergoing a revival after years of neglect. It would burn down in 1936, but now hosted concerts and talks.

Dietrich's other parish, St. Paul's German Reformed Church, served a working-class population in London's East End, traditional Cockney territory. This church stood on Goulston Lane, where in 1888, police had discovered Jack the Ripper's fourth victim, Catherine Eddowe, along with anti-Semitic graffiti written in chalk on a wall: 'The Juwes [sic] are not the men to be blamed for nothing."[2]

Dietrich's East End congregation's members had largely assimilated into English culture, often speaking English as a first language. He would frequently preach to them in his heavily American-accented English,[3] and

---

1. Bonhoeffer, *DBWE 13*, 23. The context of this letter is Barth's letter berating Bonhoeffer for leaving Germany when he was needed there for the church struggles.

2. "Jack the Ripper." The message may have been a hoax, but then, as in the 1930s, London became the destination for many Jews fleeing persecution, although in the 1880s they were fleeing from Russia.

3. Zimmermann and Smith, eds., *I Knew*, 95.

join them on hikes and picnics as they escaped the crowds, cobblestones, and coal smoke of the city's East End.[4]

Dietrich lived in the affluent Forest Hills, his rooms stretching across the attic level of his church's manse. Although his quarters are often described as two rooms, he had at least a large dining room, a study, and a guest room, as well as his own bedroom and kitchen.[5] A spacious, overgrown garden "reverting to wilderness" surrounded the home,[6] which leased most of its space to a German girls' school under the direction of a Fraulein Witte. The home, made of pale brick, stood at the top of steep lane of similar houses all lined in a row. Built in the 1860s, at the height of the British Empire, the houses reflected the fading glory of a once-great power.

The Bonhoeffer parsonage

Not long after arriving, Dietrich confessed a source of guilt that had been gnawing at him. He had not exaggerated in telling Barth that events in Germany had "frightened" him, and he poured out his feelings in a letter to Sabine, racked with regret that he had not preached at Gert's father's funeral: "it is a matter of constant remorse to me that at that time I did not simply accede to your request . . . . How could I have been so horribly timid?" He noted her tactful silence—"you . . . have not said anything to me about it

4. Bonhoeffer, *DBWE* 13, 2–3.
5. Bethge and Gremmels, *A Life in Pictures*, 73.
6. Bosanquet, *The Life and Death of Dietrich Bonhoeffer*, 131.

. . . ."—and expressed his deep anguish: "It haunts me now as something quite dreadful . . . that now can never be made good. Today, therefore, I must simply beg you to forgive me for my weakness . . . ."[7]

He wrote of yearning for an end to the Nazis, "so deep a longing for that real and ultimate peace in which sorrow, the injustice, the lies and the cowardice are at last truly brought to an end," and repeated his refrain: "I think so often of you, even though I only write infrequently."[8]

Yet all was not misery. Paula sent furniture, including the Bechstein grand piano, a treasured item despite the Bechstein family's close ties to Hitler.[9] Paula also hired Dietrich a housekeeper.

Sunshine burst into Dietrich's life when his friend Franz Hildebrandt, a tall, slim Lutheran pastor with a mother of Jewish descent, joined him in the manse. The two had met right before Dietrich defended his dissertation in December 1927. With this fun-loving, musical, and argumentative friend, whose outgoing personality put Dietrich at ease, Bonhoeffer maintained the familiar contours of the life he had led with his family in Berlin—sharing meals, piano playing, singing, conversation, and storytelling, with the addition of theological debates and endless joking.[10] The brick building, damp and drafty, lacked central heating, so the two fed coins into a gas heater in a futile attempt to stay warm, while dodging the ever-present mice that infested the building.[11] Between the laughter and talk, Dietrich sniffled, sneezed, and coughed with frequent colds. Germany's predicament, as well as Sabine's, preoccupied him, and he travelled back to Berlin often. If in Manhattan he had spent huge sums telegraphing his family, here he phoned home so often that, according to local legend, the phone company reduced his enormous bill.[12]

On Christmas Day, 1933, Wolf Zimmermann joined Dietrich and Franz. Wolf shivered through morning baths in the drafty manse but loved the

---

7. Leibholz, *The Bonhoeffers*, 75.
8. Ibid., 75–76.
9. Hitler particularly charmed Helene Bechstein, who introduced him into Munich high society and purportedly wished he had been her son. Not surprisingly, given the boost the family gave him, the Bechstein became Hitler's favorite piano. The flat couldn't have been too small if it could accommodate such a piano, which the family had purchased before Hitler became a force to be reckoned with.
10. Zimmermann and Smith, eds., *I Knew*, 78.
11. Eberhard Bethge, *DB: A Biography*, 328.
12. Wind, *A Spoke in the Wheel,* called it a "quantity rebate" (81).

magnificent 11 o'clock breakfasts he shared with his friends.[13] Piano playing and animated, argumentative conversations often lasted into the wee hours.

Dietrich plunged into exploring London. He made friends with another German expatriate pastor, Julius Rieger, and together the two went to movies and out for Chinese food, a cuisine Dietrich "particularly relished."[14] In the 1930s, the average Londoner did not eat Chinese, so Dietrich would have rubbed shoulders with the avant-garde in settings that offered such atmospheric touches as Chinese lanterns, real ivory chopsticks, and vivid Chinese wall murals. The *Shanghai Restaurant's Cookery Book* from 1936 contained recipes for "prawn rolls, sharks' fins in soup, fried duck, lobster omelette, fried rice with crab, pork cubes with sour sweet sauce, [and] chicken chop suey" as well as "Birds Nest in Whole Chicken," boasting one-ounce bird nests sewn into a whole boned chickens rinsed out with gin.[15]

Dietrich found himself drawn to London's National Gallery of Art on Trafalgar Square.[16] Another friend noted that Dietrich played tennis—in part to "get his weight down, a matter that rather worried him."[17]

High-spirited Hildebrandt made fun of Dietrich's housekeeper Berta Schulze (today we would call her a personal assistant). Dietrich had met Schulze in Berlin in the mid 1920s, when both were senior theology students under Dr. Harnack. Schulze was "phenomenally gifted in historical and theological knowledge."[18] Peers recognized Harnack had offered her the honor of an invitation to his private seminar in 1929, as he had Dietrich.[19] Berta supported Dietrich's remarkable academic achievement of writing two dissertations by age twenty-one by "tirelessly track[ing] down quotations for his work and help[ing] in the library."[20] She also wrote summaries for him on the Protestant and Roman Catholic church relationship and the workers' movement.[21]

Although part of Harnack's inner circle, Schulze's ties with the professor lacked the personal connection of Dietrich's. Harnack's niece was Dietrich's sister-in-law, Emmi Delbrück. The Delbrücks, the Harnacks, and

13. Zimmermann and Smith, eds., *I Knew*, 77.
14. Clements, *Bonhoeffer and Britain*, 26.
15. French, "London's Chinese Restaurant Scene in the 1930s."
16. Clements, *Bonhoeffer and Britain*, 26.
17. Zimmermann and Smith, eds., *I Knew*, 81.
18. Bethge, *DB: A Biography*, 68.
19. Ibid., 137.
20. Ibid.
21. Bonhoeffer, *DBWE* 9, 570.

the Bonhoeffers lived on same the block. Harnack himself, the picture of a genial German professor with his wire-framed glasses and tufts of white hair on either side of his bald head, would often walk chatting with Bonhoeffer through their leafy suburb to the train station—one that would later become notorious as a deportation point for Grunewald's Jews.[22] "For Harnack, Bonhoeffer was a highly valued pupil," Schulze said years later, and "one noticed this in the way he treated him. It was not customary in Harnack's seminars to receive praise."[23] Other students remember Dietrich challenging Harnack, politely but persistently.[24]

Dietrich called on Berta when he needed help. On January 5, 1932, he wrote to Friedrich Siegmund Schultze about a translation project that "someone nearby [Schulze], a friend of mine who does this kind of work extremely well and reliably, and would do [it] out of friendship. I of course, would check every questionable passage myself . . . I just don't have time to do every bit of it myself . . . ."[25] So was Schulze, a brilliant scholar, reduced to free translator by a man ten years her junior—who promised to check up on her.

Schulze's status became even more marginal under the Nazis, who were ideologically committed to returning women to the home.[26] A single woman in her late thirties with a PhD, Berta found more and more doors closed. Starting in 1933, National Socialist legislation limited the number of female staff in higher education to 10 percent.[27] Beyond that, Hitler himself denounced women's equality as "a symptom of depravity on par with parliamentary democracy," stating that "equal rights for women means that they receive the esteem they deserve in the sphere nature has assigned to them."[28] As the Nazi Dr. Kurt Rosten asked, typifying the Nazi's sentimental concept of womanhood: "Can woman conceive of anything more beautiful than to sit with her beloved husband in her cozy home and to listen inwardly to the loom of time weaving the weft and warp of motherhood through centuries and millennia?"[29]

---

22. Rumscheidt, "Harnack, Seeberg, and Bonhoeffer," 211.
23. Ibid.
24. Ibid.
25. Bonhoeffer, *DBWE* 13, 87.
26. Grunberger, *A Social History of the Third Reich*, 240.
27. Aycoberry, *The Social History of the Third Reich*, 116.
28. Grunberger, *A Social History of the Third Reich*, 253.
29. Ibid., 254.

Little wonder Berta agreed to work for her younger peer, managing his affairs and acting as his secretary. She must have arrived soon after Dietrich, as by January, three months into his stay, she had become the butt of jokes.

Berta had "intentions" toward Dietrich, thought Hildebrandt.[30] Berta's attentions, whether designed to "catch a husband" or simply part of a conscientious and detail-oriented personality, led Hildebrandt to mock her in a poem he sent to Dietrich as a 28th birthday gift: "Berta, however,/ I pray thee/ Beg thee as well/ Leave her behind."[31]

In her birthday letter to her son, Paula also referred to Berta: "We could just as well have sent the package last week, but I was worried about the cake. You'll be thinking that I sound like Berta!"[32]

According to Hildebrandt, Berta's apparent romantic interest "led to her dismissal."[33] But who dismissed her and when? From Bertha, who survived to 1987, we hear only a polite silence.

Among other bourgeois perks, Dietrich flew often from London to Berlin at a time when air travel was the domain of the wealthy. While the loud and bumpy rides left Dietrich uneasy, planes catered to a well-to-do clientele with plush seating, wet bars, wood paneling, and solicitous stewards. This, along with frequent phone calls, kept him in close contact with family. Both von Dohnanyis, with Christel, and Walter with Susi, came to visit.[34] While the living quarters were not what these well-heeled Berliners were used to, Dietrich made up for it with music and hospitality.

London pleasures included Dietrich's friendship with George Bell, the bishop of Chichester, with whom he shared a February 4th birthday and a consuming interest in the German church struggle. He visited the bishop at his home, Chichester Palace, enjoying "the great high rooms with their open fireplaces . . . ."[35] The top-hatted twosome also dined together at the exclusive Athenaeum Club, where Bell was a member, the building a neoclassic

---

30. Bonhoeffer, *DBWE 13*, 95.

31. Ibid., 95. One hopes "behind" is not meant as a double entendre.

32. Ibid., 100. Indeed, Paula does sound solicitous, sending Dietrich a birthday package that includes a pillow "stuffed very firmly, to use for your back on the couch," the aforementioned cake, a brass bowl, and a picture.

33. Ibid., 95n. Without identifying Schulze, Keith Clements, in *Bonhoeffer and Britain*, notes the hazy stories of a housekeeper who has to be dismissed for "religious dementia" and also one with supposed designs on Bonhoeffer. "Possibly these are variants of the same story," Clements writes (26).

34. Bethge, *DB: A Biography*. Christel and Susi remain nameless to Bethge, referred to as "their wives" (328).

35. Leibholz, *The Bonhoeffers*, 113.

square brightened by a frieze that ran around its exterior, recreating the Elgin marbles on a bright Wedgewood blue background. Class played its part. Bell liked the "well bred young German, who never got so carried away that he forgot his good manners."[36]

Bell had long mixed religious vocation with a love of the arts, support for the labor movement, and service to the poor. Like Dietrich, he had a fascination with Gandhi. Bell had, as well, been in Germany while the Protestant Church was debating its connection with the German (Nazi) Church, and had witnessed Nazi church anti-Semitism first hand.

One of the most charming descriptions of Bonhoeffer—and one that captures him at his charismatic best—comes from the bishop's wife, Henrietta Bell: "He was an especially attractive, vigorous, lively man with plenty of rather unruly chestnut hair and bright, eager blue eyes. And I remember after he left [a meal at Chichester Palace] saying, 'Well, that really was a very unusually attractive person.'"[37]

In 1934, as Dietrich enjoyed life at the heart of the British Empire, Sabine and Gert remained on edge in an increasingly frightening Germany. They bought a car in case of "urgent need." They left Göttingen, where the stigma of being Jewish clung, as often as possible, staying in Berlin or traveling abroad.[38] They discussed emigration.

In a letter from London, Dietrich expressed his anxiety over Sabine's daughters' schooling, sounding cold and haughty as he was wont to do when frightened. In school, first Marianne, and later Christianne, endured catty remarks from teachers and students. One child called out to young Christiane, "Your father is a Jew," an open insult in those times. Every day on the walk to school the girls passed under a sign saying "the father of the Jew is the devil." A newspaper box across from the school sold *Der Sturmer*, the virulently anti-Semitic newspaper. "The elder schoolchildren thronged in front of this," Sabine remembered.[39] Their father's Jewish blood barred the girls from the Hitler Youth, a relief to the parents, but isolating for the daughters.

"I am so very sorry you are having anxieties about the children," Dietrich wrote to Sabine. Why not, he asked, put them in the car and send them to stay in Berlin with the grandparents or an aunt or uncle? "I really don't understand this," he said, his stock phrase to express emotional distress.

36. Bethge, *DB: A Biography*, 361.
37. Clements, *Bonhoeffer and Britain*, 32.
38. The Jewish Confessing Church member Victor Klemperer, though he could ill afford to do so, also bought a car, and with his Aryan wife was pleased to travel to places like Berlin, where Victor could pass as Aryan.
39. Leibholz, *The Bonhoeffers*, 77.

Late one night in 1934, the Leibholz phone rang unexpectedly. The family froze in fear as each shrill ring reverberated. Only the Gestapo would call at that hour. Was Gert about to be sent to a concentration camp? When they finally answered, they heard Dietrich's cheery voice on the other end of the line, ready for a chat from London. "I am sorry," he wrote later, "that . . . I gave you such a fright during the night, and in fact it was exceptionally stupid."[40]

People in Göttingen began to cross the street when they saw Gert coming. Like other non-Aryans, he was banned from entering the university. Rather than protest the discrimination, many Aryan faculty members approved.[41] In this, Göttingen was not unusual; like the clergy in the Protestant Church, the university system was conservative, if not reactionary, and lecturers often taught nationalism and anti-Semitism. "Most professors were fanatical nationalists who wished for the return of a conservative, monarchial Germany," wrote journalist William Shirer. These professors found the Nazis "too rowdy," but accepted the dictatorship.[42] Peter Gay characterized the universities as "nurseries of a wooly minded militarist idealism and centers of resistance to the new in art and social sciences . . . ."[43] Victor Klemperer, an assimilated Dresden Jew banned from teaching, wished that certain professors could be left hanging from the highest lamp posts for their betrayal of human decency.[44]

Many professors clung to their jobs, pledging allegiance to the regime despite its criminality and hostility to intellectualism. One professor called it "a scene of prostitution" as one university after another fell behind Hitler when opposing him could still have made a difference.[45] Meanwhile, Sabine worried about Gert, and Dietrich pondered his next step.

---

40. Ibid.
41. Ibid, 74.
42. Shirer, *The Rise and Fall of the Third Reich*, 251.
43. Gay, *Weimar Culture*, 3.
44. Klemperer, *I Shall Bear Witness*, xix. Klemperer's journal accounts of living as an assimilated Jew and ousted professor, protected by an Aryan wife, provide valuable insight into Sabine and Gert's experience.
45. Shirer, *The Rise and Fall of the Third Reich*, 251–52.

10

Battles and Choices

IN ENGLAND, DIETRICH CONTINUED to throw himself into the struggle against the Reich's Aryan vision of Christianity, which marked his first entry into pitched battle with a real adversary. The stakes were of the highest magnitude: civilization or barbarism, peace or war, Christianity or Nazism. He entered into the fight with youthful passion and determination, where, for all the importance of his cause, he sometimes sounded as if he were plotting strategy for a snowball fight—or one of the backyard battles he and Sabine had once waged against Klaus.

"I believe what has happened up to now has been only preliminary skirmishing," Dietrich wrote from London in an undated circular letter in 1934. "The second, real battle is coming and will break out somewhere else altogether and we will no longer be able, or be allowed, to fight it out with the same fresh and cheerful militancy. Instead, this second struggle about Christianity will be won by those who can suffer all the way through it. It will lead to the complete splintering and shattering of the so-called opposition fronts . . . ."[1]

In January 1934, Julius Rieger, companion on so many excursions to films and Chinese restaurants, joined the Nazi Party, hoping to have a stronger voice from within than without. Yet in February, when Bishop Heckel arrived in England from Germany to get the renegade German pastors in line, including insisting they support excluding Jews from the church, Rieger joined Dietrich and another pastor in walking out of the meeting. Heckel threatened, vaguely, to revoke passports and charge oppositional pastors with disloyalty to the Reich.[2] And so the preliminary skirmishes proceeded.

Almost alone among his Protestant clergy friends, Bonhoeffer grasped that Hitler could not be reasoned with, bargained with, or "educated." "We have tried often enough—too often—to make Hitler aware of what is going on. . . . Hitler [will not] . . . listen to us; he is obdurate, and as such, he must

1. Bonhoeffer, *DBWE* 13, 190.
2. Barnes and Barnes, *Nazis in Pre-War London*, 106–7.

compel us to listen—it's that way round. The Oxford Movement was naïve enough to try and convert Hitler—a ridiculous failure to recognize what is going on. We are the ones to be converted, not Hitler." [3]

Thus Dietrich wrote Sutz, indignant and frustrated. He knew that Hitler understood only power—and he urged uncompromising displays of church strength that would force Hitler to back down.

Hitler, in fact, privately expressed the contempt that Bonhoeffer believed his peers invited with their attempts at appeasement and compromise: "[Protestants] will submit," Hitler said. "They are insignificant little people, submissive as dogs, and they sweat with embarrassment when you talk to them."[4]

In May, concerned pastors led by Barth hammered out the Barmen Declaration, which openly opposed the Nazification of German Protestant churches. Thus began the Confessing Church, a body that stood for orthodox Christianity in the face of Hitler's Reich Church. Although he did not attend Barmen, Dietrich contributed background work on the Declaration and became a staunch member and supporter of the Confessing Church, pushing it to take ever stronger stands.[5]

Dietrich returned to Berlin on June 18, 1934, less than two weeks before the Röhm Putsch, a time when Berlin was swept with secret excitement that Hitler's tyranny was on the verge of collapse: "With each hot June day the rumors gained detail. In bars and cafés, patrons engaged in the decidedly dangerous pastime of composing and comparing lists of who would comprise the new government."[6]

On Sunday, June 17, Von Papen, a close friend of Hans von Wedemeyer, whose life would intersect with Dietrich's in yet unimagined ways through his mother-in-law and daughter, delivered a shocking speech—written for and imposed on him by his advisors—criticizing the Nazi overlords. "The Government," Papen said, "is well aware of the selfishness, the lack of principle, the insincerity, the unchivalrous behavior, the arrogance which is on the increase under the guise of the German revolution."[7]

Though we have no record, there can be little doubt that the Bonhoeffer family was alight with hope that the end of a black period of German

---

3. Bonhoeffer, *DBWE 13*, 218.

4. Shirer, *Rise and Fall of the Third Reich*, 238.

5. As noted in the Introduction, providing a full history of the Confessing Church, which has been thoroughly done before, is beyond the scope of this book. Bethge's *Dietrich Bonhoeffer: A Biography* and Barnett's *For the Soul of the People* are both good sources. Barnett highlights the role of women in the church struggle.

6. Larson, *In the Garden of Beasts*, 283.

7. Ibid., 284.

history was in sight—or that, at least, as von Papen's speech urged, the Nazis would rein in their fanatics. "All old and intellectual Germans are highly pleased," the American ambassador, Dodd, wrote in his journal of June 20.[8] According to historian John Wheeler-Bennett, then in Berlin, "It is difficult to describe the joy with which it [the speech] was received in Germany. It was as if a load had suddenly been lifted from the German soul. The sense of relief could almost be felt in the air."[9] One wonders if Dietrich, Sabine, and Gert were together in Berlin during these heady days, Dietrich hoping the sword would soon stop dangling over his sister's head. Newspapers in London and elsewhere treated the speech as a "sensation."[10]

By Sunday, June 24, Dietrich had returned from England. Perhaps both his sense of foreboding and his faith were encapsulated in the baptismal homily he delivered in London that day: "Nobody can foretell the future, and it is no use doing it. But however dark it seems to be, there is only one man who is free of every fear—the man who believes that God is his help."[11] Revolt against the Nazis had been in the Berlin air—and even after Hitler ruthlessly slaughtered his opponents during the Röhm Purge of June 30–July 2, 1934, Dietrich would not give up hope for a domestic overthrow of National Socialism. One senses that in the midst of his small sermon, written in English and initially addressed to a "joyful day, indeed, when a mother and her child together give their lives into the hands of Jesus Christ," Dietrich began to dwell on his own fate, so bound up with Germany's, and thus moved to a rhetoric of "man" and strength before returning at the end to the love of the mother and her child. The next Sunday, he would speak out strongly, in coded language, against the Nazi regime.

Although the relationship had sputtered in 1928, Dietrich remained in touch with Elisabeth Zinn. She saved thirteen of the London sermons he sent her.[12]

After attending the ecumenical conference in Fanø, Denmark, in August 1934, Dietrich took a circuitous route back to London, stopping for a few days to visit Sabine in her Göttingen home before heading to a session of the Reich Council of Brethren in Wurzburg.[13]

---

8. Ibid., 287.
9. Ibid., 285.
10. Ibid., 286.
11. Bonhoeffer, *DBWE 13*, 364.
12. Bonhoeffer, *DBWE 14*, 134. We have them because Zinn saved them.
13. Bethge, *DB: A Biography*, 391.

Since the 1920s, inspired by Tafel,[14] Dietrich had dreamed of India. Now, before the huge fireplace at the bishop's palace or ensconced in comfortable chairs in the Athenaeum, Bell and Bonhoeffer discussed India and late in 1934, Dietrich revived plans to make the long trek there. While his mother, grandmother, Christel, and Sabine supported his quest, most of his German male peers didn't understand his fascination. Even his more enlightened clergy friends, those who opposed the Aryanization of the German church, couldn't comprehend why he would want to study Gandhi's techniques of nonviolent resistance. Franz Hildebrandt and Karl Barth, among others, discouraged this interest.[15]

Bell, who knew Gandhi, understood Dietrich's yearning and wrote a letter of introduction.

"Dear Friend," Gandhi wrote Dietrich in the fall of 1934, "if you . . . have enough money for return passage and can pay your expenses here . . . you can come whenever you like."[16]

Dietrich now attempted to be more intentional in his plans than he had in the winter and spring of 1931, when, as an enthusiastic student in New York, he had taken to scouring shipping offices looking for cheap ways to get to Asia. Despite his heavy expenses telegraphing home, he had tried to economize by eating at coffee pots, low-cost restaurants where a down and outer could get a cheap meal.[17] Christel had pushed him then, advising him to borrow money from their parents: "If you accept a position here immediately and promise not to marry soon, you can pay it back . . . I have a feeling they are sympathetic."[18]

Yet for all his inquiries and efforts, by April 12, 1931, he had abandoned his plan. It was "just too far," he wrote to his grandmother.[19]

This time would be different. Always careful about his dress, in London Dietrich accepted "tropical suits" (ironically probably not that different from what Sabine had called the "tropical" garb of the brownshirts) from

---

14. In 1928, his grandmother wrote to Dietrich, encouraging him to visit India (ibid., 105).

15. Bethge, *DB: A Biography*, 407. "People in Berlin regarded his Indian scheme as thoroughly eccentric." Interestingly, however, Wilhelm Niesel, head of the preacher's seminaries in the Old Prussian Council of the Brethren, recalls, in *I Knew*, that Gerhard Jacobi, president of the Berlin Brethren's Council, pushed for Bonhoeffer as director of a seminary on the basis of his having been "profoundly influenced by Gandhi, a reason that "somewhat surprised" Niesel (Zimmermann and Smith, eds., *I Knew*, 145–46).

16. Quoted in Bethge and Gremmels, *A Life in Pictures*, 87.

17. Zimmermann and Smith, eds., *I Knew*, 44.

18. Bethge, *DB: A Biography*, 147.

19. Bonhoeffer, *DBWE 10*, 293.

Theodor Lang, a parishioner at his Forest Hills church and the first secretary at the German embassy, who had formerly been stationed in Singapore. Lang's wife altered them to fit him.

"I would like to see still one more great country in order to judge whether the solution will possibly come from there—India; for otherwise things appear to be beyond repair, the great death of Christendom seems to have arrived," Dietrich had written in 1931, the dire situation in Germany on his mind.[20] In a letter to Edward Sutz from May 17, 1932, he expressed the same wish: "I can hardly think of [the Manhattan year] without experiencing a great desire to travel again, this time to the East."[21] And tellingly, it was to his grandmother he wrote in 1934, in the midst of the renewed effort to travel: "Before I settle down permanently anywhere, I want to try once more to go to India. Recently I have occupied myself intensively with the issues over there, and I believe one might learn very important things. In any case it often appears to me that there may be more Christianity present in the 'heathenism' than in our whole established church."[22]

In London, Dietrich heard Gandhi disciple Mira Bai speak, possibly at the nearby Crystal Palace. Once called Madeline Slade, this admiral's daughter had given up her possessions and spent time in prison in pursuit of freedom for India.[23]

Dietrich perhaps subscribed to "Orientalism," which found its popular expression in notions of flying carpets, maharishis wearing turbans embedded with rubies, and magic potions hidden in six-armed Vishnu statues. In Edward Said's reading, the West lumped together all the widely disparate cultures of the "East" as a monolith[24]—such was the mystique, if illusion, of the "Orient" in popular culture. Among more educated people, the "Orient" held the promise, which Dietrich yearned for, of a purer faith expression. Yet this mythic, mystic view of the "exotic East" held only a tangential relationship to reality, its dark, smoky aesthetic perhaps closer to Leni Riefenstahl's vision of the Nuremberg rallies than anything in Asia.

---

20. Peck, "The Significance of Bonhoeffer's Interest in India," 438.
21. Ibid., 437.
22. Ibid., 439.
23. Bethge, *DB: A Biography*, 407.
24. See Said, *Orientalism*. While Bonhoeffer's interest in India and Gandhi seems completely in earnest and accords with his pacifism, fascination with Eastern religions and Gandhi in particular was a vogue amongst the intelligentsia of this period, and like Chinese food, would in 1950s and '60s Europe and America be taken up by the masses. Nick Carraway's dry recounting of Gatsby's confused Orientalism in *The Great Gatsby* pokes cruel fun at the phenomenon.

After a year coping with dismal London rains, and a run of colds, Dietrich was—at least in his dreams—drawn to "the distant, fertile, sunny . . . world of India."[25] But now Germany also beckoned. Gerhard Jacobi, head of Berlin's Brethren Council and a Confessing Church member, thought Dietrich's interest in Gandhi "could be of great use in shaping" a church community and offered him the directorship of a Confessing Church seminary.[26]

Dietrich faced up to his decision: Gandhi's ashram in India or the seminary in Germany? Going to India would fulfill the dreams of his mother and grandmother, as well as his own long-held yearnings—and would safeguard him from Nazi Germany. On the other hand, directing the seminary would offer him the chance to establish a monastic community that could potentially revitalize Christianity in his homeland.

Dietrich chose Germany.

Dietrich wrote to Sabine and Gert for Gert's birthday in November 1934: "I have made myself very much at home here [in London] and yet naturally my life's work does not lie here. I do not like leaving, but more from certain feelings of security that are very *bourgeois* [Bonhoeffer's italics] and these must certainly not be allowed to become a major factor, otherwise life will no longer have any real value at all and there will no longer be any joy in it either."[27]

Now he wrote a revelatory letter to his brother, Karl-Friedrich, having accepted the seminary position: "I do believe that at last I am on the right track, for the first time in my life." His faith in his Sermon on the Mount theology was immense: "Here alone lies the force that can blow all this hocus-pocus [Nazism] sky high—like fireworks."[28]

---

25. Bethge, *DB: A Biography*, 440.

26. Zimmermann and Smith, eds., *I Knew*, 145. Elisabeth Zinn was Jacobi's vicar at this time, so it's possible she encouraged him to offer Dietrich the position.

27. Leibholz, *The Bonhoeffers*, 89. A slightly different translation of the same letter appears in Bonhoeffer, *DBWE 13*, 242, where "quite ordinary" substitutes for "bourgeois."

28. Bonhoeffer, *DBWE 13*, 285. Dietrich tried to juggle both India and the seminary. Although in the end he was willing to spend only a few weeks in India, the travel time there and back made the trip impossible. Instead Bonhoeffer visited religious communities in Britain.

PART III
The Incomparable Year

— 11 —
New Ground

THOUGH BERLIN NOW BRISTLED with swastika banners and machine gun-toting youths with Nazi armbands riding in the backs of open trucks, in 1935 Dietrich traversed a city largely unchanged in the two years since the Nazi takeover. The classical columns and arches along broad boulevards still proclaimed imperial ambitions from the days of the Kaisers.[1] The city still hummed with life and energy, if of a different sort from the chaotic Weimar days. Office workers jammed the cream-colored streetcars. Red double-decker buses, similar to London's, crisscrossed the city, along with red and white elevated trains and dark red and cream-colored commuter trains, in almost incessant, mechanized motion. Only the affluent owned cars, which competed in the traffic circles with horse-drawn carts and scores of bicycles. Below ground, red and white subways ran day and night.[2]

Once hungry, Berliners now ate well. Most factory workers bought a subsidized hot lunch at work for about $2.[3] Higher status employees, such as secretaries, would buy the milk and hot dogs wheeled around their offices on carts or bring a lunch in the ubiquitous Berlin briefcase. Commuters in a hurry could grab an orange or banana from a street cart heaped high with produce. Businessmen might catch a quick lunch at Aschinger, the Berlin equivalent of New York's Horn and Hardart automats, or hop into a bar for a "small beer" with pea soup and bacon or bockwurst and potato salad. Someone of Dietrich's class, looking for a more refined meal, would order a light lunch of coffee, cold cuts, and two soft-boiled eggs in a glass in a coffeehouse, or dine at one of the city's hotels or a fine restaurant that served wine in addition to beer.[4]

1. Friedrich, *Before the Deluge*, 6.
2. Lubrich, ed., *Travels in the Reich*, 184.
3. Ibid., 185. A cheap hot lunch was a perk, but more importantly, a way for a government obsessed with food and remilitarization to cut the fats workers put on their sandwiches.
4. Ibid., 185.

Yet life had changed. By 1935, Hitler had swept away Weimar's giddy, gritty, and glittering experimentation in art and social arrangements. Cross-dressing, homosexuality, and nudity had slipped entirely underground, "American" decadence had been outlawed, the streets were orderly, and an uneasy stability sustained by terror replaced the dizzying feeling that "one was dancing on a volcano."[5] Perhaps most notably, unemployment had fallen from 6 million in 1932 to 1.5 million.[6]

Kay Smith, whose maid had once asked to eat the runny remnants of a breakfast egg, was back in Berlin after a twelve-year absence. Weimar's gritty decay was gone: "no more shabby fronts and broken fences . . . the crowds . . . well dressed . . . well nourished." But Smith also noted the "tension."[7]

During Dietrich's springtime arrival, he would have been greeted by birds: sparrows twittered amid the traffic of the Kurfürstendamm, the crowded artery that cut across the city, where the elegantly dressed Paula still liked to stop and relax over coffee and cake or soup and a small meat pie, after a day of shopping—and where she would tip the wait staff generously.[8] In Berlin, birds unusual in urban centers congregated: magpies, nightingales, and the black-feathered, yellow-throated diving grebe. Swans floated peacefully in the canals outside the Charlottenburg Palace. The metropolis remained a land of parks, gardens, and waterways. Wild boars and deer still ran loose in its woods, once royal game preserves. Berlin, in the words of Heinrich Hauser, writing in the 1930s, was a "green" city long before that color had ecological connotations, a city with as many trees as people, where the balconies of the apartment houses bloomed extravagantly with flowers.[9] Few places, however, would have been as garden-like as Dietrich's parents' house in Grünewald, where he reentered a spacious and familiar world.

One of Dietrich's hopes was that by helping to build a powerful Confessing Church that would stand firm against Nazi anti-Semitism, he would help establish a safe haven for Sabine and Gert, whose situation grew more dire with every passing month. To do so, he would now enter what seemed a wholly male world, although it was infused with Paula's spirit—and women, including one of particular importance, would come to support it.

On April 17, Dietrich reported for work as director of a preacher's seminary under the auspices of the Old Prussian Council for the Brethren,

---

5. Ibid., 189.
6. Gole, *Exposing the Third Reich*, 145
7. Ibid., 144.
8. Leibholz, *The Bonhoeffers*, 9.
9. Friedrich, *Before the Deluge*, 4–5.

earning 360 marks a month, a comfortable salary.[10] He hardly had time to catch his breath: he was under immense pressure to find a home for his new seminary.[11] He and the tall, slim, deceptively sepulchral Hildebrandt, still high-spirited and joking, still his closest friend, drove through Brandenburg, an area just south of Berlin, checking out possibilities. Nothing suited. Just as they were about to accept temporary housing in Berlin, not the most desirable setting because of its heavy Gestapo presence, good fortune struck. The Rhineland Bible School in Zingst offered them temporary sanctuary.[12] Characteristic of him when he knew what he wanted, Dietrich wasted no time heading towards his destination.

On a raw, windy night, Dietrich arrived at Zingst with twenty-three seminarians, a mere three days after learning that the Bible school existed. Leaving the train station, the all-male group hiked half an hour through "impenetrable darkness" to reach their destination on the chilly shores of the Baltic.

Warmth, light, and steaming fried potatoes greeted them at the school's musty conference center. After dinner, the group shared communal Bible reading and sang hymns. They were excited, on fire—not seminarians going through school to get a good job in a secure field, but young men deliberately choosing a path through the Confessing Church, an institution at odds with the state. They risked their futures, sure they were doing God's work.[13] Some had already been interrogated, arrested, or imprisoned.[14]

For six weeks, the group lived in drafty thatched-roof cabins amid the sandy dunes, shared an outhouse, and attended classes in the dilapidated half-timbered center, built years earlier by "the Bible Circles of the Baltic." Their grounds, a mile from Zingst, ran from the beach to the edge of the adjoining heath.

The rough and ready setting, more summer camp than seminary, worked in the students' favor. The relaxed environment led them to overcome the "superfluous rigidity" normal in German life and to bond.[15] Not many seminaries offered the possibility of a race down the beach for

---

10. Bethge, *DB: A Biography,* 424. For an inflation calculator, see http://fxtop.com/en/inflation-calculator.php.
11. Ibid., 417.
12. Ibid.
13. Bonhoeffer, *DBWE 14,* 87.
14. Ibid., 24.
15. Ibid., 87.

a dip in the icy cold Baltic.[16] Not many offered a director as young and unconventional as Dietrich.

No other houses were in sight. On clear days, students could see the Baltic island of Rügen in the distance. In this lonely outpost, on a cold, windy peninsula far north of Berlin, Dietrich and his pupils breathed in salty air, listened to the cries of the birds, and focused on God and each other. Between classes, the young men hiked on the windy shore, played ball, and held outdoor worship services amid sand dunes where coarse grasses grew. Sometimes they sang, perhaps a setting for four voices by Josquin des Pres.[17] Surely, when Bonhoeffer played his gramophone recordings of Negro spirituals brought back from America[18]—a way to open the subject of Negro oppression in the US, which Dietrich had promised his Harlem friends he would discuss in Germany—his students must, for a few moments, have felt transported to another world.

---

16. Ibid., 22.
17. Bethge, *DB: A Biography*, 425.
18. Holland, "First We Take Manhattan, Then We Take Berlin."

— 12 —
New Arrival

ARRIVING A DAY LATE, a lanky, handsome young man with an infectious smile strolled onto the beach near Zingst. We might imagine him, albeit fully clothed, arising like Venus from the sea, but in fact, he came from the shore. He was twenty-five, tall, and athletic, with a gift for music and theology. Some of the seminarians, theologically sophisticated and well-heeled, knew Dietrich from University of Berlin circles, but this newcomer, Eberhard Bethge, had to ask someone to point out his director, so young he blended in with the other seminarians.

Dietrich invited the new arrival for a walk on the "yellow, sandy shore of the Baltic." Eberhard was taller than him, with broad shoulders, long limbs, a wide mouth. Next to him, Bonhoeffer looked rounder, balder, and more professorial in his wire-framed glasses, though Eberhard would later remember him as "powerfully built . . . with lively blue eyes."[1] As they strolled side by side along the breezy shore, Dietrich asked Eberhard about his home, his family, and his friends. Eberhard had never experienced such personal interest from a professor.

Eberhard might have talked of his father Wilhelm, who had been a pastor in the small farming village of Zitz where Eberhard grew up. To the young Eberhard, his father, floating lofty in the pulpit and often sought out for advice, seemed "like the king of the village."[2] When his father died, fourteen-year-old Eberhard, whose hero worship never had a chance to be tempered by the conflicts of adolescence, gladly followed in his footsteps. In his social milieu, unlike Bonhoeffer's, a pastoral career was admirable, not idiosyncratic.

Eberhard had initially supported Hitler. "During my childhood in the Second German Reich, the greatest thing that could happen to me was when my father would drive us children to Potsdam once a year—Potsdam, with its Garrison Church and memorials to Frederick the Great, with the

---

1. Leibholz, *The Bonhoeffers*, 42.
2. Bethge, *Friendship and Resistance*, 1.

soldiers singing 'Now thank we all our God' after the Prussian defeat of the Austrians in 1757. Those are very strong, lasting childhood impressions, which were why we at first welcomed the political events of 1933," Eberhard later wrote.[3]

In welcoming this messianic, militaristic leader, Eberhard was hardly alone. The German Lutheran Church had wholeheartedly supported World War I and, like other German institutions, had been devastated by the defeat. Not only did the surrender undermine the clergy's belief that God sided with Germany, it brought changes that appeared catastrophic: The Empire was dissolved, and the monarchy abolished. The Lutheran Church rejected democracy on theological grounds, believing that if the legitimacy of the state derived from God, it must come down to the people through a divinely appointed monarch, not up from the masses. Hence, democracy was heresy. Initially too, the provisional government established in 1918 wanted to separate church and state. For a short time, the clergy lost its power to oversee state schools. The government was also on the verge of ending subsidies to churches, instead proposing to tax them, when a public outcry stopped this.

In fact, the Weimar Constitution granted the churches the privileges they had enjoyed under the Kaiser. However, the damage had been done. The Lutheran Church had locked itself into viewing the Republic as a deadly enemy,[4] and turned from democracy to a romanticized German past of "blood and iron and simple, heroic piety." Luther's popularity surged during the Weimar period, when modern Lutherans aggressively adopted him as representative of a distinctly German rather than European or Enlightenment spirit: "The irrational, dark and mysterious elements in Luther, and therefore in the whole Germanic race, were idealized." The church cast Luther as a conservative alternative to Calvin, one of the hated French, who was linked with decadent democracy and a Western European rationalism designed to oppress the Volk spirit.[5]

Unlike Dietrich, Eberhard had not distinguished himself as a scholar. Some of his teachers despaired of the happy-go-lucky youth who seemed better at crafts than applying himself to academics. "I urgently advise you to allow your son to take up a practical trade at Easter . . . [even though] it is Eberhard's wish to become a pastor," one teacher wrote to his mother. "Whether

---

3. Ibid., 2.
4. Klan, "Luther's Resistance Teaching," 439.
5. Ibid., 440–42.

Eberhard is up to these demands naturally cannot yet be determined, but I doubt it."[6]

Studious or not, Eberhard pursued theology, and in 1933 immediately understood, as did his friends, that while they might support Hitler, they couldn't support the new Reich Church. Like so many in the German clergy, they believed Hitler was simply misguided. "We dreamed," wrote Bethge, "that Karl Barth might have a word with him [Hitler] some time and then everything would be different."

In October 1934, the Confessing Church announced it would not follow the dictates of the Nazified German Church. Eberhard and fourteen of his friends were giddy with excitement. They pressed their director to pronounce their Wittenburg seminary, the very spot where Martin Luther had denounced Catholic heresy, part of the Confessing Church.[7]

Instead, the director expelled them.[8]

Young and carefree, they failed to grasp how antithetical their orthodox Christianity was to National Socialist aims. Most of them still believed in Hitler's ability to save Germany, if only he would correct his theology.[9] They should have been frightened but instead celebrated when Swiss and English newspapers printed their story.[10]

Their open opposition to the Nazi church lit up their spiritual lives. As civil rights activists would later sing "we shall overcome," they sang "Keep us in thy word, O Lord/and do deflect the enemies' sword." Eberhard's cousin and best friend Gerhard Vibrans wrote of the power they felt rising from "an insurmountable wall of prayer."[11]

At least one seminary instructor tried to cool their ardor: if there had once been a Hellenization of the Christian faith, he asked, why not a Germanization? The young theologians remained unmoved.

Luckily for them—and worried mothers and girlfriends—the Confessing Church immediately swept them into its new seminary. Thus, Eberhard, recently broken up with a fiancée, found himself on a windy beach.

The next day, preaching in the sandy Rhineland Bible center, Dietrich turned the notion that faith leads to obedience on its head, stating

---

6. de Gruchy, *Daring, Trusting Spirit*, 4.

7. Bethge, *Friendship and Resistance*, 15.

8. Ibid., 3. The year before, Bonhoeffer had been driven to Wittenburg with two friends and had handed out leaflets decrying the Reich church. But apparently he had no contact with Bethge or his friends.

9. Ibid., 19.

10. Ibid., 16.

11. Ibid., 17.

in a lecture that "only the obedient believe."[12] Eberhard felt a thrill of recognition, for he and his friends had just experienced a renewal of faith through obedience.

Eberhard's presence brought joy to the seminary brothers, including Dietrich.[13] As Dietrich wrote in a letter to Eberhard, still half-envious, much admiring and self-effacing almost a decade later: "I don't know anyone who does not like you, whereas I know a great many people who do not like me." And then came the weighing: Eberhard "open and modest," Dietrich "reticent and rather demanding."[14]

Eberhard and Dietrich quickly drew together. A love of music bound them: Dietrich's niece Renate Bethge would later write that with Hildebrandt, Dietrich talked theology; with Eberhard he made music.[15] Yet Eberhard also had a talent for theology, revealed early on in his sermon on Isaiah 53's suffering servant. More importantly, Dietrich and Eberhard were joined by a deeper bond and one harder to articulate—a rejection of Nazism and a vision of Christianity so profoundly at odds with their culture that it propelled them forcefully from the ordinary lives they had known.

On June 2, the seminary held a service at the village church in Zingst. Dietrich preached, then prayed and collected an offering for Confessing Church clergy.[16] The service electrified the congregation, especially when Dietrich read the names of pastors imprisoned in concentration camps, moving some to tears.[17] Soon afterwards, the Nazis arrived, alerted that the seminarians had taken an illegal collection.[18]

Meant to intimidate them, a Nazi interrogation instead drew the seminarians closer. As days passed, they enjoyed the "splendid summer weather, the sea, and innumerable lilies of the valley in the woods," Dietrich wrote to a friend in England. For Pentecost, Dietrich declared a four-day holiday: "It's a very fine thing to celebrate these festival days in a community like this, where we are all of one mind." Dietrich's contentment overflowed as he experienced a period of "brotherly love ... obedience ... discipline ... unshakeable joy. ... I have rarely celebrated Pentecost with so much joy and hope."[19]

12. Ibid., 4.
13. Bonhoeffer, *LPP*, 156.
14. Ibid., 189.
15. de Gruchy, *Daring, Trusting Spirit*, 17.
16. Bonhoeffer, *DBWE 14*, 55.
17. Ibid., 845–46.
18. Ibid., 59.
19. Ibid.

— 13 —
Finkenwalde

BESPECTACLED SEMINARIAN WALTER KOCH hurried through the Stettiner Station, suitcase in hand, hat on his head. Like most Berliners, he was at home in the busy railway station, where express trains travelled continuously to and from the eastern regions of Germany. Curious about Finkenwalde and anxious to meet Bonhoeffer, Koch, the well-heeled Berliner, pushed his way onto a crowded train.

For Koch, whose road to Finkenwalde would change his life in unforeseen ways, the adventure began almost as soon as the train left Berlin. Koch squeezed past people crammed in the narrow train corridors, swaying as the train picked up speed. He peered into the glass windows of the compartments, looking for an empty seat. He happened to stop, struck, in front of a compartment where four young men sat eagerly talking with a fifth, who had the highbrow air associated with a scholar. Impulsively, Koch slid open the door and asked if the group were traveling to Finkenwalde.

The conversation stopped abruptly. Why would somebody—a stranger on a train to Stettin—ask if they were going to Finkenwalde? The passengers exchanged uneasy glances. In these days, when every neighbor was a spy, what did this man know about them and why was he here?

Dietrich was the first to pull himself together and speak. "Yes indeed, we are going to Finkenwalde. Why does that interest you?"[1]

Koch introduced himself. After the dead silence, cheerful—and no doubt relieved—shouts accompanied this introduction. A burst of questions followed: Why would he think to ask them if they were going to Finkenwalde of all places? Did they look "theological"? How could that be? They thought they looked "normal."

"I knew it somehow—[that you were] the brethren," Koch told them. He then went on to explain how he had seen the eerily ubiquitous Dietrich twice the previous day in two different parts of Berlin, once on the street at the Zoo, a bustling section of downtown Berlin, another time at a café in

---

1. Zimmermann and Smith, eds., *I Knew*, 113.

Dahlem, the quiet, upscale, leafy suburb on the western edge of the sprawling capital.[2]

Koch's journey to Finkenwalde had passed through a Reich Church course earlier in the year. Forty of the forty-five would-be ministers showed up either in SS or SA uniforms. There, a Nazi church official told them: "Germany has experienced its new Pentecost. When Hitler came, there was a wind from heaven. The banner with the swastika that flies before all of us is the Holy Spirit; its fire, which inspires us and welds us together in a hitherto unprecedented community, is the one great miraculous community of the people which no longer knows any classes or states. What the first disciples had experienced at Pentecost and the enthusiasm which had gripped the German people today were the work of the one and the same Spirit of God which we did right to call holy."[3]

Many believed this story. Koch emphatically did not.

Koch arrived for the seminary's second session. Earlier, on June 24, 1935, the seminarians had moved from their temporary residence in fragile huts on Zingst's empty beaches to a sturdier manor house-turned-school in the village of Finkenwalde. The school stood near a branch of the Oder River and north of a sweep of green beech forests, a setting ideal for walks and water sports.[4]

---

2. Ibid., 113.
3. Wind, *A Spoke in the Wheel*, 100.
4. Bethge, *DB: A Biography*, 425.

The site of Finkenwalde has now been turned into
a Bonhoeffer memorial. A train still goes past it.

They found the new seminary building itself scarcely habitable. The back of the grounds, where the grass grew long, was scarred by a gravel pit.[5] When the advance group arrived in June, they found a "veritable pigsty—"[6] and a "repugnant" woman living in one wing, who had "set up a kind of a brothel."[7]

---

5. Ibid., 426.
6. Zimmermann and Smith, eds., *I Knew*, 146.
7. Bonhoeffer, *DBWE* 14, 23.

The advance group made initial repairs on the building—cleaning, hammering, starting a garden, and gathering supplies—while the rest of the seminarians waited in Greifswald youth hostels.[8]

Dietrich's connection to privilege—and to Paula—added touches of luxury, including the well-travelled Bechstein. In the open fireplace of the main hall, Dietrich placed his copper brazier from Spain. He hung his icon from Sofia, much admired by Eberhard, and every week displayed different Rembrandt Bible etchings from an edition he owned.[9] Dietrich also brought his entire theological book collection to Finkenwalde to create a library, an act of generosity much admired, though it may also have been a way to help Paula have less to worry about as she organized the upcoming move from Grunewald to the new house in Charlottenburg.

Much of Finkenwalde's communal life took place in three large rooms on the ground floor. Dietrich held classes in a lecture room with a U-shaped arrangement of tables. A comfortable dining room doubled as a twice-daily devotional room. Here, the seminarians relaxed over meals on dark-stained chairs around dark-stained tables, reproductions of two of Dürer's apostle paintings looking down at them from one wall. Generous outpourings from the community meant the seminarians dined on potatoes, bacon, ham, eggs, sausage, cucumbers, and pears. At night, a simple wooden candelabra spread a soft glow when the group gathered for devotions.

The most "beautiful" room of all was the commons, furnished with comfortable leather armchairs, Dietrich's Bechstein, and a second grand piano donated by another seminarian. Here the group gathered for evening discussions, as well as music, readings, and Sunday games.[10] In this room, as at Zingst, Eberhard showed his talent for making friends. He had both an "infectious liveliness"[11] and a steadiness of character that kept him largely free of depression.[12] In contrast to Dietrich, he was "more ebullient, more outgoing, more embracing" of life.[13] As Hildebrandt's high spirits had done, this warmth and extroversion put Dietrich at ease, and he continued to draw closer to his new friend.[14]

8. Bethge, *DB: A Biography*, 425.
9. Ibid., 426.
10. Bonhoeffer, *DBWE 14*, 110–11.
11. Wind, *A Spoke in the Wheel*, 111.
12. de Gruchy, *Daring, Trusting Spirit*, 33.
13. Ibid., 144.
14. Ibid., 208.

Soon they were almost inseparable, a fact noticed—and sometimes resented—by the other seminarians, one of whom referred disparagingly to Eberhard as "the representative of the führer [i.e., Bonhoeffer]."[15] Vibrans saw with mixed feelings his own close friendship with Eberhard threatened by his cousin's role as the "chief's favorite."[16]

Dietrich led the seminary by example, helping in the kitchen and even making a seminarian's bed. Services around the dining table began and ended the day, with a sequence of mediation, Bible reading, and singing followed by prayers and the Lord's Prayer, and on Saturdays, a sermon.[17] The most difficult task for many seminarians was the daily silent meditation on a Bible verse in the Quaker tradition, perhaps borrowed from Dietrich's two visits to the Quaker retreat center Selly Oak in Birmingham.[18]

Dietrich proclaimed Sunday a day of rest. At first, the students disdained the leisure activities Bonhoeffer encouraged for that day; later, following Dietrich's example, they threw themselves into table tennis, swimming, and music.[19] Dietrich reigned as ping-pong champion.[20]

Seminarian Hans-Werner Jensen noted Paula's influence on the seminary: "What an example Bonhoeffer set for us in his close attachment to his mother! There was hardly a day when he did not have a long-distance talk with her, across those hundreds of miles to Berlin. I doubt he would have been such a pastor to his brethren without this constant readiness to listen to his mother."[21]

As his mother had done in their Berlin home, Dietrich integrated culture into seminary life. Dietrich read Annette von Droste-Hülshoff's "The Jew's Beech Tree," undoubtedly meant as a critique of Nazism, aloud to his seminarians. Eberhard sang Schütz, or Psalms 70 and 47, while Dietrich accompanied him on the piano: "that was what you [performed] best," Dietrich would later write to him.[22] Dietrich played Chopin, Brahms, and Beethoven, especially improvised excerpts from the Rosenkavelier[23] as well

---

15. Ibid., 17.
16. Ibid.
17. Bethge, *DB: A Biography*, 428.
18. Ibid., 412. "I liked it very much there," he wrote on a postcard.
19. Zimmermann and Smith, eds., *I Knew*, 127.
20. Ibid., 110.
21. Ibid., 154.
22. Bonhoeffer, *LPP*, 134.
23. Bethge, *Friendship and Resistance*, 5.

as Bach.[24] He was an expert sight reader, and soon the seminary was filled with the romantic, tempestuous strains of Brahms or Beethoven concertos, swelling eerily into the countryside. Sometimes Bonhoeffer would improvise passionately or play too hard, losing himself as he hammered away loudly on the keys.[25]

24. Bethge, *DB: A Biography*, 429.
25. Zimmermann and Smith, eds., *I Knew*, 124–25.

— 14 —
Murmurs of War

Not long after the seminary opened, Bonhoeffer's supervisor, Wilhelm Niesel, popped in for a visit. Though he worried that the Finkenwalde atmosphere was "too spiritual" after hearing a lecture by Bonhoeffer that "astonished" him by its dryness—do the candidates ever get a chance to go to the movies, he asked[1]—he enjoyed rowing one afternoon on a nearby lake. This outing triggered a memory, and he recounted a story of a "fat boy" in a white sweater capsizing a boat on Berlin's Kleine Wannsee lake, a resort area with sandy beaches, boating, golf, and shooting in southwest Berlin. Niesel and his party had already come ashore with hopes of getting a coffee at a nearby garden restaurant when the accident occurred. The boy in the boat was Dietrich, aged twelve or thirteen.[2]

The visit to the lake near Finkenwalde brought home the militarism that surrounded the seminary. After rowing, the group climbed a hill, which offered a view of runways where fighter planes were constantly taking off and landing in a roar of propellers and engines. "There too," noted Niesel, "a young generation was in training, but for a kingdom which had even then begun to reveal its hardness and cruelty."[3]

Remembering his childhood home, Dietrich opened Finkenwalde's doors to guests. Housekeeper Erna Struwe with her white hair and crisp full-length white apron or sensible button-down dress helped make this possible. Not surprisingly, visitors included Dietrich's brothers-in-law Hans von Dohnanyi and Walter Dress. We have no record, however, that Sabine ever came. Perhaps she anticipated the all-male environment as too overbearing. She would later write in relief that English men actually listened to women, and then delivered an uncharacteristically strong criticism of German patriarchy: "In sharp contrast, many German men will often not

1. Zimmermann and Smith, eds., *I Knew*, 146.
2. Ibid., 145. It would be interesting if this were the birthday outing Dietrich took with Susi.
3. Ibid., 146.

allow a woman so much as a single word, frequently interrupt her, sometimes tease her, and frequently deliver long, instructive monologues at her without finding out first if she wishes to hear them."[4] She would continue to let Dietrich meet her on her own turf.

To his German seminarians, Dietrich's pacifism, the fruit of his Manhattan year, was perhaps his most astonishing trait. It caused heated arguments,[5] especially with Hitler's rearmament openly underway. When Quaker physicist and pacifist Herbert Jehle visited Finkenwalde, seminarians accused him of naivete for opposing violence.[6] Rumors of "terrible heresies" swirled around the seminary: talk of "Catholic practices, enthusiastic pacifist activities and radical fanaticism" drew curious visitors to its doors.[7]

Another Finkenwalde practice that attracted attention was "its daily and detailed reading of the Psalms—unusual within the German Evangelical tradition."[8] This represented a refusal to bow to Nazi pressures to abandon the Old Testament. But for all the swirling gossip from outside, the seminarians found their joy—amid frequent contention—in a life centered around the Bible, drawn close by what one seminarian called the "urgent" task of building a Christian community that would be a bulwark against "the waves of the evil spirit . . . [against the] terror . . . of the evil, angry adversaries . . . ."[9]

In August, 1935, Bethge joined a contingent that, with Bonhoeffer, biked through parts of Pomerania visiting isolated Confessing Church pastors. The group ended up at the Baltic, relaxing for a few days by the sea. Meanwhile in an August 30, 1935 letter to pastor Hans Thimme, Dietrich, ever eager to promote Finkenwalde hospitality, offered the seminary as the site of a regional conference, praising its "lovely forest, and water, with a boat!"[10]

Dietrich's vision for Finkenwalde included a House of Brethren—seminarians who would stay on past their course of studies and live at Finkenwalde. They would provide emergency pastoral services as needed, support the work of the Confessing Church, and help new seminarians

---

4. Leibholz, *The Bonhoeffers*, 108.
5. Bethge, *DB: A Biography*, 431.
6. Ibid.
7. Ibid., 433.
8. Ibid., 434.
9. Bonhoeffer, *DBWE 14*, 111–13.
10. Bethge, *DB: A Biography*, 434.

build community. In September 1935, the first six of the Brethren, including Eberhard, settled into private rooms at Finkenwalde.

Finkenwalde's location drew Dietrich out of his Berlin culture and towards the conservative Prussian aristocracy. It also brought him into the world of the Pomeranian Council of Brethren. He worked with Stefanie von Mackensen, wife of the vice president of Pomerania and manager of the Council of Brethen's office. The council's offices on Politzer Strasse became a focal point of the seminarians.[11]

The seminary filled an emptiness in Dietrich's psyche, giving him, for the first time since Sabine's marriage, a firm ground on which to stand. Like Coleridge, who'd dreamed of—and even prepared for—a Utopian community in Pennsylvania, and Van Gogh, who invited Gaugin to Provence in a futile attempt to start an artist's colony, Dietrich sought fellowship with likeminded people. In June, he had written from Zingst that "the work here is very satisfying and fulfilling and indeed makes each of us happy . . . ." After the first Finkenwalde semester ended, he wrote: "The summer of 1935 has been the fullest time of my life, both from the professional and the human point of view."[12]

The two new people who would have the most profound impact on the last decade of Bonhoeffer's life entered his orbit through the seminary. The first, Eberhard Bethge, was already becoming central to him; the second, soon to make her grand entrance, was Ruth von Kleist-Retzlow, born a Pomeranian countess of Zedlitz and Trützschler.

---

11. Ibid., 438.
12. Bonhoeffer, *DBWE 14*, 60.

15

First Encounter

ONE MORNING IN EARLY September 1935, sixty-eight-year-old Ruth, prone to wearing long floral dresses with her white hair pulled in a bun on top of her head, found her way to the new seminary at Finkenwalde, arriving for Sunday services.

She had passed the seminary in August when she had been driven through Finkenwalde with a caravan of cars to set up housekeeping in a grand apartment in Stettin with six of her grandchildren. Her pigtailed granddaughter Maria, age eleven, later Dietrich's fiancée, "squeezed amid hams, heads of cabbage, carrots and duffel bags," had glimpsed it too.[1]

Since arriving in Stettin, Ruth had received an appeal for help from Finkenwalde. She had, as well, read some of Dietrich's work. Now she would meet him in person.

The white-haired matriarch did not arrive alone. She swept the grandchildren who lived with her onto the train for the twenty-minute ride to Finkenwalde.[2] The seminary stood a few blocks from the village center, where Ruth and her brood marched off from the Finkenwalde station that the Nazis had newly refurbished.

The newcomers worshipped with the seminarians in the Finkenwalde's school gym cum chapel where light from a window reflected on walls draped in coarse cotton. The sun lit the plain cross. A simple cloth covered an altar flanked by candles and flowers. A modest pulpit stood in a corner.[3] Painted in gold on one wall the Hebrew word *Hapax*, meaning "once and for all,"[4] perhaps reflected Dietrich's desire that the church take a decisive stand against Nazism.

Granddaughter Ruth Alice, Maria's older sister, later recalled the "lusty singing"[5] of the seminarians, table tennis in the garden by the long, ivy-cov-

1. Pejsa, *Matriarch of Conspiracy*, 205.
2. Ibid., 208.
3. Bethge and Gremmels, *A Life in Pictures*, 145.
4. Bethge, *DB: A Biography*, 426.
5. Bismarck and Kabitz, eds., *Love Letters*, 306.

ered school, and a simple lunch around a horseshoe-shaped table brought from a glassed solarium. Ruth remembered, however, that they couldn't stop for lunch that first visit, as the cook in Stettin was preparing them a meal. In her recollection, they stayed for lunch the following week.[6] Maria, a future mathematician, counted the number of times Dietrich said "God" during that first sermon—sixty-eight in all.[7]

Ruth, forthright, energetic and emotionally intense, was, like Dietrich, passionate about breathing new life and spirit into the church. Her independence of mind had immediately led her to support the Barmen Declaration. She had recognized from the start the heretical nature of the German Nazi church, and by 1935 was the delegate to the Belgard District governing body of the Confessing Church. Believing that a spiritual malaise had overtaken Germany, Ruth was excited by the seminary's spiritual energy and focus on the centrality of Christ. She asked questions with such "ardor" that Dietrich, with his typical reserve, was initially taken aback, though he wished his students shared her intense intellectual curiosity.[8] Later, though in her late sixties, she would, inspired by Dietrich, take up Greek.

Ruth threw herself into supporting Dietrich's cause, finding money, furniture, and a huge variety of supplies for the seminary. When Finkenwalde needed food, Ruth and her extensive network were on hand, providing potatoes, meat, vegetables, and eggs. Phone calls to Junker estates brought in garden tools, kitchen utensils, and books. With her passion for their cause and welcoming apartment open to them as second home, she became "Aunt Ruth" to the "brothers." Koch, a welcome dinner guest during this period because he knew French, a language her grandchildren practiced while dining, described her cultured home as "a contrast to the brown demon [the Nazis], which filled the streets and squares of the town with its noise . . . with the sanguinary speeches of those who prepared the Germans for war—civilians and troops alike—under the slogan: Might before Right."[9]

Ruth increasingly pulled Dietrich into her east Prussian world, where aristocratic tradition and large landed estates provided a hedge against the shrill Nazi intrusions. As Bosquanet put it, "his aristocratic dignity and unconstrained air of authority appealed to men who possessed the same qualities; and for Bonhoeffer, hours spent with these families in their gracious homes, where deep and simple piety and leisured culture spoke directly to a large area of his many-layered being, were among the most precious of his joys during the period at Finkenwalde."[10]

6. Pejsa, *Matriarch of Conspiracy*, 209.
7. Ibid.
8. Bethge and Gremmels, *A Life in Pictures*, 358.
9. Zimmermann and Smith, eds., *I Knew*, 114.
10. Bosanquet, *The Life and Death of Dietrich Bonhoeffer*, 184.

— 16 —

Ruth

RUTH, BORN IN 1867, had spent her life in the landed Prussian aristocratic circles into which she now drew Dietrich. Like Bell, she and Dietrich shared a birthday, February 4, a fact that had special significance for the twin Dietrich. Without Hitler, he and Ruth might never have met, though, as fate would have it, Ruth's father, Count Robert Zedlitz, the former Prussian culture minister, had sometimes visited Paula's childhood home in Breslau.[1]

Ruth lived at the apex of a pyramid in which 3 percent of the Prussian population owned 40 percent of the land and ruled their vast holdings with the pomp of medieval kings. She was a Junker, described thus in 1943 by historian A. Whitney Griswold: "Numbering not more than a few thousand families, this proud, medieval cult of virtue and the sword has largely dominated Prussian politics since the thirteenth century and, through Prussia, profoundly influenced the whole course of German history. Until its power is broken and it has been converted to the ways of the present century . . . [freedom] will be smuggled into Germany with difficulty and that unhappy nation will continue to renounce the world as the Junkers' ancestors, the Teutonic Knights, did before them."[2]

It was Ruth's Christianity, rather than any renunciation of the Junker way of life, that led her in a radical direction.

On Christmas Eve of 1882, when the twentieth century's horrors were unimagined, fifteeen-year-old Ruth walked with her brother Rob and sister Anni to a Christmas church service. Snowflakes fell gently, lit by a backdrop of soft yellow lantern light. Here, the siblings "accidentally" ran into twenty-eight-year-old Jurgen von Kleist, a slim, handsome officer and landowner. Rob introduced Jurgen to Ruth. Guided by an unspoken message that he was her family's choice for her husband, Ruth promptly fell in love.[3]

1. Bethge, *DB: A Biography*, 7.
2. Griswold, "The Junkers."
3. Pejsa, *Matriarch of Conspiracy*, 17.

At sixteen, Ruth's confirmation into the Lutheran Church launched her into the season of balls and dinners that marked her coming out. With her high spirits and good looks, she had no trouble filling her dance cards, "those brightly colored folded papers that hang from [the] . . . wrist by satin ribbons."[4] By age seventeen, with newly bobbed brown hair and a low-cut gown, Ruth attracted so much attention that her brother Rob warned her "severely" during the Christmas holidays not to become a coquette and ruin her marriage prospects. All she wanted, however, was to wed Jurgen von Kleist.[5]

The two met publicly at dinners and dances and chatted during a rowboat ride, flitting in and out of each other's sphere. Ruth sought marriage because it was expected—and because she wholeheartedly believed in it. Like the Bonhoeffer women, Countess Ruth's only conceivable destiny was marriage and childbearing. Stark, unspoken threats hovered over single women: unmarried aristocratic ladies filled Prussian Protestant convents. Yet Jurgen did not propose.

Ruth waited, something she would forever hate to do.

In the fall of 1885, eighteen-year-old Ruth spotted a letter amid the mail at her mother's place at the table in the vast dining room. She snatched it and ran to the library, where she tore the envelope open with eager fingers to find a marriage proposal: "Will you trust me for your entire life?" For a dizzying moment Ruth thought "she saw God." Her mother hurried after her to the library. Ruth threw her arms around her. Then, immediately, Ruth sent Jurgen a telegram—"Yes, come," inside herself saying, "yes, yes, a thousand times yes!" That evening Jurgen arrived as Ruth waited in an upstairs room, first in darkness, then lighting two lanterns that cast extravagant shadows on the drapes and walls. Entering, Jurgen swept Ruth into his arms, holding her almost without breathing, and caressing her "ceaselessly." Her parents expected a traditional spring wedding. Ruth pressed for and won a winter date.[6]

On her nineteenth birthday on February 4, 1886, seventy guests arrived to the Red Hall, her father's reception room for receiving official visitors, including the revered Kaiser. Her mother wore a white Empire gown, while her father pinned a host of medals over his formal attire. With servants opening the grand oak double doors to every guest, her parents regally received each friend or relative.

---

4. Ibid., 19.
5. Ibid., 20.
6. Ibid., 22–24.

Once the guests had assembled, Ruth and Jurgen wed before an altar brought in from the family chapel.[7] The room was brought alive by the splendor of hothouse flowers and a welter of hanging banners in Ruth's family colors of black and gold. A wedding photograph shows Ruth standing with her arm linked to her slim new husband. She has an open, round face framed by wavy dark hair. Beside her, Jurgen manages to look gentle despite a stiff collar, a large handlebar moustache, and severely side-parted hair.

Ruth began her married life in an apartment in the town of Köslin, where Jurgen had a government job. She had a son, Hans Jurgen, ten months after her marriage, in November 1886. She bore five children, three in the first five years of wedded life. Following her father-in-law's death, the couple took over the family's remote eastern estate at Kieckow near the Baltic Sea.

Jurgen died in 1897 at age forty-three. Now a widow, thirty-year-old Ruth moved to a large apartment in Stettin, as she later would with her grandchildren, so her children could attend school there. She visited Kieckow two days a month, but otherwise left its operations to a bailiff. Kieckow would pass to her son Hans Jurgen as soon as he was of age. She would become dependent on him financially and would be expected to subordinate her own needs to his decisions.

Ruth left stories of her life behind in a memoir of her early life, called *Meine Ehe* (*My Marriage*). These autobiographical fragments offer her own dramatic recounting of her courtship, marriage, and life thereafter. She cast herself as the headstrong heroine of her own story in a way that offers insights into her character and preoccupations—including a preoccupation with marriage that she would later bring to bear on Dietrich.

Responsibilities gripped the widowed matriarch. By 1907, Ruth's oldest daughter Spes (*hope* in German) was old enough to debut. Spes, fully her mother's daughter, sallied off grandly to Silesia for a winter season of dinners and balls. Her grandfather, Ruth's father, hoped to marry her to the cultured and wealthy Count Limburg-Stirum.[8] Ruth eagerly supported this match. Spes, however, rejected the count's proposal, imperiously informing her grandfather she would not marry a suitor who was one-quarter Jewish and "even looks it!"

In 1908, Spes tried again to evade a marriage offer, this one made during the Stettin season by Walter Stahlberg, a wealthy industrialist. When Spes entered the Stettin flat and told her mother that she planned to become

---

7. Ibid., 26–28.
8. Bismarck and Kabitz, eds., *Love Letters*, 302.

a pianist in Berlin instead of marrying Walter, Ruth burst into sobs, tears rolling down her cheeks, her body contorting in anguish. Marriage, Ruth gasped to Spes, was not such a bad idea, and without a dowry, Spes was wrong to turn down offers from eligible suitors. Surely Walter would support her career as a pianist.

Spes changed her answer to yes.

Following Ruth's histrionics, Walter asked Ruth to release him from the engagement. Ruth shouted that he had injured and insulted her daughter, then stormed out—and sent Spes to him.[9]

The couple married. Spes had little in common with her industrialist husband fifteen years her senior. The marriage failed, and eventually the couple would divorce. None of this would deter Ruth's matchmaking.

Like many of the Junker estates, Kieckow ran deeply into debt, and the grand Junker families, though they spent more austerely than their counterparts in western Germany, often found themselves strapped for cash. This would have disastrous results, as many of the Junkers would in the end gamble on Hitler as a way to preserve their traditional lives. But that problem loomed in the future. Ruth now faced immediate concerns: how would she marry her two remaining, undowered daughters?

Ruth approached this task head-on. She and a nearby aristocratic widow, Hedwig von Bismarck, joined forces and arranged for the marriage of Ruth's second daughter, Maria, to Hedwig's son, Herbert. Then, in 1918, as World War I ended, Hans von Wedemeyer, owner of the Pätzig estate, approached Ruth, exploring the possibility of marrying her youngest, Ruthchen. Ruth responded favorably, attracted to the handsome young man.

Ruth, always a steamroller, left nothing to chance. She asked each party separately if they loved the other. Each replied no—because they'd hardly spoken. Hans believed that love would grow. Shy Ruthchen tried to sidestep Hans during his visit by insisting she had bookkeeping work to do. Ruth nevertheless arranged for a wagon ride around the Kieckow grounds the next day, planning to put herself in one wagon with the coachman and a companion, Ruthchen and Hans alone in another.

The two older sisters, on hand to help run the estate during the war, protested. Ruth was ruthlessly railroading Ruthchen into marriage, just as she had them. "Just because the mother is captivated by this young officer in uniform doesn't mean that she should hand over her daughter on a silver platter."[10] Unhappily married Spes, second daughter Maria, and even

9. Pejsa, *Matriarch of Conspiracy*, 103.
10. Ibid, 141.

their sister-in-law Mieze united to defend Ruthchen against Ruth's assault. Ruthchen herself insisted she had to spend the next day—payday—with the estate's workers instead of with Hans.

Ruth remained adamant, unclouded by doubt. Hans was Ruthchen's "prince charming," just as Jurgen had been hers. The workers could wait for their pay.

Ruthchen and Hans sat together in the wagon, bumping around the estate, but Hans didn't propose. That evening, when Ruth pressed her daughter about marrying, Rutchen replied that she was "unsure" if she wanted to commit her life to a stranger.

The next day, Ruth's machinations shrouded in mystery, the two were betrothed.

Hans wanted an immediate wedding. Ruth agreed and so it was. On November 17, 1918, the young couple married in the Kieckow church, and, by Ruth's account, "all who are present agree that no bride in history ever looked as radiant." The next morning the newlyweds set out in a snowfall for Pätzig, Ruth delighted to have married her final daughter without a dowry.[11]

---

11. Ibid., 142–43.

— 17 —
Collision Courses

BUT RUTH WAS MORE than simply a matchmaking matriarch. As World War I ended, she, along with almost everyone else, struggled with the trauma of defeat, along with the shock to her monarchist's sensibility that democracy had come to Germany. In 1919, her world turned upside down, Ruth turned to new trends in Bible interpretation, including the work of Karl Barth, who insisted on the centrality of Jesus Christ to Christianity. "Ruth," wrote her biographer, Jane Pejsa, began "to see quite clearly that her role . . . [was] to reconstruct the foundations—both spiritual and secular—to which this family . . . [could] cement its traditional ethical and moral values."[1]

In 1925, two books among many appeared: *Mein Kampf,* and Ruth von Kleist-Retzow's own manifesto: *The Responsibility of Landed Property in This Social Crisis,* an examination of the role of the rural aristocracy in the democratic age. To Ruth's mind, God had ordained the Prussian aristocracy to control the land, thereby establishing nineteenth-century social arrangements as immutable. "Hand in hand with the land goes a veritable sea of responsibility that must be shared by all who live on it," she wrote, including the local pastor and the peasants. "If there is suffering, if there is disorder, if there is injustice in our village, we must all share the responsibility . . . . The landowner has royal duties and royal responsibilities. . . . he must day and night keep in mind the well-being of his land and his people . . . ."[2]

Ruth described the life of the landowner as not so easy "nor so comfortable as it first seems," though it was arguably far more comfortable than the life of a peasant. She defended "race, blood and soil," echoing popular sentiments: "We are obligated to fight and to suffer together—for ourselves, for the German nation and for this land that God has given us!" Even Dietrich had expressed such ideas as a youth pastor in Barcelona in 1928—and Hitler had latched onto them with more sinister intent in his own much more successful 1925 book. Nor could Ruth see, as Griswold did, that "the

1. Pejsa, *Matriarch of Conspiracy,* 148.
2. Ibid., 161–62.

great entitled estates have no possible justification other than the maintenance, for political reasons, of a small, privileged caste . . . imprisoned in its own archaic economy and social system."[3]

In 1931, as Dietrich taught at the University of Berlin, Raba, Spes's daughter and Ruth's oldest grandchild, studied there. She joined the Nazi Party and quickly rose up the ranks. Tall, confident, blonde haired, and aristocratic, Raba became leader of the Party's female students, with an office next to Joseph Goebbels, and her own part-time secretary.[4] The party tapped Raba, the model Aryan, to be a speaker at its 1931 youth rally in Berlin. Then someone discovered she was one-quarter Jewish, "the stain" on her father's side. Raba was stunned.

The Nazis forced Raba to resign her leadership position. Soon after, she quit the party, changed her name, and began attending church. Her father could still, in 1931, have records of the family's Jewish blood purged from the Provincial Registry. "In Stettin, we Stahlbergs still count for something!" he declared to Raba's mother as he delivered the papers that hid their children's Jewish ancestry, and the fact that his great-grandfather had been president of a synagogue.[5]

Trouble continued after the Nazis rose to power. Many Prussian landowners became Nazis. But some, including members of the von Kleist family, not only Ruth but her son Hans Jurgen, and her cousin, Ewald von Kleist-Schmenzin, as well as Maria's father, Hans von Wedemeyer, rejected Nazi anti-Semitism, as well as the party's ultra-violence, idolatry of the state, and reliance on propaganda. Like other Protestant aristocrats, Maria's father scorned Hitler for his lower-middle-class, Austrian roots. As time went on, both the Grunewald intellectual culture and the old Junker families would divide over Nazism, some loving it, some loathing it.[6]

One fateful morning early in 1935, the ten-year-old granddaughter of one of Ruth's relatives' Junker neighbors went to school and repeated comments her seventy-year-old grandfather had made about the Nazis. After the seventy-year-old was arrested and held for two days for questioning, Ruth's children decided to move their own children out of earshot. The von Wedemeyers, von Bismarcks, and von Kleists chose Ruth as the children's caretaker. They pooled their resources so that their six oldest could attend

3. Griswold, "The Junkers."
4. Ibid., 177.
5. Ibid., 183–85.
6. Bethge and Gremmels, *A Life in Pictures*, 94.

school in Stettin while living with Ruth in an apartment the three sets of parents would finance.

Ruth initially balked at the idea that she should single-handedly run what she would later call a boarding school, when she'd rather be tending to her flowers, her letter writing, and her theological studies. She wondered if she had the stamina to take on six lively young people, but as a dependent, her role had been decided by the family. Characteristically, she rose to the occasion.[7] She rented a large ground floor Stettin flat at 103 Politzer Strasse, down the street from the offices of the Prussian Council of the Brethren, where Ruth's friend, Nazi Stefanie von Mackensen, helped resist the German Christian Church.

Ruth furnished her airy rooms, which opened into each other through French doors, with her blue sofas, her cupboards, and her carpets. She rotated between the flat and her dowager cottage on the Kieckow estate. The grandchildren she oversaw included three von Wedemeyer children: Ruth-Alice, Max, and the lively eleven-year-old Maria, along with Spes and Hans Otto von Bismarck and Hans Friedrich von Kleist. A photo of all six shows Maria, the youngest of them, in a floral print dress that matches her sister's, her dark hair in a braid down her back.

Ruth continued to despise what she had early identified as Nazism's anti-Christianity. As a follower of Barth, she had quickly grasped that the Nazis would destroy the Christian church.

Ruth had a formidable personality. Her granddaughter, Ruth-Alice von Bismarck, described her as "headstrong and temperamental."[8] Eberhard Bethge, with whom she would become the tightest of domestic conspirators, recalled her as one who spoke her mind "with refreshing forthrightness."[9] To Werner Koch, Ruth was "one of the most remarkable women of her time . . . Pomeranian aristocracy of the best kind . . . standing up to the last for truth and right . . . everything always rooted in and always nourished by the Holy Scripture."[10]

On September 15, an urgent call came to Finkenwalde from Hildebrandt, now working as assistant pastor for the Confessing Church's outspoken Martin Niemöller: how would the Confessing Church respond to the newly unleashed Nuremburg Laws that stripped Jews of their rights? The call brought Dietrich and others seminarians, including Eberhard, to the Steglitz-Berlin

---

7. Pejsa, *Matriarch of Conspiracy,* 204.
8 Bismarck and Kabitz, eds., *Love Letters,* 301.
9. Bethge, *DB: A Biography,* 439.
10. Zimmermann and Smith, eds., *I Knew,* 114.

Confessing Church Synod from September 23–26. Dietrich and Eberhard heckled from the gallery as the synod refused to challenge the Nuremburg Laws—or even the Aryan clause—in any effective way. Marga Meusel, a Protestant deaconess, drafted a resolution of solidarity with all Jews, not just Christian Jews, but her proposal didn't even make it onto the agenda.[11] Meanwhile, the new Reich church head, Hanns Kerrl, had issued the first "emergency measures" of the new act "for the settlement of the German Evangelical Church," which would by December make Finkenwalde illegal.[12]

Dietrich returned from the conference to Finkenwalde with Sabine's fate weighing on him. As Bethge put it, Dietrich had "personal reasons for his shame at the weakness of his church" in condemning anti-Semitism. Since the passage of the Nuremberg Laws, Dietrich had been distressed and the Bonhoeffer family in a quiet uproar, trying to decide how best to protect Sabine and Gert. The family urged emigration. To the couple, "the thought that they might have to emigrate into an uncertain future was almost unbearable; their sense of helpless grew."[13]

Dietrich remained staunchly and visibly close to Sabine and her family while others shunned them. Although her husband and her children identified as Christians, their Jewish ancestry barred them from membership in the German Church, as it did Hildebrandt, adding urgency to Dietrich's quest to keep the Confessing Church open to Jews. At this point, too, neither Grete, Dietrich's sister-in-law, nor brother-in-law Dohnanyi had been cleared of the "taint" of Jewish blood.

Yet despite the Confessing Church's failure of nerve, for the seminarian these continued to be happy, heady times. As Heinrich Vogel, who ran the Confessing Church seminary in Berlin recalled, "They were all young people who were setting their future at stake, eventually their freedom and their lives, in order to study theology. And all were shaped through that decision, that either/or . . . the cross or the swastika."[14]

A remarkable spirit of optimism hovered over Finkenwalde, as it had over Zingst, though Dietrich would later emphasize the difficulties of communal living. Even after the Confessing Church had made a weak stand at Steglitz, the group continued to believe that a tiny remnant could save the world. "I cannot and will not deny my decisive years," Eberhard would later write, "in which I was filled with theological renewal, with the renewal of

---

11. de Gruchy, *Daring, Trusting Spirit*, 19–21.
12. Bosanquet, *The Life and Death of Dietrich Bonhoeffer*, 173.
13. Bethge, *DB: A Biography*, 490.
14. Barnett, *For the Soul of the People*, 87.

knowing how and why I am a Christian. And I still believe today the Christ figure is and will remain central in my life."[15] Ruth also found the seminary a miracle, something only God could have dropped into the lap of a woman who at sixty-eight thought life had passed her by.

---

15. Bethge, *Friendship and Resistance*, 13.

PART IV
Reconfigurations

— 18 —
New World

ONE DECEMBER DAY, EBERHARD found himself sitting in Dietrich's sister Christel's parlor, struggling to make small talk with this upper-class Berliner, the wife of Hans von Dohnanyi. As he had warned Eberhard he would, Dietrich had closeted himself with Hans, a dissenter working close to the Nazi power center, to discuss aspects of the church struggle. Eberhard, left alone with Christel, became acutely aware that Dietrich's forthright sister was annoyed at having to entertain him. She would have much preferred to be in the study with the two men. Eberhard spoke mechanically, hardly knowing what he said, in "anguish" over being foisted on an unwilling hostess. He felt every inch the provincial, out of his realm. The sense of awkwardness lingered, and this most social of men wondered why Dietrich would leave him in such an uncomfortable situation. At the same time, he felt excited to be close to people important enough to believe they had the power to effect change in the world.[1]

Dietrich had bestowed a great honor on Eberhard in taking him home to Berlin for the Christmas holidays and introducing him for the first time into the Bonhoeffer circle. For the Saxon "country boy," Dietrich's home meant a sudden ascent into a world of chauffeurs and maids, diplomats and scholars, international travel, tennis matches, horseback riding, weekends at country estates, and visits to the homes of countesses who happened to double as aunts. For the youth who had felt the lash of his frugal mother's disapproval when he wished to take a boat trip down the Danube from Vienna to Constantinople, and her "shame" and disappointment when he, to her mind, wasted money on a trip to Paris,[2] the freedom with which the Bonhoeffers spent, the nonchalance with which they travelled and surrounded themselves with beauty—Goethe's cabinet, an icon from Sofia—was intoxicating.

---

1. Bethge, *In Zitz gab es keine Juden*, 104–5.
2. de Gruchy, *Daring, Trusting Spirit*, 2.

At this point, he "really could not imagine that I would one day belong to their world." Yet possibilities were opening in front of him. "My contact with the Bonhoeffers began to initiate a change." Because of the political situation, he began meeting people who would normally have been entirely out of his sphere.[3]

"As a matter of course," Dietrich soon took his Eberhard with him to Göttingen to meet and be vetted by Sabine and Gert. Crucial to Eberhard's future, though she would later write of it offhandedly, Sabine "greatly liked" him.[4] Paula and Karl also came. As the family gathered in Sabine's living room, with its grand piano and gracious furniture, Karl, joined by Sabine and Gert, urged Paula to sing. At last she agreed, and with Dietrich accompanying her on the piano, warbled "The Two Grenadiers" in a youthful voice. Here at last, the ice broke: Eberhard, until this moment miserably out of place, sank into a comfortable connection with his own life. His father used to sing this song, and, as young boy, it had moved him to tears.[5]

The introduction of Eberhard into Dietrich's circle coincided with Dietrich's parents' move to a new home on Marienburger Allee in Charlottenburg. The much smaller house, closer to downtown Berlin than Grunewald, stood at the end of a quiet street. With woods on one side, the situation offered privacy. It represented the parents' retreat into what Bethge would call a more tightly controlled world—one that would become part of a conspiracy to overthrow Hitler. Next door, Dietrich's sister, Ursel Schleicher, moved with her husband and children into an almost identical house, one that would become central to more than one conspiracy.

While the Bonhoeffers designed their house themselves and had never shown any interest in modernist forms, it's clear the traditional architecture adhered to the National Socialist aesthetic—and that as Aryans, the Bonhoeffers could move with ease in Nazi Berlin. Dietrich, the sole unmarried child, had a spacious attic bedroom, bath, and alcove as his domain. The parents included an apartment on the second floor for grandmother Tafel, a space Sabine and her family would later use on their frequent visits.[6]

Music and politics mixed in the family, musical evenings becoming both a cover for political talk and a pleasure in and of themselves. At the next-door Schleicher home, Eberhard participated in the music and became gradually aware that he was meeting political contacts from all walks of life,

---

3. Bethge, *In Zitz gab es keine Juden*, 104.
4. Leibholz, *The Bonhoeffers*, 103.
5. Bethge, *In Zitz gab es keine Juden*, 106.
6. Leibholz, *The Bonhoeffers*, 76.

from former trade unionists to Prince Louis Ferdinand, second son of the deposed Wilhelm II.

When not a center of political resistance, the Bonhoeffer home became a refuge from National Socialism. It remained an oasis of the old culture, holding onto a traditional, pre-Nazi way of living and being. Finkenwalde students liked to visit, having learned that Paula, even more than Dietrich, would offer a fount of support and advice.[7]

In early 1936, Karl Bonhoeffer's dean tried to persuade the faculty "to join the [Nazi] party as a group."[8] Karl refused, but near retirement, he chose distasteful compromise with the regime he abhorred. In doing so—staying on as psychiatrist in the Chief Court for Freedom from Hereditary Disease—he was able to ameliorate some of the excesses of Nazi eugenics.[9]

Yet the compromises sat uneasily with the family.

In late October 1935, grandmother Tafel had written to Dietrich from his older brother's Karl-Friedrich's house where she had gone to be out of the way while Paula and her sister Elisabeth managed the move to Charlottenburg. In her letter, Tafel expressed her distress over a Bonhoeffer cousin's husband's forced emigration due to the Aryan laws: "This fifty-four-year-old man is traveling around the world looking for work so he can finish raising his gifted, well-behaved children . . . it was one of those rare beautiful families and now it has been destroyed. . . . These things are affecting everything, even down to the details of family life!"[10]

Ruth, though much younger, reminded Dietrich of this frail and fading grandmother. Both were strong, outspoken women. Both fervently embraced Christianity, and both thought for themselves, with little tolerance for religious cant. Ruth shared Tafel's "vivacious and lively-minded" spirit and "never tired of 'giving thanks to God' despite the falsehood and shame of that [National Socialist] time."[11] Both women were unbending in their rejection and disdain of Hitler's vision. As their relationship grew closer, Dietrich would sometimes call Ruth Grandmother, even though Ruth was closer in age to his parents.

Ruth's support of Finkenwalde mirrored Tafel's fervent promotion of Dietrich's never-realized journey to India to learn more about Eastern

---

7. Bethge, *Friendship and Resistance*, 74–76.
8. Leibholz, *The Bonhoeffers*, 81.
9. Ibid., 83.
10. Bonhoeffer, *DBWE 14*, 107.
11. Bosanquet, *The Life and Death of Dietrich Bonhoeffer*, 49–50; Zimmermann and Smith, eds., *I Knew*, 115.

religions, where Tafel had spoken frankly of living through him. As Ruth rounded up money for Finkenwalde, so in 1928 had Julie Tafel sent money to Dietrich for India. As Ruth encouraged the growth of the seminary, so had Tafel, in 1932, prodded Dietrich to start a youth club for the poor in Berlin. As Dietrich once wrote to Julie about the church struggle: "It is becoming ever more evident to me that we are to be given a great popular national church, whose nature cannot be reconciled with Christianity,"[12] so he would write to Ruth about his continuing church battles, knowing that in her he had found a soulmate. Ruth lived vicariously through Bonhoeffer and his projects—and as with Tafel, Dietrich confided in her.

Tafel, already in failing health, died of pneumonia fewer than four months after Dietrich met Ruth. On January 15, 1936, Dietrich delivered his grandmother's funeral address, doing what he deeply regretted not having done for Sabine's father-in-law. Tafel represented "the obligation to stand by a promise once it is made . . . uprightness and simplicity in public and private life . . . her last years were clouded by the great sorrow she endured on the account of the fate of the Jews among our people . . . . She was the product of another time and another spiritual world, and that world does [not] go down with her to the grave."[13]

Memories of Tafel would remain vivid for Dietrich all his life. They surfaced in his prison fiction, which illustrates poignantly the young Dietrich's craving for the adult reassurance Tafel provided. There, his semi-autobiographical character Martin, living in a house that was a recreation of Bonhoeffer's Grunewald home, turned to his beloved grandmother for help: Martin worried that he might look ridiculous to other people but not realize it. "One didn't talk about such personal things" to parents or older brothers. When the grandmother, however, offered kind reassurances, Martin was "overjoyed."[14]

It was to Tafel that Dietrich had sent a detailed and heartfelt letter about his visit to Bethel, a Christian community and hospital for people with epilepsy, knowing she would understand. As he attended a church service there, he glimpsed in those suffering epilepsy one of his "lightening

---

12. Bosanquet, *The Life and Death of Dietrich Bonhoeffer*, 127.

13. Bethge, *DB: A Biography*, 506. Bethge's translation does not include the bracketed note. Bonhoeffer, *DBWE 14*, puts the "not" in brackets because of confusion as to whether or not it should be there (911). Given how strongly Bonhoeffer struggled to hang on in prison to the past life Tafel represented and also based on the defiance of the funeral sermon itself, I believe Bonhoeffer meant to say that her world did *not* go down with her to the grave.

14. Bonhoeffer, *DBWE 7*, 83.

flashes" of the view from below: "they cannot be master of themselves and must be prepared every moment from their illness to seize them." This, Dietrich ruminated to his grandmother, "may perhaps reveal to these people certain actualities of human existence, in which we are in fact basically defenseless."[15] Soon Hitler would try to euthanize these epileptics as useless eaters, illustrating the impassable differences in world view between him and people like Julie and the grandson she had helped form. As Dietrich put it in his funeral service: "We cannot imagine our lives without her."[16]

From Julie's example, Dietrich tried to incorporate into his life the following lessons: Accept God's will. Bear your burdens. Focus on what is real. Do what is necessary and reasonable. Remain inwardly cheerful. Affirm life.[17]

After the funeral, back at Finkenwalde, Dietrich went from depression to influenza. Bethge, in his biography, attributes the depression—what Dietrich called his "accidie, tristitia"—to the burdens of Finkenwalde leadership.[18] Yet, whether Bethge recognized it or not, we may link Dietrich's feeling of sadness and darkness to grief for his beloved grandmother.

After his grandmother's death, Dietrich turned more fully to Ruth to provide the support and nurture Tafel had once offered. The past became, as so often for Dietrich, a template for the future. This does not mean that Ruth could ever replace Tafel—but she did help fill an empty space. Years later, Eberhard would mock Ruth's sense of religious connection to Dietrich: "the great 'sensation of spiritual encounter with you' (sorry!)."[19] Ruth, however, would continually characterize the relationship with Dietrich as one of the high points of her life, the spark in her old age that made her feel young again. In prison, Dietrich would long for letters from Ruth. For all three, the connection was deep. Ruth and Eberhard, with Sabine, came to form Dietrich's innermost circle.

---

15. Bosanquet, *The Life and Death of Dietrich Bonhoeffer*, 126.
16. Bonhoeffer, *DBWE 14*, 909.
17. Ibid., 910.
18. Bethge, *DB: A Biography*, 506.
19. Bonhoeffer, *DBWE 8*, 356.

— 19 —
Days of Love and Hope

IN THE SUMMER OF 1935, Sabine learned details of concentration camp life from sister Christel. Sabine, horrified, refused to hear more. One night, the doorbell rang at 11 PM, a typical time for a Gestapo raid. Sabine, "terribly frightened," urged Gert to escape through the back garden, amid its many fruit trees. As she opened the front door, two "SA" men extended their arms toward her, heiling Hitler.

They only wanted information.

Sabine heard from a friend in Munich of anti-Semitic and anti-Catholic slogans painted on cars: "Do not buy from Jewish swine" and "Jesuit means parasite."[1] Relentless anxiety gnawed at her. Still, the Leibholzes remained in place. Sabine's Munich friend moved to London and later hanged himself.

Despite the Nuremburg laws, times of respite occurred. Two men who worked at their bank, one Christian, one Jewish, let Sabine's Jewish family illegally exchange the same amount of foreign currency as Aryan customers.[2] This allowed the family to travel abroad.

For one magical winter month, the family stayed in Grindelwald, Switzerland. In this time before widespread tourism to the Alps, the family enjoyed the quiet, unharried beauty of mountains and snow. "Softly gliding rides in the sleigh with the snorting horses before us, great flakes of snow falling soft and quiet, a profound stillness, black pinewoods, the lights shining from distant windows" created a land of enchantment. The girls practiced skiing. "Never a brownshirt in sight!"[3] Sabine could sleep again at night.

The family also travelled to Locarno for more than a month, and to the Netherlands, where Gert's brother Hans had emigrated. Hans and his wife lived in The Hague, and the Leibholzes considered moving there. Yet

---

1. Leibholz, *The Bonhoeffers*, 78.
2. Ibid., 79.
3. Ibid., 80–81.

they continued to return to Germany, despite the "iron band" that seemed to tighten around Sabine's heart every time she reentered her homeland.[4]

Even given the increasing pressures both twins felt from the National Socialists, in his letter to her to celebrate their joint thirtieth birthday in 1936, Dietrich sounded flush with optimism—despite the fact that in December, Nazi church leader Kerrl had, among other prohibitions, banned the Confessing Churches from collecting money or ordaining pastors.

"We think that after the Olympics many matters will be clarified.... Don't you think the last ten years have been deeply rewarding for us? You know that in spite of everything I would rather be alive today than 30 years ago. I wonder whether this is not also the same with you, Sabine, and with you both—provided, that is, one can manage a little beyond the personal dimension...." Dietrich asked whether "here and there... and specifically among our [sic] children... character formation is not being achieved?" He was "thinking a great deal about Grandmama's death. It was like the end of an epoch!" He noted they could learn from her way of living. "Let each of us wish the other that as brother and sister we may continue to remain as close to another as we have been up to the present.... Certainly," he added thoughtfully, "we still have great need of one another."[5]

The closeness he felt to Sabine contrasted with some of the strains suggested in a letter to sister Susi. Writing in response to the birth of her son, he said, "During the past few years, things were not really as they should have been—and it was, as I clearly recognize, my own fault."[6] He thanked her for asking him to be a godfather but a few months later expressed a thinly veiled annoyance at the timing of the baby's baptism, writing, "Could you not delay the baptism for eight days?... I hope things can be arranged so I can be with you...."[7]

As for Ruth, she brimmed with joy as Dietrich joined her in her Stettin apartment, overflowing with cake, flowers, and telegrams, for her sixty-ninth birthday tea party, which coincided with his thirtieth birthday and the fiftieth anniversary of her wedding day.

It would be interesting to know what Sabine's response was to the question of whether she would rather have been alive in Nazi Germany than thirty years prior, but as so often, she falls tactfully silent on the topic her brother has introduced. Instead, in her memoir, she quotes his letter

---

4. Ibid., 81.
5. Ibid., 92.
6. Bonhoeffer, *DBWE 14*, 81.
7. Ibid., 104–5.

and immediately launches into a story about the terror she experienced at the time. Implicitly, her answer is an emphatic no. No longer were Dietrich and Sabine sharing the same thoughts; no, she was not glad to be alive in a place where people marched in the streets chanting about wanting Jewish blood on their bayonets, where she was terrified that Gert would end up in a concentration camp.

As Sabine's life narrowed and dwindled into one of lost friends, isolation, anxiety about the future, and day-to-day fear, Dietrich's expanded. The wanderer and exile found his purpose in Germany and the lonely male twin ripped in half found the closest of friends in Eberhard and entered a new world through Ruth.

Years later, Dietrich remembered celebrating his thirtieth birthday with Eberhard at Finkenwalde, the first of many they would share. They sat before the fireside.[8] "You had given me," Dietrich wrote, "as a present the D major violin concerto, and we listened to it together; then I had to tell you a little about Harnack and past times; for some reason or other you enjoyed that very much, and afterwards we decided definitely to go to Sweden."[9]

The Sweden decision involved the whole seminary. After they had all gathered around the open fire where Dietrich's copper brazier from Spain gleamed, students quizzed Dietrich about Barcelona, Mexico, and London. Then they asked for a birthday gift from their director: A trip to Sweden. He agreed, leaving the group giddy with excitement. Dietrich made plans with rapid-fire speed so that the Reich government would not have time to interfere. Dietrich would later repeatedly call this time "quite wonderful years."

In January, the timing coinciding with Eberhard having passed muster with his family, Dietrich set about ending his relationship with Elisabeth Zinn. In his popular biography, Eric Metaxas describes Zinn as Dietrich's "first love," asserting that they were possibly even engaged, but that seems entirely unlikely.[10]

In the fragment we have of a January 27, 1936 letter to Zinn, Dietrich ruminated on his move away from self-centered narcissism and pride, as well as his growing understanding of the Sermon of the Mount, and his effort to lead a "holy life." "My calling is quite clear to me," he wrote. "I must follow the path." The risks are clear: "Perhaps it [the path] will not be a long one."[11] Years later, in prison, he would write to Eberhard of this path, saying he'd never regretted it.

8. Bonhoeffer, *LPP,* 143.
9. Ibid., 143.
10. Keith Clements also makes this claim in *Bonhoeffer and Britain*.
11. Wind, *A Spoke in the Wheel*, 110. See also Bonhoeffer, *DBWE 14*, 135. In this

Much of our information about the Zinn relationship comes from Dietrich's 1944 prison letter to his fiancée Maria, a strange and elusive epistle. Dietrich writes that he and Zinn didn't realize a possible attraction until a "third person" who "thought he was helping us" pointed it out. "We then discussed the matter frankly, but it was too late. We had evaded and misunderstood each other for too long. We could never be entirely in sympathy again, and I told her so. . . . Two years later she married and the weight on my mind gradually lessened."[12]

The letter is less a description of a love affair or engagement than an exposition of Dietrich's alarm—and distaste—at a relationship with an old family friend suddenly framed as a romance. He expressed annoyance at the mysterious "third person" who forced him to acknowledge what he'd been evading. He doesn't explain why this revelation meant that he and Zinn could never be "in sympathy" again. The idea appears to have come from Dietrich alone: "I told her so." The passage suggests Dietrich's flight from the relationship rather than a mutual agreement that it had run its course.

Zinn herself, in correspondence with author Renate Wind, described the relationship as a professional friendship.[13] "During the church struggle there was not so much reflection on the difference between men and women in the Confessing Church as they both belonged together in a common battle and on one front," Zinn wrote.[14]

As he had done with Sabine, Dietrich treated the highly intelligent Zinn as a friend he could confide in freely, share ideas with, and cajole into doing favors for him. What Zinn wanted is less clear. "It is far from certain," Wind writes, that Zinn, who died in 1995, had any expectation of romance and marriage from Dietrich. Zinn married Gunther Bornkamm, the New Testament scholar, in 1938, two years after Bonhoeffer ended the relationship—and despite have danced so near to an extraordinary woman, Dietrich, rather than disappointed to lose her, was relieved at her marriage.

---

letter to Zinn, Dietrich cites Philippians 1:23: "For I am hard pressed between the two, having a desire to depart and be with Christ, which is far better." Given the exuberance for life he is expressing to others at this period, such as Sabine, this death wish is possibly a bid for sympathy.

12. Bismarck and Kabitz, eds., *Love Letters from Cell 92*, 66.
13. Ibid., 109.
14. Ibid.

20

Squaring off against the Führer

AT A NAZI PARTY rally on March 11, 1936, Hitler walked solemnly between throngs of the faithful. He stopped, raised his arm heavenward and cried to the now silent crowd that their faithful comrades, killed for upholding the National Socialist cause, lived as ghosts all around them, marching with them in spirit. Foreign traveller Denis de Rougemont, who attended the rally, experienced an epiphany: "I thought I was going to a mass [political] meeting . . . but it is worship that they are engaged in! And it is a liturgy that is unfolding, the great sacral ceremony of a religion I am not part of . . . I have understood. . . . What I now experience has to be called the sacred horror."[1]

Dietrich understood the sacred horror, as he had from the start. He continued to call for Christians to draw a line and stand firmly on it, even if it meant suffering. He had witnessed firsthand the fruits of "cheap grace," the concept that he had acquired from Adam Clayton Powell Sr. at the Abyssinian Baptist Church in Harlem.[2] Cheap grace meant easy platitudes and feeling virtuous through churchgoing while ignoring glaring injustices.

In the 1920s, Dietrich's older brothers had criticized him for pursuing a career in a weak institution. Bonhoeffer had recognized the church's weakness and hoped to change it. A church grounded in the Sermon on the Mount, as he had written to his brother, could blow the Nazi regime sky high. Yet what both he and Hitler saw—in reality—was the decay.

"I promise you," said Hitler, "that if I wished to, I could destroy the Church in a few years; it is hollow and rotten and false through and through."

---

1. Lubrich, ed., *Travels in the Reich*, 87–88.

2. Holland, "First We Take Manhattan, Then We Take Berlin." Cheap grace was the concept that grace could be had without "the price of following after Jesus." In *Discipleship*, Bonhoeffer wrote, "Cheap grace means grace sold on the market like cheapjacks' wares. The sacraments, the forgiveness of sin, and the consolations of religion are thrown away at cut prices. Grace is represented as the Church's inexhaustible treasury, from which she showers blessings with generous hands, without asking questions or fixing limits. Grace without price; grace without cost!" (43).

One push and the whole structure would collapse . . . I will give them a few years reprieve. Why should we quarrel? They will swallow anything in order to keep their material advantages . . . we need only show them once or twice who is the master."[3]

After the war, Confessing Church leaders were "haunted" by whether an early, stronger resistance could have achieved results—exactly the kind of principled opposition that Bonhoeffer promoted. For at times during the early years, when the German public showed outrage over persecution of the church, the Nazis had backed down.[4] Even much later, during World War II, the Nazis stood helplessly by while almost the entire Norwegian Lutheran pastorate resigned from the church rather than see it Nazified. With principled resistance, Norway managed to save more than half its Jews. Likewise, Bulgarian citizens collectively opposed anti-Semitism, with the king himself volunteering personally to lie down on the railroad tracks in front of the deportation trains. Such outcry helped save 50,000 Bulgarian Jews. Finland also stood up for its Jewish population, even when the Nazis threatened to starve the country in retaliation. "'We would rather perish together with the Jews,' Finland's foreign minister told the astonished Heinrich Himmler."[5]

From February 29 to March 10, 1936, Dietrich defied the regime: without permission he took his seminarians on the ecumenical birthday trip to visit churches in Denmark and Sweden. In response, the German Ministry of Culture revoked Dietrich's right to lecture at the University of Berlin.[6] Undeterred, Dietrich offered seminary Bible studies on the "Jewish" books of Ezra and Nehemiah and began writing *Discipleship*.

In April 1936, Dietrich and Eberhard visited Ruth, while her grandchildren holidayed between school terms with their parents. Ruth called these "the most wonderful Easter days in my little country house, because Bonhoeffer and Bethge were with me for twelve days. . . . What riches it was for me can hardly be expressed in words."[7] For Dietrich, the rambling cottage called Klein Krössin proved an idyllic retreat. "What wonderful times I've had at Krössin!" he would later write.[8]

---

3. Barnett, *For the Soul of the People*, 44.
4. Ibid., 72.
5. Sider, *Nonviolent Action*, 24–25.
6. Bosanquet, *The Life and Death of Dietrich Bonhoeffer*, 174.
7. Ibid.,184.
8. Bismarck and Kabitz, eds., *Love Letters*, 74.

Klein Krössin, in the woods on the edge of Ruth's son's Kieckow estate, had once served as the bailiff's home. It was long, rambling, half-timbered building, where one could envision Snow White living with the seven dwarves. On one side, its windows looked out onto a garden, on the other side, to a forest. The house had three large guest bedrooms, called Hope, Joy, and Contentment. Ruth slept in the fourth bedroom, which doubled as her study, complete with a large writing desk.[9]

Ruth raised geese, known to wander in and out of her kitchen, and her smoked goose breasts were coveted Christmas presents. In the warmer months, Ruth enjoyed entertaining in her garden, with its purple clematis, lilies of the valley, and creeping phlox. She had her round tea table placed under the shade of a large oak tree and spread with an embroidered tablecloth spun from Kieckow flax. On festive occasions, perhaps including a visit from Dietrich, Ruth served Baumkuchen, a Christmasy pastry shaped like an evergreen tree, filled with almonds and covered with chocolate.[10] Here Dietrich worked on his latest book, *Discipleship*.

As even Confessing Church leaders scrambled to compromise with the regime, Hitler persisted in hounding the church. During the spring, a group of Nazis attacked and beat up a Jewish pastor named Willy Sussbach. Dietrich brought Sussbach to Finkenwalde to recuperate.[11] In May, when the Confessing Church demanded the Nazi Party stay out of church affairs, the government responded with a crackdown, arresting hundreds of pastors, killing one, and confiscating church funds.[12] Curtailing church activism fell under the auspices of the Gestapo, which worked to crush any pockets of opposition that challenged National Socialist ideology.

As early as February 1936, as his birthday letter to Sabine hints, Dietrich pondered how to use the international attention that would focus on Germany during the summer Olympics to force the regime to back away from persecuting the church. With the Olympics in mind, the Confessing Church delivered a memo to the Berlin Chancellory on June 4, 1936—with Bonhoeffer's imprint all over it[13]—timed to elicit a response before the August Olympic games. The writers hoped that Hitler, to preserve his international prestige, would affirm his government's good intentions toward church and society.

---

9. Pejsa, *Matriarch of Conspiracy*, 153.
10. Ibid., 174.
11. Bethge, *DB: A Biography*, 540.
12. Shirer, *The Rise and Fall of the Third Reich*, 238.
13. Wind, *A Spoke in the Wheel*, 119.

Initially meant only for Hitler's eyes, the memo protested laws that "muzzled" the church and insisted that Christians were morally obligated to oppose persecution of the Jews. The writers also addressed issues beyond the church, such as the legality of concentration camps and the corrosive effects of widespread spying and eavesdropping.

Hitler, not one to be manipulated, never responded.

In the meantime, the June publication of Bonhoeffer's lecture "On the Question of the Church Community" caused an uproar, earning Dietrich the "fanatic" label in some Confessing Church quarters. His line, "whoever knowingly separates himself from the Confessing Church in Germany separates himself from salvation," spread "like wildfire throughout the German churches."[14] Dietrich couldn't have been more surprised by the reaction to a simple repetition of what he had been saying for the past three years. Now, Dietrich wrote to Barth, the clergy "are getting terribly excited about it."[15]

During the 1936 summer solstice, the unflagging Rougemont attended one the of Nazi's beloved nighttime bonfire celebrations, spectral, smoky, and spooky. He heard what he called a "liturgy, another recitation of a narrative of defeat and redemption: "We were lying in the mud, oppressed and humiliated. . . . But the old Germanic legend tells us a liberator will come down from the snowy mountains . . . . The old legend has become reality! He has come to awaken his people!"[16]

On July 17, a London paper published an article about the Confessing Church memo, still unacknowledged by Hitler. On July 23, a Swiss paper printed the entire memo. Hitler flew into a rage. Most in the Confessing Church, already far to the right of Bonhoeffer and his cohorts, raced away from the fallout.

Werner Koch, the young seminarian who had recognized the "highbrowed" Bonhoeffer on the train ride to Stettin, and Ernst Tillich—both close associates of Bonhoeffer—had leaked the memo abroad in frustration over the lack of official German response to it. Yet despite Hitler's fury at the incident, an eerie stillness fell.

Meanwhile, a comic incident with the "brothers" occurred at the beginning of August, when Dietrich took a group of seminarians on a three-day beach retreat to the shores of the Baltic. He described the accommodations as "frightful . . . . Five to ten ancient field cots in a room. Stale air." More importantly, the villa was not in an isolated spot like Zingst, conducive to

---

14. Bethge, *DB: A Biography,* 520.
15. Ibid., 521.
16. Lubrich, ed.,*Travels in the Reich,* 89.

contemplation, but "*right in the middle* of the swimming activities" (emphasis Bonhoeffer's).

Friend Helmut Gollwitzer remembered that Dietrich "again and again in his conversations evoked the vision of a religious order living in voluntary celibacy."[17]

Another, Hellmut Traub, recalled that Dietrich "loved the word Zucht—discipline or self control."[18] But the seminarians were clearly frustrated by their leader's prudery. "All hell broke loose," in Dietrich's words, one evening after devotions as seminarians mounted a sexual rebellion. Wolf Dieter Zimmermann, who had followed Dietrich to Finkenwalde, opened the complaint session. Dietrich learned that five seminarians had gone out after dinner and been, in his words, "overwhelmed by temptation . . . indeed by an unbearable desire for pleasure, dancing, girls, etc. Two then went off with girls with whom they had spoken. Nothing else happened. But a terrible onslaught of nature against the word emerged."

At 11 that night, Dietrich went for a beach walk with Zimmermann only to be stopped by four other seminarians who demanded a talk with him "now." The group settled in the sandy darkness. "We sat facing each other. I let them speak, one after another and was silent. There were wild outbursts of sexual desire against the word of God. They spoke in completely frank language. . . . The five stood against me and themselves . . . it was clear how serious things had become. I was overwhelmed. All I could do was pray to myself and ask the Lord Jesus to step in." The episode passed, but the dumbfounded Dietrich wrote to Eberhard: "I have to be there with the brothers every moment; after yesterday you can understand why!"[19]

During the summer, Dietrich read a verse in a Berlin bookstore: "At the end of the Olympiade/We'll beat the CC [Confessing Church] to marmalade/Then we'll chuck out the Jew/The CC will end too."[20] That rhyme expressed the sentiments of Oberscharführer Schröder, Eichmann's superior in dealing with the "Jewish question," who wrote on August 28, 1936: "The Jew as a person is a 100 percent enemy of National Socialism, as proven by the difference in his race and nationality. Wherever he tries to transmit his work, his influence and his world outlook to the non-Jewish world, he discharges it in hostile ideologies, so we find it in Liberalism . . . Marxism, and not least also in Christianity. These ideologies then accord with a broader concept of Jewish mentality."[21]

17. Zimmermann and Smith, eds., *I Knew*, 143.
18. Ibid., 157.
19. Bonhoeffer, *DBWE* 14, 229–30.
20. Bethge, *DB: A Biography*, 536.
21. Dawidowicz, *The War Against the Jews*, 86.

— 21 —

Friendship

DIETRICH AND EBERHARD HAD cheerfully planned an August 1936 holiday together before the start of a church conference in Chamby, but when Eberhard invited his brother and his cousin Vibrans to join them Dietrich responded coldly. "Naturally, if you would like it. . . . But it was something of a surprise to me. Do you believe it is good for the four of us to travel?" As it happened, Eberhard's brother dropped out, but anxiety about Vibrans laced Dietrich's letters to Eberhard: "If Gerhard [Vibrans] can get accommodations elsewhere, that would be another matter entirely. Like you, I think the three of us making the trip would be wonderful . . . but every decision, every change of plans, etc. can cause more friction among three people than between two . . . things sometimes happen . . . . Moreover, we cannot do much for Gerhard financially on this trip."[1] A few days later, he suggested that he and Eberhard travel alone together in Switzerland then split off, with Eberhard to travel with Vibrans, Dietrich to head to Finkenwalde.[2] Finally he wrote, "I am trying to think of a way not to disappoint Gerhard."[3]

Despite Dietrich's disinclination, Vibrans came along. Tensions rose. When Dietrich left Vibrans waiting in the car while he and Eberhard made a visit, Vibrans referred to himself as a "third wheel," angering Dietrich. In a restaurant afterwards, Vibrans became aware of Dietrich's "great nervousness and irritability." He didn't know what he had done until he and Eberhard went to the post office together so that Eberhard, ever tactful, could fill him in.

Dietrich later wrote to Vibrans to apologize. The apology letter itself still emanates some of the emotional sting of the vacation: "I have spoken to Eberhard about what you told me. He agreed with you. This hurt me very much at first." Eberhard, grateful for the warm and welcoming friendship the Vibrans family had shown him after his father died, was no doubt

1. Bonhoeffer, *DBWE 14*, 226.
2. Ibid., 233.
3. Ibid., 235.

mortified to have had his cousin repaid by rudeness from Dietrich. Thus the apology came at Eberhard's behest, from Eberhard's intervention on behalf of his cousin, and reflected Eberhard's growing influence on Dietrich. Dietrich wrote to Vibrans, "I now understand that I perturbed you during our time together" and apologized both to Vibrans and Eberhard.

Explanations followed: "I am aware that this is not an excuse," Dietrich explained, "[but I was] absolutely at the end of my tether." He was "happy" Vibrans came along but irritated that Vibrans characterized himself as "the third wheel." Eberhard was annoyed that Dietrich laid down travel "conditions" with Vibrans, but the letter doesn't outline what the conditions were. Dietrich defended these conditions as bringing "clarity in all circumstances" rather than as a sign of "unfriendliness."

Dietrich added a postscript that suggested the easy conviviality of the seminary days had ended: "We also have to remember that we are no longer students and that each of us now brings along more personality traits than we think or want."[4] Vibrans irritated Dietrich. He had tried to sidestep traveling with him, and he'd attempted for Eberhard's sake to get along with him, though perhaps part of the annoyance was jealousy that the two were so close. If Eberhard had been invited to cross the portal into the magic world of the Bonhoeffers, Vibrans most surely had been stopped at the door.

In his deferential response to Dietrich, Vibrans in turn apologized that "I offended you ... unintentionally." He explained the comment about being the "third wheel" as a joke—"only kidding"—and said he dropped it immediately when he saw it irritated Dietrich. Vibrans insisted that he "never would have thought to take offense" at being left in the car while Dietrich and Eberhard made a visit, because it was Dietrich's "right to take only Eberhard."

Vibrans response also signaled in "a few revealing sentences, his acceptance of the very special relationship" between his two friends.[5] He called it a "unique relationship." Before the trip, he may have suspected how things stood, for he had ribbed Dietrich in a June letter: "But what happens if Eberhard must leave? Then your name will once again stand in heaven [as] a lonely star . . . . Endless elegies could demonstrate to you how I view my *womanless* existence as an equally joyless one"[6] (emphasis Vibrans). If before the trip he had suspected that Dietrich's interest in Eberhard as more than ordinary friendship, now he believed he knew. He was ready to step

---

4. Ibid., 246

5. de Gruchy, *Daring, Trusting Spirit*, 29–32.

6. Bonhoeffer, *DBWE 14*, 195.

aside, to appreciate the past, and to accept "what is present and always will be."

In the meantime, "how self-evident it has become to me to discuss important matters with you," Dietrich wrote Eberhard. Dietrich would later write, in a letter full of apologies, "I ask myself, did I in some way alienate you from your old friends? I don't believe it; rather it was your path that led you in a different direction."[7]

Vibrans's words about a special or unique friendship echo codes used for gay relationships in Weimar Germany. Gay groups had exploded during Weimar, despite the infamous Paragraph 175 that criminalized homosexuality. These groups often used the word "friend" as a euphemism, such as in "Friendship" and the "Male Friends Club" or the "Friendship Association," which was "a social space for homosexuals where they could talk, have fun and exchange thoughts."[8]

Under Weimar, the energized gay community had several branches. One, headed by sexologist Dr. Magnus Hirschfeld, sought to legitimize gay men as a "third sex," somewhere between male and female. In contrast, vigorously opposed to any branding of gay men as effeminate, reactionary Adolf Brand's *Gemeinschaft der Eigenen* or Community of the Self-Owned or Special, defined gays as hypermasculine warriors and fetishized the male form.[9] (He was not the only one to hold this view. Ernst Bluher, for example, promoted a male-only society, male "clubs" and male-to-male physical relationships.)[10]

In Brand's view gay men exemplified physical fitness and vigor. Brand, who detested the Weimar democratic experiment, excluded women from his circles, finding them debilitating to the hypermasculine psyche. His publication, *Der Eigene*, its circulation carefully restricted, celebrated Greek art, especially nude male sculptures, romantic poetry, nudism, and heroic descriptions of male bodies and male friendships. It remained in print until 1933.[11] Vibrans's words "unique" and "special" conjure Brand's "unique" or "special" male relationships.

In these early days, Bethge tried to sidestep the friendship's deeper implications. He attempted to define "friendship" one way, Dietrich another. Bethge understood a holiday among "friends" as open to others, the more

7. Bonhoeffer, *DBWE 8*, 185.
8. Crouthamel, "'Comradeship' and 'Friendship,'" 112.
9. Ibid.
10. Theweleit, *Male Fantasies*, vol. 1, 27.
11. Crouthamel, "'Comradeship' and 'Friendship,'" 111.

the merrier. Dietrich wanted to vacation with Bethge alone, the two of them a couple. The timing of Dietrich's break with Zinn indicates that Eberhard was the "third party" who suggested to Dietrich he might be in love with her, most likely Eberhard's attempt to deflect some of Dietrich's needs by encouraging him to pursue a woman. Dietrich, instead, as we saw, broke with Zinn. Eberhard wanted Vibrans to join their twosome as another friend. Dietrich pushed Vibrans away.

Dietrich and Eberhard soon traveled alone to Italy for a carefree holiday. They celebrated Eberhard's birthday in Florence.[12] They visited Rome via the Simplon Pass. Dietrich, "once again entranced by St. Peter's," tried to share with Eberhard what the "magnificent building" meant to him,[13] and together they viewed Melozzo da Forli's paintings of angels in the Vatican Museum.[14] Eight years later, in Italy with the German army, Eberhard would write to Dietrich of "sitting near the place [Rignano, below Monte Soratte on the Via Flaminia] where we saw the seven hills in the glimmering twilight after the hot car journey . . . ."[15] Later too, when Eberhard found himself stationed in Naples, Dietrich would write, cryptically: "I remember, too, how in August 1936 you rejected in horror the idea of going to Naples."[16] They saw the village Radicofani together, on the Via Cassia.[17] By September 13, having stopped in Zurich and Basel, Dietrich and Eberhard arrived back in Finkenwalde.

Nobody in the Confessing Church knew what the regime's next move would be. Dietrich kept up everyone's spirits and spent generously on the Finkenwalde brothers in a way he had not been willing to do with Vibrans. He radiated cheer, full of "infectious joie de vivre." He paid for two seminarians to fly to Berlin, fulfilling their dream of air travel, then a rare luxury. He handed out tickets to the Olympics, and on hot days, as he had always done, cancelled classes for trips to the beach.[18]

In a wedding sermon that spring of 1936, he might have been expressing his own condition, both with Sabine before they were torn asunder and now with Eberhard: "Nothing in life gives us greater joy than being together with a person whom we love and with whom we see ourselves as

12. Bonhoeffer, *DBWE 8*, 260.
13. Bethge, *DB: A Biography*, 554.
14. Bonhoeffer, *DBWE 8*, 219.
15. Bonhoeffer, *LPP*, 186.
16. Ibid., 340.
17. Ibid., 224.
18. Bethge, *DB: A Biography*, 541–42.

one. Because we have that other person, we are able to rejoice even amid external cares."[19]

Judith Butler, in *Gender Trouble*, challenges the notion of dividing the world into "gay" and "straight." All sex and gender is socially constructed, she argues, and is not innate but "performed." Most women and men "act" in the way women or men are expected to act in a given culture. As people "perform" their gender, these performances, repeated over and over, become accepted as the "natural" attributes of each sex. How can they fail to be "natural," when so many of each gender behave, repeatedly, in the same way? Butler calls this seemingly "natural" assumption of gender "heteronormality." As she puts it, "There is no gender identity behind the expressions of gender . . . identity is performatively constituted by the very "expressions" that are said to be its results."[20] Societies reinforce these "normal" traits because it is in their interests to regulate the chaos of sexuality. The "homosexual," either gay or lesbian, then becomes the "other" against which heteronormality is defined, the necessary corollary to "straight" sexuality.

In Butler's lexicon, "gay" becomes a confining grid placed over a person who performs gender in what the dominant culture has decided is an atypical way, more a method for heterosexist society to label its own anxieties and define norms than a category that is meaningful in its own right. So, without trying to label or "box in" Bonhoeffer, we will look at the ways he conformed and refused to conform to performing within the gender norms of his family and his culture.

Gender performance, of course, becomes more complicated in the context of the distorted world of the Nazi totalitarian state, which worked to "synchronize" all private behavior according to Nationalist Socialist ideals. It's also important to note that although his sexuality has raised questions, most Bonhoeffer scholars and biographers have chosen to place him unequivocally into a narrative of heterosexual performativity—against the evidence.

Dietrich lived outside of mainstream German gender norms for his times—for either the Nazi world or the pre-World War I culture he idealized. He alone among his siblings never married—this in spite of his deep affinity for doing things the Bonhoeffer way. As scholar Clifford Green states, "Bonhoeffer's family embodied for him a tradition and culture of standards, ethics, and ways of behaving that extended from household life to public

19. Bonhoeffer, *DBWE 14*, 914.
20. Butler, *Gender Trouble*, 33.

responsibility. It was a conscious part of who he was, and he expressed it often in letters."[21]

While Dietrich's childhood gave him many advantages and a confident demeanor that served him well, it did not equip him easily for life outside the confines of a rigid pattern his family paradigm mapped out for him—and which he, all the same, had increasingly realized would not be his "ground." Despite events from costume balls to ice-skating evenings meant to throw him into contact with suitable young women, we have no evidence of a love affair, either from afar or close at hand, no unrequited love, no Beatrice, no woman stringing him along or breaking his heart or slipping from his grasp, no tempestuous romance, no fleeting sighs; only, after Sabine married, a friendship with a cousin who looked like his twin sister. He did not respond to the women thrown across his path who would have made suitable wives, such as Walter Dress's sister, a companion among others on one of his wandering excursions—or Zinn, an ideal candidate with her many ties to his family. Unlike his siblings, when he did get engaged it was to a woman eighteen years younger, from far outside the close Berlin circles where his siblings found partners.

As for the Nazi world, it took nineteenth-century patriarchal norms to extremes. On the surface, as Richard Grunburger writes in *The Twelve-Year Reich: A Social History of Nazi Germany*, "restoring the family to its rightful place" was a Nazi "battle cry" and meant a notion of family as "male-centered and authoritarian."[22] By the late 1930s, the concern with procreation reached "ludicrous proportions," including reminders to employees that their duties to the state did not end when they left the office. The average age of marriage dropped by two to three years during this period.[23] Yet despite the multiple pressures to marry and procreate, Dietrich stayed single.

Bonhoeffer's ostensible rationale for remaining a bachelor was that he had, in such harsh times, to devote himself fully and without reserve to the church's struggle: "For a long time he thought he would have to forego marriage in order to devote all his energy to the urgent problems facing the church and the state."[24] This rationale collapses quickly, however, in the face of his later engagement to Maria von Wedemeyer, during a time when the threat of imminent arrest was most profound and would seemingly have made staying single more, not less, urgent.

21. Bonhoeffer, *DBWE 7*, 4.
22. Grunberger, *A Social History of Nazi Germany*, 234.
23. Ibid., 240.
24. Bonhoeffer, *DBWE 7*, 217.

— 22 —
"Convents" and Concentration Camps

IN 1936, MARIA VON Wedermeyer arrived at Altenburg in eastern Germany and saw her new home, a castle sitting on a hill, the Magdalenen-Stift boarding school. Maria entered boarding school at twelve, an age she would later confide was "too young."[1] "I would never," she would write in 1944, when she was not yet twenty, "approve of my sisters leaving home before the age of thirteen." However, she would insist that no matter how homesick, "I never seriously wanted to go home again for good."[2]

A Protestant school for aristocratic girls, Altenburg had traditions that harkened back two centuries. Interestingly, its founder, Henriette Catharina, Baroness von Gersdorff, was the grandmother of the deeply religious Count Zinzendorf, who had protected and supported the Moravian church of Dietrich's governesses.

At the end of a long hallway on the upstairs floor, from a window looking out over the drive, the girls watching for the postman would have glimpsed the pigtailed newcomer making her entrance. Once there, Maria quickly blended in with the other girls, donning the school uniform of a long blue dress covered with a black pinafore. Like the other students, she was forbidden hair ribbons, jewelry, or other personal ornaments. Any books that did not belong to the school were confiscated, food packages from home were divided among all classmates equally, and individual items, such as family photos, were locked in a cupboard. The girls could not eat candy. They followed a rigorous academic regime and adhered to strict Protestant religious teachings, while portraits of early school luminaries stared down upon them.[3]

---

1. Bismarck and Kabitz, eds., *Love Letters*, 179–80.
2. Ibid., 180.
3. Ibid., 299.

For all her initial homesickness and awareness that she was sent away too young, Maria appreciated the school's old-fashioned rules: "You mustn't expect the school to conform to modern educational principles—the parents can do that . . . I'm bound to agree with the headmistress that rollicking around is out of keeping . . . . Once upon a time you . . . wore ankle-length skirts . . . it was still like that in my day!"[4]

Energetic Maria thrived at Magdalen-Stift, excelling at math, enjoying illicit games of cops and robbers (despite agreeing that rollicking was wrong), and finding a friend in teacher Jutta von Kuhlberg.[5]

At this time, Maria's father Hans, a far-right conservative Christian, and a former staff member to von Papen—Hans resigning before the Röhm Putsch killed his successor—found himself accused by the Nazis of "antisocial behavior." If convicted, he would lose his right to run Pätzig, the family estate purchased for him by his father. Hans eventually won his case, but the family became more fearful, drawing in on itself.

While her father clashed with the regime, Maria lived in an environment as cloistered from the realities of the Nazi revolution as any could be in 1930s Germany. With its unchanging traditions and deep Christian roots, the school remained resistant to the new Nazi world view. What Maria would imbibe most from this education was neither modern individualism nor violent totalitarianism but an old-fashioned ethic of subordinating oneself for the good of the community.

On October 6, 1936, the Gestapo belatedly arrested Ernst Tillich for distributing a memorandum critical of the Nazi government to the foreign press. Friedrich Weissler, a Protestant of Jewish descent who happened to be taking care of one of the two copies of the memo, was arrested with Tillich. Both men found themselves in Berlin's Gestapo prison on the Alexanderplatz.

On November 13, 1936, Werner Koch was arrested and sent to the dank Gestapo prison for his part in distributing the memo that had challenged the government prior to the Olympic games. Dietrich put Koch's fiancée Dita under Ruth's care.[6]

At Christmastime, Dietrich sent Koch greetings from "Brother Glocke"—Bishop Bell,[7] a sign that important foreigners were aware of his arrest. On Feb. 13, 1937, Koch, Weissler, and Tillich arrived at the recently constructed Sachsenhausen concentration camp, an hour north of Berlin,

---

4. Ibid., 190.
5. Ibid., 299.
6. Bethge, *DB: A Biography*, 541.
7. Ibid.

confronting a situation more dire than a stint in a Gestapo jail. Here, they passed through a walled outer prison courtyard with immaculate lawns, the commandant's lovely house graced with a goldfish pond and peacocks, perhaps glimpsed the nearby brick SS barracks, then entered under the ironwork "Work will make you free" gate into the camp's inner bowels.

Like the other camps, Sachsenhausen operated outside of the law. As part of an SS recruit's training, a more experienced officer would choose a random victim and beat him to death in front of the new officer to demonstrate the guards' power.[8] Walls were nine feet high, buttressed by an electrified barbed wire fence. The entire inner camp was under surveillance by an SS man in a tower (later more towers would be added) armed with a machine gun. Guard dogs often accompanied the booted and well-dressed SS officers on their rounds amid the prisoners, who were vulnerable in their thin, striped uniforms and wooden shoes.

Inside the camp, the three Confessing Church members were separated. Weissler was put in the Jewish barracks, where chances for survival were slimmest. Accounts conflict: In one story, he died six days after entering the camp from abuse, "under the boots of Blockführer Zeidler."[9] In another account, he lasted four weeks, at which point his wife was notified he'd hanged himself; she thought that impossible, and according to an eyewitness who accompanied her to see his body, saw he had been murdered.[10]

Koch, although an Aryan political prisoner, found himself assigned to a punitive work detail. Called "the pope" by the guards, he was attacked by two SS officers, who cried—"The pope. The lazy swine! He needs a rest! . . . Put his head nicely on the ground."[11] Koch was thrown down, and two "green" prisoners—career criminals at the top of the camp hierarchy—were ordered to shovel a pile of sand over his head.

"I just thought, 'So this what it is like to die. I tried not to cry out, not to free myself, not even to pray. I simply let it go over me.'"[12]

---

8. This information was imparted to the author during a tour of Sachsenhausen and also appears in Wind, *A Spoke in the Wheel*, 121: "The arbitrary torture and murder by the SS staff claimed countless victims." However, this power, at least at times and apropos certain inmates, had limits. According to testimony in Victoria Barnett's *For the Soul of the People*, a Confessing Church legal brief accusing "persons unknown" of Weissler's murder led to two SS guards being imprisoned for several weeks, one of them hanging himself (84).

9. Wind, *A Spoke in the Wheel*, 120.

10. Barnett, *For the Soul of the People*, 84.

11. Wind, *A Spoke in the Wheel*, 120.

12. Ibid., 122.

At the last moment, a higher up intervened: Koch must be spared because of the uproar raised over Weissler's death. Koch and Tillich, both privileged sons of well-heeled Berlin families, were allowed—for the moment—to survive.

Yet paradoxically, the intense relationships forged under Nazism, heightened in a way impossible under ordinary circumstances, led Ruth, although distressed deeply by Koch's arrest, to continue to find these times invigorating, crackling with Christian renewal. In a letter similar to that Dietrich had sent Sabine as the year opened, Ruth was able to write to Dita Stockman amid all her troubles that the "Word of God has never been so 'filled' as it is now."[13]

---

13. Bosanquet, *The Life and Death of Dietrich Bonhoeffer*, 184.

— 23 —
What Will It Be?

For her seventieth birthday in 1937, Ruth took a European trip with an ease that would soon become impossible for more than half a century. She drove with her son Hans Jurgen to Kohlberg on the Baltic and then to Marienbad in Czechoslovakia. Later daughter Spes joined Ruth for a journey to Silesia, "incredibly lush this year . . . simply glow[ing] with prosperity."[1]

As 1937 progressed, the Nazis propagandized more aggressively against the church. On February 12, Kerrl, the minister of church affairs, told a group of clergy that arguments that Christianity "consists of faith in Christ as the son of God . . . makes me laugh."[2] Kerrl also ridiculed the Apostles' Creed—"True Christianity," he stated, "is represented by the Party . . . the Führer is the herald of a new revelation."[3]

Meanwhile, Nazi Alfred Rosenberg, an "outspoken pagan," dreamed of eradicating "the strange and foreign Christian faiths imported into Germany in the ill-omened year 800." The Nazis planned on expunging pastors, crucifixes, saints' pictures, and the Bible. *Mein Kampf* would replace the Bible as "the purest and truest ethic." On Nazi church altars "*Mein Kampf* would lie with a sword to the left . . . swastikas would replace crosses."[4]

On June 17, 1937, pastor Martin Niemöller preached twice because of the number of people who flocked to hear him.[5] On June 27, 1937, Niemöller again addressed an overflowing crowd with subversive ideas in a totalitarian state—"We must obey God rather than man."[6] Visiting Berlin from London that June, as Confessing Church sermons attracted ever larger audiences

---

1. Pejsa, *Matriarch of Conspiracy*, 222.
2. Shirer, *The Rise and Fall of the Third Reich*, 239.
3. Ibid.
4. Shirer, *The Rise and Fall of the Third Reich*, 240. See also Barnett, *For the Soul of the People*, 26.
5. Zimmermann and Smith, eds., *I Knew*, 99.
6. Shirer, *The Rise and Fall of the Third Reich*, 239.

amid clergy arrests, old friend Julius Rieger met with Dietrich and Hildebrandt, first at the Stadtkrug Restaurant at the Zoo and later at the Stettiner Station, to be briefed amid crowds on the real state of church affairs in Germany. Dietrich wanted Rieger to relay the truth about church persecution to Bell. Rieger, although still a Nazi Party member, exchanged his train ticket for a plane ticket for fear of being arrested at the border, and flew back to London.[7]

On July 1, 1937, Eberhard and Dietrich arrived early in the morning at Niemöller's brick home in the quiet Dahlem suburb of Berlin, eager to discuss the recent rash of clergy arrests. Else Niemöller, normally smiling and bright-eyed, answered the door distraught. Earlier that morning, the Gestapo had arrested her husband. Dietrich and Eberhard rapidly discussed the situation with Mrs. Niemöller, Franz Hildebrandt, who now served as Niemöller's assistant pastor, and pastor Eugen Rose, who happened to be on the scene. Then, one of them glanced out a window of the imposing house and saw a fleet of sleek black Mercedes—an unmistakable sign of the Gestapo—heading their way.

As the Gestapo officers got out of their cars, Dietrich, Franz, and Eberhard raced to the back door to escape. A Gestapo agent, in hiding, jumped out, blocked their path, and pushed them back into the house. Soon more Gestapo agents pounded on the front door.

Searched and put under house arrest, the three men and Else sat quietly in the parlor while agents spent seven hours searching the property, poring over Niemöller's papers and finding 30,000 marks for the Confessing Church in a safe hidden behind a painting.[8] Through the parlor curtains, Dietrich could see his own family's limo cruising slowly up and down the leafy block, Paula's face pressed to the window.[9]

Ruth was distraught at Niemöller's arrest. He had confirmed two of her grandsons. How, she wondered, does one protest injustice in a place as brutal as Nazi Germany? Feeling as trapped as anyone, she consoled herself by writing letters to Else Niemöller.[10]

Little did any of them know that Hitler himself had "had a ... fit of rage" at Niemöller's "rebellious sermon" of June 27th—"we must obey God rather than man"—and had personally ordered his arrest and life imprisonment.[11]

---

7. Zimmermann and Smith, eds., *I Knew*, 100.
8. Bethge, *DB: A Biography*, 579.
9. Ibid., 580; Bosanquet, *The Life and Death of Dietrich Bonhoeffer*, 185.
10. Pejsa, *Matriarch of Conspiracy*, 223.
11. Speer, *Inside the Third Reich*, 98.

Niemöller, a conservative, a Nazi Party member, and a World War I hero, had, like the young Bethge, welcomed Hitler's ascent to power and the demise of the Weimar Republic. He had vehemently opposed democracy, communism, and the labor movement, and in 1920 led a group of students against workers in the Ruhr Valley.[12] He had, however, become disillusioned with Nazism and later became famous for stating: "First they came for the communists and I didn't speak out because I wasn't a communist . . . then they came for the Jews and I didn't speak out because I wasn't a Jew, then they came for me and there was no one left to speak out for me."

Martin Bormann, one of Hitler's closest intimates, fanned the leader's fury against the church, which Bormann himself despised. Bormann would take advantage of the interminable lunches at Hitler's mountaintop estate, the Berghof, as guests sat around a dining room table in plush armchairs and gazed, stultified with boredom, out picture windows at mountain views.

"Bormann had developed a special technique for . . . thrusts [against the Church]," Albert Speer recalled. "He would draw one of the members of the entourage into telling him about seditious speeches a pastor or bishop had delivered, until Hitler finally became attentive and demanded details." Bormann then pretended he didn't want to tell, while Hitler would insist on dragging the story from him. Finally, Bormann would begin reading passages from a "defiant" sermon or letter. "Frequently," Speer noted, "Hitler became so worked up that he began to snap his fingers—a sure sign of his anger—pushed away his food and vowed to punish the offending clergyman eventually. He could much more easily put up with foreign indignation and criticism than opposition at home. That he could not immediately retaliate raised him to a white heat, though he usually managed to control himself quite well."[13]

"'Once I have settled my other problems,' [Hitler] occasionally declared, 'I'll have my reckoning with the church. I'll have it reeling on the ropes.'"[14]

Although Hitler instigated Niemöller's arrest, the Gestapo had largely been given free rein. As William Shirer noted, quoting an SS officer, "As long as the police is carrying out the will of the leadership, it is acting legally." Whoever was arrested, beaten, or killed deserved the treatment, as far as the state was concerned. Not surprisingly, the Gestapo's appearance often terrified ordinary people, a situation made worse by the stiff black uniforms

---

12. Theweleit, *Male Fantasies*, vol. 1, 22.
13. Speer, *Inside the Third Reich*, 123.
14. Ibid.

with their skull and crossbones death head insignias, an image taken from the former Prussian emperor's cavalry guard.

Dietrich, Eberhard, and Hildebrandt must have feared further trouble, but after their long wait in the parsonage, they were released. According to one story, Else, left alone with her husband arrested and her house upended by the Gestapo, heard the sound of voices outside her window. It was the women's choir of her church singing a chorale to comfort her.[15]

Franz Hildebrandt conducted services at the Dahlem Church in Niemöller's absence and continued to collect money illegally to support the Confessing Church. On August 8, the church planned a service of intercession for Niemöller. People began to arrive, only to find that police had cordoned off the building. A spontaneous demonstration broke out, rare in Nazi Germany, leading to 250 arrests. Franz Hildebrandt was among the arrested, and his Jewish ancestry put him in acute danger. He spent three weeks in prison and afterward, with the Bonhoeffer family's help, including making sure, via Bell, that news of his plight was published in the *London Times*, he moved to England.[16] Rieger found Hildebrandt housing and a job.[17]

In July 1937, after a wave of arrests of former Finkenwalde students, Dietrich enlisted Ruth to invite the wives of the arrested men to stay with her at her Klein Krössin cottage.[18] Ruth continued her weekly correspondence with Werner Koch's fiancé, Dita Stockmann, who was "closest to her heart," and warmly urged her to visit.[19]

In August, 1937, Dietrich began preparing three of Ruth's grandchildren for confirmation, meeting with them in the Stettin apartment as part of his weekly trip to Finkenwalde. In between his visits, the boys rode their bicycles to the seminary for further instruction.

Maria von Wedemeyer, his future fiancée, still brushed past Dietrich as the most peripheral of players, virtually unnoticed by him. One story has Maria, on school holiday from Altenburg, watching the confirmation class of three older cousins in Ruth's ground floor Stettin apartment. Noticing the class members doubling over trying not to laugh, Bonhoeffer whirled around. Behind him, on the other side of a pair of glass French doors,

---

15. Bosanquet, *The Life and Death of Dietrich Bonhoeffer*, 185.
16. Bonhoeffer, *DBWE 15*, 26.
17. Bethge, *DB: A Biography*, 405, 581.
18. Ibid., 583.
19. Pejsa, *Matriarch of Conspiracy*, 222.

thirteen-year-old Maria sat cross-legged, mimicking his gestures and making exaggerated faces.[20]

In September, Eberhard and Dietrich vacationed in Grainau and Konigsee, German resort towns near Austria in the foothills of the Alps, but bad weather sent them to Sabine's home in Göttingen early.[21]

For some time, Stefanie von Mackensen, the Pomerian Confessing Church's administrative secretary, helped protect Finkenwalde. Married to a prominent Nazi, Mackensen was a conservative nationalist who had joined the Nazi Party in 1932[22]—and who, odd as it seems in hindsight, believed Christianity and National Socialism could be reconciled. In what historian Victoria Barnett calls a "strange situation," Bethge identified Mackensen, the Nazi, as the "backbone" of the Pomeranian Confessing Church, and the one responsible for allowing Finkenwalde to remain open as long as it did.[23]

Mackensen hoped to force the Nazi party either to explicitly reject or accept Christianity. When asked "Whom would you obey? The Jew Christ or Adolf Hitler?" she chose Christ, at which point it was "demanded" she leave the party. She insisted she be thrown out, on the basis of having been accepted with everyone's full knowledge of her faith. She wanted the party to avow it had broken with Christianity; it would not—a stalemate ensued. Mackensen would remain a Nazi. As Mackensen tried to convey to Barnett in an interview from the 1980s, it's "impossible" for post-war Americans to understand the German mind-set of the 1930s.[24]

While in Göttingen with Sabine and Eberhard, Frau Struwe, Finkenwalde's housekeeper, called. She had learned through an informant that the Gestapo would close Finkenwalde the next day. Again, Ruth proved invaluable. After Dietrich phoned her, she insisted that her grandson, Alexander (Alla) Stahlberg, remove the Bechstein grand piano immediately. By evening, the piano was in Alla's apartment,[25] just ahead of the September 28, 1937 Gestapo arrival. When they heard formally that the doors had shut permanently at the seminary, Dietrich and Eberhard, at loose ends, returned to the Bonhoeffer home on Marienburger Allee.

Berlin was not without its compensations. Eberhard and Dietrich celebrated friend and clergyman Wilhelm Rott's release from prison by attending

20. Ibid., 224.
21. Bethge, *DB: A Biography*, 583.
22. Barnett, *For the Soul of the People*, 42–43.
23. Ibid., 43.
24. Ibid., 42–43.
25. Pejsa, *Matriarch of Conspiracy*, 225.

an opulent *Don Giovanni* at the State Opera, and, at the end of October, heard a festival of German church music. While painters, writers, actors, and directors fled abroad, many German musicians chose not to emigrate. Thus, as Shirer explained, "One could hear during the days of the Third Reich, symphony music and opera performed magnificently . . . . The excellent musical fare did much to make people forget the degradation of the other arts and so much of life under the Nazis."[26] To Dietrich, the festival brought together a gifted group of composers who "as part of the process of inner emigration"[27]—a common strategy for dealing with the Nazis—had turned to religious music. Thus, the two men lived in a strange, bifurcated world, much as Sabine and Dietrich had after World War I. As close friends suffered in prisons or concentration camps, never far from Dietrich or Eberhard's thoughts—and even physically close to them just north of Berlin at Sachsenhausen—the two enjoyed the luxuries that an international city offered its favored sons. Meanwhile, Sabine feared for her husband's life, and Dietrich worried for his sister and her family. In November, Dohnanyi learned of Hitler's secret plans for war, and this brother-in-law so close to Dietrich may at this point have entered into active conspiracy against the regime.[28]

In December, Dietrich's *Discipleship* was published, and Ruth ecstatically purchased thirty copies, forming a study group for the book.[29] The work, Bonhoeffer's classic exposition of Sermon on the Mount Christian living, rejected grace without sacrifice.[30] Sentences such as "not hero worship, but intimacy with Christ" (not far from the words that incited Hitler's wrath against Niemöller) attack the Hilter cult. At the same time, Dietrich would later use his book's defense of Romans 13—the Bible verse commanding Christians to obey earthly authority—as evidence of his loyalty to the Nazi regime, even as he was deeply involved with conspiracy against it.

Yet for all these stirrings beneath the surface, Karl Bonhoeffer could write on December 31, 1937, sitting in his ground floor study overlooking his now frozen back garden, that the Gestapo shutdown of Finkenwalde had its "good side"—"we had Dietrich and his friend Bethge with us for a number of weeks."[31]

---

26. Shirer, *The Rise and Fall of the Third Reich*, 242.
27. Bethge, *DB:A Biography*, 586.
28. Stern and Sifton, *No Ordinary Men*, 57.
29. Pejsa, *Matriarch of Conspiracy*, 225.
30. While Bonhoeffer's term "cheap grace" comes from Dr. Clayton Powell Sr., it also sounds much like "worship without sacrifice," one of Gandhi's "seven deadly sins."
31. Bethge, *DB: A Biography*, 586.

By Christmas, the two had returned to the seminary, now relocated into East Prussia. There, Dietrich wrote to his mother, the group had treated itself to "real beeswax candles . . . we're doing splendidly."[32]

---

32. Bonhoeffer, *DBWE 15*, 26–27.

PART V
Decisions

— 24 —
Troubles

By November 1937, twenty-seven former Finkenwalde seminarians had been imprisoned. To add to the strain, 1938 opened with Dietrich's arrest by the Gestapo. Dietrich had gone to the Dahlem parish hall for a meeting with approximately thirty other Confessing pastors. Then, as he calmly wrote, "After only a half hour, officials from the Gestapo appeared, took us all in large police vans to Alexanderplatz; we were interrogated."[1] The interrogation lasted seven hours.[2] Already banned from teaching at the University of Berlin, Dietrich now found himself banned from Berlin.

To Bethge, circumstantial evidence—missing diary pages from a trip to Berlin in February 1938—indicate that Bonhoeffer might have been stepping over the line from religious to political resistance at that point.[3]

Against a background of heightened surveillance and suppression of church groups, Dietrich insisted, as always, that compromise with the Reich Church was impossible. Meanwhile, the Confessing Church continued to crumble. Without Finkenwalde, in 1938 Dietrich's focus moved to running two underground "collective pastorates" of seven to ten trainees in east Pomerania.[4] Because these men were officially "apprentices" to sympathetic pastors (although Bonhoeffer was in charge of their training), their positions were legal. In this way, Dietrich hoped to keep educating seminarians.

Bonhoeffer's ten seminarians arrived at their new homes in two remote villages in eastern Germany. Köslin, a town of 30,000 some 100 miles northeast of Stettin, welcomed the "apprentices" who moved into a vicarage not far from the massive St. Mary's Church in the town center. Twenty-five miles farther east in the smaller town of Schlawe, with the help of a sympathetic church superintendent, Eduard Block, Dietrich and Eberhard both became

1. Bonhoeffer, *DBWE 15*, 38.
2. Bethge, *DB: A Biography*, 598.
3. Ibid., 626.
4. Ibid., 588.

assistant pastors of yet another St. Mary's church. This church stood on a hill near two old town gates and looked down upon quaint rows of houses built around a cobbled square. The town became Dietrich's official address.[5]

Another set of apprentices lived even farther east, in the tiny parish of Gross-Schlönwitz. Far from a railroad line or amenities, the pastors-in-training rode bikes and saved to buy a motorcycle or a car.[6] Bonhoeffer himself purchased a motorcycle and used it to travel the east Prussian countryside, perhaps donning goggles and a leather helmet. Maintaining his characteristic busy schedule, Bonhoeffer travelled weekly between the two apprentice parishes.

Not everyone welcomed the new collective pastorates. Gerhard Lehne, a self-described sensualist who enjoyed laughter with friends and—reminiscent of the Nazi ethos—"wild songs by a burning fire"[7] more than theology, "shuddered" with dread as he approached the remote seminary house at Gross-Schlönwitz for the 1937-38 winter session. Expecting "the stuffy air of theological bigotry," what he found surprised him: not only support for his theological work but "open-mindedness and love for everything that makes even this fallen creation still worthy of love: music, literature, sports, and the beauty of the earth; a generous style of life that favorably combined the culture of old homes with the uninhibited forms of a community of young men—last, not least, a man in charge whom one can indeed admire without reservation."

Lehne remembered fondly the "afternoon coffee and bread with marmalade . . . the blue plush and the copper teakettle . . . the stillness and simplicity of life on a Pomeranian estate." The pattern established at Finkenwalde—drawn in part from Dietrich's youth in Paula's house in what now seemed a golden age—continued. The texture of the life was Christian but bourgeois, the community warm and welcoming. Eberhard, "a good comrade," could "laugh so heartily," while Frau Struwe and the "brothers" did their part.[8] For Lehne, these "peripherals" brought the gospel to life. And here too, Dietrich thrived. As Dietrich would write in his directions for his successor, running the collective pastorates was "one of the most gratifying tasks in the Confessing Church."[9] In letters, seminarians shared with Dietrich both their admiration of him and their own vulnerabilities.[10]

5. Bethge, *DB: A Biography*, 590.
6. Ibid., 591.
7. Bonhoeffer, *DBWE 15*, 128.
8. Ibid., 128–29.
9. Ibid., 171.
10. See, e.g., Bonhoeffer, *DBWE 15*, 96.

That same February 1938, while Dietrich fumed in frustration at the Berlin travel ban, Ruth insisted that he invite his parents to Klein Krössin.[11] Thus, the Berlin university couple and the Junker aristocrat met for the first time, the Bonhoeffers staying in the guest room Joy at Ruth's cottage. Here Dietrich heard the news from his parents that although the ban was not lifted, he could, due to his father's influence, travel to Berlin for family visits.[12] Dietrich now intensified what had always been a nomadic life. His centers of operation became his parent's Berlin home, where Paula, as always, supported the church struggle—and Sabine often visited—and Ruth's Klein Krössin cottage. Both Dietrich and Eberhard, alone or together, liked to escape to Ruth's hideaway, only a few hours by train from Berlin but seemingly in another world. In the room Ruth kept reserved for him, Dietrich would continue, when time permitted, to work on his manuscripts.

Niemöller, who had been in prison since July 1, went on trial February 7, 1938. After his conviction on March 2 and sentence of seven months in prison for misusing the pulpit, the authorities released him because he had already served his time while awaiting trial. He had hardly left the courthouse, however, when the SS swept him into "protective custody," as Hitler's special prisoner, sending him to Sachsenhausen concentration camp. His fate had been sealed since the end of June, for "in a bellow Hitler [had] ordered Niemöller to be put in a concentration camp and, since he had proved himself incorrigible, kept there for life."[13]

Dietrich's brother-in-law Walter Dress became Niemöller's successor in the Dahlem parish.

The same March that Niemöller disappeared into protective custody, Hitler announced the Anschluss that merged Austria into Germany. At the end of March 1938, Dietrich and Eberhard traveled together to Kieckow so that Dietrich could confirm the group of Ruth's grandchildren he'd been preparing since August, including Maria von Wedemeyer's older brother Max. At about the same time, two-thirds of Confessing Church pastors offered what for many was a deeply anguished and morally compromising "birthday present" to the Führer: taking the oath of allegiance to him—a gift which Hitler received with contempt, saying through Martin Bormann that it had no meaning.[14]

---

11. This is Ruth von Kleist-Retzow's account, according to Pejsa; however, a postcard to his parents dated 27 January, 1938 attributes an idea of coming to Stettin to them (Bonhoeffer, *DBWE 15*, 36).

12. Pejsa, *Matriarch of Conspiracy*, 226.

13. Speer, *Inside the Third Reich*, 123, 98.

14. Bethge, *DB: A Biography*, 601.

Ruth, heavily involved in the affairs of the Old Prussian Council of the Confessing Church, wrote an anguished letter to Eberhard—but meant for Dietrich's eyes too—about the Confessing Church, which backtracked on the oath after the fact: "The counsel of the Old Prussian Union *not* to take the oath for the time being! I froze within from outrage. Now, after everyone has sworn it, except for three who were on vacation.... I find it so dreadful that the blood freezes in my veins.... When I think of the crisis of conscience that the individual pastors went through until they finally swore the oath with a wounded conscience, my heart stands still. And now they simply communicate the facts.... They should be utterly *destroyed* by the recognition that they offered false leadership.... Mrs. von Mackensen was also very irritated.... I should not be writing any of this, but I'm still seething."[15]

Dietrich shared Ruth's sense of betrayal over the Confessing Church's loyalty oath to Hitler, an event so deeply painful that it was "like a gash in his own flesh that would only heal with difficulty."[16] The Sermon on the Mount-based church he had hoped could blow National Socialism sky high had sniveled before Hitler once again. Dietrich had campaigned vigorously against the oath—but others discounted him since he was not drawing a salary from the state. Yet the oath-taking only proved Hitler correct: the church, a once formidable institution, could now be controlled through fear of losing its comforts. Dietrich felt deeply and personally ashamed.[17]

Even as late as 1938, the church failed to comprehend the state's hostility to it. The Nazis closed parochial schools, took religious instruction out of the state schools' curriculum, made school prayer optional, and increasingly vilified, persecuted, and arrested pastors and priests. By 1938, even school Christmas pageants, a German staple, were forbidden.[18] This was the logical extension of National Socialist politics: Since neither the Catholic nor the Protestant church would synchronize entirely with National Socialist aims, Hitler marginalized and excluded them. Eradication was his goal.[19]

Yet it was as though the Confessing Church—like much of the country—was under the kind of spell cast in German fairy tales. In fact, Dietrich would use the word *spell* twice in a letter during this time period to describe the Church's situation.[20]

---

15. Bonhoeffer, *DBWE 15*, 68–69.
16. Bethge, *DB: A Biography*, 603.
17. Ibid.
18. Nicholas, *Cruel World*, 70.
19. Bonhoeffer, *DBWE 15*, 564: "At the very latest, from the spring of 1937, even Adolf Hitler himself was 'finished with the churches.'"
20. Ibid., 31, circular letter of January, 1938 to the brothers: "Why have voices in Pomerania complained for months that our church lies paralyzed, as if in a spell..."

Following the confirmations of Ruth's grandchildren, in mid-April Dietrich and Eberhard took a two-week holiday together in Friedrichsbrunn in the Harz Mountains,[21] the place of deepest personal resonance for Dietrich, as well as a spot near Sabine's Göttingen home. In the brick vacation house not far from the main street of the town, yet also near the woods, Eberhard and Dietrich could together tramp through forests and mountain paths familiar to Dietrich, symbols of a more settled past, searching for mushrooms, enjoying lakeside picnics, and reading at night by kerosene lamp.

Dietrich would later write, "In my imagination I live a good deal ... in the glades near Friedrichsbrunn, or on the slopes from which one can look beyond Treseburg to the Brocken. I lie on my back in the grass, watch the clouds sailing in the breeze across the blue sky, and listen to the rustling of the woods. It's remarkable how greatly these memories of childhood affect one's whole outlook; it would seem to me impossible and unnatural for us to have lived either up in the mountains or by the sea. It is the hills of central Germany, the Harz, the Thuringian forest, the Weserberge, that to me represent nature, that belong to me and have fashioned me."[22]

Eberhard, now accepted into the innermost circle of the Bonhoeffer family, though he still saw himself as an outsider, as well as into Ruth von Kliest's upper-crust world, corresponded with both Paula and Ruth on a frequent basis, often as a stand-in for Dietrich. He and Dietrich talked together "for hours at a time."[23]

At the close of May 1938, Hitler revealed his plans to annex Czechoslovakia to his top officials.[24] In August, Ruth's friend and cousin, the balding and mustached Ewald von Kleist, every inch the 1930s aristocrat, traveled to England and met secretly with Churchill to ask him to stop Hitler. This was an act of high treason on Ewald's part. But at that point, it didn't matter: Churchill was out of power.

From June 21–25, Dietrich and Eberhard took forty-five pastors to Zingst for a Bible study on temptation meant to help them hold firm against a campaign to persuade them to join the Reich Church.[25] The National Socialists promised paid jobs in churches, a settled life, and relief from the fear of arrest and persecution, as long as the pastors accepted the Party ver-

---

and, in the same letter, "Jesus Christ alone can break the spell" (35).

21. Ibid., 41.
22. Bonhoeffer, *LPP,* 211.
23. Ibid., 220.
24. Bethge, *DB: A Biography,* 628.
25. Ibid., 593.

sion of Christianity: nationalist, Aryan, militaristic, anti-Semitic, and Hitler worshipping.

Dietrich sent Paula a characteristic postcard from Zingst. "I didn't get around to writing. But I'm doing quite well. In the coming week I'll spend a few days vacation in Rowe by the sea."[26] He also mailed a brief card to Dita Stockman, Koch's fiancée, expressing solidarity and signed by all pastors on the retreat.[27] After the retreat, he and Eberhard headed to Rowe.

This same August in 1938, fourteen-year-old Maria stayed with Ruth and two cousins in Stettin. Ruth found that Maria had "an unbounded love for life, and seizes each moment as if it were the first and the last. One might say she is a child of the earth, without affectation and with a life-giving energy that can be felt by all who come into her presence."[28]

Her gift in mathematics and her looks blossomed. As Ruth noticed and photos show, Maria resembled the young Ruth, with the same dark hair, down-turned eyes, and round, open face. Like her grandmother, she was lively, spirited, forceful, stubborn. Ruth began to pay more attention to her.[29]

Ruth's correspondence with Eberhard increased, as he had more time for her than Dietrich did. She also began working on a book for her grandchildren, *Why Should One Read the Bible?*, answering questions they had asked over the years.[30] She sent parts of it to Eberhard to critique. At this point too, Dietrich switched strategies and began to drop his overt resistance to the regime's anti-Christian religious agenda.[31] And, more than ever, as 1938 moved forward, a long-simmering concern bubbled to the surface: Sabine and her family's situation.

---

26. Bonhoeffer, *DBWE 15*, 43.
27. Ibid., 43.
28. Pejsa, *Matriarch of Conspiracy*, 282.
29. Ibid., 232–33. This may indicate that Ruth was pondering a marriage between Maria and Dietrich as early as 1938.
30. Ibid., 233–34. This was political act in a country that discouraged Bible reading.
31. Bethge, *DB: A Biography*, 628.

— 25 —
Escape

BLOODTHIRSTY NAZIS MARCHING UP their street belting out songs about killing Jews and anti-Semitic newspapers on sale across from their daughters' school seemed not enough to persuade Gert and Sabine to leave Germany. Frustrated, brother-in-law Hans von Dohnanyi continued to pressure them to emigrate, sharing his growing list of anti-Semitic atrocities.

The stories of atrocity unnerved Sabine, but the idea of fleeing Germany wrenched her. It meant moving far from family and the world she knew. The practical considerations intimidated her: Gert, before he had been forced into "retirement," had been a professor of German constitutional law, a field not likely to be marketable outside of Germany, especially in the midst of a worldwide depression. Further, because of currency restrictions, they could only leave the country with very little money. In addition, Gert's depression meant he was often unable to think through decisions. When he could concentrate, Europe's weakness appalled him. Would it make sense to emigrate, only to have Germany conquer their new home? Finally, like many who stayed too long, the couple remained hopeful that the regime would collapse.

When the Sudetenland crisis erupted in the summer of 1938, the pressure mounted on Gert and Sabine to leave before war broke out. For Jews, the summer of 1938 unleashed "a tidal wave of terror."[1] The SS newspaper *Das Schwarze Korps* declared that if war came, the price for the Jews would be "total annihilation."[2] Yet only when Hans passed on the information that Jewish passports were soon going to be required to bear a J, meaning Jews could be stopped at the border and prevented from crossing, did a move become imperative.

On August 23, 1938, the worried Leibholz couple drove to Berlin to consult with the senior Bonhoeffers. On August 25, the German army went on parade in Berlin, unveiling, amid legions of marching soldiers, a huge

1. Dawidowicz, *The War Against the Jews*, 99.
2. Bethge, *DB: A Biography*, 681.

field gun, "a big, motorized Bertha," to the applause of the crowds.[3] War hung in the air. On the 26th Sabine wrote to Dietrich, explaining a lapse in her correspondence as due to her own lack of "peace of mind." As the pressure had mounted unbearably on Gert to do what he most dreaded, leave Germany for good, "he had no longer been able to maintain his old equanimity" wrote Sabine. "Ultimately the resilience of the nerves simply gives in. At the moment it's hard to think all the way through all the decisions that need to be made, and that makes one so nervous." She confided to Dietrich that Gert was "sleeping so badly." The burdens of both large decisions and day-to-day life fell on Sabine's shoulders: "So I must hold down the fort for two, and sometimes it's not very easy to keep in mind matters as divergent as existential questions and pressing worries alongside the large and small concerns and wishes of the children."[4]

Sabine and Gert came back to Göttingen from Berlin on the 27th, then returned to Berlin on September 4. On September 8, they arrived in Göttingen with Dietrich and Eberhard in tow.

Daughter Marianne, now eleven, had been aware all summer that her family might flee and that the plans had to be kept absolutely secret. On September 9, the nanny was getting the girls ready for school when their mother hurried in, announcing that the family was going to Wiesbaden and would return on Monday. Sabine instructed the nanny to dress the girls in two sets of underwear each.[5]

Marianne knew. The family never went to Wiesbaden, and the girls never wore extra underwear.

Marianne raced into the Edenic orchard garden on a glorious sun-drenched day to say goodbye. Back in the house, she dared only to bid farewell to the downstairs rooms, for fear the adults would realize she knew. She slipped two tiny dolls she had prepared in anticipation of this journey into her pocket, complete with baptismal certificates, birth certificates, and passports, a poignant reminder of how important documents had become in Nazi Germany. Bigger toys, she knew, would take up too much precious space.

"Uncle Dietrich" had brought a car, so they set out together in a caravan, the two girls in the back seat of their parents' Ford. The adult couples changed places frequently, driving first one car, then another, as they headed to the Swiss border. Marianne and Christiane sang songs with Dietrich and "Uncle" Eberhard. They enjoyed the warm sun, blue sky, and beautiful countryside with the car's top down on a splendid day.

3. Shirer, *Berlin Diaries*, 123.
4. Bonhoeffer, *DBWE 15*, 63.
5. Leibholz, *The Bonhoeffers*, 85.

Meanwhile, at the Nuremburg rallies, the Nazi leaders made dire threats against Czechoslovakia. The Bonhoeffer cars sped as fast as they dared toward the border, the adults fearful that war would break out that day.[6]

Marianne sensed "complete solidarity among the four grownups."[7] Uncle Dietrich seemed his normal self: "very strong and confident, immensely kind, cheerful and firm."[8] With Dietrich and Eberhard there, the mood remained light. The group stopped for a roadside picnic as they wended their way through the Black Forest, perhaps eating fruit from the Göttingen orchard. Then, as evening approached, the atmosphere tensed. The cars stopped. The girls and their parents said goodbye to Dietrich and Eberhard. The family drove off. Marianne watched out the back window as the two men stood waving, becoming more and more tiny until at last a hill cut them off from her view.

Originally, Dietrich and Eberhard had planned to vacation with Sabine and Gert in southern Europe. Now that holiday had been scuttled: Dietrich and Eberhard needed to keep a low profile to avoid army recruitment, which meant staying away from borders.[9]

The Leibholz car sped up as night fell, shrouding them in darkness except for the glow of the headlights. "We have to get across the frontier tonight; they might close it at any moment," said Sabine. Everyone fell silent, concentrating on the drive ahead, hoping they would be able to convince the border officials they were going on vacation.

They arrived at the Swiss border late at night. The girls pretended to be sleepy and grouchy. Sabine donned a long brown suede coat, the Nazi color meant to "sooth" the border patrol. The guards, tired, waved them through with little notice. They passed from Germany without incident and, in that instant, were free.

"The sense of liberation after leaving German soil and entering a free country was so overwhelming," wrote Marianne years later, "that an echo of that feeling still returns now, so many years later, whenever I cross the German frontier into Switzerland."[10]

Dietrich and Eberhard drove back to Sabine's house in Göttingen.

That same day, September 10, 1938, Göring gave a speech near the climax of the Nuremburg rallies, whipping up the party loyal: "This miserable pygmy race [the Czechs] without culture—no one knows where it

---

6. Shirer, *Berlin Diaries*, 125.
7. Leibholz, *The Bonhoeffers*, 86.
8. Ibid., 87.
9. Bonhoeffer, *DBWE 15*, 64–65.
10. Leibholz, *The Bonhoeffers*, 87.

came from—is harassing a cultured people and behind it is Moscow and the eternal mask of the Jew devil."[11]

In the stillness at Göttingen, the laughter of his nieces and the voice of his sister now memories amid the Biedermeier furniture, the grand piano, and the fruity scents wafting in from the orchard—or perhaps from the bottled fruit still stored on dusty basement shelves—Dietrich, with Eberhard close by, would work on *Life Together* through the month of September. In it, he would ruminate on his experience in the now-dissolved Finkenwalde community, good and bad, harsh in his refusal to idealize that which had been dearest to his heart. Very probably Sabine's absence—an absence that must have been haunting amid scents and scenes he associated with her—colored his assessment of the community experiment, which had not changed her fate nor blown Nazism sky high.

He would write in this book, though he would not always follow this advice, that "God does not will that I should fashion the other person according to the image that seems good to me, that is, in my own image; rather in his very freedom from me God made this person in His image."[12]

Dietrich drew creative inspiration or security from Ruth and Sabine's homes—he did much of his writing within their protective embrace. At Sabine's home, Eberhard kept him company, while the cook, Lena, ran the house.[13] Dietrich decided he and Eberhard would visit Sabine in London as soon as she was settled.

Though their destination was England, the Leibholzes initially lingered in Zurich at the Kurhaus-Zurichberg,[14] a modestly priced stucco-and-gable-roofed spa with a wrought-iron balcony wrapped around the second floor. This spa, on the outskirts of Zurich, had been founded by Susana Orelli-Rinderknecht, a leader in the temperance movement at the turn of the century. In a beautiful and, at that time, isolated location on a hill above town, the spa offered misty views of the Alps wrapped in a white fog that contrasted with the blue of Lake Zurich. Nearby, goats grazed in a field.

Lingering made sense. On September 12, Hitler gave a speech at the Nuremburg rallies filled with threats toward the Czechs, but not an outright call for war. Colonel Hans Oster, a Christian who detested the regime, plotted with other army officers and upper-class dissidents, including Hans von Dohnanyi, to depose Hitler when he declared war on Czechoslovakia, a war

---

11. Shirer, *Berlin Diaries*, 126.
12. Bonhoeffer, *Life Together*, 77.
13. Bonhoeffer, *DBWE 15*, 99.
14. Ibid., 72.

they knew to be a gamble and likely to be unpopular. The Bonhoeffer family waited for a coup.[15]

On September 14, Ruth wrote to Eberhard of some of the continuing joy the Finkenwalde seminary—even after it was shuttered—brought into the life of a lonely old lady: "What this fellowship with Finkenwalde means!" she wrote.[16] She would also convey her frustration with her *Discipleship* study group:

"Please tell Dietrich that I almost despaired under the burden of *Discipleship*. With 'costly grace' it seemed to me that I met with not only a lack of understanding but also a lack of interest. And then I was disheartened by the impression that there was nothing but literary interest and that no sense of belonging together grew.... But yesterday evening with the "Beatitudes" was obviously better. The material may in general be too difficult for people who are accustomed to thinking very superficially about religious matters .... And still these evenings are now my whole delight!"[17] The letter ended with the mention that Maria's father, Hans von Wedemeyer, drafted into the army, would leave for duty Saturday.

Ruth continued to be "deeply affected" by Finkenwalde's closing and the seminarians' move 120 miles from Stettin, especially, Bethge said, because she and her study group "always had some question" about *Discipleship*. Dietrich, however, kept her involved, sending worn people "from his own circle" to Klein Krössin and Han Jurgen's nearby manor house to recuperate. The "hospitality was unlimited; anyone who Bonhoeffer recommended was accepted at once."[18]

From Sabine's house, Dietrich wrote Sutz, his Swiss friend, on September 18: "To my great relief my sister with her husband and children are in Zurich for several weeks ... you might be hearing from them sometime. Please be good to them then! If you could visit them sometime without too much difficulty, that would be especially nice."[19]

Sabine and her family went into downtown Zurich frequently to read the newspapers. By the 19th, the news broke that England and France would not defend Czechoslovakia, instead insisting the beleaguered country turn over the Sudetenland. The hoped-for coup was dashed, as the plotters feared that without a war, the regulars in the army would not back them against Hitler. In fact, the public hailed Hitler as a wily hero for getting the

15. Bethge, *DB: A Biography*, 663.
16. Bonhoeffer, *DBWE 15*, 68.
17. Ibid., 68.
18. Bethge, *DB: A Biography*, 595.
19. Bonhoeffer, *DBWE 15*, 72.

Sudetenland without bloodshed. Sabine and Gert, longing to return to Germany, watched their possibilities dwindle.

With world war receding, Sabine and Gert waited to see if Gert would indeed be required to have his passport marked with a J.

— 26 —
Changes

The Bonhoeffer parents were to telegraph with a code word, *passt*—"suitable or convenient"—if new passport rules went into effect. On October 5, the telegram came saying, "Your coming is not convenient," so the Leibholzes knew that they couldn't return. The weather was "magical" in this fairy-tale land of mountains and lakes but the couple, their hopes extinguished, watched the scenery through a heartsick haze, "as a sick man experiences what the weather is like from his bed."[1]

In November, sister Ursel arrived with packages and Sabine's luxurious fur coat flung over her arm. She took the girls, who wouldn't be affected by the passport rule, back to Germany to stay in Berlin with their grandparents until their parents were established in England, and drove their almost brand-new car back to Göttingen, a car enough of a rarity that its absence would be noticed.

Finally, in November, the weather gray and cold, Sabine and Gert travelled through France, their spirits low. At Calais, they boarded a boat to cross the channel to a place neither of them had ever been nor had any desire to move.

England, wrote Sabine, "received us in a fog." Gert was seasick as they crossed the channel: "pale as a corpse and sick as dog," she wrote to Dietrich.[2] Almost exactly five years after Dietrich's arrival, they made their dazed way through the crowds in Victoria Station to arrive at Miss Sharp's boarding house in southeast London, near the Manse in Syndeham where Dietrich had once lived.

A photograph shows Sabine and Gert in their room at Miss Sharp's. The ceiling is high and two of the room's big, broad windows are in view, as is the edge of the bed. The couple sits near the windows, Sabine sewing, Gert at a desk. Seemingly calm, the couple's life could hardly have been in greater upheaval.

1. Leibholz, *The Bonhoeffers*, 87.
2. Bonhoeffer, *DBWE 15*, 77.

Dietrich jumped into Paula-like activity to help them establish a foothold in London, sending off a flurry of letters to his many friends there, both English and German. Although grateful to him, Sabine couldn't hide all of her distress, writing to him of the drafts and rattlings from the three windows in their boarding house room, and of the perpetual cold and damp. All of this was exacerbated by anxieties over Gert's employment prospects— they had heard of a former German judge working as a street sweeper—and money worries.

But in London, Sabine felt safe: "England relieved our souls. It was as though a crushing weight fell away: the anxiety for the lives of my husband and children." The economic deprivations—no car, no servants, cramped quarters—"seemed quite small and unimportant."[3] Relief ran deeper when, a few days after they arrived in England, they heard reports of Kristallnacht or the Night of Broken Glass, November 10, 1938, when the Nazis burned and looted Jewish homes, businesses, and synagogues across Germany, Austria, and the Sudetenland.

Dietrich discussed Kristallnacht with his seminarians in Köslin. Some of them saw it as part of "the curse which had haunted the Jews since Jesus's death on the cross." Dietrich "rejected this with extreme sharpness." To him, the destruction of the synagogues was "a case of sheer violence." Today the synagogues, he said, tomorrow the churches.[4]

Another friend remembered that around the time of Kristallnacht, Dietrich was driven by "a great inner restlessness, a holy anger."[5]

The Göttingen newspaper celebrated the "temple of the vindictive god of the Jews" going up in flames, stating "there must be nothing in this city to remind us of this race," while the British papers reacted with horror. Gert's brother Peter was forced to hand over his textile factories and flee Germany.

The move to London brought little positive joy to Gert and Sabine. Disorientation, unemployment, culture shock, and money problems were preferable to concentration camps and gas chambers, but they were not what the couple had anticipated when they'd married. Under Nazi law only 5 percent of their capital could be taken from Germany. Sabine had her fur coat, a string of heirloom pearls, and fourteen trunks of goods, but the bulk of her wealth was left behind.

---

3. Leibholz, *The Bonhoeffers*, 97–98.
4. Zimmermann and Smith, eds., *I Knew*, 150.
5. Ibid.,153–54.

Dietrich corresponded with them cheerfully, encouraging them to visit his friends, especially Bell. "Everyday, I think of you often," Dietrich wrote.[6]

Sabine was shocked to run into an old friend, his head shaved bald, who had just arrived in England after a stay in a concentration camp, still too terrified to talk about his experiences although he was in a foreign country, out of the Gestapo's reach.[7]

As Sabine adjusted to London, Werner Koch continued in Sachsenhausen, where he'd been almost two years. Whatever Sabine's privations, though undoubtedly a jolt to someone from a privileged background, Koch's were of another magnitude. Koch endured long roll calls in the freezing cold, which involved having to stand unmoving in thin clothes as all the prisoners were counted. He was subjected to a relentless work regime, ever-present physical brutality, the shock of witnessing sadism on a daily basis, and a bewildering array of humiliating rules and regulations meant to reinforce the gulf between SS guards and inmates. He survived in part from aid offered by imprisoned "Reds" who had formed a help network—odd bedfellows, as most Confessing Church pastors feared and opposed communists.[8] Further, Koch came from well-heeled connections, and his friends from the outside exerted pressure. He was also fortunate in landing in the camp before World War II began, when the food, if inadequate and unwholesome, was not yet at starvation levels, and overcrowding not rampant.

Ruth continued to offer aid, moral support, and prayer to the distressed families of imprisoned Confessing Church pastors, who were never far from her thoughts. "I hear," she wrote to Dita in early March, 1938, "that N. [Niemöller] has been taken to Sachsenhausen where Koch was [sic—he was still there] . . . . Oh, my heart is sore for one and the other."[9] Ten days later she wrote, "The misery of it all rushes upon me, again and again."[10]

After his release on December 2, 1938, Koch received two letters from Ruth: "What can I say?" she wrote, "I am overwhelmed with joy about the good news."[11] A long telegram from Dietrich on December 9 echoed Ruth's words and used *indescribable*, Dietrich's favorite word for an intense overflow of emotions: "The joy is indescribable. That which we have hoped and

---

6. Bonhoeffer, *DBWE 15*, 79.
7. Leibholz, *The Bonhoeffers*, 100.
8. Wind, *A Spoke in the Wheel*, 122.
9. Zimmermann and Smith, eds., *I Knew*, 119.
10. Ibid.
11. Ibid.

prayed for from day to day has become real. It is still like a dream to me ... I'm now looking forward to only one thing, namely, to see you as soon as possible, so that it will be entirely certain for me that you are once again among us."[12]

As Dietrich drove Koch to a vacation in Pomerania to recuperate, he quizzed him about the concentration camp experience. Discussing what happened in the camps was illegal, but the conversation could be had safely in a moving car—and as Koch talked, Dietrich imagined himself in the same situation.[13]

Sometime before Koch's release, Dietrich and Sabine's aunt, Elisabeth von Hase, arrived to keep watch over the Leibholz home in Göttingen. Around that time, servants sent a chest of goods, including her violin, to Sabine in England. This aroused Nazi suspicions and led them to search the premises. Aristocratic, arrogant, and Aryan, von Hase, her fair hair wound in a garland of plaits around her head, put the Nazis "in their place." However, they had the last word, detaining the tall, elderly woman under house arrest for eight days after finding a copy of a book of Rosa Luxembourg's letters under the pillow in her bedroom. Worried, Dietrich arranged to move some of the more valuable furniture and goods from Sabine's house to Ruth's, lest they be confiscated.[14] And while Sabine remembered the freezing of her bank account,[15] another version of the story says that Dietrich continued to receive 170 Reichmarks each month from Leibholz funds at the Commerzbank in Göttingen.[16]

The Christmas season brought a wave of homesickness to Sabine, "an overpowering longing for woods and beautiful paths, for forest glades and the smell of trees and earth."[17] The German forests were not to be, but shortly before Christmas, her parents brought her daughters to Holland, where the family reunited. They spent Christmas together in Haarlem "at an enchanting house" of Paula's cousin, the countess Mucki Koenigs-Kalckreuth. Dietrich wrote to Sabine of "being extraordinarily happy" about her meeting with their parents and her children at Mucki's, the word *extraordinary* indicating his level of worry at her circumstances.[18] Sabine, ever the artist,

12. Bonhoeffer, *DBWE 15*, 90.
13. Wind, *A Spoke in the Wheel*, 122–23.
14. Leibholz, *The Bonhoeffers*, 99.
15. Ibid.
16. Bonhoeffer, *DBWE 15*, 113.
17. Leibholz, *The Bonhoeffers*, 99.
18. Bonhoeffer, *DBWE 15*, 85.

visited the Franz Hals museum with her father and also "saw the Brueghels; my father took a special interest in the Flemish physiognomy as shown in these pictures."[19] Together, the family walked the snow-covered streets in temperatures that dipped below zero,[20] charmed by the city's picturesque beauty.

For ten blissful days Sabine enjoyed her parents, but not Dietrich, who decided to delay his visit until she was back in London. From home, Dietrich continued to write letters to friends in England, trying to smooth the way for his sister in a country increasingly crowded with refugee Germans, where a depressed and unemployed law professor with a poor command of English was likely to be the least of anybody's concerns. "I shall be grateful to you then for each kind word that keeps her from impatience and worry," Dietrich wrote of Sabine to Julius Rieger, still a pastor in England.[21]

From Holland, Paula sent Dietrich a card to Berlin, with instructions for the housekeeper, Miss Kate, and Sabine's wish that Eberhard, accepted as someone to whom such a request could be made, sell her "car with the baggage" in Berlin.[22]

19. Leibholz, *The Bonhoeffers*, 100.
20. Bonhoeffer, *DBWE 15*, 98.
21. Ibid., 94.
22. Ibid., 98.

27

War Worries: 1939

IF 1938 HAD BEEN a terrible year for Sabine, so it had been for Dietrich. The climate of relentless persecution led pastors who had formerly opposed the Nazi church to break ranks, worn down by fear and insecurity. Stark differences arose between those who were legal pastors and could count on reliable employment and those who could not.[1] Although Dietrich poured his not insubstantial energies and resources into shoring up the remnant of the Confessing Church, his pastors became exiles in their own land, surviving tenuously in remote places.

In January 1939 Sabine and her family had another respite from cramped quarters, staying as the guests of Bishop Bell at his palace. It was the last gasp of a fairy-tale aristocratic world that would fade after the war. Sabine enjoyed the "great high rooms," blazing fires, and "well-trained" servants who brought steaming cups of morning tea to their bedrooms. Breakfast downstairs was porridge, bacon, eggs, toast, orange juice, and more tea. Servants served a festive[2] dinner to the many invited guests at a long table in the huge dining hall, with what Sabine deemed the "largest fireplace I ever saw in England."[3] Bell chose little Christiane as his dinner partner, a special honor to the family.[4] After dinner, as in her childhood home and as Dietrich had done at Finkenwalde, the guests read aloud Shakespeare, in this case *Antony and Cleopatra*, everyone taking a part. In a letter to Dietrich, Sabine wrote of the Bell's "very decent, humane way of living."[5]

---

1. Bethge, *DB: A Biography,* 607; see also Bonhoeffer, *DBWE 15,* 29: After 1935 candidates for the ministry who studied and were ordained within the Confessing Church were considered "illegal" and denied jobs, salaries, and pensions by the official German Evangelical Church. After 1937 official church authorities offered "legalization" proceedings to these candidates; this meant a de facto repudiation of their examinations and ordinations by the Confessing Church.

2. Bonhoeffer, *DBWE 15,* 113.

3. Leibholz, *The Bonhoeffers,* 101.

4. Bonhoeffer, *DBWE 15,* 113.

5. Ibid., 117.

This interlude perhaps offset some of Sabine's worries that her daughters, now thrust into the small, ugly quarters at Miss Sharp's, would "never again have a chance to acquire an eye for beauty in household things."[6] She awaited Dietrich's visit, which she hoped would coincide with their February birthday. Meanwhile, she wrote of aching bones from damp beds and keeping the girls home because their chilly school made them sick.

Dietrich longed, as he put it, to visit England. Ever in motion, he had returned to London for an ecumenical conference two years earlier, but now the need to make contact again seemed urgent. War talk in Germany, already at a pitch, heated up unabated. In January, 1939, Paula wrote to Dietrich: "On our nearby display kiosks, the military conscription was announced for those born in [190]6 and [190]7."[7] Paula wondered if Dietrich, born in 1906 but technically now a Pomeranian, not a Berliner, would be drafted. She worried that possible conscription meant Dietrich would not be allowed to go to England.

The draft posed a moral dilemma for Dietrich, a Christian pacifist, especially given his disgust with the government on whose behalf he would be required to fight. To avoid conscription, Dietrich began to think about time in the US. As he wrote to Bell, "I find it difficult to do military services under these conditions and *yet there are only very few friends who would approve of my attitude*"(emphasis Bonhoeffer).[8]

January saw Dietrich and Eberhard on vacation, due to a generous gift from Sabine. "I thank you greatly for your Christmas present, which made a very lovely ski trip possible for me. It was once again utterly wonderful in the snow."[9] In the same letter to her, Dietrich writes of possibly modernizing his parents' Friedrichsbrunn summer home. Whether this was financed by Gert and Sabine is unclear, but very possible, given the context of Dietrich's letter: "We are now thinking about installing light and central heating in the cottage, so that it will also be suitable for a longer winter stay for our parents—but I find that this is much more important now than setting myself up well. That can indeed come later; so I gladly wanted to help the parents somewhat through giving this up."[10] Sabine urged again that her car and home be sold; since currency restrictions meant that only 5 percent of the proceeds could leave the country, presumably family members would be the

6. Leibholz, *The Bonhoeffers*, 98.
7. Bonhoeffer, *DBWE 15*, 113.
8. Bethge, *DB: A Biography*, 637.
9. Bonhoeffer, *DBWE 15*, 99.
10. Ibid.

beneficiaries, though Bethge, ever functioning as the faithful family helper, smuggled money to Sabine and Gert in the uncut pages of new books. He would make a careful slit in one page and insert the bills. To communicate receipt of the money, Gert would mail back a postcard from London's National Gallery.[11]

On February 1, Dietrich sent Sabine a birthday letter to London:

> I am thinking in these days especially of you and your family and would like to celebrate with you. How often have we intended to celebrate our birthday together once more. Now everything has changed. Recently it occurred to me that there are some laws in the research on twins—I believe only that they do not apply in our case—that certain twins often have the same life experiences, even when they don't even live near each other. I must say that to a certain degree that appears to be true, in particular when we compare ourselves with our siblings. In any case the lives of both of us have recently been different from what one had expected, even when each life has its own path. In this respect perhaps we can understand our present paths through life particularly well. It is basically one and the same thing that has so decisively determined our life and given it this unexpected turn. However that may be, in any case we will think of each other a great deal on the fourth and expect less from all kinds of good wishes than from the genuine advocacy on behalf of each other. I am already looking forward greatly to seeing you again.[12]

Dietrich's letter signals his perception that he and his twin faced a singular destiny, religious persecution having come crashing down across both their life paths. Interestingly—and in alignment with his emphasis on action over cheap grace—he wishes them to become active advocates for the other, rather than passive recipients of well wishes.

And yet even this letter breathes the air of Nazi Germany—Dietrich alludes to not being able to phone Sabine. "I have had frequent visits lately, and that makes this phone business, as you will understand, unnecessarily costly."[13] Sabine would have known instantly that, in a family willing to spend vast amounts to stay in touch, the "cost" was not monetary. The "visits" were surveillance—and Dietrich feared his phone being tapped.[14]

---

11. Ibid., 251.
12. Ibid., 123.
13. Ibid.
14. Ibid.

— 28 —
London Redux

In February, shortly after their mutual birthdays, Ruth and Dietrich met in Köslin, and, over a civilized and celebratory repast of tea and cakes, discussed Dietrich's possible conscription. Ruth insisted that Dietrich not declare as a conscientious objector: she rightly feared he would be executed as a traitor.

Ruth continued to use her many well-placed connections to help him. Bonhoeffer's official address was in Schlawe, Köslin, where one of Ruth's von Kleist relatives was a recruiting officer. Ruth called her cousin, helping to postpone Dietrich's military service, allowing him to visit England.[1]

Dietrich and Eberhard headed for London on March 10, 1939. The visit would last five weeks. They took the night train to Belgium, where, worried that they would be stopped at the border and detained in Germany, Dietrich was unable to sleep.[2]

That was not what he expressed, however, in the postcard he sent Paula almost as soon as they arrived:

> Dear Mama,
>
> The trip was fine again, the water was calm, the sleeper car comfortable in every respect. We slept well and arrived here so quickly that the trip was a pleasure. This just for today.
>
> Greetings to you from your grateful Dietrich[3]

Dietrich and Eberhard's March 11th arrival energized Sabine. She had always liked Eberhard, and she quickly fell into her old intimacy with her brother. Dietrich's strong and sunny presence encouraged and renewed her. "It was as if we were suddenly upheld by someone."[4] Dietrich pulled the

1. Pejsa, *Matriarch of Conspiracy*, 242.
2. Bethge, *DB: A Biography*, 638.
3. Bonhoeffer, *DBWE 15*, 153.
4. Leibholz, *The Bonhoeffers*, 103.

family out of cramped rooms for sightseeing and visits to his old friends, including a joyful reunion with Hildebrandt. "Dietrich wanted to introduce us everywhere," wrote Sabine. He taught them all, including his nieces, "to throw the feathered arrows at a target,"[5] that is, to play darts. Further, he was bursting to share England with Eberhard.

Together, the Leibholzes, Dietrich, and Eberhard took a whirlwind tour of London: St. Paul's, the Tower, Buckingham Palace, Hampton Court, and Kew Gardens. While watching a film which Bethge calls *Queen Victoria*, with the Viennese-born actor Adolf Wohlbruck (anglicized to Anton Walbrook) in the role of Prince Albert, Dietrich shed frustrated tears that Germany threatened England with another war.[6] The film he saw was most likely *Sixty Glorious Years*, the 1938 sequel to the popular 1937 *Victoria the Great*, both idealized retellings of the queen's—and Britain's—story.

The male lead, Wohlbruck, who had worked with Max Reinhardt, the exiled Jewish director, found it prudent after 1936 to make a home for himself in England because of his sexual orientation.[7] And Sabine recounts an odd story—odd, because Dietrich was not in the least prone to courting unnecessary pain: While watching an unnamed film, but possibly *Sixty Glorious Years*, Dietrich struck a match to light a cigarette and the whole box caught on fire. "Although the flame flared up quickly, he simply held the box in the palm of his hand," Sabine wrote in her memoir. "He was burned over the whole palm of his hand."[8]

On March 14, 1939, a few days after Dietrich and Eberhard's arrival in London, Slovakia declared its independence from Czechoslovakia. "There goes the remains of Czechoslovakia," wrote Shirer.[9] On the 15th, the German army occupied Bohemia and Moravia.

Yet for all the troubles on the continent, "the English spring of 1939 was magical," [10] Sabine wrote. "The forsythia and dark mauve lilacs bloomed enchantingly, luxuriantly, in the old gardens in Forest Hills and the daffodils gleamed from the broad expanses of the parks."[11] The weather allowed the adults to sit in Miss Sharp's garden or play ball with the girls when they

---

5. Ibid., 103.

6. Bethge, *DB: A Biography*, 648.

7. Cox, "Career," on Anton Walbrook: Wohlbruck's "screen persona, like his English, was always perfectly poised and controlled . . . with only a hint at the great sublimated energy that he seemed to hold taut just below his skin."

8. Leibholz, *The Bonhoeffers*, 105.

9. Shirer, *Berlin Diaries*, 159.

10. Leibholz, *The Bonhoeffers*, 103.

11. Ibid., 105.

weren't enjoying a German meal together at the Schmidt Restaurant or gathering with other German expats at Han Priess's bookstore near the British Museum.

Dietrich discussed with Sabine, his oldest confidant, what he should do if drafted, the kind of conversation, as he had told Bell, he could not easily have in Germany, where military duty was a sacred calling. Sabine agreed that the only possibility for Dietrich, if pressed, was to join the Army Medical Service. "To take up arms in Hitler's war was simply out of the question," Sabine wrote.[12]

Although he had steered his sister and brother-in-law to Miss Sharp's, Dietrich was shocked at the Leibholzs' accommodations, telling Sabine they were "extremely inadequate,"[13] and advising the family to move "somewhere decent," the kind of arrogant language he typically used when upset.

At London's Caledonian market, amid its open-air stalls, Dietrich bought Sabine "an Indian divan cover made out of blue cloth and embroidered with gold thread 'so that you have at least one beautiful thing to look at in your room.'"[14] During that same excursion, Dietrich and Eberhard had an exchange. Eberhard, ever the musician, wanted to buy a wind instrument, apparently with Dietrich's money, but Dietrich squashed the idea, saying that given the restrictions on taking currency out of Germany, it should all be spent on his sister. This was the kind of gesture Sabine remembered, as it meant she felt protected. The hauteur with which Dietrich apparently addressed Eberhard was again characteristic of his speech when distressed. Sabine doesn't record Eberhard's response—was he mortified at this rebuke, made aware of his dependency? He would later write that "at this time [1939] I was still remote from the Bonhoeffers [without official marital status], but an admirer of the unity and strength of this family."[15]

In England, Dietrich quickly met with Bell, traveling to his friend's well-appointed palace to discuss his moral objections to serving in the army. Dietrich and Eberhard also visited Oxford to promote ecumenical ties.[16] The Leibholzes accompanied them and Gert had the opportunity to meet with political economist William Beveridge.[17] On the south coast, Dietrich

12. Ibid., 105
13. Ibid.
14. Ibid., 106.
15. Ibid, 105.
16. Bethge, *DB: A Biography*, 641.
17. Ibid., 641. Bethge identifies the man Gert met with as Arthur Beveridge, but in all likelihood he meant William Beveridge. William Beveridge, who had established academic relief council that helped displaced German Jewish academics find work, accepted a position at Oxford in 1937. It would make sense for Gert—or Dietrich on

sought out Reinhold Niebuhr, who was also in England. After this meeting, Niebuhr telegrammed the United States and arranged for Dietrich to be offered a job, adding urgency to his request by stating Dietrich was "slated to go to a concentration camp."[18] Dietrich faced no such immediate danger, but the words had their intended effect.

Even when his official business had been concluded, Dietrich lingered in London, wondering if it wouldn't be best to let the war catch him abroad, together with his sister[19] and his closest friend. But it was not to be: when Paula and Karl told Dietrich the war was delayed yet again, the two men headed home.

On April 18, 1939, as Dietrich and Eberhard entered the Charlottenburg neighborhood where Dietrich's parents lived, they ran into a parade for Hitler's fiftieth birthday marching past the local technical college.[20] Hitler's actual fiftieth birthday arrived two days later and Berlin celebrated with a huge, triumphant goose-stepping pageant of troops marching amid waving seas of red and black swastika banners.

April also coincided with the final move of the "collective pastorate," to Sigurdshof, a picturesque if small one-and-half story half-timbered farmhouse on the estate of Ruth's relative, von Kleist of Wendisch-Tychow. Here, the seminarians escaped the incessant war din of the cities. The house lacked electricity, central heating, or running water. Sigurdshof's pastors fetched water from an outdoor pump and read by kerosene lantern and candlelight. Compensations included use of the estate's fishing boat and tennis courts.[21]

Heavy wooden shutters could be closed over the small windows to seal out wintry drafts, while lush rustic ivy grew around the windows. An overhanging roof and climbing plants sheltered a courtyard. Behind the house, the Wipper River flowed, and beyond that a great forest merged with the Bismarck lands to the south.[22] The forest hid a large log shed, a convenient refuge when the Gestapo came to call.[23] Their faithful housekeeper, the white-haired Frau Struwe, moved with them, continuing as one of the lesser-sung heroes who helped keep the Confessing Church alive. Finances

---

his behalf—to have sought out an interview with Beveridge, a natural figure to help a German Jewish refugee professor.

18. Bonhoeffer, *DBWE 15*, 173.
19. Bethge, *DB: A Biography*, 648.
20. Ibid., 648.
21. Ibid., 591.
22. Ibid.
23. Zimmermann and Smith, eds. *I Knew*, 158.

remained precarious, the illegal seminary receiving no support from larger church institutions.

Never had the seminarians been in a place so remote, its physical location reflecting their psychological remove from Nazism. The few who remained saw the hope and buoyancy that had characterized the Finkenwalde days dim, but at the same time, the farmhouse was an oasis of peace in a country coming more and more to resemble a huge army base.[24] Helmut Traub, who took over for Dietrich when he headed for America, described Sigurdshof as "almost an idyll . . . inviting us to concentration and work."[25]

On his return to Germany, Dietrich had requested permission from military recruiters to spend a year in the United States. Instead, he was ordered to report for duty May 22, leading to a flurry of communications back and forth with his friends in the US. Finally, in desperation, he asked his father to intervene. Dietrich received his year's reprieve.[26]

Another visit to Sabine launched Dietrich on his journey across the ocean. The thirty-three-year-old Dietrich left Eberhard with a will, handwritten on a card, which lent a note of solemnity to his leave-taking: "Herewith I declare that Pastor Eberhard Bethge, presently living at Sigurdshof via Zollbrück, Schlawe District, has full right of disposal over my entire possessions."[27] He also gave his motorcycle to Eberhard.[28]

Ruth wrote to Dietrich on the eve of his departure: "My prayers will accompany you on your way, and the joy will be very great when you return home. This certainty will always stand by you, when perhaps sometimes in foreign lands it does become very lonely."[29] Ruth continued by alluding to what it had meant to her that Dietrich had brought her closer to God through the church struggle, creating between the two of them "something of value that will not die."[30]

"Greet Eberhard," instructed Ruth. "The two of us will now become even closer to each other. I am very glad that he is there." The short letter also contained an oblique apology for the "forgetfulness" of Dieter von Kleist, whom she had contacted at the Military Recruiting Office, a forgetfulness that had prompted Karl Bonhoeffer's phone call to forestall Dietrich's army

24. Ibid., 158.
25. Ibid..
26. Bethge, *DB: A Biography*, 634–35.
27. Bonhoeffer, *DBWE* 15, 171.
28. Ibid., 172.
29. Ibid.
30. Ibid., 173.

call-up.³¹ And finally, characteristic of Ruth, even at this moment, she requested help for a friend. ³²

On June 2, Dietrich boarded his flight to England. A postcard from Eberhard soon followed: after returning from a film in Berlin, *Katja, the Uncrowned Princess,* that he saw with friends and relatives, "I felt the 'loneliness' . . . in the absence of the verdict of a conversation partner." Then he added, "What a fine airplane you had."³³

The leisurely flight stopped in Amsterdam en route to London. Dietrich wrote Eberhard a postcard from the air: "Now we are flying over the Channel with a wonderful glowing sunset. It is 10:00 p.m. and still very light. I am doing well. You all will now be sleepy and heading to bed. I thank you for everything." And with a simple clarity, he summed up his position and the dilemma that would preoccupy him as he headed west: "My thoughts are between you and the future."³⁴

Dietrich arrived in London, joining Sabine and her family for a short stay. On June 6, he sent Eberhard another postcard from England: "Many thanks for the first short greeting. How nice that you could celebrate the departure with a movie. Today in the city I often thought of our days here together, National Gallery, portraiture, etc. The Daily Texts these days give me great pleasure, and I am happy to have them from you."³⁵ He ended by alluding to his hope that Eberhard would emigrate either to England or the US: "I have initiated the necessary steps for the invitation in the autumn. But you must still write me whether you would prefer to visit Sabine and me for a short period or Sabine for a longer period. Greet everyone!"³⁶

During his short stay in England, Dietrich visited Bell, and on June 7, a scant four days after his arrival, he boarded the *Bremen* for Manhattan, along with Karl-Friedrich. Karl-Friedrich had been offered a professorship at the University of Chicago and would explore moving from Germany. Sabine saw them go happily: When war came, she thought, Dietrich would pave the way for her family to leave England, so uncomfortably close to Germany. "Their departure," she wrote with characteristic understatement, "was not without consolation for us."³⁷

---

31. Ibid., 174.
32. Ibid., 173.
33. Ibid., 174.
34. Ibid., 175.
35. Ibid., 176.
36. Ibid.
37. Leibholz, *The Bonhoeffers,* 110.

— 29 —
Sailing Away

A PHOTO FROM THE trip shows Dietrich reading and sunning on a *Bremen* deck chair, a cloth cap on his head, a portrait of relaxation and ease, Karl-Friedrich beside him. The *Bremen*, a mighty state-of-the-art German ocean liner with two great smoke-billowing chimneys, carried passengers across the Atlantic in a rapid-fire four to five days. The ship boasted spacious cabins, ample amounts of lifeboats and chaise lounges, an outdoor pool that, because it was located between two boilers, stayed warm even in winter, and a first-class restaurant offering panoramic views of the sea through walls of glass. Stewards in their uniforms with many buttons waited on the first-class passengers, though since 1938, all the Jewish employees had been fired.[1] In July 1935, the steamer had made international news when American antifascists boarded the ship, docked in the New York harbor, and ripped down its swastika flag, sending Hitler into apoplectic fury.

His first day shipboard, June 7, Dietrich shot off a happy postcard to Eberhard, "greatly delighted" with a letter (now missing) he had received from his friend. He promised to write more soon, characterizing his current postcard as "a final faithful greeting"—and wrote cheerily of his journey: "The cabin is very roomy, and otherwise, too, there is a wonderful amount of room on the ship. The weather is glorious, and the sea utterly still."[2] Salty air filled his lungs and sea breezes cooled him as he strolled the decks. As he wrote, he assumed that Eberhard would move either to England or the US.

But by the 11th a note of uncertainty had crept into his diary: "If only the doubts about my own path were overcome."[3]

June 12th marked the end of the quiet journey on placid seas, filled with reading and thoughts, and already some loneliness, as Dietrich

---

1. Huchthausen, "The SS Bremen Article."
2. Bonhoeffer, *DBWE* 15, 178.
3. Ibid., 219.

dreamed of meals, swimming, and ping pong with friends back home.[4] On disembarking, he was met by Paul Macy of the Federal Council of Churches and ushered to the Parkside Hotel, but soon after took up residence at Union Theological Seminary, emptied of students for summer break.

Dietrich, now a prominent guest, roomed in the prophet's chamber, a large cavern with a high barrel ceiling. Matching casement windows mirrored each other at either end of the long room, each window made of leaded glass and each window almost a three-sided bow—the far panes angled slightly—but too narrow for a window seat beneath. Dietrich paced the room and smoked. Out the front window he could look over Broadway, down the narrow corridor of 121st Street. From the back he had, as he wrote, "a lovely view of the Quadrangle. I had forgotten a great deal; but everything came back quickly, right up to the smell of the house."[5]

A fountain stood in the center of the now empty Quadrangle, water spilling from what looked a small crenellated cake plate into a larger one and then to the largest of all. Bonhoeffer in his notes from the period didn't elaborate on what memories flooded back to him as he wandered the small campus, but one can imagine him haunted by the ghosts of Jean Lasserre, the Frenchman who'd turned him to pacifism during their discussions of the Sermon on the Mount, Frank Fisher, who'd brought him to the Abyssinian Baptist Church and introduced him to the black community, Erwin Sutz, now safely ensconced in Switzerland, who less than a year ago had asked to visit Sabine and Gert in Zurich. Dietrich had often mentioned in his letters and reports the almost constant conversations at the seminary. He'd likened it to living in a youth hostel. But such sociability was not available in 1939 on an empty campus during summer break, nor in nearby faded Harlem, suffering from the long Depression.

By June 13th, when no letter from Eberhard had yet arrived, Bonhoeffer wrote, "it is entirely clear to me that I must go back."[6] Late in the afternoon of the 13th, Dietrich met Henry Sloane Coffin, president of Union Theological, at Grand Central Station, and took the train with him to his country home in Lakeville, Connecticut, discussing the state of church and theology in the US for much of the ninety-minute journey.

Coffin's country house was in the mountains of Lakeview, an area replete, Dietrich noted, with "cool and lush vegetation." For the first time in his life, sitting in the garden with his hosts as the light faded, Dietrich saw

---

4. Ibid., 178.
5. Ibid., 220.
6. Bonhoeffer, *DBWE 15*, 220.

the magical flicker of fireflies sparkling in the air. "Utterly fantastic sight," he noted.

His hosts received him cordially but inwardly he felt alone and adrift. "For all that," he wrote, "only Germany, the brothers, are missing. The first solitary hours are hard. I don't comprehend why I am here, whether it was sensible, whether the outcome will be worth it."[7]

He was preoccupied with "the work at home. Almost two weeks have passed now without my knowing anything from over there. That is hardly bearable."[8] Despite the gracious setting, breakfast on the verandah, good company, and the cooling freshness brought on by a nighttime downpour that broke the oppressive heat, by the 15th Dietrich was confiding to his journal, "I would not have thought it possible that one at my age after so many years abroad can become so agonizingly homesick. . . . The full force of self-reproaches about a wrong decision comes back up and is almost suffocating. I was filled with despair."[9]

On the end of this same day, however, he wrote to Henry Leiper of the Federal Council of Churches about Eberhard in terms that indicated, despite his journal entries, he still considered remaining in the States—if Eberhard could be with him. He used the term *personal* three times:

> Finally, let me add a very personal remark. My best friend in Germany, a young confessional pastor, who has been working with me for many years, will be in the same conflict with regard to military service etc. at the latest by next spring, possibly in the fall of this year. I feel it would be an utmost disloyalty to leave him alone in Germany when the conflict comes up for him. I should either have to go back to stand by him and to act with him or to get him out and to share my living with him, whatever it be, though I do not know if he would be willing to leave Germany. That is a last personal, but not only personal reason, why I feel bound to keep my way-back open. I am sure, you will appreciate that this is a duty of "Bruderschaft" which in these times one just has to fulfill.[10]

On the 16th Dietrich visited the New York World's Fair with all its grand pavilions, but saw it dully: "Overall no particular impression." He oddly dismissed the Russian pavilion, a prime example of totalitarian architecture with its massive tower topped by a worker holding aloft a communist

7. Ibid., 221.
8. Ibid., 222.
9. Ibid.
10. Ibid., 184.

star, as "completely bourgeois." Dietrich found most of the other pavilions "too commercial" and the "Temple of Religion" building "dreadful, a movie theater." His relief was to return home to his hot, empty Union chamber: "Finally evening.... One is less lonely when one is alone."[11]

Still no word from Eberhard. Dietrich expressed his agony: "Only fourteen days ago today from Berlin... I wait for mail! It can hardly be endured. I will probably not stay long.... Then, on the other hand, I tell myself: it is cowardice and weakness to run away from here now. But... I cannot be alone abroad. That is utterly clear to me."[12]

11. Ibid., 223.
12. Ibid.

— 30 —
Agony

"I am living in the loveliest area of Manhattan, directly on the Hudson and somewhat above the city. But it is probably even lovelier to live high up in one of the skyscrapers (the highest is 360 meters!). Again and again, the general impression of New York is indeed stunning, the skyscrapers, the masses of people from all nations and races milling about, the host of churches and chapels," Dietrich wrote to his parents on June 17.

Yet the silent Eberhard at Sigsurdhof never strayed far from his thoughts: "But basically I have already become so accustomed to rural life that I often really long for it."[1]

Three more days passed. Still no letter from Eberhard. Agony. "Without news from Germany the whole day, from mail to mail, waiting in vain. It doesn't help to get angry and write letters in that mood."[2]

On the 20th, mail arrived from Germany to hot, sticky New York: a letter from parents, booklets from Stettin. Still nothing from Eberhard. In apparent desperation, overtaken by fear Eberhard was using the separation to abandon him—and knowing time was of the essence to get Eberhard to the States before the war, he mailed a short postcard in an envelope to Elisabeth Bethge, Eberhard's mother, asking her to deliver an enclosed card to her silent son.[3] At this juncture, Dietrich told Leiper he would definitely return to Germany.[4] Even at the cost of leaving Sabine to her fate in England, he would go home.

---

1. Bonhoeffer, *DBWE 15*, 201.
2. Ibid., 226.
3. Ibid., 193.
4. Ibid., 226. Since Dietrich knew that Sabine and Gert hoped he could pave the way for them come to the US, it's odd that Dietrich never mentions work for Gert in any of his letters to friends and colleagues in the US. It's possible he knew Gert's English wasn't up to par, but otherwise inexplicable that he didn't try to find Gert patronage. We have one cryptic passage in a letter to his parents: "By the way, Karl Friedrich and I had a long conversation with Gert before his departure. It was necessary" (*DBWE 15*, 215).

On June 21st, a stiflingly hot day, Dietrich visited the Metropolitan Museum of Art by himself, especially enjoying the El Grecos.[5] On June 22, he continued ill at ease, "I am sorry about my decision [to return to Germany] mostly because of Sabine."[6]

Yet, "for a German over here it is simply no longer to be endured; one is simply torn apart. To be here during a catastrophe is simply unthinkable, unless it is meant to be. But to be guilty of this oneself, to have to reproach oneself for having gone abroad unnecessarily, is certainly crushing. We simply cannot separate ourselves from our fate."[7]

On this interminable hot day of June 22, the second longest day of the year, Dietrich sat smoking and sweating in his prophet's chamber, skyscrapers in the distance, thinking of the cool woods and wilds of Sigurdshof. Still awaiting a letter from Eberhard, he wrote an anguished, "Why do I not hear anything?"[8]

Meanwhile, at the Olympic Stadium in Berlin, 100,000 Berliners had just attended an eerie nighttime solstice celebration. Hitler Youth and "maidens" carrying torches had formed a huge oval around a central bonfire. Amid the spooky light, tramping feet, and crackling fire, Goebbels made an ominous speech, threatening Poland.

The 23rd passed, again with no letter from Eberhard. Finally, on the 24th, two and a half agonizing weeks after the last communication, the hoped-for missive arrived. "Finally mail," Dietrich wrote in response to Eberhard's letter. "That is a great liberation."[9]

After mentioning a visit to Ruth in Stettin, Eberhard's blithely cheery letter painted a picture of life at Sigurdshof: "we just had our first tennis game . . . . If only you could be with us. You had hardly left when we saw three fat wild boars in the twilight on the bank of the Wipper—we felt somewhat funny. Shortly before, we had already bagged an over-one-half-meter-long adder, whose stripped skin now adorns the room." More importantly,

---

5. Ibid., 228. The Met's collection of El Grecos includes paintings that one can imagine of interest to Dietrich: a dreamlike vision, a view of Toledo, and a striking elongated portrait of an elderly man called Spirit and Paradox. Dietrich had, according to Bosanquet, fallen in love with El Greco when in Spain (*The Life and Death of Dietrich Bonhoeffer*, 68). Interestingly, however, the artist may have been a common upper-middle-class taste in that era: William Shirer also expresses a special liking for El Greco in the *Berlin Diaries*.

6. Bonhoeffer, *DBWE 15*, 229.

7. Ibid.

8. Ibid.

9. Ibid., 230.

Eberhard listed obstacles to leaving Germany: staffing difficulties in the Confessing Church, an unwillingness on the part of superiors to let him go, and other uncertainties. "One would perhaps profit more from visiting Sabine. While, of course, to visit you would bring more of a change of pace. I don't know at all what I should do," he ended.[10] If Dietrich were single-mindedly, obsessively devoted to a reunion with Eberhard, no matter what the cost, Eberhard was equivocal—and that, given the urgency, was tantamount to a refusal to emigrate.

On the same day as his letter to Dietrich, Eberhard wrote more formally to thank Paula and Karl for all the hospitality they had shown him. He noted Paula's influence on Dietrich in modeling for him how to respond gracefully to a multitude of requests. He also apologized for a communication mix-up that meant he, Eberhard, had not received their request to drive them on vacation (one wonders if he perhaps became tired of functioning as the family valet and simply ignored the request), and alluded to possible problems with leaving the collective pastorate to come to Berlin.[11]

On June 26, Dietrich hinted in his journal his awareness of the vital stirrings" that drove him: "Today I happened to read from 2 Tim. 4:21 'come before the winter'—Paul's plea to Timothy. Timothy is to share the suffering of the apostle and not be ashamed. 'Come before the winter'—otherwise it might be too late. That is haunting me the whole day. We seem to feel like the soldiers on leave from the front who, despite all that awaits them, push to return to the front. We can't come free of it. Not as if we were necessary, as if we were needed (by God!?), but simply because our life is there and because we desert our life, annihilate it, if we are not part of things there. It is not at all something pious, but something almost vital. But God acts not only through pious impulses but also through such vital stirrings as well. 'Come before the winter'—it is not a misuse of the Scripture if I allow this to be said to me. If God gives me the grace for that."[12]

Still anxious to return to Germany, Dietrich decided on June 30 to travel on July 8 with Karl-Friedrich, thirty days ahead of his earlier plan. The decision made, his lethargy left and his liveliness returned—and with it his characteristic engagement in the world around him.

Eberhard now responded to Dietrich's evident reproaches with excuses—"Perhaps you can picture for yourself how I have been absorbed by matters here.... Three times, every week on Saturday, I was in Berlin, which in the heat was not a little exhausting (counting your trip as well),

---

10. Ibid., 179. The allusions to Sabine meant moving to England.
11. Ibid., 181–82.
12. Ibid., 232.

and in addition took care of work and order here."¹³ We see too a pattern of Dietrich's hunger for his friend and Eberhard's tact—Eberhard praised *Life Together* and affirmed that Dietrich was remembered and missed. Yes his evasiveness kept Dietrich needy and insecure.

The letter continues an ongoing conversation about money—in response to what must have been Dietrich's queries or offers, Eberhard assures him he has enough funds: "With the financial matters, that can wait; at present your parents are still away. By the way, I just paid the full price for the dictionary [that the two had hoped to split the cost of]. I am still doing quite well. The trip recently to the wedding went smoothly; I could ride there and back from Berlin with my cousin Karl-Friedrich in the BMW . . . ."¹⁴ The chatty letter moves from talk of theology to the people back home. Eberhard had visited Ursel, who lived next door to the Bonhoeffers, then noted "I slept in our room."¹⁵ Eberhard mentioned that Ruth had sciatica and declared firmly, "I would like to invite Mrs. Von Kleist here soon," without any of the "what should I do" equivocations he had about coming to America. He reported that Mrs. Struwe was "doing quite well" and now getting along with Eberhard, indicating there had been some trouble.¹⁶

On July 5, Dietrich noted in his journal that he wished he could stay in the States an extra four weeks. "But the stakes are too high. Letter from Eberhard, great joy."¹⁷ In this latest letter, dated June 29th, Eberhard wrote: "Believe me, the prospect of seeing you again sooner indeed fills me with very great joy, despite all appreciation for the tempting offers and the difficulty of giving it up. It will be good to be together again! But how will it happen? Where do I come? I must certainly pick you up somewhere!" He carefully carved out spaces apart for himself, such as for his sister's mid-September wedding, and noted, "I can imagine how you sometimes feel. Your letter conveys to me, I believe, a very vivid impression." Apparently the "vivid impression" was not wonderful, as evidenced by the "but" and "nonetheless" that followed: "But I nonetheless took great pleasure in your careful and detailed reports." The whole map of his life again changing with Dietrich's quick return, he mentioned Karl and Paula: "I had a very detailed letter from your mother describing their vacation, with a personal greeting from your father, in reply to my thank-you letter back then. I was very pleased about it. . . . As always, one is suntanned, relaxed, and in a good mood!"¹⁸

13. Ibid., 195.
14. Ibid., 198.
15. Ibid., 197.
16. Ibid., 198.
17. Ibid., 237. Bonhoeffer uses the same phrase—"great joy"—a few days later in response to an unexpected letter from his parents.
18. Ibid., 207–8.

— 31 —
Do You Want Me?

ON JULY 8, DIETRICH sailed with Karl-Friedrich toward Europe. "It is quiet and hot," Dietrich noted in his journal. He read, talked with his brother. Karl-Friedrich too would stay in Germany, turning down the University of Chicago.

Eberhard wrote to Dietrich in London on July 11:

> Your letters with the complaint that you didn't receive anything hurt me a great deal. . . . I am truly very sorry that you had to wait so. The reasons were of course first the overwork, and last week I was not doing so well. Now today I am already writing, as your mother writes, to England so that you don't have to wait too long. I beg you please to give me some benefit of the doubt about what the new situation here demanded and not to be angry with me, so that we can look forward, untroubled and happy, to seeing each other again. Now I am completely back in shape. I couldn't explain it to myself at all, really, where this came from, for I had no particular exertions immediately behind me; the fourteen days here alone, which perhaps were more of a strain on me than I initially felt, were already ten to fourteen days in the past, but perhaps it was only then that a certain exhaustion emerged. However it may be, now I am fine again, and Mrs. Struwe is feeding me especially well. So on Sunday I was doing well again, when we had visitors, the two from the estate, Aunt Ruth with her Kieckow son and his wife. . . . I believe that you will be in demand from many quarters upon your return, but I would nonetheless say, especially since you have offered it: please come! We are immensely pleased, especially me.[1]

Sabine, however, greeted Dietrich's return on July 13th with distress. Both she and Gert were "very shocked" to hear he would go back to Germany.

---

1. Bonhoeffer, *DBWE* 15, 245–46.

"Was it madness? Did it have to be?" Sabine asked Dietrich.[2] He was "utterly convinced that it did have to be." His desire to maintain ties with his parents and "his young theologians" was "very strong."

On his arrival in London, Dietrich wrote Eberhard a letter that was filled with anticipation and yet hesitation:

> I don't think Stettin is very lovely, but one could perhaps drive home along the sea. It would be around the thirtieth, thirty-first, or first, I think. I am just figuring out that the twenty-ninth is a Saturday; does that suit you better? Perhaps particularly not? We hoped, didn't we, to have a day and a half for the return trip. But perhaps you will take me directly to the sea? So, I will count on your picking me up in any case and send you word of the details.[3]

He assumed his friend would be part of a Swiss excursion, another trip financed by Sabine's German bank account: "In the meantime, you will book the fourth to the fourteenth, won't you! By the way, Sabine wants to give us a trip to Switzerland, which I find very kind. Do try as soon as possible to apply for the necessary foreign currency; I will do so as well as soon as I arrive."

Then, reality intruded, the plaintive, tortured question following: "How should things go after the Baltic? Do you want me or not? I would really like to know."[4] Across the decades the words echo: "Do you want me or not?"

In 1932, Dietrich had written of his childhood fantasies of death. In doing so, he regarded his younger self in the third person, as if he were observing someone else from a distance: "As a boy, he liked to picture himself on his deathbed, surrounded by all who loved him, speaking his last words to them. He had often secretly considered what he might say to them at that moment. Death was nothing strange or hard for him. He would have been quite ready to die young, a beautiful, devout death. They should all see and understand that death is not hard but splendid for one who believes in God."[5]

Dietrich most likely pulled this romanticized deathbed scene from his reading, for, in middle childhood—Bonhoeffer had this fantasy before age twelve, before Walter died—stories typically structure the young person's religious understanding, as the fantastic and irrational faith of the young child gives way to an attempt to create meaning and coherence.[6]

2. Leibholz, *The Bonhoeffers*, 127.
3. Bonhoeffer, *DBWE* 15, 249.
4. Ibid., 25.
5. Bosanquet, *The Life and Death of Dietrich Bonhoeffer*, 36.
6. Fowler and Lovin, *Trajectories in Faith*, 25–26. According to the stages of faith

Bonhoeffer's death scenario, though the details are not as fully fleshed out for us, mirrors that of the angelic little Eva in *Uncle Tom's Cabin*, who has the power to bring adult and child alike to spiritual renewal as she is dying. Eva says the following before she perishes:

> "If you love me, you must not interrupt me so. Listen to what I say. I want to speak to you about your souls. . . . Many of you, I am afraid, are very careless. You are thinking only about this world. I want you to remember that there is a beautiful world, where Jesus is. I am going there, and you can go there. It is for you, as much as me. But, if you want to go there, you must not live idle, careless, thoughtless lives. You must be Christians. You must remember that each one of you can become angels, and be angels forever. . . . If you want to be Christians, Jesus will help you. You must pray to him; you must read . . ." A bright, a glorious smile passed over her face, and she said, brokenly,—"O! love,—joy,—peace!" gave one sigh and passed from death unto life![7]

It's no wonder that such a tableau, illustrating a child capturing the attention and adoration of every adult in the household—and having the power to advise and transform them—captured the hearts of children. Interestingly, however, Dietrich describes his youthful death fantasy only to dwell on how his concept of dying changed. After Walter's death, terror replaced the comforting and empowering image of a serene passage within a circle of family members.

In the newer fantasy, he has an incurable disease, but this "fact" appalls him: "His moment of understanding that death is fearful and bitter, a moment which interrupted his favorite theme for discussion and fantasy had suddenly acquired a bitter taste. Now he was silent about the beauty of a devout death."[8] The earlier dream of a romantic demise was colored with shame. He wrote that "he felt nauseated by his theatrical imaginings."[9]

Yet even at age fourteen—two years after Walter's death—he had found Max Klinger's "Vom Tode" ("On Death") lithograph cycle "the most beautiful I have ever seen."[10] Death pulled him into its orbit. Death was linked in his mind with love, community, attention, influence, respect—a

---

development outlined, in mid-childhood stories become "the major way of giving unity and value to experience."

7. Stowe, *Uncle Tom's Cabin*.
8. Bosanquet, *The Life and Death of Dietrich Bonhoeffer*, 37.
9. Ibid., 36.
10. Bonhoeffer, *DBWE 9*, 37.

vision that while macabre was also prophetic, and not entirely unusual in death-obsessed Nazi Germany. Yet if he never quite lost his fascination with dying, life drew him even more strongly, and after 1939, Bonhoeffer would increasingly devote his energies to the problem of staying alive.

If Eberhard was the main catalyst behind his return, Germany also exerted its pull, in the allure of its vital crisis. Others responded as well—among them Thomas Kelly, Hans Fallada, Thomas Wolfe—to what Wolfe called "something [barbaric] . . . in the spirit of man which he had never known before . . . [that] shook his inner world to its foundations."[11]

Quaker Thomas Kelly, who had lived in Germany from 1924-25, helping there during economic crisis, returned in 1938 as witness to another sort of crisis. Like Wolfe, he found his inner world shaken by Germany. He wrote to his wife: "Until you have lived in this world of despair and fear and abysmal suffering of the soul, you can never know [how it feels] . . . ."[12] "Suffering of the body is only the vestibule of suffering. Suffering of soul, of spirit, is terrible. . . . Dear people, how they suffer!"[13] Amid people frightened to speak out against violence and cruelty, Kelly had a spiritual awakening in Cologne Cathedral. Here, Kelly was "melted down by the love of God."[14]

He then had a rough adjustment back to the United States. The security of the serene suburbs around Haverford College, where he taught religion and philosophy, seemed "a travesty."[15] His family described him as in a "daze."[16] His heart remained with his friends in the "Blessed Community" in Germany, a place he deemed "vital."[17] In contrast, his comfortable Philadelphia surrounding seemed "humdrum," the US "pasty and artificial."[18]

Bonhoeffer in 1939 also was distressed at the triviality of life in the United States: "One sat for an hour and chatted, not at all stupidly, but about matters that were so utterly trivial to me, whether a good musical education is possible in New York, about raising children, etc. etc., and I thought, how usefully I could spend these hours in Germany."[19]

11. Wolfe, *You Can't Go Home Again*, 705.
12. Kelly, *Thomas Kelly*, 97.
13. Ibid., 100.
14. Ibid., 120. This would culminate in his book *A Testament of Devotion*.
15. Ibid., 109
16. Ibid.
17. Ibid.
18. Ibid., 108.
19. Bonhoeffer, *DBWE 15*, 222.

The German novelist Hans Fallada provides another parallel to Bonhoeffer. In 1938, Putnam, his English language publisher, arranged for him to move with his family to England. His bags packed, Fallada took a last walk around a nearby lake and decided he couldn't leave—despite endless conflicts with the regime that for him had included concentration camp stints.[20] He and Bonhoeffer shared "the only certainty" of dissenting Germans: "imprisonment or death."[21]

But for now, for all his anticipated joy at seeing Eberhard in Germany, Dietrich was in England, Sabine at the forefront.

Bonhoeffer stayed with the Leibholzes for two weeks while Karl-Friedrich, a ghostly presence on this entire journey, faded away. Perhaps like other Germans passing through in those tense pre-war summer months, Dietrich "wanted to take one last breath of fresh air"[22] before re-entering the "fine prison"[23] of Nazi Germany. As the last prewar days before the world changed irrevocably wended on, he wondered how long it might be before he saw Sabine and her family again.

London times also meant visits with old friends. Dietrich met Julius Rieger after a trip to Liberty's in South Kensington for lunch at a Chinese restaurant.[24]

When not meeting friends, Dietrich spent leisurely time with his sister. A photo from the visit shows Sabine and Dietrich relaxing on lawn chairs in the garden at Miss Sharp's boarding house. Dietrich wears a three-piece suit, Sabine her heirloom pearls, both looking happy together and at ease. Yet after almost six years of wear and tear, Sabine has transformed from an elegant young woman in a slinky silk gown to a heavier middle-aged émigré in sensible clothes.

Meanwhile in mid-July, Maria von Wedermeyer also participated in the last gasp of a culture World War II would soon obliterate. At Pätzig, her family's estate, she was a bridesmaid in her older sister Ruth Alice's grand wedding to Klaus von Bismarck. A photograph of the wedding procession[25] reveals

20. Fallada, *Every Man Dies Alone*, afterword by Rudolf Ditzen, 516.
21. Ibid., 517.
22. Leibholz, *The Bonhoeffers*, 110.
23. Ibid., 41
24. Zimmermann and Smith, eds., *I Knew*, 101. I contacted Paul French at his blog site http://www.chinarhyming.com/, and he thinks the restaurant still exists—assuming Bonhoeffer stayed for lunch near Liberty's—which French locates near the South Kensington tube stop.
25. Pejsa, *Matriarch of Conspiracy,* 248.

some of the aura of unreality surrounding the frozen Junker aristocracy at the brink of the war. The wedding couple walk arm in arm, but strangely detached from each other, both staring straight ahead. Their costumes, too, offer a study in contrast. The light catches Ruth Alice's diaphanous wedding dress so that it seems to glow, becoming translucent, showing off Ruth's slender figure beneath. A child with blond braids holds the train, which seems to merge with the bride's shimmering, gauzy veil. Ruth Alice has a ghostly, ethereal expression, a bouquet of roses held almost carelessly in one arm. In contrast, Klaus, in full dress uniform, is dark and solid, rounded helmet in place, wearing high leather boots, stiff collar, dark gloves, and dangling what looks to be a baton or narrow epee. Behind the couple Maria walks in a light, demure gown—a dress Dietrich would later particularly admire—a satin ribbon at the waist, looking down, as if willing herself not to be there. In this, the village's "last event within an order that would soon disappear,"[26] peasants lined the path to watch the bridal party pass.

For this wedding, the village church's altar, pulpit, and windowsills overflowed with flowers: larkspur, roses, and lilies from the Pätzig garden,[27] arguably as much unconsciously funereal as consciously celebratory. Prussian aristocracy packed the church, the men in full German military regalia. At the Pätzig manor house reception, Henning von Tresckow, a colonel in the German army, worried that Hitler would drag the Germans into a war against Russia which would destroy them all—and signaled his desire to overthrow the Hitler regime.[28] Meanwhile came the toast—itself subversive, if not criminal—to the aging, exiled Kaiser Wilhelm, as if time had stopped a quarter century past. A magnificent, many-course meal was followed by dancing—beloved of Maria—in the great hall where the carpets had been rolled up.

As his two weeks in London ended, Dietrich and Sabine recognized that Dietrich's return to Germany would trap the Leibholzs in England, though they "hardly touched upon it." The family saw him off on the train on July 25. Sabine called the parting—in contrast to seeing him off to America—"very grave."[29]

26. Ibid., 246.
27. Ibid., 247.
28. Ibid., 248–49.
29. Leibholz, *The Bonhoeffers*, 111–12.

PART VI
War and Conspiracies

— 32 —
Homecoming

On July 27, Eberhard arrived in Hanover to meet Dietrich. The three-hour train ride back to Berlin gave the two men the time alone that Dietrich, in particular, craved, a chance to catch up before they faced family and friends.[1]

If Pätzig existed in a strange, dreamlike stasis, Dietrich returned to a Berlin mobilizing for all-out war, surging with masses of people, and bursting with building projects, many on the monumental scale beloved of Hitler. Hitler and his cohort disdained what they considered the hodgepodge of styles that exploded in Berlin during the last years of the nineteenth century, when the town had emerged as an international capital.[2] They cleared vast areas to display their own architectural grandiosity. Hitler's new chancellery, opened in January, 1939, cost the equivalent of a billion dollars. Built to colossal dimensions, it incorporated and dwarfed what had been Bismarck's power center. Four monumental pillars supported and flanked the entrance to the severe, blank building, while on either side of the doorway large sculptures celebrated the Reich's two premier institutions, the army and the party. Albert Speer, who designed the building, understood Hitler's craving for size and so made "the long hall," twice as long as Versailles's Hall of Mirrors, installing seventeen-foot-high double doors between oversized rooms. Even Hitler's bronze inkwell was architectural, with a set of steps leading to the pool of ink.[3]

To Hitler, such designs represented a continuation of the Greek style of architecture he admired, for he believed the Greeks to be the spiritual ancestors to the Aryans: "The gigantic works of the Third Reich," he said, "are a token of its cultural renaissance and shall one day belong to the inalienable cultural heritage of the Western world just as the great cultural

---

1. de Gruchy, *Daring, Trusting Spirit*, 41.
2. Speer, *Inside the Third Reich*, 75.
3. Ibid., 159.

achievements of this world in the past belong to us today."[4] The masses, however, saw the lavish Chancellory a bit differently. A cynical joke circulated in Berlin: what do you think Hitler would have built if he had had the money?[5] As the government demolished apartment blocks, commandeered a residential section near the Tiergarten for office space, and party leaders built palatial homes, a housing shortage for ordinary people grew more acute.[6] Jews would bear the brunt of the housing squeeze.

As he traversed Berlin amid this feverish activity, Dietrich would have skirted deep construction pits while great skeletons of steel rose into the sky. Construction went on around the clock, ceaselessly subjecting guests at exclusive hotels like the Adlon to the "booming of pile drivers . . . the rattle of riveting hammers, the growling of concrete mixers and the sputtering of engines."[7] Meanwhile, Berliners could only wonder how the party leaders, with their vast palaces, had grown so rich in just six years.[8] The Bonhoeffers and Schleichers must have been relieved that they built their own new, more modest houses before the height of the frenzy.

As Dietrich and Eberhard arrived in Berlin, Paula and Karl headed abroad to meet Sabine and her family in Zandvoort, Holland. Sabine, who loved the seashore, called it "two unforgettable weeks" at the beach. Though she worried about Dietrich's fate in Germany as a conscientious objector, "the sea, the sun, the brilliance of it all, the broad sandy shore, still far from crowded at that time, the happy children—it all made that August of 1939 unforgettable."[9]

Meanwhile in Berlin, as war loomed, the city burst into a wave of decadence not seen since the late Weimar years. Government spending spiked, and Romanian, Hungarian, and Greek businessmen flooded the city. People jammed nightclubs. They drank heavily. Cabarets boomed. A spirit of recklessness prevailed as people rushed to enjoy life before war. In the words of one observer, "The people are consciously trying to drown themselves in indulgence."[10] And though prudery had been the official norm as late as 1937, by 1939 nudity had returned, from nude ballets to nude revues, with government approval, part of a plan to stimulate the birthrate. And while Dietrich had made an irrevocable decision to return to his homeland, many

---

4. Sherratt, *Hitler's Philosophers*, 24.
5. Lubrich, ed., *Travels in the Reich*, 182.
6. Ibid.
7. Ibid., 181.
8. Ibid., 184.
9. Leibholz, *The Bonhoeffers*, 113.
10. Lubrich, ed., *Travels in the Reich*, 190.

Germans disillusioned with Nazism and fearing the war to come—not just Jews—would have immediately seized Dietrich's opportunity to emigrate.[11]

In their own sphere, both Paula and Ursel had earned the "Mother's Cross" from a regime that, in the words of Dietrich's niece Renate, "pressed [women] . . . to have many children and gave them awards for breeding like cattle."[12] Both Paula and Ursel had had four or more babies, garnering them an invitation to a "solemn" awards ceremony. Paula's age allowed her to evade the event, but the family decided, in interests of prudence, that Ursel should attend. Renate remembered that "she told us some crazy things about the celebration that gave the family something to laugh about."[13]

Soon after arriving in Berlin, Dietrich and Eberhard travelled east to Sigurdshof. Though Dietrich had sent a message to say he was coming, seeing him surprised acting director Traub, who found "there was always something extraordinary about him."[14] Traub scolded him for returning to a doomed country after the efforts everyone had made to help him escape. Dietrich calmly lit a cigarette. He'd made a mistake, he said. He needed to be with the brethren. Characteristically, he and Eberhard took two groups of seminarians to the Baltic. Here, Luftwaffe planes roared ominously overhead practicing maneuvers, and a steady, disquieting stream of troops and tanks moved along Highway 2 toward the Polish border. Dietrich spent the seaside holiday encouraging his students to stand as witnesses to the reality of God's presence in the world, a reality different from what surrounded them.[15]

On August 23, as Dietrich and the seminarians relaxed on the shores of the Baltic, Hitler and Stalin entered into a nonaggression pact so they could divide Poland. That night, the Northern Lights glowed with particular intensity in German skies, shimmering in rainbow colors and deep reds, perhaps seen as a portent.[16] On August 25, England signed a treaty in support of Poland.

Up to this point in England, Sabine had often heard willingness to tolerate Nazi expansion into central Europe. People cynically remarked that a powerful Germany run by a regime fanatically opposed to communism would safeguard their way of life,[17] a sentiment also recorded by

11. Ibid., 194–95.
12. Renate Bethge, "Bonhoeffer and the Role of Women," 41.
13. Ibid.
14. Zimmermann and Smith, eds., *I Knew*, 159.
15. Ibid., 160.
16. Speer, *Inside the Third Reich*, 162.
17. Leibholz, *The Bonhoeffers*, 102.

Martha Dodd, the American ambassador's daughter in Berlin, in her memoir *Through Embassy Eyes*.

In 1939, the elite faced living reminders of the 1917 Russian Revolution in the plight of former Russian aristocrats now scraping by in European capitals as waiters, cab drivers, or stenographers. Upper-class Europeans found the threat of "bolshevism"—that they too could end up chased from their palaces to impoverished lives in foreign cities—more terrifying than Hitler's ruthlessness. Germany had, until now, appeared to offer an ever more powerful buffer between their countries and the Soviets. But once Hitler revealed himself to be Stalin's partner, sentiments changed sharply. As Sabine dryly put it, "Many had their eyes opened too late."[18]

After his seaside holiday, Dietrich cancelled courses at Sigurdshof and Köslin, both too close to Poland: His parents, now returned from Holland, had warned him that their contacts said war would soon start.[19]

On August 26, Dietrich and Eberhard returned to Marienberger Alle, remaining in Berlin into October.[20] On August 28, Dietrich wrote a letter to Sabine, still hopeful he might visit her in December.[21] On September 1, Germany invaded Poland. Hitler appeared in his rubber-stamping Reichstag before a giant wingspread eagle with a swastika in its talons. He insisted that although he "loved peace," he was responding with "courage" to provocations by Poland. On September 3 England and France declared war on Germany. World War II had begun.

Karl Bonhoeffer wrote of a mood in Berlin "radically different from [the jubilation of] 1914.... In 1939 the population had no doubt that what they were faced with was a war of aggression prepared and organized by Hitler, and for this the majority had no sympathy whatsoever."[22] William Shirer observed the same: "people in the streets ... were apathetic despite the immensity of the news which had greeted them from their radios .... Across the street from the Adlon Hotel the morning shift of labourers had gone to work on the new I. G. Farben building just as if nothing had happened, and when newsboys came by shouting their extras no one laid down his tools to buy one."[23]

18. Ibid., 102.
19. Bethge, *DB: A Biography*, 662.
20. Ibid.
21. Bonhoeffer, *DBWE 15*, 268.
22. Leibholz, *The Bonhoeffers*, 115.
23. Moorhouse, *Berlin at War*, 19.

Hitler had been wildly popular when he gained territory for Germany without a shot being fired in the Ruhr, Austria, and Czechoslovakia, but now, for many, bitter memories of the last war arose. Others thought—or hoped—the "Polish" war would pass without incident.[24]

---

24. Ibid., 19.

33

Cold Idyll, Dark Nights

IN BERLIN ON THE 3rd, the German people reacted with "horror" to the news that England had declared war. "The atmosphere here is terrible," said one Berliner, "a mixture of resignation and mourning . . . . It could not be worse."[1] While Dietrich discussed the situation with Klaus in Berlin's Eichkamp neighborhood, an air raid siren began to scream. Dietrich hopped on his bike, joining the crowds of cyclists who filled Berlin's thoroughfares. He arrived at his parent's house in five minutes. No bombs fell.[2]

On September 3, Sabine heard Chamberlain shouted down by his own party when he proposed appeasing Hitler. "Our heads were reeling," Sabine wrote, although the war had been expected. The Leibholzes, having left London, lodged in a hotel at St. Leonards-on-Sea. To save money, they rented a flat in the town. They moved to it that day, as previously scheduled, and "unpacked the trunks as in a dream." Sabine remembered seeing from her bedroom window "ships from the English fleet moving on the horizon, looking wonderfully white and gleaming in the sun. . . .The inner tension we felt was terrible. At that time I made a vow to myself never to forget that England had never wanted this war."[3] Like her mother and sisters in Berlin, Sabine faced rationing. But "I was still young and it was all interesting to me."[4]

Unlike in September 1938, in 1939 the anti-Hitler conspirators had not planned a coup. In 1938, when they planned a coup in expectation of an unpopular war, no war occurred. In 1939, when an unpopular war began, they were caught off guard.

The pressure temporarily eased on the Confessing Church as the government turned its attention to more important matters. It had surprised both Hitler and Ribbentrop that England had not backed down. Dietrich

---

1. Moorhouse, *Berlin at War*, 28.
2. Bethge, *DB: A Biography*, 663.
3. Leibholz, *The Bonhoeffers*, 114.
4. Ibid., 116.

pursued becoming a military chaplain. The ever energetic and well-connected Paula jumped into helping him.[5]

On September 27, Poland surrendered, and news of German atrocities against the Poles began to drift into Berlin. On October 6, Hitler, in a speech in the Reichstag, offered peace to England and France—a peace that had nothing to do with restoring Poland for, he declared, "The Poland of the Treaty of Versailles shall never rise again."[6]

The war crimes against the Poles shocked many in the upper ranks of the army.[7] Before the invasion, Hitler told his generals, "I have sent to the east my 'Death's Head Units,' with the order to kill without pity or mercy all men, women and children of the Polish race. Who still talks nowadays of the extermination of the Armenians?"[8] Some of Hitler's officers had participated with the Turks during World War I in eradicating Armenians through executions, long marches, and starvation, a schooling in genocide they brought to a new arena.

Hitler had already planned extermination as he delivered on his promised plans to open "living space" for an expanded German empire. The government dismissed reports of the mass murder of Polish citizens as grossly exaggerated "foreign propaganda," but the generals in the field knew the truth. General Blaskowitz, military commander in Poland, insisted that "what foreign radio stations have broadcast up to now is only a tiny fraction of what has actually happened," and called for justice. Instead, as Bethge records, "Hitler responded by recalling Blaskowitz from his post."[9]

In the typical double thinking of the regime, while killing defenseless Poles was permissible, Germans were to be cosseted. The government assured nervous Berliners that impenetrable defense systems would protect them and not a single enemy plane would ever be allowed over the city.[10]

In the capital life went on largely as usual. A full roster of entertainment, including performances of *La Traviata* and *Aida*, Goethe's play *Gotz von Berlichingen* at the Schiller theater, and Marlene Dietrich in *The Blue Angel* at the movie houses were meant to reassure people that nothing would change.[11]

5. Bethge, *DB: A Biography*, 666.
6. Moorhouse, *Berlin at War*, 29.
7. Bethge, *DB: A Biography*, 671.
8. Durkin, "Our Century's Greatest Achievement."
9. Bethge, *DB: A Biography*, 671.
10. Moorhouse, *Berlin at War*, 142.
11. Ibid., 51.

Amid this banquet of Berlin cultural offerings, much of Bonhoeffer's fall correspondence dealt with suffering. One former seminarian fell within days of the attack on Poland and other "brothers" in the army faced imminent danger of death. In October, Maria von Wedemeyer headed off for her final year at the Magdalen-Stift school in Altenburg while Dietrich and Eberhard left Berlin to meet eight new ordinands at Sigurdshof.

In mid-December 1939, Dietrich sent his mother a postcard with his laundry, wrote to her of ice skating on a frozen lake, and mentioned coming to Berlin on December 28th.[12] It's probable that the Bonhoeffer family, despite rationing, still had the traditional German Christmas dinner of carp, and equally probable that the family—and Eberhard—were forced to rub shoulders with pagan elements introduced into the holiday season, including Christmas trees topped with swastikas, pictures of a Santa Claus renamed "Solstice man," and Christmas cookies baked in the shape of the sig rune, the double lightning bolt worn by SS officers. The most devoted Nazis eschewed Christmas in favor of what was called the Julfest or Yule holiday, a celebration of the winter solstice. The Julfest celebrated the rebirth of the sun, identified with the swastika, the symbol of the rising German Reich.[13] The National Socialists even changed the words of traditional Christmas carols to expunge Christian references. The "Silent Night" lyrics became: "Silent night, Holy night, All is calm, all is bright. Only the Chancellor stays on guard, Germany's future to watch and to ward, Guiding our nation aright."[14]

In January, back in Sigurdshof with the seminarians, Dietrich wrote in a birthday note to Karl-Friedrich that they were "almost entirely cut off from the town," presumably due to the weather.[15] The coldest winter in a century paralyzed central Europe. Frozen rivers from the Danube to the Spree meant coal barges couldn't make deliveries, leading to widespread shortages. In Berlin, people sat inside in coats, gloves, and scarves. Journalists dipped frozen fingers into bowls of warm water and kept typing. Schools closed early to conserve coal, and churches were ordered to relinquish their fuel supplies and function without heat.[16]

For the far-away seminarians, the fuel shortages meant the group huddled in one room. They relied on candles rather than kerosene during the long January nights. Studying was difficult under those conditions, so

---

12. Bonhoeffer, *DBWE 15*, 291.
13. Paterson, "How the Nazis Stole Christmas."
14. Moorhouse, *Berlin at War*, 54.
15. Bonhoeffer, *DBWE 15*, 291.
16. Moorhouse *Berlin at War*, 76.

the community spent evenings playing games or reading aloud.[17] But for all the privations, Dietrich would write to his parents of his enjoyment of his remote life: "Yesterday afternoon I could not keep myself from going out right away with the skis and through the snowy woods. It was utterly beautiful, such a quiet peace, so that everything else seems uncanny. Indeed, I feel more and more that living in the countryside, particularly in times like these, is much more humanely decent than in the city. All the mass effects simply fall away here." [18]

This inner emigration, the sensation of being sealed in a snowy globe in a time and place far from the realities of Germany at war, in a community with his beloved Eberhard, created a paradise for Dietrich in this last season of seminary life.

17. Bonhoeffer, *DBWE 15*, 291.
18. Ibid., 293.

34

Winter, War, Wonder, Woe

If Sigurdshof, with its heavy snows, candlelight readings, and wild boars roaming the forests was a step back into another time, when he traveled home Bonhoeffer encountered a nighttime Berlin hushed by blackouts. As one observer described it:

> Berlin was a no-city city out there in the black. I . . . heard guttural little scraps of conversation drifting up to me, and saw the lighted ends of cigarettes bobbing along the black sidewalk. Over there, where the beacon used to flash from the top of the radio tower, there was blackness. There were no lights from the apartment windows; Berlin was as though some giant had placed a thick blanket over it, to hide the light.[19]

In the fall, people had initially congregated in central areas of Berlin, giggling in the blackness, while the buses, their windows painted blue, "rocked along . . . like enormous sea monsters."[20] In a lyrical outburst, Carl Haensel called the blacked-out Berlin a "city of dreams," bathed in a darkness that inspired the imagination.[21] But as the first weeks passed, the darkness—and stillness, for the blackout led people to talk in whispers and hushed tones—became unnerving, and people began to stay home.

A war decree, widely ignored, forbade listening to foreign broadcasts.

By 1940, Dietrich and Eberhard's relationship had fallen back into its old, companionable pattern. In February, Dietrich's application to become a military chaplain failed, despite all of Paula's connections, because chaplaincy was allowed only to veterans who had seen active combat in World War I, a rule strictly enforced even amid widespread corruption. Thus, with doors closing, Dietrich drew closer into anti-Hitler conspiracy.

19. Moorhouse, *Berlin at War*, 35.
20. Ibid., 37.
21. Ibid., 36.

Hans von Dohnanyi, who remained Dietrich's friend as well as brother-in-law, joined forces with the powerful—and to Shirer, strange—Admiral Wilhelm Canaris, the shaggy eyebrowed, devotedly Christian head of military intelligence. Canaris reported directly to Hitler, but had long been involved with plotting to overthrow the government. Bethge contends that von Dohnanyi, who had been pulled into the Abwehr or military intelligence unit in November 1937,[1] had confided in Dietrich about the conspiracy in the spring of 1938.[2] At that point, "the use of camouflage became a moral duty" according to Bethge, but Dietrich's involvement may well have still been largely passive.

Now, with the war in motion, Canaris's military intelligence office could help exempt Bonhoeffer from the draft, pretending he was needed, because of his extensive foreign connections, as a spy for the Reich. In reality he would travel abroad in counterespionage missions to communicate information about the resistance to high-ranking members of opposing governments, especially the British, still the all-important superpower in German eyes.

In early February, Dietrich managed to send a short birthday letter to Sabine despite the war, presumably via Switzerland, mentioning the cold and the snow, noting that at Sachsenhausen, where Niemöller was imprisoned, inmates had "one (or two) petroleum stoves, nothing else."[3] Dietrich wrote, optimistically, that he hoped he and Sabine could be reunited by the next year.

Eberhard's new brother-in-law, Fritz Onnasch, a seminarian who had married Eberhard's sister Margret in September, sent Dietrich birthday greetings. He wished he could share Dietrich's birthday at Sigurdshof "by the burning fireplace or in the forester's cottage with its dark oak-beamed ceiling."[4] Instead, he and his new wife visited "Aunt Ruth" in Stettin, where Ruth had gone to escape the harsh weather at Klein Krössin. February continued freezing, with snows so heavy that the seminarians had to travel by sled when they were not huddled around the tiled stove. At the end of the month, Dietrich wrote to his parents, asking Paula to buy a supply of soap on Eberhard's ration card and inquiring about Sabine. A few days later, he wrote back, having been in touch with Paula. "Above all," he wrote, "I was

---

1. Stern and Sifton, *No Ordinary Men*, 72.

2. Dramm, *Dietrich Bonhoeffer and the Resistance*, 14. Sabine expected a coup in the fall of 1938, so the conspiracy could not have been a mystery to the family.

3. Bonhoeffer, *DBWE 15*, 295.

4. Ibid., 294.

happy to hear that Sabine is indeed so fit and healthy."[5] He also considered buying his niece Renate a book of twelve wood engravings of Dürer's *The Passion* for her confirmation, though it's also possible the many mentions of art books comprised a code—even that the family was still smuggling money to the Leibholzes via Switzerland.[6]

The Nazis had begun food and soap rationing nervously in late August, fearing it would necessarily bring back memories of hunger and starvation from the last war, as well as reminders of the unrest in 1918.[7] Rather than demand sacrifices, the regime allotted the average German 2,400 calories a day, including two and half loaves of bread a week, about a pound of meat and generous supplies of sugar, fat, and jam. With their typical sting, the Nazis allowed the Jews much less. The government also restricted the Jews to shopping only in the late afternoon, when most of the stores had been emptied.

In March, Ruth heard the rumor running through Stettin that the city's Jews had been rounded up, put into boxcars and shipped to Poland.[8] No false report, this first transport of German Jews had occurred the night of February 12–13, when Nazis roused about 1,300 from their beds, allowed each to bring a suitcase, a watch, and a wedding ring, and took them by train to the Lublin area of Poland. Although this event received heavy press coverage outside of the Reich, ordinary Germans, forbidden international newspapers, relied on hearsay. The deported Stettin Jews included children, the sick, and the elderly. Once dumped from the train into Poland, a forced march to Lublin followed in the unusual cold, through almost two feet of snow. Not surprisingly, at least seventy people died.[9] Eventually, most of the rest would also perish, either through brutal living conditions or in death camps. When Berlin pastor Heinrich Gruber protested the deportation, the result was arrest and time in a concentration camp, a fate unlikely to be forgotten by other pastors contemplating dissent.[10]

In his correspondence with Sabine and Gert, Dietrich continued to dwell on the weather which provided the privacy he craved: "In recent weeks I have lived totally secluded in my little forest cottage, could only reach the next village with snowshoes, without train, auto, or telephone connections.

5. Ibid., 297–98.
6. Ibid., 298.
7. Speer, *Inside the Third Reich*, 214.
8. Pejsa, *Matriarch of Conspiracy*, 252.
9. Magid, "Lubin, Poland."
10. Bethge, *DB: A Biography*, 688.

It was quite wonderful," he wrote. "Even up to today there is deep snow here. But it will not last much longer. I thought of you all again and again during the cold here."[11] The letter also picked up a conversation from the previous July, when Dietrich had been with them in London, about "the laws of creation," still on his mind as a puzzle. While God's law could not be abandoned—such would be "enthusiasm"—Dietrich nevertheless mused that "the ultimate meaning of all law on earth is to guarantee the possibility of love in the sense of Christianity,"[12] a love both antithetical to and yet, paradoxically, dependent on biblical law. The mandates, including marriage, must not be over-historicized.

Eberhard, sitting beside Dietrich as he wrote by candlelight in the dim cottage, added a cheerful but concerned note to Sabine in the margin, indicating, if cryptically, how much Dietrich worried about a possible invasion of England: "One year ago we were constantly together! It is difficult now to imagine your new living conditions [since the Leibholzes had moved to St. Leonards-on-Sea]. And that is truly a shame. Our thoughts of you over there lack some of the capacity to imagine details, but they are now especially intensely with you and preoccupied with everything that affects you."[13]

The Sigurdshof pastorate session ended in March and the pastorate dissolved.[14] Never again would Dietrich experience the way of life he loved best: living with and directing a group of seminarians with Eberhard at his side. Dietrich and Eberhard now based themselves in Berlin from April through August. But forced separation would follow when Dietrich made a fateful blunder in East Prussia during the summer months.[15]

---

11. Bonhoeffer, *DBWE 15*, 300.
12. Ibid.
13. Ibid., 302.
14. Bethge, *DB: A Biography*, 695.
15. Ibid., 686.

35

Gert Gone

DURING THE SPRING OF 1940, Berliners celebrated war victories, yet goods stayed in short supply. Karen Blixen (also known as Isak Dinesen), the author of *Out of Africa*, visited Berlin for a month, and found the city lackluster. With "no flying footsteps, no flags a thousandfold. . . . I can only say now the city is now a sorry picture . . . monotonous, like despair itself." Dirty snow filled the streets. People wore last year's fashions resignedly: "if I have seen no rags, I have seen no elegance," Blixen wrote. Even at the posh Hotel Adlon everyone looked lost. "Humor itself" had become "anathema" and propaganda reigned: "it generates something like an obsession; it seems a kind of magic." Nazi officials took Blixen to tour the filming of *Jud Suss*, perhaps the most notorious of German anti-Semitic propaganda films. Even the fakery in a more benign film being shot, about Mary Queen of Scots, shown "in a carriage with a curtain of painted cardboard through a pile of sand which represents the moors . . ." seemed a metaphor for the Nazi sham. "Here," Blixen wrote, "I see with my own eyes Dante's hell on earth."[1]

Dietrich and Eberhard settled into the attic bedroom at the Marienberger Allee, spending long hours together there after dinner, smoking, making music, and talking. As in the fall, the theaters performed a full repertoire including Shakespeare, Shaw, and Ibsen, designed to boost morale, while the paintings adorning the oversized new government buildings showed endless depictions of idealized Germans, the men with their hands on the plough or the sword, the blonde, blue-eyed young mothers buoyant. This raised Blixen's ire: "These are the people seen through the eyes of the middle class, or rather, they are the wish and the dream of the middle class: how people should be."[2] Germans, though not Jews, who were forbidden access, strolled in the snow-covered Tiergarten, "soldiers with booted girls on their arms," families with young children.

1. Lubrich, *Travels in the Reich*, 227–32.
2. Cited in ibid., 232.

Crowds window shopped, almost the only kind of shopping still available, while Party members stood on street corners, shaking their small red boxes, collecting for the Winter Relief Fund, supposedly to aid the poor, the funds widely believed to support wild SS parties. Crowds jammed the buses, subways, and trolleys. The parades and marching formations of years past might have gone, but streams of soldiers in trucks and tanks rolled by, filling roads en route to elsewhere in this hub of an empire. Soldiers also arrived in Berlin for rest and recreation, taking sightseeing tours in horse-drawn, ten-seat carriages and indulging in the night life.[3]

Gas rationing meant more horse-drawn vehicles in Berlin, as well as tiny cars run on motorcycle engines. Only the privileged were allowed full-sized autos. This included Karl Bonhoeffer, whose well-equipped Mercedes stayed in operation because he was a psychiatrist. Ordinary Germans could use a car only under strictly regimented circumstances, and only the old, the ill, the disabled, and those returning from travel with masses of luggage could take taxis. Cars that ran on wood became one response to the gas shortage. People attached a woodburning stove to the car itself or put one on a small trailer behind it and fed in the wood "gas" by hand. Wood gas became so popular that 200 filling stations for it sprang up in and around Berlin.[4]

Moods swung wildly in Germany that spring. Enthusiasm in Germany grew when the army defeated the Norwegians, who had been supported by British and French troops. The enemy seemed simply to crumble. Although in hindsight we know England was ready to step from the center of the world stage, to most Germans, it was still the mighty power. William Shirer wrote that "it would be hard to exaggerate the feeling of triumph in the Third Reich . . . . As they see it, Germany has at last met the great British Empire in a straight fight and won hands down."[5]

Sabine, with her love of the seashore, had been delighted to move from London to St. Leonards, a town built in the nineteenth century as a charming resort on England's east coast, facing Germany. Even in the winter, the Leibholz family could sit out by the pebble beach on benches protected from the winds by "glass panels."[6]

On May 14, the family heard a rap at the door. A police officer stood before them. Gert must come with him to a refugee camp, because he was a German. No, the officer did not know where Gert was going. The girls cried.

3. Ibid., 244–45.
4. Ibid., 245–46.
5. Moorhouse, *Berlin at War*, 58–59.
6. Leibholz, *The Bonhoeffers*, 116.

Christiane made piles of sandwiches for her father, which he packed in his suitcase with other food.

Sabine's "heart was heavy." Gert was shaken and startled that he, a Jewish refugee, would be considered a security risk by the English. Both he and Sabine feared that in the all-too-likely event of a German invasion the SS would take control of the refugee camp, a frightening prospect for a Jew.[7] Now, as in Zurich in the fall of 1938, Sabine lost her heart for the beauty around her.

The days passed. Sabine heard nothing of Gert, who was not allowed to write letters. Anxious and alone, she kept bags packed for herself and her daughters in case they too were interned. She heard rumors that the English planned to deport the Germans to Canada and Australia. With the waves lapping against the pebbled shore, Sabine watched as the English tried to make the expected invasion more difficult by taking down the piers around St. Leonards, piers opened with fanfare and hullabaloo in the flush days of 1891.

The worried Mr. Griffiths, the vicar who Bell had put in charge of the German refugees in St. Leonards, visited Sabine repeatedly after Gert was taken, urging her to leave. He told her she would be shot when Germans landed. She refused, afraid that Gert would unable to find the family if she fled St. Leonards. In the meantime, Christiane, who had suffered taunts in Nazi schools for being Jewish, was now, ironically, persecuted for her long German-style braids: "You are Hitler's daughter!" some of her schoolmates told her. Sabine cut her hair.[8] When Sabine, following the German custom, hung some newly washed bedding out of the window to dry on a warm, sunny day a neighbor accused her of giving secret signals to the German navy. When Sabine scrubbed her clothes on the roof garden of the apartment building, she was again suspected of communicating with the enemy.[9]

After ten days, Sabine received a letter from Gert. He had been taken to the Huyton refugee camp in Liverpool, where conditions were rough and food scarce. The sandwiches and other food the girls had packed for him had been a godsend. To add to the misery, inmates were not allowed to read newspapers and initially not allowed to send or receive mail. Further, Nazis and Jews were thrown together willy-nilly, leading to violence.

7. Ibid., 118.
8. Ibid., 119.
9. Ibid., 120.

While in the autumn of 1939, only those deemed dangerous had been interned, by the spring of 1940, all male German and Austrian refugees aged sixteen to seventy, and some women and children, were sent to camps.[10]

Once she had received a letter and had an address for Gert, Sabine felt she could move the family to a safer location. She headed to Devon, where an elderly Mrs. Wilkinson had invited a group of German refugees to her home in Willand with its large garden. The girls promised not to speak a word of German during the entire daylong trip to Devon. They kept their word, and the journey took place without incident.

Mrs. Wilkinson had a beautiful house and Sabine enjoyed the romantic countryside with its thatched and whitewashed cottages, the front yards blooming with an array of brightly colored flowers.[11] She was again near the ocean, but this time facing west, on the other side of Britain from Germany. The days were warm and balmy, the beautiful trees like a romantic painting—but how different their circumstances from the year before when Dietrich had visited.

Sabine and her daughters, with their fourteen trunks of belongings, had only one bedroom in the refugee-filled house. Their room held a double bed for Sabine to share with Marianne, and a single bed for Christiane. Sabine felt the huge comedown. "I was glad," Sabine wrote, "my mother could not see the cramped quarters in which we had to live."[12]

Troubles continued for Sabine. After the German occupation of Holland, Sabine's brother-in-law Hans Leibholz and his wife, an "Aryan" like Sabine, committed suicide. Sabine had known them well, for Hans's work had sent him frequently to London. The shock was profound.[13]

Sabine, distressed by the Germans coming ever closer to England, found heart in Churchill's "blood, sweat, toil and tears" speech, promising the English would resist the Germans to the last person.

Dietrich's fears for Sabine spiked during the Dunkirk evacuation that moved the trapped British army from France. He delayed his visit to East Prussia, where he would be cut off from the outside world, so he could follow the news on the now-illegal BBC. Meanwhile, Ruth felt bruised by the effects of Dietrich's increased absences from Stettin. With no seminary left, he had fewer reasons to visit. During his briefer trips, she found him preoccupied.

10. Ibid., 118.
11. Ibid., 122.
12. Ibid., 121.
13. Ibid., 96.

She missed the days when nearby Finkenwalde had animated her, when the Confessing Church's opposition to the regime could still inspire hope, when her apartment was the center of optimistic strategy sessions. She wished the cheerful, high-energy seminarians still came to call, treating her as their aunt or mother. Even her grandchildren had outgrown her now defunct Stettin "boarding school," adding ever more quiet to her life.[14]

Lonelier than before and worried about her many friends and relatives in the army, Ruth poured out her "frustrations and sadness" in letters to Eberhard, who unlike Dietrich, continued faithfully to respond to her.[15] As time passed, Eberhard and Ruth, both already drawn together in orbit around Dietrich, would enter into a conspiracy of their own to secure their positions in the Bonhoeffer circle.

Not one to wallow in self-pity, Ruth reached out to Dietrich's family, inviting the von Dohnanyi children, Bärbel and Klaus, to stay with her in July at Klein Krössin. In a letter addressed to both Dietrich and Eberhard, Ruth wrote of her gratitude and relief that Alla Stahlberg, the grandson who had helped save Dietrich's Finkenwalde piano from the SS, escaped death in battle, of rereading Barth's article, "The Christian as Witness," with "great joy," and of her pain at the many war deaths among those she knew. She looked forward to the arrival of the von Dohnanyi children, "to their exuberance, and to the possibility of new connections to your family."[16]

---

14. Pejsa, *Matriarch of Conspiracy*, 243.
15. Ibid., 256.
16. Bonhoeffer, *DBWE 16*, 59.

— 36 —
Darker Hours

On June 17, Dietrich and Eberhard sat drinking coffee in an outdoor café by the Baltic when the loudspeaker, crackling with trumpet fanfare, announced France had fallen. A frenzy broke out, people cheering and climbing on chairs to sing the national anthem and other patriotic songs. The wild burst of jubilation culminated in arms raised in the Nazi salute amid repeated, rhythmic shouts of "*Sieg heil.*" Eberhard sat silent, shocked and unhappy. Dietrich jumped to his feet with the others. He hauled Eberhard up, whispering, "Raise your arm! Are you crazy?" Dietrich heiled vigorously, saying to Eberhard, "We shall now be running risks for more important things, but not for this salute!"[1] As described in Olivia Manning's *Balkan Trilogy*, German newsreels exulted at the victory:

> Out of the smoke of some lost city appeared the German tanks. They followed each other in an endless stream into the sunlight, driving down from Ypres and Ostend. A signboard said: Lille – 5 kilomètres. There seemed to be no resistance. The Maginot Line was being skirted. The break-through had been so simple, it was like a joke. And the fair-haired young men standing up in their tanks came unscathed and laughing from the ruins. They held their faces up to the sun. They sang: "What does it matter if we destroy the world? When it is ours, we'll build it up again." The tanks, made monstrous by the camera's tilt, passed in thousands—or, so it seemed. The audience—an audience that still thought in terms of cavalry—sat watching, motionless, in silence. This might of armour was a new thing; a fearful and merciless thing. The golden boys changed their song. Now, as the vast procession passed, they sang: "We do not want to be Christians, because Christ was a Jew pig. And his mother, what a travesty...."[2]

1. Pejsa, *Matriarch of Conspiracy*, 255.
2. Manning, *Fortunes of War*, 248.

In England, Sabine and the rest of the country greeted the fall of France with a stunned silence. Suddenly, the island country was alone. Sabine thought her host Mrs. Wilkinson was about to have a stroke as they heard the news over the radio in her sitting room: "she went dark red right to the roots of her hair." But like most of the English, Mrs. Wilkinson clung tenaciously to the idea that England would defeat the enemy.[3]

Meanwhile, Dietrich wrote to his parents from Königsberg, alluding to France's fall (and thus to Sabine's fate), that "behind everything we see, other experiences loom that fill our thoughts unceasingly, even into our dreams."[4] He also noted a strange and "delightful" coincidence: he was staying in his parents' old house, where Christel had been born.[5]

By the summer, the return of the victorious German troops, the parades, the ringing bells, the blaring loudspeaker announcements, and the buildings draped in seas of swastika flags built up a renewed martial din in the capital. Many were ecstatic.[6]

When an infantry division returned to Berlin from France, people went wild, "weeping and laughing from pure, spontaneous joy," as the troops, showered in confetti, paraded along the broad Unter den Linden, which was draped in red, black, and white swastika banners "forty yards long and ten feet broad." The joy was not in the triumph, according to one observer, but in the hope that the war was almost over. In "every happy heart lived the belief that this was the end of it all." The English, people said, would soon see reason and negotiate an end to the conflict. Peace would reign.[7]

On July 3, 1,100 Germans who had been interned in England found themselves on the *Arandora Star* to begin a journey to Canada. A German submarine torpedoed the ship, killing 600 passengers. Although Gert had assured Sabine he would do all her could to stay in England, she didn't know for certain whether he was on or off the vessel.

Soon after, Sabine moved to Oxford, arriving at Mrs. Harrison's boarding house with her daughters and her fourteen trunks. Again, Sabine and the girls shared a single room.

At this point, she found Gert was indeed alive and well. Now he could correspond daily, and while the air raid siren went off often, Oxford was not

---

3. Leibholz, *The Bonhoeffers*, 123.

4. Bonhoeffer, *DBWE 16*, 60. The editors note (footnote 3) that this alludes to France, and the fall of France increased Dietrich's worries about Sabine.

5. Ibid.

6. Moorhouse, *Berlin at War*, 64.

7. Lubrich, ed., *Travels in the Reich*, 238.

bombed. On July 26, Sabine received a telegram from Gert: he would be in Oxford that evening. "I was overcome with joy," Sabine recalled. "I was so excited that my heart started to beat quite wildly, and I was really afraid I would not live through the afternoon." By mid-August Gert had recovered from his ordeal in the refugee camp, and the family had only more shock to endure: One night the many bells in Oxford began to ring at once, in a wild cacophony, the signal that the German invasion was beginning. "An icy fear fell on us," wrote Sabine, but it was a false alarm.[8]

In July, when Hitler himself returned triumphantly from France, Berlin again went wild: "Hitler . . . was driven to the Reich Chancellery on a carpet of flowers. According to press reports, the mile-long route from the Anhalter Station to the Chancellery was a perfumed avenue of greens, reds, blues and yellows flanked by cheering thousands who shouted and wept themselves into a frantic hysteria as the Führer passed."

Though the Nazis often stage-managed such events, the enthusiasm that day was almost certainly genuine. Indeed, throwing flowers at Hitler's convoy had been expressly forbidden, but the crowds ignored the instruction. The celebrations continued at the Reich Chancellery, where the massed ranks of Hitler Youth and German maidens filled the air with their "incessant . . . shrill cheering." Twice Hitler appeared on the balcony of the Chancellery to greet the enraptured crowds: "Caesar in his glory was never more turbulently received."[9]

In a meeting of the Old Prussian Council in July, Bonhoeffer appeared to capitulate to "the new reality" brought on by the fall of France.[10] In fact, he was simply changing tactics—or more accurately, doubling down on his policy since 1938 of increasingly working underground.

Meanwhile, the Dohnanyi children arrived at Klein Krösse in July as did two of Ruth's grandchildren also staying nearby—Maria von Wedenmeyer's younger siblings, Hans Werner and Christine. As Ruth watched the families together, ideas continued to form in the mind of this consummate matchmaker: "how the threads might be stretched to include her own family circle."[11] Eberhard, as conscious of the precariousness of his own situation as Dietrich was oblivious, also continued to ponder how to solidify his ties with the Bonhoeffers.

8. Leibholz, *The Bonhoeffers*, 128–30.
9. Moorhouse, *Berlin at War*, 61.
10. Bethge, *DB: A Biography*, 682–83.
11. Pejsa, *Matriarch of Conspiracy*, 257.

Dietrich awoke to exceptionally bad July weather, probably heavy rains, on the Saturday of a weekend Confessing Church retreat in Königsberg. Manfred Koschorke, a chaplain, had advertised the July 13 event and sent thirty invitations to likely participants.

Dietrich arrived at the Gut Blöstau manor house in time for the 3:30 coffee hour. Due to the foul weather, the turnout was light—only seven men, including Bonhoeffer and Koschorke, and a handful of wives.

A detailed Gestapo report offers a rare glimpse of a Confessing Church event. Over coffee, Dietrich criticized Nazi treatment of Polish prisoners, insisting that once prisoners had been disarmed, they ceased to be enemies and deserved humane treatment. He condemned Nazi harassment of a German nurse who had begged for kinder treatment of Polish prisoners.[12] He criticized the interrogation of two pastors for allowing Polish prisoners to attend a worship service.

Later, after a Bible study, Dietrich described the Nazi emphasis on work as at odds with Christianity. Farmers were forced to work all day on Sundays rather than attending worship services. Dietrich insisted that the state allow people time to practice their faith. He also called on the Confessing Church to seek out young people.

The next day, Sunday, Dietrich preached on a theme dear to him: only the Confessing Church followed the narrow way of salvation.[13] Some participants brought children, so a children's sermon addressed them. Afterwards, as Dietrich repeated his remarks about treating Polish prisoners humanely, the Gestapo burst in and broke up the meeting, which was illegal under new ordinances.

The Gestapo had no interest in the women, who were not counted or named, although they had participated in the discussions. They interrogated the men until two in the afternoon, but couldn't establish that they had spoken subversively or collected money, also an illegal activity.

Once the Gestapo had left, the group ate dinner and discussed ways to handle a Gestapo interrogation, such as the need to speak as ambiguously as possible.[14] Afterwards, the retreat moved to the estate of Baron Eberhard von Meerscheidt-Hüllessem, a Confessing Church supporter, where the participants sang hymns, had a discussion about death, and Dietrich again preached, contrasting the Christian notion of death as an evil to the National Socialist framing of death as heroic.

---

12. Bonhoeffer, *DBWE 16*, 65.
13. Ibid., 66.
14. Ibid., 67.

Unknown to anyone there, one of the retreat goers, a humanities professor named Bracks, was a Gestapo informant. In his report, Bracks wrote with a candor and a level of detail that Dietrich and his cohort dared not about their activities.

The Gestapo report did not "reproach" Bracks for his efforts, even though none of his damning allegations—the threat to state security in criticizing the Polish policy, the opposition to the Nazi conception of work, the taking of an offering—could be proven during the interrogation. Instead, Bracks was commended for not exposing his loyalties, thus increasing Confessing Church trust in him.

On July 16, two days after the Gestapo interrogation, Dietrich wrote his mother a seemingly cheerful, mundane letter from Königsberg, filled with chitchat: he was sending her some unused ration stamps, Eberhard was back in East Prussia, and the inevitable laundry was coming home. He had concerns that a bottle of hair lotion that came open in his suitcase had "once again ruined my jacket," possibly a coded message he'd been in trouble, and he offered news about staying with Ruth later in the month.[15]

Five days later, he again wrote Paula: he was coming to Berlin to talk to Hans, cancelling his plans to visit Ruth. Apparently, the Gestapo raid had shaken him sufficiently that he planned to discuss with his brother-in-law an assignment in military intelligence.[16] To the continuing irritation of the Gestapo head, Himmler, the Abwehr remained outside of Gestapo authority.

Bethge offers a slightly different version of events. In his account, Dietrich discovered that local residents were unnerved because they had seen Russian troops on the former Lithuanian frontier, near the Memel River, which then formed the border between Lithuania and easternmost Germany. As a result, Dietrich cancelled his visit to Ruth in order to discuss the matter with Dohnanyi in Berlin. Whatever the instigation—almost undoubtedly a combination of worry about the Gestapo intrusions and the realization that he had found a plausible reason to act as a spy in East Prussia (an opinion with which Dohnanyi concurred)—early August marks a definitive, traceable step toward Dietrich becoming an active participant in the resistance movement. At the end of August, he traveled to gather more information about what was occurring on the Lithuanian border, even though he was not yet formally a part of military intelligence.[17]

15. Ibid, 61.
16. Ibid., 68.
17. Bethge, *DB: A Biography*, 697–98. Interestingly, these reports of Soviet troops massing on the border lead credence to revisionist history that says the USSR was planning an attack on Germany.

On August 26, Dietrich wrote from Königsberg to Eberhard: "I think very much now of your birthday. I could not stand that you would receive nothing at all from me. So you will be receiving a package, and I hope you will find joy in it. It is the sixth birthday we will celebrate together, as it were—nearly a fifth of your life! That is something. I think back with gratitude on these past years and with confidence on those yet to come."[18]

On September 4, 1940, however, bad news arrived: Dietrich learned he was banned from any public speaking due to "subversive activities"—and learned he had to report his whereabouts to the police on a regular basis. The speaking ban was not fatal, but the requirement to report his whereabouts was, wrote Bethge, a "deadly blow . . . to be avoided at all costs." Dietrich protested and got no response.[19]

Dietrich's new restrictions, however, became Ruth's boon: Dietrich spent a month with her at Klein Krössin, working on his *Ethics*, waiting for Dohnanyi to return from Italy where he was formalizing plans for Dietrich's entry into military intelligence.[20]

For Ruth, it was the long, leisurely visit she had "been dreaming about for years, ever since she met her dear friend,"[21] the kind of visit, but longer, that Dietrich and Eberhard had made during Easter of 1936. She put Dietrich in the guest bedroom Hope, and to his intense gratification asked him to lead a daily Bible study for her household.[22]

Klein Krössin was ideally isolated and difficult to access, in the middle of a Junker estate where—in a country where class differences had hardly disappeared despite the National Socialist "revolution"—the Prussian aristocracy routinely snubbed the Nazis.[23] This isolation allowed Dietrich the luxury of listening unimpeded to banned BBC broadcasts about the bombing of Britain in a comfortable cottage with fat geese wandering in and out of the kitchen. Dietrich continued to worry about Sabine and her family. Dohnanyi had told him of the planned invasion of England, code named Operation Sea Lion.

The long visit also gave Dietrich the opportunity to meet with men in Ruth's circle, such as Ewald von Kleist, who were part of the resistance.[24] Surely Sabine and Gert's fate added urgency to Dietrich's hopes for an over-

18. Bonhoeffer, *DBWE 16*, 72.
19. Bethge, *DB: A Biography*, 697–98.
20. Ibid., 700.
21. Pejsa, *Matriarch of Conspiracy*, 258.
22. Bethge, *DB: A Biography*, 697.
23. Pejsa, *Matriarch of Conspiracy*, 259.
24. Ibid., 258.

throw before disaster fell. On October 9, near the end of his stay, he wrote to Eberhard in Berlin. Sabine was much on his mind, but he rejoiced in Klein Krössin's rhythm of work and worship, the daily prayer and exegesis, a world that spared him the "spiritual, physical and mental hardships resulting from disorder."[25]

He meant Sabine when he referred to "a rough autumn storm" that left him "quite depressed," the storm an allusion to German bombing raids over England preparatory to invasion.[26] He continued with musings deeply revelatory: "My thoughts travel often to Sabine and to you these days. I feel a remarkable sense of closeness to each of you, in contrast to my thoughts of other people."[27]

Sabine and Eberhard, the two closest to his heart. A year before he had made a choice and had picked life with Eberhard over saving Sabine from a possible Nazi invasion of England. The decision, as he alluded, haunted his dreams. He wrote of it stiffly: "When one has the feelings that others expect something of him and one has fulfilled these expectations so poorly, then an awareness of guilt lodges in one's memory, as well as a simultaneous longing for forgiveness and for being able to help again."[28] But then he brushed away those cobwebs. He anticipated receiving a "chest and five boxes" of Eberhard's. "We can ... unpack them together. How are you doing financially? And in the air raid shelter?"[29]

---

25. Bonhoeffer, *DBWE 16*, 78.

26. Ibid., 78. In *DB: A Biography*, Bethge suggests that Dietrich uses the same storm phraseology to refer to the Battle of Britain in an August 10, 1940 letter to his parents (1001).

27. Bonhoeffer, *DBWE 16*, 78.

28. Ibid., 78–79.

29. Ibid., 79.

— 37 —

Exile in Ettal

Dietrich's question to Eberhard about the air raid shelter, if wry, was not casual. By fall, 1940, British bombings had begun over Berlin. On August 28, bombers for the first time killed civilians in the city.[1] When more raids followed, Hitler's outrage in a speech in early September expressed his typical mind-set: "Should the Royal Air Force drop two thousand, or three thousand, or four thousand kilograms of bombs, then we will now drop 150,000; 180,000; 230,000; 300,000; 400,000; yes one million kilograms in a single night. And should they declare they will greatly increase their attacks on our cities, then we will erase their cities!"[2]

In September 1940 the British bombed Berlin nineteen times. On October 7, two days before Dietrich's question to Eberhard about air raids, the British had attacked so early—shortly after 10 pm—that people were out on the streets, caught by surprise.[3]

Meanwhile, Dietrich spent the four-week period at Ruth's pondering his future. Having blundered so badly with the Königsberg retreat, he needed now to keep a low profile, but his past left a dangerous trail—more dangerous than he knew. By the end of his stay, he had finally decided to actively join the Abwehr as a double agent.

While Dietrich and Ruth's upper-class cohorts plotted yet another coup, Hitler's popularity surged. By 1940, Hitler had reduced unemployment, built the autobahn, restored order to Germany, and offered support to traditional families. After the deprivations of World War I and the economic shocks of the Weimar years, life had stabilized for the average German. This occurred despite a fascist state where the government and the industrialists worked together to suppress wages, an employee could not quit a job without a boss's approval, and surveillance was ever present. Now, with the

1. Moorhouse, *Berlin at War*, 140.
2. Ibid., 140–41.
3. Ibid., 143.

expansion of the German empire into the Ruhr, Austria, and Czechoslovakia, and the victories across Europe, many hailed Hitler as a miracle worker.

Dietrich's decision to participate in a resistance focused on assassination was all the more daring given Hitler's increasingly messianic status. Bonhoeffer would not be part of killing a mere political leader, but, in the eyes of many, Germany's spiritual savior. As one German remembered, "The Führer was . . . an idol that was emulated and served."[4] One woman, seeing Hitler in an open car, responded to his (to her) good looks: "He had beautiful blue eyes, like an Enzian (a flower) and was suntanned." Another woman's daughter remembered her mother walking in Berlin and suddenly finding herself close to Hitler's motorcade: "She . . . raised her hand . . . He nodded to her and waved." Then the SS pushed the mother away. The daughter—albeit telling the story from a postwar perspective—recalled her mother "feeling strangely" in Hitler's presence and later saying, "That man is extremely dangerous. He has eyes that you can say father to. But what's behind those eyes?"[5]

Why would an avowed pacifist get involved in a plot to kill? Dietrich himself struggled with that decision. He had been severely disappointed in the Confessing Church's tepid challenge to Nazism. He rejected Kantian moral absolutes and decided that his own moral purity meant less than helping to bring down the regime.

Dietrich did not flinch from the possibility that in plotting assassination he was participating in a sin. Yet, frustrated by the many Christians he encountered who felt their Christian ethics had nothing to do with politics, or who believed that they could maintain personal salvation through churchgoing, confession, and communion while closing their eyes to the injustices all around them, he saw little alternative but to take action. He was part of the elite in the country, to whom much had been given and from whom much was expected: who but he and his cohort should shoulder the responsibility of challenging Hitler? Should they not, in Luther's formulation, sin boldly? Finally, the double threats of conscription and possible arrest by the Gestapo hovered close.

Dietrich's sister-in-law, Klaus's wife Emmi Delbrück Bonhoeffer, supplied a rationale for the family's logic in supporting a coup, couching it in a story: While standing in a line to buy vegetables, she mentioned to a friend some Nazi atrocities she'd heard about. The saleslady in the store overheard her and said loudly, "Frau B, if you don't stop spreading such horror stories, you'll end up in a concentration camp too, and then no one can help you."

---

4. Johnson and Reuband, *What We Knew,* 338.
5. Ibid., 339.

Emmi came home and told her husband what had happened. He was upset: "'You are completely mad. Please understand that a dictatorship is a snake. You step on its tail, it bites you on the leg. You have to crush its head. . . . Only the military can do that.'"[6]

For Dietrich, according to Bethge, the decisive moment had been the fall of France. As Confessing Church friend Wilhelm Rott would write, "The belief of many of our circle that the clash of weapons would bring catastrophe on the regime had been shattered. We would have to adjust ourselves to Hitler's rule, at any rate for a long time."[7] The next impetus to action came in the form of the travel restrictions on Bonhoeffer. And behind it all, possibly even more real, was the growing "storm" swirling over Sabine, and the "longing . . . to be able to help again."

In the fall of 1940, no longer a *"Stiftsfraulein"* or "convent-girl" in an ankle-length skirt at the Magdalen-Stift, Maria entered Elisabeth von Thadden's Wieblingen School. The school, normally in Heidelberg, had been moved to Tutzing in Bavaria because authorities had decided it was too close to the Maginot Line.

Von Thadden, the school's founder, was formidable, courageous, and uncompromising. When her mother died, this nineteen-year-old, the oldest child, managed the family estate and took care of her younger siblings for eleven years. When her father remarried in 1920, to a woman five years younger than Elisabeth, the thirty-year-old left for Berlin to study education. The Weimar Republic granted enterprising women unprecedented opportunities, and Elisabeth studied progressive education.

In 1926, the chance came to lease the empty castle Wieblingen near Heidelberg. With an inheritance in hand, von Thadden leapt at the opportunity, quickly getting the licensing necessary, and opening the school's doors in 1927 to a class of thirteen girls. The stucco structure, with its green-shuttered windows and orange-tiled roof, housed and schooled the students in the same building, which overlooked a cobblestone courtyard surrounded by a high wall.

Von Thadden offered the "best and brightest"[8] girls the same quality of education as upper-class boys. She did so while grounding her progressive educational methods in Christian ethics. She aimed to train her students

---

6. Barnett, *For the Soul of the People*, 182. This echoes testimony at the Nuremberg trials, where some insisted that only a military coup could have dislodged Hitler.

7. Bethge, *DB: A Biography*, 683.

8. Pejsa, *Matriarch of Conspiracy*, 281.

to think for themselves, behave with compassionate morality, and become emancipated women, all goals anathema to National Socialist aims.

Photos show the middle-aged and unmarried von Thadden with her dark, wavy hair either pulled severely back into a bun hidden behind her head—or cut as short as a man's. The hairline recedes and von Thadden wears a man's dress shirt with a pointy collar and a silk tie. Only her eyes, visionary and far away, show any softness.

The von Wedemeyers and von Kleists had as little interest as the Bonhoeffers in creating "emancipated" daughters. Neither Maria nor her older sister Ruth Alice had any expectation of stepping out of traditional gender roles. As far the Junker families were concerned, a woman's role as wife and mother was a settled affair. However, the attraction of the school would have been immense: von Thadden was a Prussian aristocrat and a strong Protestant with ties to the Confessing Church. More compelling to families that dreaded the influence of Nazism on their children, von Thadden despised National Socialism and even as late as 1940, when sixteen-year-old Maria arrived, was outspoken in her disdain.

Students noted the contemptuous way von Thadden would adopt the Nazi "heil Hitler" salute, raising her arm and then flicking her wrist limply, as if shooing away a fly. Despite pressure, she enrolled Jewish students, and even, on occasion, helped them with tuition, presumably a response to their parents' loss of ability to work.

Around the time Maria arrived, drama erupted when a student denounced von Thadden to the Gestapo. Authorities threatened to close the school for its failure to hang a portrait of Hitler, as well as for reading the psalms—considered Jewish—during worship services. At that point, von Thadden decided to take the school back to Wieblingen, where she hoped her good reputation would protect her.

Assertive, athletic, and academic, eager to please, and used to living away from home, Maria soon found her place as a leader at the school.

As the fall progressed, Dietrich made arrangements with the Confessing Church for a research and writing sabbatical, which freed him for working on his *Ethics* and making resistance contacts.

The leave of absence meant the Confessing Church—already severely financially strained—cut his salary. Dietrich had been never good with money. As Bethge with his typical tact put it, "His inadequate talents for the essentials of bookkeeping caused considerable difficulties for the Council of Brethren [his employers] in their dealings with the tax authorities, and occasionally led to his having to answer further inquiries."[9]

The Gestapo focus on Bonhoeffer became so threatening that in November, Dohnanyi and others decided he'd be safest in Munich, away from his old haunts.[10] Dietrich's aunt, Countess "Ninne," offered him the use of her Munich home and address, so that he could register as a Munich resident—an address which offered the added protection of association with the aristocracy—and from there, he applied for "indispensable" (meaning draft exempt) status due to his intelligence work for the High Command of the Wehrmacht.[11]

When Dietrich arrived in Munich in November 1940, none of his military issues had been settled, but his time had been freed and the process of keeping him out of the army was in motion. From Munich, Dietrich moved near, and then into, the monastery of Ettal, Paula's idea,[12] to work on *Ethics*. Because of fears of attracting unwanted Gestapo attention, Dietrich for a time would stay fixed in this one place, highly unusual for him. As a result, he and Eberhard would have their longest separation to date. Eberhard would live in Berlin working for the Gossner Mission and traveling to east Prussia on Confessing Church business while Dietrich remained—sometimes impatiently—in Ettal. This separation led to frequent letters, a window into the relationship of this couple. As Eberhard would later write, "we put more into words this year."[13]

Ettal had been founded by the Benedictines in 1330. The original Gothic double abbey that had consisted of separate of communities of men and women, as well as a house for Teutonic Knights, had burned down in 1744. The marble edifice Dietrich encountered, rebuilt in a Baroque Italianate style, could be considered incongruous in an Alpine valley surrounding by mountain peaks, near a quaint German town of stucco and gables. This newer abbey included a lavish white marble church with a curved front flanked by towers. The interior was filled with white and pink marble trimmed in gold, with a huge crystal chandelier suspended on a long chain from the top of the church's large dome. Clear glass in Palladian windows that formed a circle just below the painted dome let in floods of light that spilled on

---

9. Bethge, *DB: A Biography*, 701.

10. Ibid., 700.

11. Ibid., 700–701.

12. Bonhoeffer, *DBWE 16*, 97: "Ettal was actually your idea, dear Mama. I have not forgotten that."

13. Ibid., 143.

the brilliant white marble, gold ornaments, and extravagantly gold-framed paintings adorning the church's walls. Marble statues of patrons, accented with gold, stood in niches or on pedestals flanking huge paintings, while the marble and gold pulpit was ornately carved and decorated with twisting figures. The setting overflowed with opulence, displaying earthly splendors meant to conjure the vast riches of heaven.

Dietrich stayed—at least for a time—at the Hotel Ludwig der Bayer, facing the monastery, a typical stucco rustic German building with shutters and cozy attic bedrooms.

At Ettal, Dietrich was a guest of the Abbot, Angelus Kupfer. This exile put him in contact with Roman Catholics resisting the regime, including priest Rupert Mayer, who the Nazis "kept at" the abbey from 1939–45 to stop his anti-Nazi preaching.

These Catholics, together with his contacts with Ruth's Junker aristocrats in the resistance, pulled Dietrich in a politically conservative direction.[14] Although he had once supported Weimar's democratic republic and even been called a socialist, Dietrich increasingly fell under the influence of people who interpreted the experiment in German democracy as a disaster. These (mostly) men, rooted in a nineteenth-century ethos, looked back to the glory years of the pre-World War I German Empire and saw a hereditary king at the helm. An intellectual voice for the resisters, Bonhoeffer now began to articulate a rationale for an at least temporary return to monarchy in the post-Hitlerean world.

In mid-November, as Dietrich settled into Ettal, he wrote to Eberhard: "I eat in the refectory, sleep in the hotel, use the library, have my own key to the cloister, and yesterday had a good and long talk with the Abbot. In short I have everything that one could desire. The only things missing are a desk, and what in these nearly six years has become a matter of course, the exchange of my impressions with you.... Come in December!"[15]

Unlike during Dietrich's 1939 month in Manhattan, letters shot back and forth between the two, some touching on money, which Dietrich treated as theirs, not his own: "Guess what?' wrote Dietrich after his arrival in Munich. "In the side pocket of my briefcase I found two hundred marks. Shall we use it for our Christmas trip? Or shall I send you something very nice? Half of it is yours, in any case."[16] Dietrich, hoping to track down information on royalties from his books *Discipleship* and *Life Together*, asked Eberhard: "I found out I earned 764 RM in March and April 1939 (when we were away).

14. Bethge, *DB: A Biography*, 723.
15. Bonhoeffer, *DBWE 16*, 86.
16. Ibid., 82.

Do you remember if we ever received it? . . . Say, did we already give Mama the taxes for November?"[17] "Your mother," responded Eberhard, "thinks she remembers the 1939 money . . . . She also said you have quite a nice sum accumulated there."[18]

Christel brought her children to Ettal in late November to escape the Berlin air raids.[19] Such raids, once unthinkable, had become routine.[20] Nazi officials ordered children to be "sent to the countryside," an awkward way to avoid saying "evacuated."[21] Officials wanted children moved under the authority of the Hitler Youth, an idea clearly anathema to the Bonhoeffers. But enrolling the children in the monastery school under Dietrich's watchful eye was acceptable.[22]

Small details abound in the correspondence. Dietrich added a postscript to his November 23 letter to Eberhard regarding Vibrans's upcoming marriage, to take place on the eve of Vibrans's departure to the front: "I was very pleased and amazed at Gerhard's decision. Now of all times!"[23]

17. Ibid., 103.
18. Ibid., 116.
19. Ibid., 87.
20. Moorhouse, *Berlin at War,* 159.
21. Ibid., 186.
22. Bonhoeffer, *DBWE 16,* 93.
23. Ibid., 90.

— 38 —
The Foretaste of Paradise

PHILOSOPHER GEORGE SANTAYANA'S BEST-SELLING autobiographical novel, *The Last Puritan*, translated into German, would exercise a strong hold on Dietrich's imagination. Santayana, famous for noting that those who forget history are condemned to repeat it, called his surprise hit a "memoir in the form of the novel." By the time Eberhard wrote to Dietrich about it, Dietrich had already finished the book. "I have sometimes recognized myself in Oliver. Do you understand that?" Dietrich wrote of the book's protagonist.[1]

Dietrich's meaning here is cryptic, though the phrase "do you understand that?" (one Ruth uses as well) highlights a special emphasis. Like Dietrich, Oliver came from an upper-class background, and like Dietrich, he chose a peripatetic life. But more interestingly, Oliver's sexuality is ambiguous, and he enters into intense homoerotic friendships with two men. *The Last Puritan* includes a nude swimming scene between Oliver and the handsome, but socially inferior, Jim Darnley, who manages his father's yacht. Oliver is impressed with Jim: "What a chest, and what arms!" Darnley, we find, had been discharged from the English Navy for "immoral" behavior with other sailors.

Santayana probably had a same-sex orientation.[2] In letter a little later on, Dietrich would again mention the novel to Eberhard: "How far are you with Oliver?" he asked. Dietrich criticized Oliver for pouring himself out without being convinced of the meaning of what he was doing and thus missing the "authentic and utterly unique" path. "In regard to God and human beings, he never risks everything, and as a result he becomes lonely, even ridiculous. In its asperity it's a haunting book . . . . We will have to talk about it again sometime."[3] Later Zimmermann would run into Dietrich on

1. Bonhoeffer, *DBWE 16*, 128.
2. "George Santayana."
3. *DBWE 16*, 140.

the streets of Berlin, and the two would have an eager conversation about the book, initiated by Bonhoeffer.[4]

Early on, as he pondered his months away in Ettal, Dietrich fantasized about renting "a small apartment in the mountains" but decided it would be "very lonely." His thoughts instead roved to he and Eberhard reuniting: "How lovely it would be if there were something we could do together. Can you think of anything?"[5] He enjoyed Ettal's monastic rhythms: "I experience its regularity and silence as extremely beneficial to my work. It would certainly be a loss . . . if this communal life preserved for 1,500 years was lost, something those here consider entirely possible." Two days later he would write, "The ordered life is very good for me, and I am amazed at the extent to which in the seminary we did similar things quite on our own."[6]

Christmas presents were part of the entwined lives of the two men. Now, however, the war complicated the season. If in normal years, Germans gave each other clothing, candy, perfumes, and soap, rationing now made this almost impossible.[7] Like most Germans, Dietrich and Eberhard worked with what was available: Dietrich advised Eberhard not to worry unduly about presents for his parents, but instead to give them a book Dietrich had already purchased. "December 30 is Mama's birthday anyway. We can still find something for her together."[8] Dietrich thought "the flask . . . very nice for your [Eberhard's] mother," adding, "Didn't you want to send your mother a little picture?" He also wondered what to buy Eberhard's sister, Margret, and her husband. Later he decided a historical novel, *Adelheid*, "would be lovely [for them] . . . from both of us." Ruth posed a bigger problem: "I will have to look around in Munich some more," but "if necessary, simply a nice letter would do."[9] "Shall we perhaps give Hans [Dohnanyi] something together?"[10] He ended up presenting his father a thermometer, and his mother sugar, an item rationed and hard to find. Both gifts, he admitted, were "somewhat odd."[11] For Eberhard, a two-pound sausage came from Christel.[12] Dietrich,

---

4. Zimmermann and Smith, eds., *I Knew*, 189–90. From a twenty-first-century perspective, the novel reads as a period piece, because the story it tells and characters it describes seem, even if autobiographical, not real. Yet it struck a chord with Bonhoeffer, another indication that our frame is not his frame.

5. Bonhoeffer, *DBWE 16*, 83.

6. Ibid., 87, 89.

7. Moorhouse, *Berlin at War*, 55.

8. Bonhoeffer, *DBWE 16*, 104.

9. Ibid., 110.

10. Ibid., 95.

11. Ibid., 111.

12. Ibid., 110

however, did not buy gifts for his siblings, instead sending the money for gifts to the wives of seminarians at the front.

Perhaps the most anticipated Christmas present for Dietrich was Eberhard's visit, a subject Dietrich had raised from his first arrival at Ettal and continued to press: "As time goes on, there is so much to tell you and talk over with you that it is high time that we just meet." The house in Friedrichsbrunn called to him, and he repeatedly mentioned it. "My parents are staying in Berlin for Christmas.... But perhaps you and I could still go to the Harz anyway?" Anticipating Eberhard's likely objection that he would need to see his own mother: "Perhaps your mother could also come? Just an idea!?"[13] But in the end, Eberhard visited Ettal, and so anxious was Dietrich that his friend travel in comfort—and not renege on making the journey—that he had his parents send their chauffeur out early in the cold December of 1940[14] to stand in line for a sleeping berth ticket. It was to no avail: "Papa... informed me that it was impossible to get a sleeping car.... Even though the chauffeur was sent at 8:30 a.m. the first possible day, people were already standing in line; moreover, the military grabbed up a lot of the tickets, etc." Dietrich instead offered advice to make the eleven-hour train ride comfortable: bring books and a thermos of coffee. Trains were likely to be crowded, and after dark it could be difficult to read by the "dim, blue light" in the compartments.[15] But Dietrich was determined not to lose the visit under any circumstances, even if he had to take the risk of attracting Gestapo attention by moving: "if it all should become too much for you, then write to me, and I will meet you somewhere else."[16]

Eberhard did arrive, and the two hit the Alpine slopes to ski, something the ever-athletic Eberhard had been eager to do.[17] Having secured Eberhard "together as before,"[18] Dietrich's thoughts turned to Sabine in a Christmas letter to his parents: "This year we will again be thinking primarily of Sabine, Gert and the children... we regret that we can do so little. But I believe that when our hands are utterly tied something better is at work...."[19]

Apart after Christmas, the two men laced solicitous advice and musings to each other throughout the letters: "I saved a sausage for you....

---

13. Ibid., 99, 100.
14. "Winter 1940/41."
15. Lubrich, ed., *Travels in the Reich*, 216.
16. Bonhoeffer, *DBWE* 16, 105.
17. Ibid., 111.
18. Ibid., 101.
19. Ibid., 111.

You need to make sure you're eating well," Dietrich urged.[20] Using *incomparably*, a favorite word to describe the relationship, Dietrich wrote, "truly, how incomparably easy and pleasant our way has been even through these past years, in comparison with all that has weighed others down for years," calling the circumstances, even in the midst of war, "the very foretaste of paradise."[21]

In his circular letter to the Finkewalde brothers he also spoke to a double reality with which he struggled, perhaps excoriating himself more than anyone for his tendency to be living the good life—and offering some insight into how he viewed recent history. For him, neither the rise of Hitler nor the new outbreak of a new war but the start of war in 1914 had "shattered life."[22] The Nazi era simply intensified a process that had begun years before. The current war served "only as a newly sharpened clarification" of what Germany had been enduring for years. Like time-lapse photography, it compressed and made evident what already existed. The war was not the evil but the fruit of a pre-existing evil.[23]

As if describing himself, he wrote: "We wish to escape to some isle of the blessed: [so that we can comfort ourselves that] my life at least is lovely and joyful and harmonious! How often the parsonage and pastoral life are just such isles of the blessed. And how often we Germans have made of Christmas just such an island onto which one can escape from the actual reality of life for a few days or a few hours. How utterly our entire usual celebration of the feast, which we have decorated with all that is cozy and well loved and sweet and colorful, is oriented to this 'magic' that is supposed to carry us for a time into fairyland."[24]

Bethge understood that Dietrich was living in such a fairyland: "Bonhoeffer lived a remarkable life during the war. For weeks at a time he worked in the peaceful surroundings of the Kieckow fields or the snow covered slopes of Ettal. In terms of time alone, he had more periods of time for steady work than he had had during the Finkenwalde years. And in Berlin, not every meeting for quartet playing served conspiratorial ends.... A person who knew nothing of his involvement in the conspiracy might find his way of life in those weeks difficult to understand."[25] Indeed Dietrich might well have looked like a typical Nazi collaborator, living in ease as others suffered—but such was not his intent or his fate.

20. Ibid., 89.
21. Ibid., 88.
22. Ibid., 105–6.
23. Ibid., 106.
24. Ibid., 107.
25. Ibid., 705.

— 39 —

Human Hearts in 1941

DIETRICH REMAINED AMID THE dramatic scenery at Ettal as 1941 opened, sometimes oppressed by the majestic, cloudy surround of mountains that blocked the already scanty winter light in the valley. By the end of January, all his wishes had materialized: he was declared indispensable as a civilian, he formally became an unpaid part of the Munich military intelligence office, and the requirement that he constantly register his whereabouts with the police was temporarily lifted.[1]

As Dietrich's life restabilized, Ruth collapsed in her Stettin apartment on a January morning. Her cook called the doctor, and, with a houseguest's help, got Ruth into bed. The doctor arrived and diagnosed a small stroke. A few hours later, Ruth's son Hans Jurgen appeared in Stettin, having been phoned. To "his astonishment," neither the cook nor the doctor opened the door but an older man Hans Jurgen had never seen. When Hans Jurgen learned this houseguest was a Jew his mother had been harboring, he abruptly ordered the man to leave. The man disappeared, never to be heard of again. This odd, fleeting memory would haunt him.[2]

Eberhard meanwhile had moved from Dietrich's attic bedroom in the Bonhoeffer house to an apartment in the charming half-timbered Burckhardthaus in the Dahlem section of Berlin. The Gossner Mission operated the house, which became the first home of his own. His mother, who visited, was delighted: "she . . . was very surprised and pleased by my nice, lovely apartment. I was quite proud of it," Eberhard wrote to Dietrich.[3] Eberhard nevertheless visited the Bonhoeffer family frequently. Dietrich also asked him to manage his finances as his upcoming spying trip to Switzerland came closer.

Sabine and the possible invasion of England still weighed heavily on Dietrich's mind, and he used the code name "Christiane" to refer to England:

1. Bethge, *DB: A Biography,* 700.
2. Pejsa, *Matriarch of Conspiracy,* 259–60.
3. Bonhoeffer, *DBWE 16,* 137.

"Is Christiane truly expecting us soon?" But above all he was still aglow from the Christmas visit from Eberhard: "how wonderful that you were here. I am still nourished by it." And then the darker afterthought: "I piled a great heap of requests and discussions on you. In retrospect I am sincerely sorry about this."[4] Gifts too remained important, as Dietrich continued in his bountiful role: "I shall be sending you a package with all sorts of things, including some surprises."[5]

Finding food became an increasing concern throughout the letters. When Dietrich sent a goose to Ursel, he asked her to "preserve some" for Eberhard.[6] Eberhard brought "a small piece of pound cake" to Dietrich's parents, noting: "Even in the most peaceful times it would have been considered excellent."[7] With the onset of the war, the government replaced real coffee, as essential to Germans as tea to the British, with an unpopular substitute made from roasted malt or chicory. This freed real coffee up for the troops. Genuine coffee therefore "assumed the status of a . . . currency."[8] Dietrich received such a prized gift from Switzerland: "The wonderful coffee arrived recently, and I am not the only one who was delighted," he wrote.[9] Dietrich went so far as to suggest that the wife of a recently imprisoned Confessing Church member would react with "much joy" to some coffee. People, he wrote, "are extremely grateful for the smallest things!"[10]

Dietrich longed to reunite with Eberhard, hoping to see him in Berlin after the Swiss trip: "You must plan this! My parents will probably not be at home at that point. If it becomes too difficult at our house, I could probably move in with you for a few days . . . " he wrote on January 27.[11] On February 14th: "I can easily arrange myself around your schedule. . . . I am especially looking forward to music with you. How wonderful that you [have] learned to play the flute. That is a great enrichment of our relationship. . . . You are reimbursing yourself for restaurant meals there, aren't you? Otherwise it would be too much." He again invited Eberhard to Ettal, extolling the beautiful weather: "Frost, sun, but no snow. . . . I miss having a partner! You see, you

---

4. Ibid., 137.
5. Ibid., 129.
6. Ibid., 121.
7. Ibid., 141.
8. Moorhouse, *Berlin at War,* 86.
9. Bonhoeffer, *DBWE 16,* 192.
10. Ibid., 193.
11. Ibid., 131.

simply must come back."¹² On February 19: "Now it will be the end of March before we see each again, ten weeks! This often seems so absurd to me."¹³

Dietrich's desire to go with Eberhard to Friedrichsbrunn reemerged repeatedly as well. On February 8: "It has now been more than four weeks since you departed from here! Perhaps we could meet in Friedrichsbrunn ... I would like that very much. Think about it!"¹⁴ On February 19: "I would be eager then to go with you to Friedrichsbrunn over Easter. Can you not arrange to have some sermon around Easter so that you could be in Friedrichsbrunn for a day or two? For by then there will be a great deal to tell and to discuss." On February 22, "Can you not arrange the visits ... in such a way that Friedrichsbrunn becomes the base, and I come along here and there? That would be a magnificent idea! Make it happen."¹⁵

Now that Vibrans was marrying, Dietrich was generous: "Despite his unprepossessing façade, ... He is truly a fine, deep, and intelligent fellow." Then the tantalizing bread crumbs trail off into the black hole of ellipses: sentences of a "particularly intimate nature" that Dietrich writes about Vibrans, and then "intimate" words about Eberhard that are omitted by the editors from the published record—Dietrich ends with "Please throw this part of the letter straight into the trash!"¹⁶

As February opened, Dietrich still remained tucked within the high peaks of the Alps, breathing the achingly cold, fresh air amid the snow. He loved his birthday, as Eberhard was well aware. This birthday, Dietrich's thirty-fifth, led to a flurry of mail: "Don't forget Aunt Ruth's [also February 4] birthday! Or mine either, please!" Dietrich pleaded, only half jokingly, on January 31st.¹⁷

Eberhard responded with a warm letter: "It certainly does feel odd to me that I should wish you a happy birthday in writing. This is the first time since 1935—no, the first time ever." He thanked Dietrich for the friendship, for "your care and faithfulness ... availability in all personal and professional needs, intellectual and spiritual generosity and partnership, sharing of neckties and shoes ... ." Then "the package last evening. Say you rascal: what a fabulous hat! I had not the slightest inkling.... And the extra treats!

---

12. Ibid., 154–55.
13. Ibid., 162.
14. Ibid., 145.
15. Ibid., 163.
16. Ibid., 131.
17. Ibid., 133.

So now I shall sort through all my treasures with reckless abandon. Otherwise I would need a warehouse." He mentioned he would visit "Aunt Ruth."[18]

Dietrich wrote a "birthday letter" back to Eberhard: "What wonderful days we have had on the various February 4ths, in Finkenwalde, in Schlönwitz, and Sigurdshof! . . . that the two of us could be connected for five years by work and friendship is, I believe, a rather extraordinary joy for a human life. . . . I wish for myself in this new year all of this may continue to be so, and increasingly more so . . . ."

And the apology, a recurrent theme: "You have also patiently withstood the severe tests of such a friendship, particularly with regard to my violent temper (which I too abhor in myself and of which you have fortunately repeatedly and openly reminded me), and have not allowed yourself to be made bitter by it."[19]

Eberhard wrote back of his "joy" at the letter and "pain" that he had no gift waiting for Dietrich in Ettal. Wartime shortages meant that Eberhard could not assemble the traditional German "birthday table," presumably to be mailed, of flowers, gifts, and treats.[20] Nevertheless, Father Johannes from Ettal showed up to visit Dietrich with a bottle of schnapps, two cakes, and an azalea. Letters from his parents cheered him. Dietrich wrote to Eberhard on his actual birthday with an effusive outpouring, his "awareness that without a morning hymn outside my door, as you have arranged for me over the course of the years, and without morning and evening devotions together and personal intercession, a day like this is actually without meaning and substance."[21] Eberhard responded: "I was filled with the loveliest and liveliest birthday thoughts of you."[22]

In another letter Dietrich resisted an ongoing theme in their relationship as Eberhard sought breathing room by suggesting to Dietrich he expand his circle: "You wish me good stimulating friends. . . . it is a great gift . . . yet the human heart is created in such a way that we seek not the many but the one particular other and rest there."[23]

18. Ibid., 134–35.
19. Ibid., 136.
20. Ibid., 143.
21. Ibid., 138–39.
22. Ibid., 141.
23. Ibid., 139.

— 40 —
Conspiracies

IN EARLY FEBRUARY, EBERHARD saw Ruth in Stettin, arriving with a precious half-pound of real sugar, six carnations, and a volume of Kierkegaard.[1] Then on a Saturday soon after her birthday, he visited her sick bed. Ruth lay propped up amid her birthday splendor of flowers and letters, suffering what he thought to be the flu, though it may have been a continuation of her stroke.[2]

Eberhard's visits had a purpose. If Dietrich were being pulled deeper into the anti-Hitler conspiracy, these friends had their own agenda: Eberhard had decided to marry. Few were better suited to promote his plans than Ruth.

As Eberhard would recall, he would peer out the window of Dietrich's attic bedroom in Berlin, into the Schleicher's yard next door: "the window of that room looked out over the garden of the neighboring house at number 42, where the presence of the Schleicher children [including adolescent Renate] became for me more and more exciting and attractive."[3]

---

1. Bonhoeffer, *DBWE 16*, 142.
2. Pejsa, *Matriarch of Conspiracy*, 260, and Bonhoeffer, *DBWE 16*, 149.
3. de Gruchy, *Daring, Trusting Spirit*, 63.

"The window of that room looked out over the garden of the neighboring house at number 42, where the presence of the Schleicher children [including adolescent Renate] became for me more and more exciting and attractive," wrote Eberhard Bethge. This view from the attic bedroom would have looked down on yards more richly planted than today.

Eberhard sent Dietrich a letter on Valentine's Day, 1940, as unseasonable spring weather filled the air, forwarding Dietrich's mail with a warning: "Don't be surprised at the one from Aunt Ruth. On both visits we had discussed the ever popular topic of marriage; that is the explanation."[4] A week later, Dietrich wrote back, "Many thanks for your letter from my room. It always gives me joy when you are there. It is wonderful that you were at the Schleichers for music making! . . ." Here, the letter is ellipsed, once again "a few sentences of a particular intimate nature" omitted according to a footnote.[5]

In his biography of Bonhoeffer, Bethge offers seemingly endless details about church struggle, theology, and conspiracy, but the eventual paired engagements of the best friends to teenaged girls slip into the narrative as almost an afterthought. However, even without his help it's possible to discern the outlines of Eberhard's courtship.

4. Bonhoeffer, *DBWE 16*, 152.
5. Ibid., 162.

By 1940, Eberhard recognized he was in an untenable position, connected intimately with the Bonhoeffer family as a "friend," a position, as he would later write, without any public or legal status. Marrying a Bonhoeffer would create a secure situation for him, making him less dependent on Dietrich's patronage. A wife would aso create boundaries to keep Dietrich and his explosive temper at bay, while marrying into the family would at the same time keep the two friends close. Finally, it would be difficult for Dietrich to fight such an alliance, as Eberhard might otherwise marry out of the Bonhoeffer circle. As all of Dietrich's sisters had long since married, niece Renate, the oldest of the next generation, was Eberhard's obvious choice.

He and Ruth talked.

His future might rely on Renate, but for the moment Eberhard's attention was focused on Dietrich. He sent his friend a gift.

"I am utterly at a loss for words in response to the birthday present that just arrived today! It is truly beyond all bounds, completely impermissible, and nevertheless a tremendous joy," wrote Dietrich. "The cordial cups are still sitting here on my desk, and I keep glancing at them in disbelief. Clearly you have spent months searching and eventually turned your whole wallet inside out to give this joy to me. . . . They are precious vessels intended for precious contents; I shall take good care of them and use them eagerly and often, and they will surely last well beyond my lifetime. How wonderful to have received them from you of all people! I shall drink the first glass to the constancy of our friendship."

Others unconsciously hit close to the mark, as Dietrich recorded, writing to Eberhard, "Everyone admires them and suspects that they are a wedding present; they expect great revelations from me. Unfortunately, I had to disappoint them."[6]

For, though he talked in his circular letters of waking up to the realities brought on by war, Dietrich had found his bliss, and would have—indeed wished—to float on unchanged with Eberhard, even as Eberhard began to plot marriage to Renate. If Dietrich could have stopped time—if it could forever have been Eberhard and him, young and vigorous, running the seminaries, racing on the beaches of Zingst, snowshoeing on the edge of the forests near Sigurdshof, skiing in Ettal, lounging by the lake in Friedrichsbrunn, smoking, talking, and playing the piano in his attic bedroom, with frequent side trips to Sabine and Ruth—he would have done so. He yearned to be with his dearest friend, making music, playing tennis and bridge, traveling, eating, sharing life and talk.

6. Ibid., 163.

Dietrich and Eberhard would often talk, smoke, and make music in Dietrich's attic bedroom. For all the family prestige, this was a modest room, more "man den" than lush habitat.

In longing for stasis—or the past—he reflected one strain of National Socialism. In an act of sheer will, the Party imposed a nineteenth-century aesthetic—and world view—on a captive population, the "spell," the false "magic" Dietrich alluded to. From women kept in the home in braided coronets to veneration of the moribund Junker culture to erasing modern art in favor of second-rate nineteenth-century realist paintings, the Nazis had bottled up their culture. Meanwhile, they pursued world conquest from the vantage point of outmoded Malthusian notions of scarcity, empire building that had run its course, and a backward-looking pseudoscience of racism.

But another strand of Nazism sought to destroy the traditional Christian ethic as well as institutional Christianity. In 1941, Catholics in leadership urged German families to make their home "a small house of God," in order to fight the attacks on Christianity in the public sphere. Bishop Clemens of Munster told parents bluntly of the bias in Nazi school history books: "You will be horrified at the lack of regard for historical truth with which the attempt is made to fill inexperienced children with a distrust of Christianity and Church, yes, with hatred of a belief in Christ!"[7] In 1941, Alfred Rosenberg's paper "Culture and Religion in the Third Reich" revealed a plan, like so many others the Nazis proposed, in which celibacy would be

---

7. Nicholas, *Cruel World*, 71.

outlawed, priests would be replaced by "athletic Nazi officials," and Adolf Hitler would become the new head of the church.

There was a "30 point plan" for a Reich Church centered entirely on "race and nation," eradicating the "strange and foreign Christian faiths." After characterizing the current clergy as parasites who "love . . . the sweet bread they eat," this plan envisioned a hard, astringent purity: "The National Reich Church does not acknowledge the forgiveness of sins. . . . A sin once committed will be ruthlessly punished by the honorable and indestructible laws of nature and punishment will follow during the sinner's lifetime."[8]

On February 24, Dietrich set out for Switzerland on a spy mission, ostensibly surveillance for the regime, in reality to make contacts for the resistance. He seemed hardly to notice the beauties of Zurich's mountains and lake, where two and half years earlier Sabine and Gert had spend such anxious days hoping for a coup. He wasted no time in contacting Sabine on his arrival, however, writing what he described to Christel as "two long letters," but afraid "for her [Sabine's] sake" to write more.[9]

His words of longing poured out in English, which would cause less trouble for Sabine than German were they intercepted: "You cannot imagine my joy to be able to write to you directly after this long period of silence . . . . Our thoughts and more than that our prayers were with you every day." Again, he waxed hopeful that the war would not last more than another year. "I am longing," he ended, "for the day when we will meet again in unchanged fellowship and in the old spirit."[10] In fact, much of his correspondence from Switzerland was laced with his concerns for Sabine, mentioning her in both of his letters to Bell, and taking the time to write his old comrade in social work from 1932, Anneliese Schurmann, on Sabine's behalf. Anneliese, who had immigrated to England because of her Jewish ancestry, was now a student of Anna Freud. Bonhoeffer, in a comedy of errors, mistakenly thought Anneliese had gone to Brazil and addressed the letter to Brazil. After thanking her "for all that you have written us about Sabine," he asked: "Might you not know of something nice for him [Gert] in Brazil? The last few letters sounded rather depressed. Please keep your ears open as to whether a man like him might be needed somewhere."[11]

---

8. Ibid., 71.
9. Bonhoeffer, *DBWE 16*, 183.
10. Ibid., 166.
11. Ibid., 175.

Back in Germany on March 24, Dietrich stayed with his parents in Berlin, yearning to be on hand for the coup he believed imminent. He arrived home, however, to a problem he had not anticipated.

— 41 —

City Life, Country Life

DIETRICH HAD RETURNED TO a Berlin rife with rumors about where the Reich army would next strike. Allied air raids had resumed after a drop the first three months of the year, and Berlin was still shockingly short of ordinary goods, as most supplies were diverted to the army. The government cut meat rations in 1941, but by that time rationing was largely theoretical. As one Berliner wrote: "We started out with four pounds of rice a month, which was cut to one pound—and not a store in Berlin had any rice to sell. We had ration cards for oil, eggs, peas and beans. None of these articles was to be found, ration card or no . . . ."[1]

Shelves and shelves of the grand department stores stood dusty and empty. In early February, Eberhard had been unable to find the board game he wanted for Dietrich's birthday. Everyday items—shoe strings, suspenders, toilet paper, canned goods, and rubber bands—had disappeared. "Things which one could not buy in German stores: shaving soap, electric wire, candles, any metal object, phonograph records . . . , typewriters, electric razors, electric water heaters, clothing of all kinds . . . , furniture, thread (one spool a month), many kinds of paper and stationery, color film, vanilla, spices of all kinds, pepper, gelatine, leather goods, buttons, cigars," wrote one observer. Soap too, was all but impossible to find. Tomatoes and oranges were gone, while women stood in long lines for ordinary produce.[2]

For propaganda purposes, shops windows often displayed items they did not have, and in grand hotels, such as the Kaiserhof, colored water filled liquor bottles.[3] A fine meal, however, could still be had at the exclusive Horchers, where high-ranking Nazis—Göring especially—and their guests could order pickled herring, lobster salad, fried chicken, ice cream with real

---

1. Moorhouse, *Berlin at War*, 85.
2. Ibid.
3. Ibid., 86.

chocolate sauce, and the coveted real coffee, not to mention the restaurant's specialties, wild game and flambé.[4]

The bombing raids continued to disrupt Dietrich's routine, as they had earlier in the war, leading him to appreciate his remote country retreats all the more. No coup materialized.

But beyond all this he confronted a particular new problem: the regime refused him membership in the Reich's Writer's Guild, and banned him from publishing due to his subversive activities.[5] He was not alone. The paper shortage brought on by the war offered Goebbels the opportunity to stop the church press, excepting official Reich Church outlets.[6]

The war also gave the government leeway to double down on the church itself, which Hitler had "reeling on the ropes" as he had promised. After talking with Dietrich in Switzerland about the state of the church in Germany, Willem Visser't Hooft, secretary of the World Christian Student Association, released a report outlining the gradual hemming in of Christian clergy through imprisonments, house arrests, mandatory twelve-hour workdays (which made it impossible to attend services), and bans on speaking and preaching. The goal was to "make the church into an innocuous sect which . . . cannot exert any influence in public life."[7] Children evacuated from cities offered another opportunity for the National Socialists: they were in "the grip of the state" and taught, for instance, that bishops were "racketeers" and the pope an "arch-racketeer."[8]

While Bethge later dismissed the effects of the writing ban, it's clear that it raised financial concerns. Dietrich had been using the royalties from *Discipleship* and *Life Together* to meet expenses, which included helping Eberhard. Soon after the ban, he wrote to the Pastors' Emergency League, asking for salary compensation for his work as a Confessing Church pastor.[9]

At Easter in early April and then again near the end of April, Dietrich visited his beloved Friedrichsbrunn, but without Eberhard, despite Dietrich's repeated requests. Instead, his parents joined him for his Easter stay. After they left, he wrote of chopping wood for a "break" and thanked them for the trip: "It was quite lovely to spend a few quiet days with you up here.

---

4. Lubrich, ed., *Travels in the Reich*, 249.
5. Bethge, *DB, A Biography*, 730.
6. Bonhoeffer, *DBWE* 16, 177.
7. Ibid.,176.
8. Ibid., 178–79.
9. Ibid.,195–96.

I haven't had that for a long time."[10] He hoped Eberhard could pick him up at the Grunewald train station, as the family continued to be allowed to use the Mercedes.

Dietrich drew sustenance from the woods around Friedrichsbrunn.

Bombing raids over Berlin had again tapered off, but in April, the first of three huge flak towers arose, this one near the Zoo, not far from Dietrich's parents' home. Built on the grand scale beloved of National Socialism, the 128-foot-high tower surged above the nearby Zoo train station and much of the city. Two hundred-thirty feet long, the concrete building resembled a medieval fortress, and bristled with anti-aircraft guns. Meant to hold 8,000

10. Ibid.,186. Also see 682.

people, it included an air raid shelter and a hospital ward, and stored such treasures as the bust of Nefertiti.[11]

Meanwhile, Dietrich lived a seemingly quiet life. In April, his Abwehr protection allowing him to travel more freely, he went back and forth twice between Friedrichsbrunn and Klein Krössin, where he saw Ruth, once in mid-April, and then at the end of April.[12]

In May 1941, the Nazis removed von Thadden from her school, accusing her of "endanger[ing] the state." Von Thadden moved to Berlin to work for the Red Cross. Maria stayed on at Wieblingen.

On June 22, 1941, Hitler invaded the Soviet Union. Hitler's strategy included killing as many Eastern Europeans as possible to free up food and land for the Germans. As usual, a strange logic undergirded the cruelty: Germany was only supplying 83 percent of its own food needs. "Russia is our Africa," Hitler said, envisioning it as a vast colony to exploit. His model, in fact, was based more closely on North America, where Europeans had conquered, and then eradicated, most of the native inhabitants, forging a new society, as Hitler understood it, "on the basis of racial superiority." National Socialist ideology required that Germans lay aside what it understood as a false, sentimentalized compassion and steel themselves to clearing Eastern Europe of Slavic and Jewish populations through mass murder—except for those needed for slave labor—to allow for Aryan expansion.[13]

While Dietrich worked on his *Ethics* at quiet Klein Krössin, the Nazi propaganda machine shot into high gear in Berlin and elsewhere. Announcers shouted news of the Russian invasion through scratchy loudspeakers strung along roads all over the country, including the Unter den Linden and Kurfürstendamm in Berlin. Interrupting programs with trumpet and drum roll fanfare, newscasters commanded everyone to stand in silence while invasion progress reports were read.[14] Lest anyone miss the news over the loudspeakers or in the papers, sound trucks drove up and down the streets blaring announcements: first 322 "Red" planes had been shot down, then 2,582. Brest-Litovsk, Kaunas, Dvinsk were taken. War, some noted, had become entertainment.[15]

The atrocities at the heart of the invasion—the murder and starvation of civilians, as well as the execution of Soviet army officers, soldiers, and prisoners of war—revolted many career German military officers, just as

---

11. Moorhouse, *Berlin at War*, 309–10.
12. Bonhoeffer, *DBWE 16*, 682.
13. Fritzsche, *Life and Death in the Third Reich*, 153–55.
14. Lubrich, ed., *Travels in the Reich*, 250.
15. Ibid., 251.

the invasion of Poland had done, and added new urgency to assassination plans. Yet with the initial victories in the East, Hitler's stature grew. Further, although Dietrich, among others, tried to negotiate secretly with the British for a conditional surrender should the conspirators manage to assassinate Hitler, Churchill was unmoved. He saw no signs of an effective underground and no reason to promise anything.

Shirer wrote, "One marvels at these German resistance leaders who were so insistent on getting a favorable peace settlement from the West and so hesitant in getting rid of Hitler until they had got it. One would have thought that if they considered Nazism to be such a monstrous evil as they constantly contended—no doubt sincerely—they would have concentrated on trying to overthrow it regardless of how the West might treat their new regime."[16] As Churchill was to say, "They must do something, like the Belgians and Dutch, Norwegians and French, before we are prepared to believe even in their existence."[17]

Yet the German conspirators perceived their situation as more complicated—they were not occupied by a foreign power but were the conquering power. Hitler might be a monster, but he was their monster. Further, he enjoyed such solid popular support that any coup carried the risk of making him a martyr and reviving the "backstab" theory from World War I. The conspirators also remembered the humiliating Versailles treaty, and felt justified in seeking reassurances that Germany would be treated honorably in defeat—and thus far, they had no guarantees.

The shock of the atrocities, however, motivated some undecided generals to join the conspiracy, including Claus Schenk von Stauffenberg. Stauffenberg, a man of rare decision among the elite, would eventually prod the conspirators into action.

In the middle of June, Dietrich wrote a short note to Bell from Berlin, presumably transmitted via Sutz in Switzerland, to tell him that Martin Niemöller was well and to thank him for his care of Sabine.[18] At the end of June, Dietrich returned to Klein Krössin. He took breaks from *Ethics* to walk in Ruth's garden, and, despite the wet summer, again appreciated the peace of rural life away from blare of air raid sirens, exploding bombs, and the rat-a-tat of anti-aircraft fire, all ruining nerves and sleep. Yet he thanked

---

16. Shirer, *The Rise and Fall of the Third Reich*, 1018.
17. Dramm, *Dietrich Bonhoeffer and the Resistance*, 158–59.
18. Bonhoeffer, *DBWE 16*, 193.

his parents for hosting him in Berlin "for so long and especially also that Eberhard could be there too."[19]

In this letter and one that followed in early July, Dietrich tried to persuade his parents to visit Ruth, offering to put them up at a nearby inn. "The food supply here is still actually at nearly prewar levels," he wrote them in June. By July 5th, he assumed his parents had received Ruth's letter of invitation and hoped their visit would coincide with the arrival of Ursel's children. Ruth had invited the Schleicher daughters to visit, including Eberhard's love interest, Renate.[20]

Since her stroke the past winter, Ruth had been walking with a cane. She put the Schleicher girls in the guest bedrooms Joy and Contentment under the eaves of the cottage. On balmy days, the girls had the run of the grand Kieckow estate, but the rainy summer often kept them indoors. In the evenings, the Kieckow granddaughters, Ruthi and Elisabeth, came over for charades, while on wet afternoons, Ruth would give the Schleicher girls some of the precious stock of stationery she kept on hand for Dietrich, encouraging them to write letters home. Ruth did her best to work her not inconsiderable charm on Renate.

By now, Ruth had moved from clandestine machinations to openly supporting a match between Eberhard and Renate. Eberhard had "recently declared his intentions," while Renate, not quite sixteen, "had found her way into Ruth's heart." As for the marriage, "everything waits on the parents' approval and Renate completing the gymnasium." This union, which, if the parents allowed it, would bind Eberhard tightly to the Bonhoeffers, increased Ruth's own resolve that she too be connected to the family: "She wonders if it will ever be possible for anyone from her own family to cross the invisible line that separates them from the Bonhoeffers of Berlin."[21]

Later in the summer, the Schleicher parents visited. In August, Rüdiger wrote to Dietrich and the elder Bonhoeffers of his admiration for Klein Krössin. "Mrs. Von Kleist was so very kind; she showed us not only her own home and estate but also Kieckow, where we became acquainted with her son's family, such likable people—that is actually quite an understatement . . . I can attest sincerely to Dietrich that I was quite taken with even these Pomeranian noble elite types." Yet Rüdiger also questioned the lack of freedom of the lower classes in this Junker world. The younger Schleichers

---

19. Ibid., 193–94.
20. Ibid., 194.
21. Pejsa, *Matriarch of Conspiracy*, 264.

thrived, "looking very cheerful and radiant," wrote Rüdiger, in part due to the "excellent cuisine" at Klein Krössin.[22]

For Ruth, this July was a last refuge before a time of great sadness, which had fallen even as Rüdiger wrote his letter home.

---

22. Bonhoeffer, *DBWE 16*, 204.

42

Horrors and Joys

"I am living as in a dreamworld," Ruth wrote to Eberhard in a birthday letter to him on August 24. She was reeling, heartsick over the loss of two grandsons on the Russian front. "And almost daily we hear of those who are newly fallen. Each piece of news rips the wound open again." The sense of German war responsibility lay heavily on her and she wrote in words Dietrich would echo: "Somehow one doesn't want to be excluded from the inexorable fate and guilt that has come upon us . . . . When our news speaks of the 'unimaginable losses' that we are inflicting on the enemies, I experience this like a knife to my soul." For the first time, she questioned her beloved friends' avoidance of military duty: her conviction that all must share the guilt "makes me uncertain . . . concerning your path and Dietrich's during these times. Do we not belong within this entanglement and must we not employ our spiritual energies without considering the cost—at the very places where the battle is fought? Would we not proceed on our way more confident of our goal if we did not evade this final contact?"[1]

In contrast, Dietrich's two birthday letters to Eberhard remembered the past, so frequently a theme: "[On the 28th] I shall think of so many lovely trips together, especially in 1936." He then alluded to the future: "What could I wish for you for this new year but . . . that in your personal life you can make a plan for the future that at present is still denied to us? And I see how these wishes for you, are at the same time, my own wishes. It is impossible to imagine how it will be a year from now."[2]

A fleeting yet tantalizing hint that Dietrich was preoccupied with the changes that might come should Eberhard marry emerges in a Zimmermann recollection. One day during the war he met Dietrich in Berlin, and Dietrich had on his mind "the ethical problem of marriage and family." Dietrich resisted the commonplace idea that "marriage began with being together in the flesh." He told Zimmermann "that aspect was not decisive,"

1. Bonhoeffer, *DBWE 16*, 210.
2. Ibid., 211.

then wondered if monogamy was truly a Christian demand, since the patriarchs "had lived in a different way." Dietrich asked: "[Since] in marriage everything is permitted; what else is permitted over and above that?"[3] In *Ethics*, Dietrich also touched on marriage and sexuality. For him, Christianity was rooted in the body—he noted *bodily* resurrection after death—and he wrote that sexual pleasure could not be designed solely for procreation. "For if the body is an end itself, then there is a right to bodily joys, without having to subordinate them to a further, higher purpose. . . . The joys of the body are a sign of the eternal joy that is promised human beings in the presence of God." Speaking more directly to sexuality, he wrote, contradicting his assertion of sex as the symbol of the fall in *Creation and Fall*: "Sexuality is not only a means of procreation, but . . . embodies joy." He quoted Ecclesiastes 11:9: "Rejoice young man while you are young . . . . Follow the inclination of your heart and the desire of your eyes, and know that for all these things God will bring you into judgment."[4]

Yet it can't be coercive sexuality: "to encroach upon my body is to intrude into my personal existence."[5] Later in the volume he defines rape as "forcible use, by illegal power, of another's body for one's own purposes, especially its sexuality."[6] Once again, he insists boundaries must be respected. Shame enforces boundaries: "shame expresses the essential freedom of the human body with regard to sexuality. To destroy the feeling of shame is to dissolve all sexual and marital order, in fact any communal order at all."[7]

His concern with marriage and its limitations went back at least a decade. As theologian Lisa Dahill points out, Dietrich interrogated marriage in Prague in 1932, before the crisis of Nazism hit.[8] Dietrich, later responding to Eberhard's articulation of the invisibility of a same-sex relationship, would both rail against its lack of status and in prison continue developing

---

3. This is a problematic statement without more context— and possibly an esoteric comment that only an in-group would understand. Reiterating and expanding on *Creation and Fall*, in *Ethics* Bonhoeffer locates the conscience as the self-reflective dividing line between what is permitted and prohibited and continued to take a dim view of conscience as that which, if relied on wholly as a guide, elevates humans into a distorted relationship of presumed equality with God (Bonhoeffer, *DBWE* 6, 307–8). At the same time, in this conversation, he appeared to be groping for a more open definition of marriage. Here, of course, he is not talking about conscience, but discerning what is permitted.

4. Bonhoeffer, *DBWE* 6, 186–87.

5. Ibid., 188.

6. Ibid., 214.

7. Ibid.

8. Dahill, "'There's Some Contradiction Here.'"

his nascent queer theology—something he had begun to do in Prague in 1932, before the crisis of Nazism fully hit.

Dahill notes that in his July 1932 lecture in Czechoslovakia, Bonhoeffer critiques a one-to-one correspondence between the ideal of the Lutheran orders of creation—the institutions of family, work, government, church believed handed down by God—and the *manifestations* of these orders in society. Instead, Bonhoeffer emphasized, as he would all his life, the fallenness of the contemporary world, and the way this fallenness infused the divine orders with brokenness and distortion: "From the perspective of Christ we must recognize the entire world as a fallen world; we do not know its original orderings any longer. There now remain only orders of preservation oriented toward Christ, and to the extent that we determine an order to be no longer open for Christ, that order must be broken. *There are no orders that are holy in themselves.*"[9] Bonhoeffer thus reacted, even before the National Socialist victory, to propaganda attempts to use the orders to justify both violence and Aryanism (the National Socialists insisted that violence would "purify" the orders by eradicating the decadence that had crept into them and also insisted on racism as integral to God's plan for the world). In a 1932 summer seminar called "Is There a Christian Ethic?" Bonhoeffer focused on the social constructions of marriage, arguing that "every order is . . . mutable and destructable, including monogamous marriage."[10]

From these orders—the institutional arrangements understood theologically to be handed down from God—Bonhoeffer shifted the focus to the centrality of Christ. Not the order itself—not the form—determines its value, but the extent to which it is infused with and conformed to a Christ-like sensibility—loving, humble, peaceful, other oriented. Searching for a ground to stand on in a society relentlessly organized around heterosexual monogamy, Bonhoeffer groped to break open marriage in ways that allowed in Christ's love. Dahill rightly understands this as allowing a critique of patriarchal marriage, the dominant form in Germany in the 1930s, but it equally opens, as Dahill notes, the possibility of a more radical reformation of the marriage mandate to include other forms of loving, Christ-centered relationships into—or in Bonhoeffer's later formulation, alongside—this order of creation.[11] A decade later, too, Bonhoeffer would return to the man-

---

9. Bonhoeffer expands on this theme in his *Ethics*, writing, "The woman is given to the man as a 'companion,' as his 'counterpart' . . . and they become one flesh." This is not for an end—the mechanistic production of babies, but a "blessing" in itself (210n8).

10. Dahill, "'There's Some Contradiction Here.'"

11. Ibid., 81: Dahill writes, "Gender-bending, queer-friendly, female-oriented forms of life today: are they really so much more disruptive than Jesus' own welcoming of prostitutes and sinners, lepers and tax collectors, Gentiles and demoniacs? There's

dates and their mutability in *Ethics*, writing that "because the son of the first human beings, Cain, was born far from paradise and became the murderer of his brother, here, too a dark shadow falls over marriage and family in this our world."[12] In his pinpointing of patriarchal, heterosexual matches as potentially a "shadow," fallen, imperfect and open to reformation, Bonhoeffer has sown a first seed for a more open definition of marriage.[13]

While Ruth grieved the many dead young soldiers on both sides, Dietrich sent cheerful notes to Eberhard en route to Switzerland, urging him to "let [Pastor] Reimer give you the honey that he promised me and keep it entirely for yourself . . ." but then, on second thought: "If possible, I might want some of it." In another letter, he dwelled on wishes for joy, hopeful Bible verses, and good food: "At noon I ate a festive meal in your honor. By the way, this miserable guest-house feeding, which has sunk to new lows even here, has again made me aware of how dreadful you have it in Berlin . . . . If anything should come of the side of bacon from Kieckow, I would also like to request a piece of it." He urged Eberhard to use his rations cards, which he would not need while in Switzerland, but noted, "how dull the good food in Switzerland will be for me, all alone."[14] He would, in fact, enjoy the Swiss food: real coffee, real chocolate, good cuts of meat.

Dietrich's double life continued. On one level Dietrich continued as the privileged Aryan, beneficiary of Hitler's revolution. On the other hand, as the war continued to grow more brutal, he worried about the fate both of Sabine and of friends at the front—and he continued, while avoiding conscription, to be torn over his path.

In his August letter to his seminary brothers, he spoke of the many who had already died in the Russian theater, mentioning Ruth's grandsons, Hans Friedrich, and Jurgen Cristophe, whose death had been such a blow. Dietrich had confirmed these grandsons a few years back, along with Max von Wedermeyer, during those happy days when the young Maria mimicked him in the Stettin flat. He mentioned as well four former seminarians who had fallen and four other friends dead in battle, a total of ten dead in or close to his circle. "Whomever God has called is someone God has loved," he wrote, but as quickly added "the devil also has a say in death" and

---

no space in the world Christ creates for fixed hierarchies of social class, male privilege, inherited elites; Bonhoeffer grasps this in his capacity to write so powerfully of this transforming call of Christ, even as he simultaneously resists letting this disorienting divine power call into question the male social privilege he clung to."

12. Bonhoeffer, *DBWE 6*, 71.

13. Though Bonhoeffer can sound Platonic, he is focused on the here and now.

14. Bonhoeffer, *DBWE 16*, 211.

therein he located a paradox—death is both what God wills and doesn't will. Bonhoeffer was plagued as well by the thought of writing cant: "There are times in which everything is so bewildering and so distressing that any direct word seems to us to destroy the mystery of God . . . ."[15]

In Bethge's view, Dietrich felt shame at being alive and safe when his Finkenwalde brothers were falling and suffering. He "felt even more ashamed," Bethge wrote, when he received letters from the front from those who thanked him for having forced them to memorize Bible verses at Finkenwalde: "One has to live with the texts," wrote one seminarian. "I am very grateful now for your having kept us to it."[16] First his brother Walter had died in a war, and now his "brothers" were putting their lives at risk: Who was he that he should be thanked by them?

The loved ones in danger spread across many fronts, and during the fall trip to Switzerland, Dietrich caught up again with Sabine. He wrote to her from Zurich, conveying how close he continued to feel to her: "The more difficult it becomes to keep close contact with one's friends abroad the more one feels the inseparable fellowship with them."[17] He wrote to Bell, still concerned about Gert's ongoing depressed state and its impact on Sabine: "she is worrying a little about the future of her husband. I do not think there is any particular reason for depression on her side. . . . I should let you know that I am a little troubled about their inner balance. If you would be good enough to inform them of my letter to you and to encourage them, I would be very thankful to you indeed."[18] He spoke to Swiss friends of his wish for "the total elimination of the Nazi system."[19]

In Switzerland, he stayed with friend Adolf Freudenberg, who had been instrumental in getting *Creation and Fall* published years before. Since even the affluent couldn't find decent clothing in wartime Germany, Freudenberg's wife took Dietrich clothes shopping in Geneva. The Freudenbergs had noticed that Dietrich, always concerned about keeping up his appearance, "clearly suffered [in his 'aesthetic feelings'] from his worn and shabby clothing." When Mrs. Freudenberg helped him buy new shirts and underwear, he was "joyful and grateful."[20] Another time, his sensibilities came into play when the Freudenbergs took him to "a romantic but rather dingy beer

15. Ibid., 207–8.
16. Bethge, *DB: A Biography,* 703.
17. Bonhoeffer, *DBWE 16,* 217.
18. Ibid., 224.
19. Bethge and Gremmels, *A Life in Pictures,* 124.
20. Zimmermann and Smith, eds., *I Knew,* 169.

garden" that was usually popular with German guests. Dietrich, however, disliked the poor service and the stray animals—a cat, dog, duck, and turkey—begging for food. These, remembered Adolf, "offended his sense of beauty and dignity, and we soon left." When they took him to their summer house at Lake Champex, he relaxed and hunted for mushrooms while appreciating "the freshness and scents of early autumn, which is so bright and colorful in the Wallis Mountains."[21]

21. Ibid.

43

Shadows

IN AN OXFORD CRAMMED to the bursting, Sabine, Gert, and the girls felt fortunate, in 1941, to rent a small house from a railroad ticket seller who'd joined the army. In a letter to the senior Bonhoeffers, Gert called the house "Little Castle by the Railroad."[1] "The furniture," wrote Sabine, "was in unspeakably bad taste, but this was no longer of any concern to us."[2] The home's second living room became a study for Gert, the girls had a yard to play in, and for the first time since the move to England, the family and its fourteen trunks had privacy and room to spread out. Because of the general housing shortage, they paid twice the normal rate of rent. But they were, wrote Gert, "happy to be free of boardinghouse life, at least for the time being."[3]

    The family's financial circumstances meant that Sabine tended to the house and yard without any hired help, a circumstance sure to be of concern to the parents, though Gert airily reassured them that "this way we don't have any aggravation with personnel, and everything is cleaner and better, and Sabine wonders sometimes what our maids actually used to do." The money they had set aside was sufficient: "We don't need to buy much due to careful provisioning, and since we occasionally also receive things here or there and our reserves are not yet depleted, things have been going quite well so far." Barring a crisis or the war dragging on too long, "we shall continue to manage somehow." Of more concern to Gert was Sabine's depression when alone. Gert hastened to add that Sabine seldom was alone. Even Christiane's presence was enough to cheer her. But the fiction only stretched so far: "Actually, is there anything that can be done for this?" he wrote his father-in-law. "She thinks it is perhaps also an inherited trait.... She already

---

    1. Bonhoeffer, *DBWE 16*, 343.
    2. Leibholz, *The Bonhoeffers*, 130.
    3. Bonhoeffer, *DBWE 16*, 343–44.

spoke to Dietrich about this some time ago."[4] Dietrich, of course, had his dark, brooding moods.

If both Gert and Sabine suffered mentally, they knew they had reasons to be thankful: Oxford experienced no bombing, Gert had a full ration card, which would not have been the case for him as a Jew in Germany, and their fears of concentration camps and other horrors had eased. They enjoyed the beautiful and quiet gardens of St. John's College as well as the international community that gathered in the university town. But still they longed to be home. "May poor Uncle Rudi [their code name for the war] soon depart this life, and may divine providence bestow on us in the not too distant future the hour in which we shall all see each other again," wrote Gert.[5]

In the fall of 1941, Nazi leaders gathered at Wannsee, the resort area of lakes and waterside cafes near southwest Berlin where the young Dietrich had once capsized a pleasure boat. Here the final solution to the Jewish "problem" was formalized: genocide. Hitler commented that he knew even the best Nazis had "good" Jews they wanted to protect: he advised them to harden themselves against such thinking.

Dietrich returned from Switzerland to a Berlin continuing to overflow with soldiers and bulging to the bursting point with foreign workers and residents. This tangled mass of humanity lived in a city now even more rife with shortages and ever more worried about air raids. Jews, by decree, had to wear the yellow star. At least one observer expressed surprise at the number of Jews still in Germany, given the persecution.[6]

That fall, more Berlin Jews lost their homes, with 1,500 deported, proving the Stettin deportation had not been a fluke—in the end, 60,000 Jews would be transported from Berlin.[7] In addition to eradicating the Jews, the deportations served a practical purpose by helping to alleviate the Berlin housing shortage. Albert Speer, who had been displacing Jews since 1938, by 1941 had forced most Jews into overcrowded Judenhausen—or Jew's houses—in dilapidated areas of the city. Between evictions, mass deportations, and the number of Jews who committed suicide—2,000 in Berlin by fall of 1941—fresh housing stock became available.[8]

The deportations upset Dietrich, and in October he and Confessing Church pastor Friedrich Perels prepared two reports for Dohnanyi's secret files. At the same time, a sixty-eight-year-old friend of the Bonhoeffers

4. Ibid.
5. Ibid., 344–45
6. Lubrich, ed., *Travels in the Reich*, 251–52.
7. Bonhoeffer, *DBWE 16*, 225.
8. Moorhouse, *Berlin at War*, 113–15.

received an evacuation notice. "Everyone tried zealously to stand by her but could do nothing more than help her pack," wrote Bethge. She was sent to a concentration camp and given her age, no doubt selected for gassing. One pastor, Katharina Staritz, published a protest about the deportations and was immediately arrested, while some Catholic and Protestant clergy helped Jews disappear with forged papers, ration cards, and other help. However, these measures, as everyone involved knew, were wholly inadequate.[9]

The regime encouraged people to be hard. "Jews are to blame for the war," said Goebbels. "They are suffering no injustice in the treatment we give them. They more than earned it."[10] And as the Russian invasion began to go badly in October, leaving an ill-equipped German army to face a Russian winter, Hitler, characteristically, lashed out ever more violently, exacting a retribution in which he decided that no matter how much his beloved Germans suffered, the Jews would suffer more.

In their report, Bonhoeffer and Perels mentioned the health problems caused by the deportation notices—"severe attacks of illness"[11] in some cases. By the end of October, Dietrich, though protected and privileged, was himself sick, having come down with pneumonia.

Even with a month in September in Switzerland to spare him from the deprivations of the average Berliner, Dietrich had been exposed in October to the perils of the city. Since crews no longer cleaned or ventilated the overworked subway cars, they stank, especially as people had "only a cube of soap big as a penny box of matches to wash with for a month." People fainted or got off trains for air. Germs lingered. People were "white as flour, except for red rings around their tired, lifeless eyes."[12] Inadequate and unhealthy food—bread, for example, stretched with sawdust, as well as fake honey, fake sugar, and egg powder[13] took a toll. Civilians were jittery and worried, worn from nights in bomb shelters followed by days at work. "People are sick; just plain sick in body and mind," wrote American correspondent Howard Smith. To Smith, the malaise lent to Berlin the atmosphere of "a cheap, dockside dive," and was, ironically to him, concentrated in the lower-middle classes who had brought Hitler to power. But even Dietrich, part of the "airtight caste of privilege," had gotten ill. Perhaps his acute awareness that Hitler's regime was, as Smith put it, "a fine looking fat apple with a tight, red, shiny skin . . . rotten to the core . . ." contributed to Dietrich's malaise.

9. Bethge, *DB: A Biography*, 745–46.
10. Lubrich, ed., *Travels in the Reich*, 254.
11. Bethge, *DB: A Biography*, 746.
12. Lubrich, ed., *Travels in the Reich*, 275.
13. Moorhouse, *Berlin at War*, 88.

Already, Smith opined, fascism's "day [was] over. It will never again be an attracting force as it was before the world discovered its meaning."[14]

Yet even as the Nazi fairy story of superiority began openly to unravel, some continued to trumpet the Aryan myth, such as Jacques Chardonne, a French fascist and anti-communist. For him, fascism's allure came from his dream of reviving a mythic French and German folk culture.

Chardonne reflected the self-image the Nazis still clung to. Cocooned in a dreamy bubble, he enjoyed a dinner hosted in Vienna by the head of the Nazi Youth, Baldur von Shirach, the same person who years ago had removed Ruth's granddaughter Raba from party leadership for her Jewish ancestry. During the dinner, lights were turned off to create a twilight atmosphere: around tables lit "by a circlet of red candles, and decorated with a bouquet of autumn leaves, amidst splendid china from an earlier age . . . We listened to a Bach chorale . . . then a Mozart quintet, after which the pure song with its restrained resonances was repeated. The general silence, the half-darkness that shrouded the participants, the flickering of the red candles, the autumn foliage, and the really beautiful music united to create a sort of spiritual spectacle . . . . I always sensed a certain splendor in these gatherings, full of nobility and good taste, which derived not only from the décor and the music but also from a certain quality of mind."[15] Ghostly spectacle along with assertions of purity and nobility remained a Nazi aesthetic, even as the cause became ever more tattered.

Chardonne articulated the misty ideal of the SS, based on Teutonic Knights of old, but "a totally new Germanic creation . . . an order of militant monks . . . tall . . . elegant . . . joyous . . . ." They were, to him, hygienic, pure, heroic. "They live ingenuously, in total self denial, there is nothing personal about them, they do not seem to feel sorrow, or fear, or hunger or desire: they are the angels of war come down for a moment from the Nieflheim."[16]

In October, wielding her cane and barely able to see, seventy-four-year-old Ruth arrived in jam-packed Berlin. Bombing raids had tapered off during this period. Dietrich, nursed by Eberhard, convalesced. Yet Dietrich was too sick to receive his old friend. "Not seeing you was very painful for me," Ruth wrote to him when back in Stettin. She had also failed to see an ophthalmology professor from the University of Berlin, probably hoping to consult with him about her increasingly troubling cataracts.[17] However, she

---

14. Lubrich, ed., *Travels in the Reich*, 278.
15. Ibid., 267.
16. Ibid., 268.
17. Bonhoeffer, *DBWE 16*, 234.

enjoyed staying with the Schleichers. Ruth wrote to Dietrich in terms that mirrored Rüdiger's approval of the von Kleists: "It was absolutely lovely at the Schleichers. What a cultured household! And I quite proudly imagine having some claim on the dear young ladies!" She also made her way to Dahlem and heard encouraging news that Martin Niemöller fared better than could be expected in the concentration camp. Her most anguished concern focused on her grandson Alla, part of a new Russian offensive, "a terrible ordeal." She feared too for a former Finkenwalde seminarian, Arthur Rau, who had a "weak constitution" and yet had been drafted into the regional shooters, a group that guarded bridges, railroad stations, and prisoner-of-war camps. "I imagine it would be horrible for him," she wrote. She had not had time to visit with Eberhard's sister Margret, beset as she was with problems of housekeeping, rationing, and dealing with government officials. "But now," she wrote, hinting broadly, "a spare room with the two beds is always available to welcome special guests."[18]

Dietrich spent his convalescence writing, addressing the increased persecution of the church and the ever-growing casualties among his former seminarians, six more dead and four more wounded. He continued to be tormented: "How frequently we are pierced with horror when we think of the loneliness of their death. Why could we not offer them the final service of fellowship?" As he dealt with these issues, Dietrich tried to accept his role: at times "life seems meaningless to us and our time wasted, because we can not share the monstrous experience of war at the front lines." But given that he was not about to enlist, "it would be irreverent . . . to crave such experience for ourselves as well. For who knows how well he would stand up? Who wishes to provoke God's miracle? . . . We dare not let our wishes and fantasies trivialize for us the task given to us daily by God."[19]

On December 8, the US declared war on Germany. And as 1941 drew to a close, Dietrich boarded a train in Berlin the morning of Sunday, December 14, heading for Kieckow, home of Hans Jurgen. Ruth had just written Dietrich from Stettin, where she had managed, despite the paper shortage, to find him 500 sheets of typing paper, 200 sheets of scratch paper, and 100 envelopes. Where should she send them?[20]

She continued her group study of *Discipleship*. "One must read into it," she wrote to Dietrich. "Perhaps that is its greatest value. I often have the

---

18. Ibid., 234–35.
19. Ibid., 238–39.
20. Pejsa, *Matriarch of Conspiracy*, 260.

impression that . . . links have been omitted. Surely you will develop these further."[21]

Sunday night, Ruth received a phone call, telling her Dietrich had arrived in Pomerania. Monday morning she left for Kieckow, staying at the manor house rather than Klein Krössin, both to be closer to Dietrich and, as usual, to save precious fuel. Dietrich had not been expecting her until the 17th but now they would have two extra days together.[22]

Family members crowded the house for the holidays. Dietrich led morning and evening devotions for a group of forty, including servants, in the hall's great dining room.[23]

Shortly before Christmas Dietrich returned to Berlin, where Hans Jurgen, with the help of the Bonhoeffers, had gone for a gall bladder removal, leaving Ruth in charge of Kieckow. Meanwhile Dietrich tried to keep Eberhard close through music, as he had years ago with Sabine: "We also need you urgently for the singing. Without you it won't work!"[24] On December 30, Dietrich and Eberhard performed Schutz's cantata "The sower went out to sow his seed" for Paula's sixty-fifth birthday party.[25] On that December day, Ruth wrote to Dietrich from Kieckow. He had granted her the right, she said, to speak freely and "not to scrutinize all my words when something personal escapes from me . . . ." Despite the difference in their ages, she acknowledged him as her spiritual mentor, the pastor and counselor she turned to at the end of life. Once again she framed their friendship as providential: "let us both thank God for bringing our meeting to pass."[26]

Continuing into the next day, the letter spoke too of handling Dietrich's laundry: "it gives me pleasure when I can take care of something 'motherly' along the way . . . . How caring your entire family has been about my son [Hans Jurgen]. . . . Please greet your parents and especially all the Schleichers, who were so very considerate to me."[27]

All the same, 1941 ended bleakly for Germany. The German army was ill-equipped for the Russian winter and bogged down thousands of miles from home. German radio broadcast happy stories of German soldiers on the front gathering to sing Christmas carols around candlelit trees.

---

21. Ibid., 270
22. Bonhoeffer, *DBWE 16*, 248.
23. Pejsa, *Matriarch of Conspiracy*, 271.
24. Bonhoeffer, *DBWE 16*, 248.
25. Ibid., 247.
26. Ibid., 249. It's not hard to imagine that Ruth's "personal" conversation pushed him to marry.
27. Ibid. Again, "laundry" might be a code word.

Propaganda in favor of runes, swastikas, and winter solstices faded as the need to appease the public deepened. Ruth, like many others, suspected the worst. "How eerie is the great stillness that has followed the storm," she wrote, adopting necessarily cryptic wording about the Russian offensive. "What is going on? What will happen?"[28] As the year drew to the close, Dietrich went to hear Bach's "Musical Offering" at the Berlin Vocal Academy.[29]

---

28. Ibid., 249.
29. Ibid., 686.

— PART VII —
Cornered: 1942-43

— 44 —
Risks

FORMER SEMINARIAN ERWIN SANDER wrote to Dietrich on February 4, 1942—Dietrich's thirty-sixth birthday—from the Russian front: "Russia is a truly distressing country. Here the war has cast traditional conceptions about the treatment of others to the winds. In mid-January a unit of our division had to shoot fifty prisoners in one day because we were on a march and were not able to take these prisoners along. In partisan areas, children and women who are suspected of supplying partisans with provisions are disposed of with a shot through the base of the skull. These persons must be done away with in this manner because otherwise German soldiers would have to forfeit their lives. . . . We cannot give special consideration to the civilian population's store of provisions . . . including seed potatoes . . . if we are in need of them. We have had to burn down many a village in the last three weeks out of military necessity . . . . And to us soldiers the promise comes from the Sermon on the Mount, 'Blessed are the merciful, for they will receive mercy.' The contradictions are enormous . . . ."[1]

One might understand the letter as full of rationalizations—"otherwise German soldiers would have to forfeit their lives"—but the careful documenting of the war crimes—how the women and children were killed, the use of seed potatoes, the burning of villages—juxtaposed against the Sermon of the Mount, suggests Sander's desire to protest what he was witnessing.

Other letters, if omitting atrocities, painted equally bleak pictures. Shortly before his death in February, 1942, seminary "brother" Erich Klapproth wrote of the -45 degree Celsius weather: "Our clothes have been sticking to our bodies . . . . For days at a stretch we cannot even wash our hands, but go from the dead bodies to a meal and from there back to the rifle. All one's energy has to be summoned up to fight against the danger of freezing . . . . Sometimes, when we have been away from the mess hall a long time, we invade the farmhouse after the fighting and slaughter geese, hens and sheep, get filled and overfilled with sides of bacon, honey and the nice Russian

1. Bonhoeffer, *DBWE 16*, 252.

potatoes.... We often dream of being relieved, but we are now reduced already to 40 instead of 150...."[2]

Ruth celebrated her seventy-fifth birthday in 1942 amid flowers, gifts, and almost one hundred messages. Eberhard's sister Margret, living in Stettin, visited with azaleas from Eberhard and birthday greetings from Dietrich as Ruth stood at her festive birthday table.[3] "She is a treasure," wrote Ruth of Margret. Yet war and the seemingly endless death toll on the battlefield continued to fill Ruth with sadness and fear, as did her own aging. The distance from Dietrich also remained a frustration. She watched anxiously as he stepped more deeply in the world of conspiracy, often seeming tense. "So we must part from one another—I because of my advanced age and you by reason of lowering your visibility," she wrote to him in response to his birthday letter, though in fact they would remain quite close. "It does not matter so much as you may think. If only I could speak to you once more in quietness, rather than always trying to make the most out of every moment .... Is it possible you can spend Easter at Klein Krössin?"[4]

Ruth also wrote to Eberhard, thanking him for his birthday letter: "It was one of the dearest. You have a great gift in that you are able to speak from your warm heart." Repeating her constant refrain about what had been most important to her during the last seven years, she wrote, "I am so thankful for your friendship and Dietrich's, which light the evening of my life." Yet she also spoke of her frustration: "I want so to speak to either you or Dietrich in quietness. Instead, Dietrich will be at Kieckow when I can't possibly be there.... In April, I hope to be in Klein Krössin... I would be so happy if you could visit me at that time...."[5]

In March, Vibrans died on the Russian front. The news struck Eberhard particularly hard, and he would later memorialize this dear childhood friend with a book, as he would Dietrich in a much more famous book. Dietrich, too, felt the loss, if only on Eberhard's behalf—it "has been a blow to me like no other sad news in this war to date," he wrote to Vibrans's father.[6]

Despite all the human loss, the Party leadership remained in a bubble. "After only nine years of rule the leadership was so corrupt that even in the critical phase of the war it could not cut back on its luxurious style of living," wrote Albert Speer. "For 'representational reasons' the leaders all needed big

2. Bethge, *DB: A Biography*, 704.
3. Pejsa, *Matriarch of Conspiracy*, 277–78.
4. Ibid., 275–76. It's again likely that Dietrich was sidestepping her marriage talk.
5. Ibid., 277.
6. Bonhoeffer, *DBWE 16*, 256.

houses, hunting lodges, estates and palaces, many servants, a rich table, and a select wine cellar. They were also concerned about their lives to an insane degree. Hitler himself, wherever he went, first of all issued orders for building bunkers for his personal protection. The thickness of their roofs increased with the caliber of the bombs until it reached sixteen and a half feet."[7]

Hitler and his entourage lived in increasing isolation from the sufferings of ordinary Germans, a situation that boded ill for Germany as the war began to unravel.

Dietrich's personal life continued to head in directions he would not have chosen. It had been almost two years since the last seminary session at Sigurdshof had ended. The communities of Eberhard and the brothers, sites of deepest satisfaction, had scattered. He could still, to Ruth's satisfaction, retreat to Kieckow and Klein Krössin, but they were less permanent and less attractive substitutes for the seminary life he loved. Also, though Eberhard had nursed him through his pneumonia and remained close, he continued to doggedly pursue marrying Renate. And while the conspiracy offered Dietrich many advantages, from draft deferrals to the opportunity to atone for the crimes of the regime, its hallmark was paralysis.

Another blow fell when Hitler dismissed one of the conspirators, General Brauchitsch, the army's commander in chief, and took over his position himself. Yet in 1942, the plotters again regrouped. The aging General Ludwig Beck, with a balding head shaped like a light bulb and deep mournful eyes, agreed to take command of the coup. Though he had initially supported the Nazi revolution, he had resigned from the army in 1938 to protest the speed of Hitler's expansionist policies. More hope came as it became clearer that the Russian invasion was a disaster: people increasingly began to support the conspiracy.[8]

Of more immediate interest, during the previous autumn's deportations in 1941, Dohnanyi and Dietrich helped fourteen Jews flee to Switzerland. These friends, in danger of being exterminated at a death camp, included Charlotte Friedenthal, who was part of the Confessing Church's provisional leadership. The escape involved a large currency transfer. This transfer caught the attention of Himmler and earned Dohnanyi and Bonhoeffer increased surveillance by the Gestapo. Initially, the Gestapo understood the currency irregularity as an illegal moneymaking scheme. Himmler hoped it would throw Canaris's military intelligence office into such a bad light that Hitler would put it under Gestapo control.

---

7. Speer, *Inside the Third Reich*, 217.
8. Bethge, *DB: A Biography*, 751.

Wilhelm Schmidhuber, suspected of smuggling currency out of the country, was Dietrich's superior in the Abwehr. Should the Gestapo uncover Schmidhuber's role in a conspiracy, Dietrich would be in trouble.[9]

Oblivious to such machinations and finishing her final year at Wieblingen school, Maria took over classes when the regular math teacher got sick and left.[10] On March 20, 1942, Maria, class captain, graduated from a school run without von Thadden and now synchronized with Nazi ideology. Ideally, a Nazi school developed physical strength rather than intellect, and created a "really great spirit" able "to follow the lofty flight of such an eagle [as Hitler]." Such education dedicated itself to "promotion of will power and determination, combined with training in the joy of responsibility." Further, because Germans had become "broken and defenseless, exposed to the kicks of all the world," National Socialist schools must ensure that German children knew they were "absolutely superior" to all others.[11]

Ruth, hospitalized in Stettin for four weeks—a "bitter pill"—[12] because of a heart murmur, could not be at the graduation, nor could Maria's father, still at the front. The only witness was her mother, Ruthchen, who had written to Maria weekly, while single-handedly managing an estate.

Now eighteen, the newly graduated Maria was stunning, with charisma and sexuality enhancing her beauty. Her intelligence, too, was striking and unforgettable, even in the world of Nazi—and Junker—Germany that discounted female intellect. Friends, family, and coworkers described her repeatedly as assertive, beautiful, and intelligent.

Maria, publicly at least, displayed a bold personality. According to her sister Ruth Alice von Bismarck, Maria had "spontaneous vitality." [13] Brother Max wrote of Maria's "passionate temperament and extreme sensitivity."[14] Sabine's daughter Marianne described Maria, whom she met after the war, as "so vivacious, so radiant."[15]

Maria's letters and journal show her love of action, of galloping on horses and hunting, of whirling, running, jumping, dancing, and playing. As an assistant teacher, she enjoyed sliding down steps with her charges on lunch trays, and joining them for hide-and-go-seek.

9. Dramm, *Dietrich Bonhoeffer and the Resistance*, 157.
10. Pejsa, *Matriarch of Conspiracy*, 282.
11. Nicholas, *Cruel World*, 68.
12. Bonhoeffer, *DBWE 16*, 276.
13. Bismarck and Kabitz, eds., *Love Letters*, 295
14. Ibid., 298.
15. Ibid., 348.

Much like Dietrich, this remarkable woman became a victim of circumstances. Paradoxically, the supremely confident Maria was needy, a trait noticed by her close Wieblingen school friend, Doris Fahle. Doris wrote that Maria was "absolutely steadfast . . . in her views . . . firmly rooted she was in her well-established world . . . . But she was 'vulnerable.'"[16]

In a topsy-turvy war world, Maria found refuge in her grandmother.

By Easter, Ruth's frustration had reached a pitch. Dietrich and Eberhard would be at Kieckow on April 5, Easter Sunday, knowing Ruth would still be in the Karolus Hospital in Stettin. Irritated at their seeming inflexibility in accommodating her, even in her illness, she wondered if they were trying to avoid her.[17]

As her extended family gathered for Easter, Ruth, alone in her hospital room, wrote to Eberhard, sending greetings to Dietrich from "her heart." On Easter, guests and family at Kieckow cold-shouldered the Nazi church in Kieckow, instead heading in two "horse drawn vehicles" for "the little parish in the woods" in Naseband presided over by dissident Pastor Reimer. Late that afternoon, Dohnanyi phoned Kieckow with an urgent request that Dietrich head to Norway on April 10th to help orchestrate the release of Norwegian Bishop Berggrav before he could be sent to trial for refusing to cooperate with the Nazis.[18]

On Easter, the day Dohnanyi called, all the Norwegian Lutheran pastors had resigned at Berggrav's instigation. This was exactly the kind of statement Dietrich had worked for in Germany fervently, but in vain. Berggrav did avoid a trial, being kept under house arrest until the end of the war.

Dietrich liked his travel companion, Helmuth von Moltke. As they navigated Norway's fog and ice, walking and talking between a flurry of visits, enjoying a movie at Dietrich's behest and eating better food than wartime German fare, they discussed the stalled coup. Though convinced of the need to oust Hitler, von Moltke balked at the idea of assassination.

From Norway, Dietrich and von Moltke headed to Sweden, where on their arrival they "were most sumptuously fed," according to Helmuth.[19] Dietrich naturally took advantage of this opportunity to write to Sabine, still hopeful the Nazi regime would be ousted in a few months. Eberhard always hovered beside him in spirit: "My friend [Eberhard] is often with us," he

---

16. Ibid., 300. Fahle uses the English word *vulnerable*.

17. Pejsa, *Matriarch of Conspiracy*, 278. In their defense, being involved with Ruth could be overwhelming—she seldom, if ever, hesitated to pick up the phone or write letters in order to ensure she had a voice.

18. Ibid., 279–80.

19. Bonhoeffer, *DBWE 16*, 268.

wrote, "he has become a great flutist and his friendly good-humored nature is a joy to the family."[20]

Back in Berlin for a short interlude at the end of April and beginning of May, Dietrich returned to his parents' house. The food shortage had by this time grown so acute that the senior Bonhoeffers had started a garden in their backyard. Here they grew grapes, apples, pears, strawberries, peas, beans, potatoes, and tomatoes. Later they would add corn and tobacco.[21]

Most Berliners who had any land at all, even a terrace that could hold pots, had begun growing vegetables.[22] Others scavenged for wild plants and weeds, such as dandelions, nettles, and Dietrich's favorite, mushrooms. To have meat, people kept chickens and rabbits—Dietrich was especially pleased when, while he was in prison, his sister sent him a rabbit liver.

Not only was empty land converted to gardens, seemingly every remaining scrap of empty space housed the ballooning ranks of workers brought in from conquered Reich territories. As one French forced laborer explained: "Berlin was covered with wooden barracks. In even the tiniest space in the capital, there were rows of brown, wooden blocks, covered in roofing felt. Greater Berlin resembled a single camp, which had been scattered between the sturdy buildings, the monuments, the office blocks, the rail stations and the factories."[23]

Jews endured conditions one journalist described as "completely hellish." They were "hunted animals . . . . They are reminded every day, both in speech and in writing, that the Jew is the enemy of the German people. Wherever they go, gigantic posters scream this in their face . . . ."[24]

This is the Berlin Dietrich saw as he talked with a friend of both his and Sabine's from the confirmation class they had shared so long ago, Hans Bernd von Haeften. Von Haeften, a councilor in the Foreign Office, was a Confessing Church member and a pacifist. Although an anti-Hitler conspirator, von Haeften, like von Moltke, resisted the idea of killing Hitler. He and Dietrich took a long walk around crowded downtown Berlin to discuss the situation, away from the possibility of microphones and prying ears.[25]

20. Ibid., 273.
21. Ibid., 112.
22. Moorhouse, *Berlin at War*, 92.
23. Ibid., 122.
24. Ibid., 282–83.
25. Bonhoeffer, *DBWE 16*, 168–69.

— 45 —
Ruth and Maria

"I HAD ALWAYS BEEN especially close [to Ruth]," Maria wrote. "The feeling was mutual because she thought I resembled her as a young girl."[1]

Maria had been a skinny, pigtailed child of eleven when she and the then–twenty-nine-year-old Dietrich first met in the fall of 1935. He had lived in Berlin, Barcelona, Manhattan, and London and travelled to Italy, Algeria, Mexico, Sweden, Denmark, France, and Cuba. He had a PhD, had taught at a university, pastored churches, and published books. Though intelligent and energetic, Maria had hardly left the provincial backwater of Pätzig. She, for instance, knew nobody who had ever been to the United States. In her highly hierarchical Prussian society, Dietrich was fully the adult male with all the rights that entailed, Maria a child and a girl, her wishes subordinated to family needs.

Maria loved her father and her brother Max, two years older than she. Like Sabine, she remembered the excitement of Christmas, in her case not holding a twin's hand, but sitting on her father's knee, "gazing in wonder at the cracks of light from the Christmas-tree room growing brighter and brighter, and looking forward to the big treat with every fiber of my being."[2] Later, the door would open, and the children would enter the room lit by the tree's candles. They would breathe in the scent of pine, gingerbread, and candles, then open presents wrapped in tissue paper and decorated with stars.

Her father called her "Missymouse" and pulled her long braids. He accused her of spending too much time in the kitchen mingling with the servants, mimicking their dialects.

Maria, like Dietrich, fought getting lost in a large family. When her own sons were born, she wrote "My children are going to have so much home life they are going to get sick of it."[3] She remembered her own youth as she advised her sister on handling a daughter: "I'm one of those funny

---

1. Bismarck and Kabitz, eds., *Love Letters*, 330.
2. Ibid., 138.
3. Ibid., 351.

types . . . who need an inordinate amount of attention, and if they don't get it, they extract it. And a scolding is better in such cases than indifference. We've all been brought up to be a bit too 'Prussian' and 'stiff upper lip' and 'don't fuss.'"[4]

She did not get along well with her mother[5] or more ladylike older sister. "[We were] very different as children," wrote Ruth-Alice, "and frequently at odds for that reason."[6] Her mother and Maria clashed often, Ruth-Alice remembered. Maria agreed: "As Mother told me—I was always their problem child."[7]

Maria thus turned to her father. "It simply went without saying that I should tell Father *everything* while out riding with him, and that he should share in all our fun . . . ."[8]

Despite feeling overlooked within the family, Maria grew up a star player in the life of the village, a leader in the community, a dispenser of gifts at Christmas and holidays, an organizer of the village Christmas pageant, and a symbol of privilege to whom others paid deference. Because her mother found social events a strain, Maria early took on hostessing duties. She said she had more evening gowns than she knew what to do with and had danced away more than one night at a grand estate. Her bedroom was decorated enchantingly with a picture of an angel hanging above her bed, a flower piece by Brueghel and a Grunewald altar.[9] She imbibed the "stiff necked" Junker hauteur, an aristocratic penchant for command that would sometimes make her a challenging personality when she moved into different spheres.

Maria's prison letters to Dietrich would overflow with her love of Pätzig, her childhood home, an estate about sixty miles east of Berlin. Part of Pätzig was a marshy, gloomy forest, medieval in character, filled with deer, wild boar, owls, turtles, and snipes. Maria learned to ride and hunt boar early.

Pätzig's imposing manor house, surrounded by gardens, stood near the village's parsonage, church, and school. French doors, flanked on each side by rows of windows, led into the then–150-year-old home, built in the eighteenth century. The second story, roofed in orange tile and punctuated by dormered windows, offered panoramic views across pastures and the

---

4. Ibid., 356.
5. Ibid., 295. See also Pejsa, *Matriarch of Conspiracy*, 282.
6. Bismarck and Kabitz, eds., *Love Letters*, 10.
7. Ibid., 180.
8. Ibid.
9. Ibid., 40.

lake to the forest beyond. Visitors could see sheep grazing in the distant meadows and fields of rye, potatoes, wheat, and sugar beets. By the 1920s, much of the estate had been deforested to offset deep agricultural losses,[10] another indication of the fragility of the Junker economy.

The forests might have become smaller, but life had changed little in two hundred years. The village "idiot" still served an important role in village life. Strict hierarchy still reigned; people still traveled by horse, and big workhorses, reminiscent of the Middle Ages, still pulled the ploughs. In this archaic social order, young Maria grew up.

Although to the manor born, Maria was not coddled. She and her siblings' Spartan regime included a daily run before breakfast around their palatial home, to be doused afterwards with buckets of cold of water by the servants.[11] Maria hunted, stole summer fruit from the kitchen garden, and when the weather grew colder, gathered with her brothers and sisters in front of an open fire on her father's Persian cushions to eat baked apples.[12] Hans, a renowned storyteller, regaled them with tales of his own childhood.

The von Wedemeyer parents had joined the Berneuchens, a Protestant reform movement. Their friend Karl Bernhard Ritter was one of the movement's leaders. The von Wedemeyers opened Pätzig to him during the 1920s. The Berneuchens tried to inculcate joy into the grim Prussian Protestant religious holidays and sought to cultivate dependence on God's provision, hoping to inspire gratitude while glorifying God in music, prayer, and service.[13] The family wove its religion into its everyday life, gathering for prayers every morning at 8:30 AM. When needed, they sang hymns at morning prayers asking for rain or sunshine to help the crops.

For five years in a row, from ages seven to eleven, Maria went with her siblings to annual Berneuchen missionary meetings, of which she had "frightful" memories: "We found it dreadfully boring to sit in the sweltering sun and listen to stories about poor little Negro children. Not even the mountains of pastries in the intermission were adequate compensation."[14]

As soon as Ruth was released from the hospital in April 1942, she headed for Pätzig. The faithful Hans Jurgen helped her onto the train at Stettin with her cane and her cataracts. At Pätzig, Ruth watched through clouded

---

10. Ibid., 288.
11. Paradise, "Eulogy for Maria Friedricka von Wedemeyer Weller."
12. Bismarck and Kabitz, eds., *Love Letters*, 90.
13. Ibid., 307.
14. Ibid., 116.

eyes as the ever-energetic Maria, overflowing with exuberance, taught her thirteen-year-old brother, Hans Werner, to dance. The two rolled up the Oriental carpet on the floor of the Pätzig great hall. As Strauss waltzes from the phonograph filled the air, Maria and Hans Werner wound round and round the room.[15]

Ruth's frustrations with Dietrich continued unabated. Her letter of April 24, 1942, composed about the same time Maria twirled about the great hall, expresses some of her impatience with him for behaving like a teenager flitting in and out of her life: "I hope finally at the 15th of May to be at Klein Krössin. You know how welcome you are there. But I have about given up when it comes to any plans involving you and Eberhard. In all honesty, I must say it would be much pleasanter at Krössin if you were a little more serious about planning ahead for your visits.... How happy it would be for me, as you well know, if you and Eberhard could spare a little time for me while I am still here [at Pätzig]. But I won't be a beggar."

According to Pejsa, the allusion to Pätzig was telling: "This letter is the first hint that the grandmother has something new on her mind—something that has to do with the Wedemeyers of Pätzig."[16]

Ruth soon relocated to Klein Krössin, with its May gardens in bloom. She waited impatiently for Dietrich's visit. Near the end of May, Ruth sent an urgent message to Pätzig, insisting that her cataracts were bothering her and that Maria must come help her with her letter-writing and reading.[17]

Maria arrived at Klein Krössin not only to help, but to enjoy some freedom before her service year. This year, required of all young women who had completed high school, had been devised by the Party as a way to solve the servant problem. Young women would learn about homemaking and child care through working in a married woman's home. The older women would get free or low-cost help.

The government also encouraged young women to spend their service year on farms. Not only was the traditional rural life part of the Nazi ideal of blood and soil, but during the war farmers sorely needed help. The need for

---

15. Pejsa, *Matriarch of Conspiracy*, 283.

16. Ibid., 285. Letters such as Bethge's February, 1941 Valentine's missive to Dietrich: "Don't be surprised at the one from Aunt Ruth. On both visits we had discussed the ever popular topic of marriage; that is the explanation," suggest that while Maria might have been a new object, a marriage between Dietrich and one of her young relatives was probably not a "new" thought for Ruth in 1942. See Bonhoeffer, *DBWE 16*, 152.

17. Ibid., 286.

young women's labor in all areas became acute: they filled gaps in hospitals, churches and factories, farms and schools.

Maria, like others her age, faced working long hours in austere surroundings. As she noted years later, however, complaining was not an option; the stiff upper lip was the rule. It was especially hard to complain when young men her age had gone to the Russian front, including her beloved Max. In a photograph, the slim, musical youth with the sensitive mouth looks too young to fight. He seems to be playing dress-up in his stiff-collared woolen uniform with the eagle pinned to his breast, despite having been schooled from earliest youth for a military career. His visored hat, perched jauntily, appears too big for his head, ready to slip down over his eyes at the first rough movement. Trying to look brave and nonchalant with his shoulders pulled back—what Maria called "snappy"—he instead appears uncertain, unformed, too kind to fit anyone's stereotype of a ruthless soldier of the Aryan master race. When she later sent Dietrich a copy of this photo, Maria asked that he not "dislike" it. "A lot of people do . . . but I'm fond of it."[18]

That May 1942, Ruth sat with Maria amid the chestnuts in her beloved gardens. One photo shows Ruth outside the cottage, in a long Swiss-dotted dress with a large bouquet of what appear to be primroses held in her lap. She perches on a bale of straw, her scissors or knife still in her hand, a curving woven basket beside her. The picture typifies Ruth, the consummate arranger.

Meanwhile, back in Switzerland while Ruth waited impatiently, Dietrich wrote to Sabine from the small guest room of a friend's home overlooking Lake Zurich. "You know we are with you in our thoughts and our prayers every day," he told Sabine. "I have always been thinking about you during the last months, specially in the depth of winter how you were getting through the severe cold."[19]

At his hosts' home, he played the piano, impressed them with his charm and intelligence, and enjoyed taking them out occasionally to meals, which he turned into "festive" affairs. "He loved to eat well," remembered his hosts, the Salomons. He introduced them to his old Union Theological friend, Sutz, the start of a lasting friendship. One afternoon, after he'd received his mail, they found him "depressed." "Things are serious for me," he said, and left that day.[20]

---

18. Bismarck and Kabitz, eds., *Love Letters*, 155.
19. Bonhoeffer, *DBWE 16*, 284.
20. Zimmermann and Smith, eds., *I Knew*, 171–72.

46

Sweden, Krössin, Berlin

BONHOEFFER HURRIED FROM SWITZERLAND to Sweden, another neutral country, because Bell was there. With the conspiracy plans intensifying, he wished to speak to this trusted friend.

Ostensibly, Bonhoeffer's trip to Sweden assessed the Swedish church for the Nazi government and sought information about the "real relations" between Britain and its US and Soviet allies.[1] But the true reason was—again—to test how the allies would respond to high-ranking Germans toppling the Reich government. Bonhoeffer took a risk, not without misgivings,[2] and gave Bell a list of names of people planning a coup to depose Hitler. He also communicated the request that the foreign governments allow the new German government time to establish itself because "even if the men involved first had to conceal their intentions from the people," they intended to end the war as soon as possible.[3]

Bell noted in his journal Bonhoeffer's concern that Germany not escape punishment. Not surprisingly, Bonhoeffer spoke of restoring the monarchy and again suggested his friend Prince Louis Ferdinand, a man he vouched for to Bell as a Christian with "outspoken social interests."[4] Yet all this earnest talk was too little, too late.

When he received Bell's report on the conspiracy, Anthony Eden, close friend to Churchill and leader of the House of Commons, simply couldn't fathom that Bonhoeffer could have met with as high-ranking an Englishman as Bell without—at best—being the unwitting dupe of the Gestapo, at worst a genuine Nazi spy.

"What an indescribable joy to have heard from you from George! It still seems to me like a miracle," Dietrich wrote to Sabine and Gert from Stockholm on

1. Dramm, *Dietrich Bonhoeffer and the Resistance*, 167.
2. Ibid., 178.
3. Ibid., 168.
4. Ibid., 178–79.

June 1.⁵ For Dietrich, caught so long in the world of Nazi Germany—"The air that we breathe is so polluted by mistrust that it almost chokes us"⁶—the meeting with Bell almost overwhelmed him. Dietrich letter to Bell danced on air: "It still seems to me like a dream to have seen you, to have spoken to you, to have heard your voice. I think these days will remain in my memory as some of the greatest of my life." As was typical when faced with courage, humanity, or goodness, Dietrich experienced both appreciation and inadequacy: "I feel ashamed when I think of all your goodness and at the [same] time I feel full of hope for the future."⁷

Beyond all else, Bell had painted a hopeful but realistic picture of Sabine's life, relieving Dietrich's oppressive fears that her letters hid deep sufferings: "as far as he can see there is no real reason for worrying about your future," Dietrich wrote to Sabine. "He does not underestimate your difficulties and hardships, yet he will always prove a true friend."⁸

The extent to which Germany had indeed become a "vast prison," cutting Dietrich off more and more from the humane forms of life he loved, came home to him in Sweden. "My heart is full of thanks for these last days. George is one of the great personalities I have met in my life."⁹

Dietrich passed on messages to Gert and Sabine through Bell—asking Sabine if she wanted to return to Germany after the war, which he must have dearly hoped for, and promising "to do the utmost for finding position" for Gert.¹⁰

Sabine and the family were in Cambridge for Gert to give a paper, when Bell suddenly appeared. He told them he'd just seen Dietrich in Sweden and showed them documents about the conspiracy. Sabine was "shaken." All thoughts of the conference fled, replaced by terror that somehow Dietrich's name would leak out to the press in conjunction with the conspiracy. "Our hearts pounded," Sabine wrote. Knowing Dietrich had been Sweden, combined with the dangers he faced, threw Sabine and Gert into turmoil. They were, wrote Sabine, "inexpressibly weighed down by our anxieties as to how this all would end." Bell also told Sabine he had done "his utmost" to convince her brother to seek refuge in England with him. But Dietrich feared this would create catastrophe for those left behind.¹¹

5. Bonhoeffer, *DBWE 16*, 312.
6. Bonhoeffer, *LPP*, 11.
7. Bonhoeffer, *DBWE 16*, 311–12.
8. Ibid., 312.
9. Ibid., 313.
10. Dramm, *Dietrich Bonhoeffer and the Resistance*, 181.
11. Leibholz, *The Bonhoeffers*, 145–46.

His journey done, Dietrich sent Ruth word from Sweden that he would arrive at Klein Krössin, hoping to continue work on his *Ethics*.[12] Maria was already there. In so far as Ruth had planned matchmaking, she barely succeeded: Dietrich arrived the day before Maria left.[13] The setting could not have been more perfect for romance: a long balmy midsummer idyll in Ruth's enchanting flower garden, colored in vibrant violets from the clematis and creeping phlox[14] blooming outside the rambling cottage, a setting with happy associations for all concerned.

Ruth sits in her garden.

Ruth included Maria in conversations with Dietrich as an equal, not a child. In front of Dietrich, Maria spoke to her grandmother with the bold, "cocky" attitude that Ruth liked. Discussing the day with her sister decades later, Maria remembered that "the three of us got on extremely well together." When Ruth dismissed her desire to continue studying mathematics as a "silly whim," Maria, more than thirty years later, recalled that Dietrich "took it seriously."[15]

That evening, Dietrich walked alone with Maria down the cobblestone path to Kieckow in the dusky twilight. The two discussed, among

---

12. Schlingensiepen, *Dietrich Bonhoeffer 1906–1945*, 292.
13. Ibid., 286.
14. Pejsa, *Matriarch of Conspiracy*, 174.
15. Bismarck and Kabitz, eds., *Love Letters*, 330. Other accounts says she initially resented Dietrich's intrusion.

other subjects, first names, daisies, and "Lili-Marlen," a popular German war song.[16] While Ruth felt hopeless about the situation in Germany, Maria's conversation bubbled with optimism. Dietrich began "to compare and contrast the grandmother and granddaughter," finding them alike, except for Maria's hope. The socially polished Dietrich, put on the spot by feeling pressured to behave as a suitor, hardly knew "how to conduct himself."[17]

The next day, Maria left.[18]

Somewhat later, June 25, 1942, during a long train trip from Berlin to Rome, Dietrich wrote to Eberhard about Maria, clearly continuing a conversation the two men had already started about her.[19]

"I have not written to Maria," Dietrich told him, imagining his few "highly charged" moments with her would fade "into the realm of my unfulfilled fantasies." At this line, most biographies stop, but the letter continues. Thinking on paper, Dietrich backpedaled. Yes, the few moments were "delightful," but, he wrote, with some irritation, "I don't see how a meeting could be contrived in such a way as to seem unobtrusive and inoffensive to her. I couldn't expect Fran von Kleist [Ruth] to arrange it . . . because the fact is, I'm still very uncertain and undecided."[20]

Contrived—the word echoes across the years. Sitting on the train speeding toward Rome, Dietrich knew of the web that Ruth and Eberhard were spinning around Maria. He understood the plan: He should marry the young woman. The only reason Dietrich wouldn't turn to master matchmaker Ruth to "arrange it" was that he himself was a reluctant suitor. The backstory explaining Dietrich's recent sidestepping of time alone with Ruth, a woman he admired and felt especially close to, and, in prison, longed almost palpably to hear from, was almost surely the incessant, relentless pressure to marry her granddaughter.

By mid-July, the wandering Dietrich had returned from his trip to Italy, where he had written to Sabine with the hope "it won't be long before we see each other again."[21] Back in Germany, he made his way to Ruth's cottage to work on *Ethics*, both the cottage and Ruth continuing to act as a muse. He didn't run into Maria, as she was staying with her von Kleist cousins on

---

16. Pejsa, *Matriarch of Conspiracy*, 287.

17. Ibid.

18. The dating of their meeting is uncertain. According to Bonhoeffer, *DBWE 6*, Maria spent from June 2–5 at Klein Krössinn (461). According to Bonhoeffer, *DBWE 16*, 688, Bonhoeffer arrived there on June 8.

19. Schlingensiepen, *Dietrich Bonhoeffer 1906–1945*, 296.

20. Bismarck and Kabitz, eds., *Love Letters*, 331.

21. Schlingensiepen, *Dietrich Bonhoeffer 1906–1945*, 296.

their estate at Gross Tychow,²² doing national service work as a mother's helper. Yet Ruth, true to form, apparently continued matchmaking: in July Maria wrote in her diary "the catchword 'marry.'"²³ On August 10, Dietrich traveled to Magdeburg for a church conference.

In the meantime, Sabine in Oxford avoided having to become a housemaid, the fate of the more impoverished of her peers. Sabine's class feathers ruffled at the idea of upper-class German women going into service: "The women refugees, too, many of whom came from good families . . . frequently . . . had to take posts as domestic servants for English families, and their experiences were often harmful and humiliating. . . . Occasionally they were given different names, for instance, the name of the last cook employed at the house. In other words, their employers did not so much as take the trouble to accustom themselves to the new names! . . . They showed themselves incapable of understanding what it meant for someone whose social background was actually similar to theirs to be forced, for lack of resources, to accept work as a housemaid."²⁴

In late August, Dietrich was sipping tea in the garden of his parents' home when a servant called him to the phone to speak to Ruth: Maria's father, Ruth told him, had been killed on the Russian front. Dietrich would later write to Maria, "I thought I could sense from afar, at that moment, what you had lost; and I think I was able to think of you and share your grief in a genuinely selfless fashion."²⁵ In his condolence letter to the widowed Ruthchen, Dietrich didn't mention Maria, but wrote that his "thoughts go out especially to Max," Maria's older brother, who Dietrich had confirmed.²⁶ Maria broke off her national service year to return to Pätzig.²⁷

---

22. Bismarck and Kabitz, eds., *Love Letters*, 333.

23. Bonhoeffer, *DBWE 6*, 461.

24. Leibholz, *The Bonhoeffers*, 151. Even working-class women, as outlined in Margaret Powell's memoir, *Below Stairs*, found the treatment harmful and humiliating.

25. Bismarck and Kabitz, eds., *Love Letters*, 69. While Bonhoeffer, *DBWE 6* and *16* both have Bonhoeffer at Klein Krössin the week of August 18–25, the clarity of Dietrich's memory of getting the phone call in his parents' garden—"I shall never forget"— leads to the assumption that Dietrich either went to Klein Krössin as soon as he got the news or had gone to Klein Krössin, come back, and would go again, not implausible given the amount of travel he and others of his class routinely undertook. In any case, he remembered himself in Berlin the day he heard the news.

26. Pejsa, *Matriarch of Conspiracy,* 289; Pejsa (288) has Bonhoeffer in Munich, not Klein Krössin on August 25, another indication that Dietrich's visit was shorter than a week.

27. Bismarck and Kabitz, eds., *Love Letters*, 331.

On September 1, Dietrich was back at Klein Krössin, where he saw Maria once again.²⁸ It seems that Ruth pushed Dietrich to marry Maria and that the conversation went poorly. Ruth wrote to Eberhard: "In hindsight I have real regrets about Dietrich's visit here. It is as if I said too much, and even without words, made judgments on what ought or ought not to be. God forgive me if I conducted myself badly . . . . So many questions have turned up and they all need to be answered." She turned to her co-conspirator: "How happy I would be if you could resolve them with me." Ruth then mused to Eberhard: "Even if a happy marriage is cut asunder too soon [by death], still one is rewarded for an entire lifetime. Marriage is a mystery. Not every marriage is as God would have it."²⁹ In other words, Dietrich once again had tried to sidestep marriage by pleading danger: Ruth would have none of it.

In late September, Ruth arrived in Berlin, in preparation for a cataract operation. This involved a long, two-week pre-op stage in the hospital and then convalescence, a situation ideal for her relentless matchmaking. She asked that Maria come to Berlin to read to her in the hospital. Yet Ruth once again must have felt thwarted: Dietrich arrived in her sickroom on October 2 merely to pay a "farewell visit" before his trip to Munich, the prelude to a six-week journey that would include traveling to Switzerland and the Balkans on Abwehr business. In six weeks, Ruth would presumably be back in Stettin, her plans for throwing Dietrich and Maria together during hospital visits fruitless.³⁰

Maria also came to the hospital on the 2nd, and despite her grandmother having already bandied about the idea of the marriage, seemed determined to frame Dietrich primarily as a pastor and friend. Now, Maria took the opportunity to chat with Dietrich about her Aunt Spes's friend Klara Ninow, who had died an atheist. Fearing Dietrich would be "horrified" and highly disapproving, Maria was warmed at "his kindly verdict," about Klara. "That—I think—was when I first took to you," she later wrote.³¹ In her diary she wrote, "Very different meeting than in June."³²

---

28. Bonhoeffer, *DBWE 6*, 462.
29. Pejsa, *Matriarch of Conspiracy*, 290–91.
30. The cataract operation didn't take place until October 13.
31. Bismarck and Kabitz, eds., *Love Letters*, 91.
32. Bonhoeffer, *DBWE 6*, 463. If this is when Maria first "took to" Dietrich, we can imagine she interpreted what Bonhoeffer called June's highly charged moments differently. In fact, Maria describes herself as "a bit put out at first" by Bonhoeffer's presence at her grandmother's cottage (Bismarck and Kabitz, eds., *Love Letters*, 330).

While Dietrich went to Munich, Maria, who stayed in Spes's Berlin apartment, visited the Schleichers, where Hans Walter and Renate showed her around their garden. They crossed into Dietrich's parents' adjoining garden, where "the grapes were ripe, so we feasted on them." At that point, Maria looked up to see Karl Bonhoeffer watching from a window. Maria "blushed" that she was caught stealing at their first meeting.

The senior Bonhoeffers invited in Maria, Renate, and Hans Walter. They sat in the ground floor study and talked. Maria saw a picture of Dietrich's long dead brother Walter. She thought of her own brother Max, far away on the Russian front.[33]

Dietrich returned from Munich on October 14, the day after Ruth's operation, his visit to abroad cancelled for fear he would be arrested at the border. At loose ends, he saw Ruth frequently. "Ruth . . . insist[ed] that Maria be with her every afternoon and that Dietrich . . . visit at the same time." Ruth found frequent excuses—wishing to sleep or needing her bed changed—to send the two out into the hallway to sit on a bench together.[34] The hospital corridor was busy with the traffic of doctors, nurses, orderlies, and the sisters in their long habits, but the two were, to some extent, alone.

Ruth apparently openly pushed the couple together. Dietrich would later write in frustration to Maria about Ruth's matchmaking in the hospital. It caused him, and he imagined, Maria, a "painful inner burden" when Ruth expressed "things not suitable for discussion." He then burst out, "I told her countless times that I did not wish to discuss things, in fact this would do violence to both parties. . . . My conversations with her were often difficult to endure; she did not heed my requests."[35]

Maria remembered, at least initially, being blind to her grandmother's intentions, although it's hard to fathom how that could be. "Dietrich's frequent visits surprised me, and I was impressed by his devotion. We often had long talks together at this time. It was a reunion under different circumstances than in June. Being still deeply affected by my father's death, I needed Dietrich's help."[36]

"Do you remember how we went for a stroll in the corridor and talked about senile teachers, and do you remember how happy I was that you were so utterly against emigrating?" Maria would later write. "And do you remember how we hurried down the steps into the Brandenburgische Strasse

---

33. Bismarck and Kabitz, eds., *Love Letters*, 91.
34. Pejsa, *Matriarch of Conspiracy*, 291–92.
35. Bonhoeffer, *DBWE 16*, 370.
36. Bismarck and Kabitz, eds., *Love Letters*, 331.

..."[37]—the location of Spes's apartment in an elegant, tree-lined block of flats. Dietrich walked Maria home, and Maria mentioned she wished she could attend the Schleicher's "musical evening," apparently the farewell party at the Schleichers in honor of Renate's older brother, Hans-Werner, who was leaving for the front. This would have been the evening of October 14th.[38]

Maria did attend the farewell party. Dietrich may have invited her. It was the only time she would see the entire Bonhoeffer family together.

At the Schleicher's party, Maria had what she termed "a very interesting talk with Pastor Bonhoeffer. He said it was a tradition with us that young men should volunteer for military service and lay down their lives for a cause of which they mightn't approve at all. But there must also be people able to fight from conviction alone. If they approved of the grounds for war, well and good. If not, they could best serve the Fatherland by operating on the internal front, perhaps even by working against the regime .... Oh, it's all so logically clear and obvious. But isn't it terrible, when I think of my father?"[39]

At the end of the evening, Dietrich didn't accompany her home. She managed the trip alone through blacked-out Berlin. As one observer wrote of the blackout experience: "Strangely enough, it seems as if one were sinking, and there are accompanying sensations as if one were drowning. One soon becomes accustomed to moving about in the dark; but for all that, one does not escape an intermittent horror."[40]

When Maria arrived at Spes's apartment, she realized she had forgotten her key. Both Spes and the maid were out. Nobody answered the phone when she called. So she sat on stone steps outside the building to wait in the darkness.[41]

37. Ibid., 35.

38. Ibid. The text implies, but doesn't explicitly state (331) that this musical evening was indeed Hans-Werner's party.

39. Ibid., 331–32.

40. Lubrich, ed., *Travels in the Reich*, 228.

41. Bismarck and Kabitz, eds., *Love Letters*, 104.

47

Maria

THE NEXT DAY, HER diary suggests she had shared her concerns about Dietrich's lack of military service with her grandmother: "I now know that a man like Dietrich, who truly feels he has an inner mission to help his country and is a personality capable of forming an objective opinion, is right to be useful to Germany in another way and avoiding military duty as long as possible. . . . It is so easy to become a grumbler, a person who complains and carps at everything on principle and sees an ulterior motive behind it."[1]

Whatever Maria's doubts, the Gestapo, still fixated on currency issues, had by October focused on Dietrich and Dohnanyi. Whether coincidental or not, Dietrich's interest in Maria grew as he became aware of his increased danger of arrest.

One October afternoon, Dietrich invited Maria to a small restaurant near the hospital owned by Hitler's half-brother Alois,[2] decorated in rustic "old German" style with wood trim, wrought iron light fixtures, and plain white tablecloths.

Alois, who had moved from Liverpool to Berlin to capitalize on his more famous half-sibling's success, carefully complied with Hitler's policy of distancing himself from relatives, and so had little or nothing to do with Adolf. Alois was exonerated by the British, who captured him after the war, as having led "a perfectly blameless existence"—but his restaurant was, unsurprisingly, frequented by storm troopers.

As they passed the neon lights spelling out Alois on the restaurant's façade and entered, passing photos of Hitler, a waiter greeted them with a "Heil Hitler" salute. Maria, perhaps still leery of Dietrich, questioned him about dining at an eatery owned by Hitler's brother. Whatever Dietrich's feeling about rubbing elbows with the booted and uniformed SS, he brushed off her worries—the restaurant, he told her, was the safest possible place to

---

1. Bismarck and Kabitz, eds., *Love Letters*, 331–32.
2. Pejsa, *Matriarch of Conspiracy*, 292; Bismarck and Kabitz, eds., *Love Letters*, 331.

talk to her freely about her continuing grief over her father's death.³ It was also not the worst place for a man wanting to pose as a loyal Nazi to arrive with a young woman beautiful enough to attract notice.

On Sunday, October 18, Dietrich held a morning hospital prayer service for Maria and her grandmother on Ephesians 5:15–21. Maria wrote about it in her diary. During the service, Dietrich exhorted them to make the most of their time and to be grateful: "Everything we can not thank God for, we reproach him for."⁴ Maria also noted, "We must not be carried away by an idea, a popular opinion or a lazy attitude, but ought to seek the truth through the spirit."⁵ The following Sunday morning, October 25, according to one source, Bonhoeffer held another hospital prayer service.⁶ In her diary, Maria wrote that she was "unconsoled."⁷ A year later, Maria would write to Dietrich about that day, suggesting that Dietrich had visited her at Spes's Berlin apartment: "it was a year ago today that we were *alone* together for the last time. I accompanied you to the door after prayers, and I so much wanted to thank you for what you said, which moved and affected me a great deal, but I couldn't get the words out. And then you went out, and I stood there behind the closed door, angry with myself for being so self centered. Then you rang the bell again because you'd forgotten your texts. . . . I shall never forget that Sunday."⁸

Monday, October 26, Maria received devastating news: her beloved Max had been killed on the Russian front.

When Dietrich discovered Maria had left Berlin suddenly, he assumed Ruth's matchmaking, rather than Max's death, was the cause: "I then interpreted your premature departure from Berlin [on October 26] within that context and was grieved by it."⁹ All the evidence, including this, suggests that, contrary to the received narrative that she merely "notic[ed]" an "early attraction,"¹⁰ Ruth worked relentlessly to jump-start the relationship.

On October 31, Dietrich's Abwehr boss, Schmidhuber, was arrested.¹¹ During his interrogation, Dietrich's and Dohnanyi's names emerged, indicating

---

3. Bismarck and Kabitz, eds., *Love Letters*, 331.
4. Ibid., 333.
5. Bonhoeffer, *DBWE 6*, 324.
6. Ibid., 463.
7. Ibid.
8. Bismarck and Kabitz, eds., *Love Letters*, 110.
9. Bonhoeffer, *DBWE 16*, 370.
10. Ibid.
11. Dramm, *Dietrich Bonhoeffer and the Resistance*, 203.

they "played not an unimportant part" in currency irregularities and had perhaps conspired to help Jews escape the country. Two Bonhoeffer family meetings took place in November.[12]

Dietrich wrote Maria a brief condolence letter about Max on October 31, the same day as Schmidhuber's arrest, that made no allusion to the October 25th visit. One wonders why it took him five days to write the note. He asked her to "please greet your grandmother in particular once more."[13]

By now, Maria had arrived, after a short stay at Pätzig, back at her cousins' Gross Tychow. Without consulting anyone, Ruth invited Dietrich to the November 8 memorial service for Max at the Pätzig church.[14] While the sequence of events is murky, Maria's mother Ruthchen got wind of Ruth's invitation, understood it as an attempt at matchmaking and put a stop to it. Mrs. von Wedemeyer wrote to Dietrich asking him not to come to the memorial service. Maria, embarrassed at the brouhaha, shot off a letter to Dietrich on November 11, explaining that she had known nothing of her mother's request until after the fact: "I learned she had asked you not to come because of some stupid family gossip that Grandmother has rather encouraged, and which my mother regarded as a threat to her relationship with Grandmother. Fundamentally, you and I have nothing whatsoever to do with this."[15]

Now, perhaps with the threat of an arrest looming larger, Dietrich's long hesitancy about pursuing Maria suddenly disappeared. Dietrich's letter of November 13 in response to Maria's impulsive missive expressed a warmth and level of interest that shocked Maria. He wrote, "I . . . pray . . . that God may bring us together . . . soon, and very soon. Can you understand all this? Do you feel just as I do? I hope so—in fact, I cannot conceive of anything else."[16] He wrote again on the 15th, both letters frankly acknowledging the large role Ruth was playing in promoting the match, excusing it as age, asking Maria to forgive her grandmother, and expressing "horror" that Ruth might write to Mrs. von Wedemeyer about the situation at the wrong time. Alarmed at Dietrich's letters and possibly her grandmother's pressure, Maria turned to her mother. Mrs. von Wedemeyer traveled to Klein Krössin to spend an evening there with Maria, who was visiting, and Ruth, presumably

---

12. Ibid., 203.
13. Bonhoeffer, *DBWE 16*, 366–67.
14. Dietrich was at Klein-Krössin by November 7, so it was possible he had planned to accompany Ruth to the funeral.
15. Bismarck and Kabitz, eds., *Love Letters*, 333.
16. Bonhoeffer, *DBWE 16*, 370.

to sort the situation out.¹⁷ On the 19th, back in Pätzig, Mrs. von Wedemeyer telephoned Dietrich at Maria's request, asking that he not write to her daughter, but also offering to explain herself face-to-face. That gave Dietrich the opening he needed.

In the midst of all this, Dietrich went to visit Wolf Zimmermann, now married and living in a small wooden house in Werder on the Havel, about thirty miles from Berlin. The handsome, wasp-waisted Werner von Haeften was there. His younger brother was the pacifist with whom Dietrich had recently spoken. A staff lieutenant with the Army High Command, the fair-haired Werner, whose receding hairline above either temple gave him the look of an intellectual, had direct access to Hitler. He and Dietrich "talked for hours" about whether Werner should kill Hitler, Dietrich insisting Werner think it through so that Hitler's death didn't make the situation worse.¹⁸ Meanwhile, von Dohnanyi met with Manfred Roeder, a senior military prosecutor who would later become a chief nemesis, about Schmidhuber.

On November 19, immediately following Mrs. von Wedemeyer's phone call, Dietrich again sent Maria a letter: "Your mother called me this morning and told me of your wish [that he stop writing] . . . . Please forgive me if I have burdened you too greatly with my letters. . . . Do not think I failed to understand that you do not want to respond and cannot . . . . Please forget every word that hurt you and burdened you."¹⁹

Dietrich wasted no time getting to Pätzig to see Mrs. von Wedemeyer, arriving on November 24. Maria had returned to her service work at Gross Tychow. Dietrich had a tete-a-tete with Ruthchen in her late husband's study, decorated with mounted deer heads. In a letter of November 27 he described the visit to Eberhard:

"From Tuesday through Wednesday noon I was at Mrs. Wedemeyer's. Contrary to my fears that the house would have an excessively spiritual tone, its style made a very pleasant impression. She herself was calm, friendly and not overwrought, as I had feared. Gist of the discussion she requested: a year of total separation to enable Maria to find some peace. No fundamental objection to the whole thing, but given the enormity of the decision, etc. . . . My response: these days a year could just as well become five or ten and thus

17. Ibid., 464.
18 Zimmermann and Smith, eds., *I Knew,* 190–91. We don't have a date for this meeting beyond November, but a glance at the Bonhoeffer calendar we do have might put it in mid-November, probably between the 15th and 18th. One clue is that Dietrich missed a November 17 meeting of the Freiburg Circle, a resistance group discussing what Germany would look like post-Hitler, a subject of intense interest to Bonhoeffer.
19. Bonhoeffer, *DBWE 16,* 373.

represented a postponement into the incalculable; that I understood and respected her maternal authority over her daughter, but future circumstances themselves would show whether such a stipulation could be followed...."[20]

The letter marks the first unequivocal declaration of Dietrich's decision to pursue the marriage. He wrote that he could have pressured the mother, only nine years his senior, and probably forced a yes, but didn't want to take advantage of her "weakness" in light of the recent death of her husband. "I mustn't make her feel defenseless—that would be shabby of me...."[21] He ended on a practical note: "Besides, while driving around the estate on Wednesday, she spoke of its [troubled] financial position... and thought I ought to know. Well, we shall have a chance to talk about all this."[22]

Dietrich pursued his quarry in tandem with his best friend and confidante, for at this time, thirty-three-year-old Eberhard continued to press Dietrich's sister and brother-in-law to allow his marriage to the now seventeen-year-old Renate. They resisted because of her age. Bonhoeffers did not marry before twenty.

On November 27, Dietrich wrote to Eberhard that Ursel and Rüdiger had discussed the proposed marriage to Renate with Paula and Karl. "Everywhere the same—old-fashioned—ideas hearkening back to past times."[23] Given Dietrich's veneration of prewar family life, this may not have been a complaint. Yet he assures Eberhard: "If it begins to look ominous for you ... I shall in that case say something about my own situation; then for once they will consider your situation not only from Renate's perspective but also from your own. But for now, I shall hold my peace."[24]

As of November 27, Dietrich had not said a word to his parents about his pursuit of Maria or of his entering into marriage negotiations with Mrs. von Wedemeyer. Yet he had, at Ruthchen's request, informed Ruth of the details, including the demanded separation. Ruth reacted badly. "I must calm her lest she cause even more trouble," Dietrich wrote to Eberhard.[25]

That same day, November 27, Maria's mother called her daughter with news of the meeting with Dietrich and the yearlong ban on further communication. That day, Maria wrote in her diary: "Why am I suddenly so cheerful these days? I feel safe, for one thing, because I can now postpone all

20. Schlingensiepen, *Dietrich Bonhoeffer 1906–1945*, 304.
21. Bismarck and Kabitz, eds., *Love Letters*, 336.
22. Ibid., 336; Bonhoeffer, *DBWE 16*, 375.
23. Bonhoeffer, *DBWE 16*, 375.
24. Ibid.
25. Ibid., 374.

my musings, deliberations and worries till later. But shelving them certainly can't be responsible for this sense of relief. Ever since Mother told me on the phone about her meeting with Dietrich, I feel I can breathe freely again. He made a considerable impression on Mother, that's obvious—He couldn't fail to. The incredible fact remains, he actually wants to marry me. I still fail to grasp how that can be."[26]

Maria did not keep her feelings of relief a secret. Ruthchen wrote to Dietrich that Maria—as her diary entry had attested—was "relieved and happy" at the separation.[27]

Ruth, in contrast, vexed at being thwarted, continued to present a problem, "causing a good deal of trouble with her endless telephoning," as Dietrich wrote to Eberhard on November 29th.

Dietrich, having decided to take the plunge, was undeterred —though still procrastinating—and suggested in his November 29th letter to Eberhard another stratagem: "I have also considered whether—without my knowledge—you might like to write to Mrs. Wedemeyer sometime as a friend, very nice and sweet and clever, as you are able to be when you want. But this could be later; perhaps that would also be better."[28]

For all Dietrich's concern for not doing "evil" by manipulating Ruthchen into agreeing to a marriage while weakened by grief, and for all his understanding and solicitude toward Ruth, Dietrich seemed unwilling or unable to understand that it might be wrong to pursue marrying a reluctant eighteen-year-old woman suffering the double blow of recently losing both her father and her brother. That Maria, and not just her mother, might be vulnerable from the losses, on top of the ever-looming possibility of a German defeat; that it might, in fact, be a disservice to her to push his suit at this moment, never seemed to have crossed his mind. Maria, surrounded, confusingly, by seemingly loving people who did not have her best interests at heart, had only her mother as a wedge between her and their desires. Shy Ruthchen alone stood up to protect her daughter's interests.

Maria was not entirely real to Dietrich. In this most crucial of relationships, a potential marriage, Dietrich's "other" functioned as an "it"—an object—not a "thou," a human being. Yet for all his willingness to sacrifice Maria to his own needs, it would take Ruth to push the situation forward.

26. Bismarck and Kabitz, eds., *Love Letters*, 336.
27. Bonhoeffer, *DBWE 16*, 376.
28. Ibid., 377.

48

Pursuit

Despite her relief at her breathing room, by December 19, after a visit to Ruth, Maria's desires about Dietrich had flipped, and her diary records a determination to marry him.

"I thought coming home might be the one thing that could shake my resolve. I still believed I was under the influence of Grandmother, or rather, of her own unrealistic and exaggerated idea, but it isn't true. The innermost reality stands, even though I don't love him. But I know that I will love him."[1]

Maria wondered how she would be able "to forgo" her "love of dancing, riding, sport," even "pleasure" to marry someone "old and wise for his age" and a "thoroughgoing academic." Yet she dismissed reservations her mother had expressed earlier: "Mother says he's an idealist and hasn't given it careful thought. I don't believe that."[2] Even so, Maria waited, not contacting Dietrich and not telling her mother of her latest decision.

Maria went back to Gross Tychow sometime after December 19th. At about the same time, Dietrich, still the intellectual voice for the resistance, wrote an essay called "After Ten Years," noting: "We have been silent witnesses of evil deeds; we have been drenched by many storms; we have learnt the arts of equivocation and pretence; experience has made us suspicious of others and kept us from being truthful and open; intolerable conflicts have worn us down and even made us cynical. Are we still of any use?"

Plots had stirred, bubbled, brewed, dissolved, and reformed, and because the only sensible plan was to smash the head of the snake, it had been all the more important to quell suspicion by performing flawlessly as good Germans supporting the regime. Bonhoeffer, who had wanted from the start to go all out in nonviolently resisting National Socialism, had tried and tried, and by 1938 had had his heart broken. Others were like him, such as Elizabeth von Thadden, but still nothing had happened. Now, after ten years

---

1. Bismarck and Kabitz, eds., *Love Letters*, 337.
2. Ibid.

of effort and of waiting and enduring, he weighed in with his essay, striking at the heart of what was most debilitating about moral life in Nazi Germany.

He was writing for friends—and for posterity—but his impatience emerged: "Mere waiting and looking on is not Christian behavior. The Christian is called to sympathy and action, not in the first place by his own sufferings, but by the sufferings of his brethren, for whose sake Christ suffered."

He asked the question posed by so many: why the Germans had failed so miserably at "civic courage," that quality enabling standing up in the public sphere to cry out against injustice. He attributed it to the German virtue of obedience misplaced and distorted in the service of evil. He concluded: "We . . . must take our share of responsibility for the moulding of history . . . whether we are the victors or the vanquished. . . . The ultimate question for a responsible man to ask is not how he is to extricate himself heroically from the affair, but how the coming generation is to live."[3]

Bonhoeffer used the word *fairy tale* in "After Ten Years" to describe the folly of obedience to the regime, and the word was apt—people followed a regime characterized by night and fog, sleights of hand, mystic conjurings of Teutonic times, and false assertions of the purity of the Aryan superhero. The country, in a bubble, lived as if in slow motion, as if sleepwalking, as outside forces the regime unleashed came closer.

Like the Jews in Germany early on, who were forced to lie to the international press and say they were not being subjected to violence to avoid the threat of more violence, like the prisoners of the Nazis forced to thank their abusers for beating them, the duplicity that was a hallmark of Hitler's character and the regime became mirrored in the upper classes as they pretended to support what they despised. If Hitler knew, he no doubt enjoyed it.

Dietrich gave copies of "After Ten Years" to Bethge, Dohnanyi, and Oster, and hid another copy in the roof beams of Marienberger Allee 43, an odd choice given that Paula noticed—or would soon notice—how often the top floors of houses burned after bombing raids.

By the end of 1942, not only was day-to-day German life increasingly harsh, the future looked nightmarish. As 1943 loomed, would the privileged class finally act? That question danced in Dietrich's mind.

The new year, 1943, opened darkly. The Soviet army pushed closer to Germany. "The situation of the German soldiers was catastrophic and such news as filtered through the Reich about the real situation made many

---

3. Bonhoeffer, "After Ten Years," in *Letters and Papers from Prison*, 7.

people grasp for the first time . . . [that] Hitler's Germany was inexorably beginning to deteriorate."[4]

Just after the New Year, Ruth, cane in hand, boarded the crowded, foul-smelling train to Berlin, to attend Eberhard and Renate's engagement party. The two had become officially betrothed on December 20.[5] Renate was still only seventeen, and Eberhard's prospects were unsettled. We don't know why the family agreed to an engagement that violated Bonhoeffer rules about a bride being twenty, but we can guess it was a mixture of Eberhard's charm and an attempt by the families, who as yet knew nothing of Maria, to protect both Dietrich and Eberhard from any questions about their relationship now that the Gestapo was taking actively malevolent steps against the family.[6]

The spirit of the guests at the afternoon party that spilled between the homes of the Bonhoeffers and the Schleichers was "joyful"—except for Dietrich, who soon left the laughter, toasts, and singing to retreat to a quiet upstairs room to brood. Ruth noted this and "guess[ed] the reason" was that Dietrich pined for Maria. Ruth, fed up with the delays impeding her own cherished match, decided to go directly from Berlin to Pätzig to bring her weight to bear on Maria.[7]

Dietrich more likely brooded over losing Eberhard than gaining Maria, struggling with his feelings about what he would later refer to bitterly as Eberhard's "triumph." If he had been cornered into championing the marriage, he could not feel happy about it. Memories of Sabine's marriage may have flooded him.

On January 10, after Ruth's visit to Pätzig, Maria wrote in her diary: "I had 'the talk' with Mother." The conversation caused "hot, heavy tears"[8]—it is unclear whether they were her mother's, Maria's, or both. Maria expressed her "irrevocable" wish to marry Dietrich, and Ruthchen gave way. Maria still did not say she loved Dietrich in her diary, instead quoting Goethe: "And yet, what happiness to be loved." Maria hoped her mother understood that the marriage was "the proper course."[9] Mrs. von Wedemeyer's reservations remained—she, with the backing of Maria's guardian and uncle, Hans

---

4. Dramm, *Dietrich Bonhoeffer and the Resistance*, 218.

5. Bonhoeffer, *DBWE 16*, 692.

6. Whether or not the family thought Eberhard and Dietrich more than friends, they knew the Nazis often trumped up charges to discredit enemies.

7. Pejsa, *Matriarch of Conspiracy*, 295.

8. Bismarck and Kabitz, eds., *Love Letters*, 337.

9. Ibid.

Jurgen, insisted that the couple abide by a one-year postponement and agree not to announce the engagement. Maria wanted the postponement as well.

On January 13, on what would have been Max's twenty-first birthday, Maria wrote to Dietrich from Pätzig: "With all my happy heart, I can now say yes." Yet she soon qualified this statement. She acknowledged how little the two knew each other and the extent to which Ruth had brokered the relationship. "I myself am always saddened to think that Grandmother has told you only nice things about me, so you form a false picture of me."[10] She offered him an out: "if you've realized I'm not good enough . . . ." Even more tellingly, she supported the long separation: "I myself am quite convinced that I need some time to put my decision to the test." Near the close of the letter, she asked him for privacy: "This is our business alone, isn't it, not anybody's else's. I'm so scared of what other people say, even Grandmother. Can you grant this request?"[11]

Later that day, after mailing her letter, Maria visited her grandmother in Stettin. Ruth confronted her with the news that Dietrich had said he'd decided to stop pursuing the engagement. Maria, assuming she would receive a "Dear Fraulein von Wedermeyer, I regret to inform you . . ." letter from Dietrich, didn't tell her grandmother she had, in fact, just accepted Dietrich's proposal. The two strong-willed, emotional women most likely quarreled, for Maria would later write, "Oh, it was dreadful!"[12]

Sitting in his attic room overlooking the dead, winter garden behind his parent's Berlin house, Dietrich read Maria's acceptance with surprise and responded with an outrush of emotion: "I sense and am overwhelmed that a gift without equal has been given to me—after all the confusion of the past weeks I had no longer dared to hope—and now the unimaginably great and blissful thing is simply here, and my heart opens up and becomes quite wide and overflowing with thankfulness and shame and still cannot grasp it at all—this Yes that is to be decisive for our entire life."[13]

In calmer tones, but writing so quickly that in places the handwriting is almost indecipherable, he assured Maria he didn't want to "push or frighten" her. He acknowledged that he knew "for you it cannot be easy to say Yes to me." What negotiations had gone back and forth during those weeks, we can only guess, but Maria's hesitancy to marry rang clear to him. "I understand well that you wish to be alone for a time yet—I have been alone long enough in my life to know the blessing (though to be sure also

10. Ibid., 338.
11. Ibid., 339.
12. Ibid., 160.
13. Bonhoeffer, *DBWE 16*, 383.

the dangers) of solitude." And thus, rather than experiencing a "thunderbolt" of love or passion, the two entered awkwardly into their arranged and brokered engagement.

Dietrich ended the letter with a postscript about Ruth: "I assume as a matter of course," he said stiffly, "that I will say nothing to your grandmother before you wish it."

Ruth wrote to him on January 21 with a request that he visit.[14] At this point, neither Dietrich nor Maria had told her they were, in fact, engaged, so we can imagine Ruth hoped to apply pressure. On the 24th, Dietrich received a letter from Maria repeating, "I would like neither to write letters nor to receive any. I know exactly what I am asking with this. But you have my Yes, my true and whole-hearted Yes."[15] In the meantime, Dietrich had written to her, wondering why she had not responded to him: "I am not trying to push you, truly—I would much rather wait much longer." He ended with a postscript repeating his assertion: "I didn't want to rush or force anything. . . . it seems as if it were in fact God commanding us to wait until we are shown the way."[16] On January 24, in response to her letter requesting he not contact her, Dietrich repeated "I understand your insistence on being alone." He suggested that the "months of silence" be "a help to us, not a yoke."[17]

On January 24, the "mistress of Gross Tychow," Baroness von Kleist, certified that Maria had been "employed in the house and kitchen as a Pflichtjahrmadel [girl doing one year's compulsory service] until December 31, 1942."[18]

A few days later Dietrich wrote to thank Maria for a photo of herself she had sent him.

On February 2, 1943, the remains of the trapped Sixth Army in Stalingrad surrendered to the Soviets. Two days afterwards Eberhard presented Dietrich with a birthday table, complete with a gift of pictures of Napoleon, no doubt a reference to a tyrant similarly thwarted in Russia. Later, Dietrich shared champagne with Christel in the hospital, where she'd had an operation. They drank "to other times."[19] Dietrich called Ruth with birthday

14. Ibid., 285.
15. Ibid., 387.
16. Ibid., 386.
17. Ibid., 388.
18. Bismarck and Kabitz, eds., *Love Letters*, 85.
19. Leibholz, *The Bonhoeffers*, 147.

wishes and offered her what he knew would be the most prized of gifts: his engagement to Maria.

Ruth was delighted, but wrote him following his birthday phone call with barely controlled impatience at the delays in setting a wedding date, blaming them first on Ruthchen and Hans Jurgen, then writing, "Perhaps it is necessary for Maria so that she is clear in her mind. But certainly if it appears too long a time for you and for her, there are ways and means to shorten it."[20]

And thus the players were left. Dietrich had the yes he wanted. He would wed the "twin" to his niece Renate. He and Eberhard could proceed apace, each now joined to a teenaged bride. With the Gestapo closing in, Dietrich also no doubt hoped the engagement would help protect him, for connections with military families conferred legitimacy in the Third Reich. Maria had breathing room. Ruth had her cherished match. Within these layers of intrigue, Ruthchen had bought time and space for her daughter. Meanwhile, for Maria and Dietrich more than a month of silence ensued.

---

20. Pejsa, *Matriarch of Conspiracy*, 296.

49

The Noose Tightens

REMARKABLY, DIETRICH FAILED TO tell his parents of his engagement to Maria until February 4, the same day he spoke the Ruth. Given the turmoil over the engagement, and his two-and-half month pursuit of Maria, including his flurry of communication with Ruth, Eberhard, Maria, and Ruthchen, it's surprising that Dietrich never breathed a word at home. Yet it confirms that while he remained close with his parents, they were not part of his innermost circle, as they had not been when he and Sabine tapped on their joint wall as children and spoke a secret language.

The next morning Dietrich received a letter from Ruth:

> I thank you for your birthday letter, and even more for your evening phone call. I am especially thankful that I am now freed from my agonizing uncertainty. In this regard, this [marriage decision] is probably the greatest act of your life. Do you understand what I mean? I wrestle so with my own will—to remain silent, even if I am not in full accord [with the delays]. How I would have liked to send you the letter from Maria for it brought me so much happiness. However, since there has been so much mix up in this affair, I dare not. You know how it all stands, so the letter holds nothing new for you.
>
> Now my heart is so full of things I want to tell you. And still I do not know enough to be permitted to discuss it all. What you have said is sufficient for me: "I am happy and I am grateful." I repeat that to myself very much every day, and I pray to God that it turns out not just good, but very good. That I will accept you as a son [sic] when the time comes—certainly you know this without my saying it.[1]

Dietrich traveled with his beloved Eberhard a few days later: On February 8 the two went to Munich. The following January Eberhard, once again en route to Munich, would write to Dietrich about the trip: "Almost a year ago

---

1. Pejsa, *Matriarch of Conspiracy*, 295–96.

we were sitting together in the train on this same stretch of line and travelling together to Munich for the last time. It was another very good journey. You were reading Talleyrand, we ate in the dining car, I expect that I was writing to Renate again. We heard Palestrina [in Munich] and marvelled, we drank coffee with Ninne [Countess Kalckreuth] (I'll be going to see her in the morning) and managed to get hold of some very good books. We worked out money and coupons together; as always, you were very generous."[2]

Eberhard had indeed written to Renate on the train, which was delayed on the tracks, though the weather was springlike.[3] After the bookish, companionable journey, the two men strolled around Munich. Later, Dietrich read portions of his *Ethics* aloud to Eberhard. The two shared a charming hotel room, and while Eberhard wrote once again to Renate, Dietrich fell asleep.[4] It could have been Oliver and Jim Darnley in *The Last Puritan*: the years together had been enough "to establish a private current of sympathy, and heighten the sense of union in contrast to the outer world." [5]

On February 10th, 1943, Eberhard sent a letter to Renate, telling her that Dietrich had been urgently advised not to take his planned trip to Switzerland, and so would return to Berlin. People, he wrote, were "agitated" in Munich about the Stalingrad defeat. He and Dietrich debated whether to go to Ettal or instead to Metten monastery to try to find food.

"I think there are times when you wouldn't care for me at all. For instance, when I ride like a maniac and talk dialect to the farmhands . . . When I play the gramophone and hop across the floor on one foot, pulling on a stocking with a huge great hole in it. . . . I smoke a cigar because I've never smoked one . . . . Or I get up at night, put on a long dress and dance wildly around the drawing room."[6]

So Maria confided in a "letter" to Bonhoeffer written in her diary on February 3, 1943 at Pätzig, the day before Dietrich would reveal the news of their engagement. Maria clung to her adolescence and addressed her imaginary Dietrich as a father figure, musing that her upcoming nursing experience would improve her behavior, saving him the job.[7]

---

2. Bonhoeffer, *LPP*, 265.
3. *DBWE 16*, 391.
4. Ibid.
5. Santayana, *The Last Puritan*, 232.
6. Bismarck and Kabitz, eds., *Love Letters*, 342.
7. Ibid., 343.

Ruth, fully informed about Gestapo activities, and determined that her granddaughter understand Dietrich's danger, wrote to her on February 16 hinting that Dietrich might soon get arrested.

Dietrich's jeopardy increased after Stalingrad. The regime became jumpy, determined to quell dissent. Meanwhile, the University of Munich became a center of "revolt" after several students began distributing what were called the White Rose Letters, filled with anti-Nazi propaganda—and spreading them to other universities. In February, 1943, the Gauleiter of Bavaria, Paul Giesler, who had been given a file of White Rose Letters, came to the university and taunted the female students by suggesting they were too ugly to find husbands. "If some of the girls," he added, "lack sufficient charm to find a mate, I will assign each of them one of my adjutants . . . and I can promise her a thoroughly enjoyable experience."[8]

This comment caused an uproar. Angry students forced Giesler and his guard from the hall and that afternoon, the unprecedented occurred: a street protest in Munich, the first anti-Nazi student demonstration ever to occur in Hitler's Germany. Hans and Sophie Scholl, responsible for the White Rose Letters, were quickly brought before the People's Court and sent off to execution.

In Berlin on February 27th, the Gestapo rounded up more Jews and deported some 10,000 to death camps.[9] Some 5,000–7,000 Jews also slipped underground, a precarious way to try to survive in Nazi Germany,[10] albeit with better odds than deportation.

In 1942, Berlin had experienced only one British air attack. But on March 1, 1943, the idyll ended as the British unleashed one of their fiercest onslaughts, dropping double the payload of bombs that the Luftwafte had visited on London during its worst raids. Further, the British introduced the "blockbuster," an aptly named high explosive bomb that could destroy an entire city block.[11]

As the bombs fell with earthshaking explosions, the great domed roof of St. Hedwig's Catholic Church in the heart of the city took a hit and crashed spectacularly into the building. Bombers struck others prestigious downtown addresses, including Göring's Air Ministry.[12]

---

8. Shirer, *The Rise and Fall of the Third Reich*, 1022–23.
9. Moorhouse, *Berlin at War*, 285.
10. Ibid., 292.
11. Ibid., 306-7.
12. Ibid., 308.

Berliner Ruth Andreas-Friedrich noted the March 1 raid in her diary: 'The city and all the western and southern suburbs are on fire. The air is smoky, sulphur-yellow. Terrified people are stumbling through the streets with bundles, bags, household goods, tripping over fragments and ruins."[13] The raid killed nearly 500 civilians.[14]

Earlier in the war, the Nazis would send huge teams of workers to clear the rubble and rebuild after an air raid, a show of defiance meant to buoy morale and demonstrate that the attack had been futile. Now, Berliners lived amid the debris.

The Gestapo felt intense pressure to contain unrest and round up dissidents. Meanwhile, Bonhoeffer's 1942 meeting with Bishop Bell in Sweden came to light.

The Gestapo was closing in fast on Bonhoeffer and Dohnanyi over what it still thought was illegal currency speculation.

Alarmed by her grandmother's letter and subsequent hints, Maria broke her vows of silence on March 9 and telephoned Dietrich. She burst into tears over the phone. Dietrich laughed and reassured her he was fine, following up with a necessarily vague, but reassuring letter, full of mystical love language. "My heart is still beating noticeably," he wrote, directly after the call, "everything in me has been turned upside down—from joy, from surprise—but also from shock that you were worried." He tried to reassure her, saying he had spoken to Ruth "wrongly . . . you needn't worry a single moment, I myself am not at all worried."[15]

Dietrich, of course, *was* worried, both about being arrested and about the impression he'd left during the phone call that he was in a hurry to marry. "I should have said . . . I don't want to be [impatient]; and I'm not when I think it would trouble you. So it is true after all: I'm not impatient." What he would like was conversation, to "be able to say things to you and to listen to you."[16]

The love language was idealized and patriarchal: "And what an indescribable happiness it is for a man when the woman he loves stands beside him, with him, brave and patient—and above all prayerful."[17]

13. Ibid., 308–9.
14. Ibid., 309.
15. Bonhoeffer, *DBWE 16*, 392–93.
16. Ibid., 393.
17. Ibid.

50

Trapped

THE NAZIS REMAINED ON edge. On March 13, Bonhoeffer received orders to report for military duty in Munich—in response, a new position was hastily devised for him under the theory the regime would soon be overthrown.[1] That very day, Dohnanyi took part in an assassination attempt. Eberhard drove Dohnanyi to the train station in Karl's Mercedes. Unbeknownst to Eberhard, Dohnanyi's briefcase carried explosives. Dohnanyi passed these to Henning von Tresckow, Maria's uncle, and von Schlabrendorff, Maria's cousin, who put them on a plane Hitler was taking to Smolensk. However, the bomb somehow failed to detonate, and Tresckow managed to remove it from the plane before it was detected.[2]

On Friday, March 19, Junker aristocracy, Berlin intelligentsia, and former royalty met at the Bonhoeffer home. The Bonhoeffers, including Klaus and Dietrich, entertained Ewald von Kleist and Prince Louis Ferdinard of Hohenzollern, the friend Bonhoeffer kept hoping would be king of postwar Germany. Louis, part of the conspiracy, was told of another assassination attempt planned for two days hence. Amid the parklike surroundings of the Bonhoeffer home, he agreed to go on national radio to declare himself Kaiser, as soon as Hitler was dead.[3]

On Sunday, March 21, the conspirators pursued—or wanted to pursue—the assassination they had outlined to the prince. Their target was Hitler's excursion to an exhibit at the Berlin arsenal. Major von Gersdorff, urged on by Treckow, wore bombs on his own body in a plan to kill Hitler kamikaze style. That day, in a Hitchcock-like tableau, the Bonhoeffer family met at the Schleichers to rehearse the birthday cantata for Dietrich's father's seventy-fifth birthday party. Dietrich was pianist, Klaus played the cello, Rüdiger manned the violin, and Hans von Dohnanyi sang along with the warbling voices of young nieces and nephews, all raised in hymn.

1. Dramm, *Dietrich Bonhoeffer and the Resistance*, 221.
2. Ibid., 222.
3. Pejsa, *Matriarch of Conspiracy*, 301–2.

Dohnanyi's car stood ready outside the door, awaiting the news of Hitler's death. Christine von Dohnanyi whispered to Ursel under cover of the instruments: "It will go up any minute now!" But the minutes passed, and the telephone never rang. What had happened? Why was Hitler not dead? In fact, Hitler had not kept to the planned schedule, but abruptly left the exhibition after only ten minutes. Von Gersdorff had had no chance to act.

In her book on the conspiracy, Dramm raises the question of whether these attempts actually took place, quoting J. K. Roth that they might have been "wishful fantasies . . . which . . . acquired the character of fact."[4] Whatever the case, Hitler survived, leaving Bonhoeffer family members in grave danger.

Continuing to anticipate arrest, Dietrich and Dohnanyi coordinated their stories. Dietrich wrote a backdated letter on Max Krause stationery, which had not been sold since 1940, promoting himself as a spy. The letter, outlining all the ways Dietrich could use his international contacts to gather information for the Reich, was meant to explain his exemption from military service.

On March 23,[5] Eberhard and Renate married in the civil ceremony that made their union legal, although the church wedding that the family saw as the real event would not take place until May 15, the twentieth anniversary of Ursel and Rüdiger's own nuptials. Dietrich witnessed the civil service and despite his mixed feelings, remained ostensibly—and defiantly—supportive. "I've often been glad you invited me to the civil ceremony when you did," he later wrote. "I think back to the day with great pleasure and feel that I was at the decisive moment with you."[6]

Dietrich broke the vow of silence this time, writing to Maria on March 24 to ask her to visit Ruth, who was in the hospital in Stettin. Dietrich had just seen Ruth, who worried that Maria was still upset over "last winter's difficulties." Ruth hoped for some "kind and heartening words" from her granddaughter to show that the two were no longer quarreling.[7] Maria explained to Dietrich on March 26 that she was not angry but had not wanted to contact her grandmother until her plans to visit her had solidified.

On March 31, the entire family gathered at the Bonhoeffer home for Karl Bonhoeffer's seventy-fifth birthday party. How the women managed food for the occasion in such a time of scarcity is unknown. After Stalingrad,

---

4. Dramm, *Dietrich Bonhoeffer and the Resistance*, 304.

5. Bonhoeffer, *DBWE 8* has March 23 as the wedding date, 597; Bonhoeffer, *DBWE 16* has Bonhoeffer visiting Ruth that day in the Stettin hospital (693). It is possible that Dietrich attended a morning ceremony then took the train to Stettin that afternoon.

6. Bonhoeffer, *LPP*, 136.

7. Bismarck and Kabitz, eds., *Love Letters*, 346.

Goebbels had put an austerity drive into effect. Meat was scarce and saccharine continued to replace sugar, which was harder than ever to find. The icing on Berlin bakery cakes, at least to one observer, began to taste like a mixture of saccharine, perfume, and sand, probably a fair assessment of ingredients.[8]

The good food of yesteryear might have been in short supply for the party, but the house overflowed with flowers and well-wishers, congratulations and fine music.

On this festive day, the children and grandchildren sang Walcha's cantata "Praise the Lord," Gert and Sabine sent a congratulatory telegram through Sutz in Switzerland, Klaus offered the birthday toast, and Karl had the dubious honor of a note from Hitler, awarding him the Goethe Medal for Art and Science.

In the family portrait taken to commemorate the day, one wouldn't have known that Berlin was in the midst of what Goebbels had recently proclaimed a "total war," that the city had been devastatingly bombed four weeks before, that fearful Berliners were scrambling to find basic goods and going to work past smouldering ruins and starved slave labor. Everyone looks peaceful, the men in ties and jackets, the women in long dresses. A closer glance would show that celebrants were thinner and paler, the clothes from yesteryear. It was the last time they would all be together.

---

8. Moorhouse, *Berlin at War*, 88.

— 51 —
White Nurse

By the time of the birthday party, Maria had begun her nurse's training in Hanover. National Socialist ideology presented nursing as among the most suitable vocations for a woman. Nazi woman's leader Bertha Braun characterized it as an expansion of motherhood into the "spiritual realm," bringing "the idea of selflessness and self-sacrifice in[to] all areas of life."[1]

The Nazis had professionalized and standardized nursing, a profession in sorry condition when they took power. By 1938, all nurses (except psychiatric) completed a required year and a half of training, as well as a year of practical experience before being licensed. Only Aryans could become licensed nurses, though Jewish nurses were tolerated as long as they stayed among Jews.

The National Socialists had quickly brought the old Protestant and Catholic nursing orders under the umbrella of the Party. The Nazi nursing organization, founded in 1934, pledged to serve the will of Adolf Hitler, and all other nursing organizations were required to follow suit. This meant synchronizing nursing with National Socialist ideology, including an embrace of euthanasia.

According to the Nazis, survival required controlling the population to maximize the best genetic material and subordinating the needs of the individual to the needs of the collective. Thus, the ethical framework of medicine changed, and the overarching mandate moved from offering the best care to each individual to the best care for the society as a whole. The new slogans for public health became "prevention not protection," "cure not care," and "public health not sentimental humanitarianism." "Purity" meant the "strength" to make hard choices.[2]

By November 1933, the Protestant nursing orders had pledged their support to Hitler through a public telegram that stated, "Being overwhelmed by the saving grace of God given to our dearly beloved nation again through

1. Steppe, "Nursing Under Totalitarian Regimes," 14.
2. Ibid., 13–14.

your hand ... [we] pledge ... willing sacrificial service and eternal fidelity to our God-given Führer!"[3]

As with pastors in the Confessing Church, some nurses tried to oppose the system. However, since all jobs came through the state, resistance carried a high price. A few nurses managed to hang crosses in sick rooms and even encouraged soldiers to desert during the war, but risked prison or execution for their efforts.[4]

A nursing shortage at the end of the 1930s led to a massive recruiting campaign. Advertisements described a nurse as "a political solider." Next to motherhood, "a woman has no more beautiful or feminine an occupation" than nursing, proclaimed one ad.[5]

Beyond this propaganda stood the symbolism of the "white nurse" as described by Klaus Theweleit in *Male Fantasies*. This woman, usually young and always a social "better," was, like Maria, "noble, beautiful, rich." Others might try to imitate her, but as with the princess and the pea, bloodlines would reveal themselves. The real white nurse was likened to "the countess of Sythen Castle," who, "bearing herself proudly ... never lost courage" and thus inspired others.[6] She was "Mother, sister (-of mercy, nurse), and countess all in one person. Such is the holy trinity of the 'good' woman, the nonwhore. Instead of castrating, she protects. She has no penis, but then she has no sex either. Her body is 'completely enveloped in a white apron.'"[7]

The white nurse also functioned symbolically as the sister figure, which was how Dietrich wished to cast Maria. Such a sister figure stood by her brother and shared his suffering, which was not only the noblest thing she could do, but, in fact, "her destiny."[8] This conflation of fiancée/girlfriend with sister was reinforced, as we have seen over and over again, by the fact that the men around Dietrich, both family members and seminarians, tended to marry their friends' sisters or close relatives. Walter Dress was a friend of Dietrich's before he married Susi. Onnasch was a Finkenwalde friend of Bethge before he married Bethge's sister. Grete von Dohnanyi, who married Karl-Friedrich, was the sister of Hans von Dohnanyi. The list goes on, notably ending with Eberhard marrying Renate, Dietrich's niece, as close as Eberhard could come to a sister of Dietrich. In turn, Maria was the granddaughter of the dear friend that Dietrich and his cohort called ei-

3. Ibid., 18.
4. Ibid., 23.
5. Ibid., 15, 17.
6. Theweleit, *Male Fantasies*, vol. 1, 90–91.
7. Ibid., 95.
8. Ibid., 109.

ther "Mother Ruth" or "Aunt Ruth"—a symbolic mother offering a symbolic daughter in lieu of herself to her symbolic son.

The "white nurse," wrote Theweleit, was "given a preeminent role in the psychic security system of the men . . . [as] the essential embodiment of their recoiling from all erotic, threatening femininity."[9] As a white nurse, however, Maria, insistently her own person and a sexual being, would fail.

In 1974, Malcolm Muggeridge filmed a remarkable, if short, interview with Maria for a documentary on Bonhoeffer, part of his series *A Third Testament* covering "six renowned thinkers" from Augustine to Bonhoeffer.

Fifty-year-old Maria in the interview remained the person contemporaries from the 1940s described: glowing, helpful, and emanating a sincerity that, despite her confidence, could be seen as vulnerable. Still fit and beautiful, she faced Muggeridge wearing a form-fitting short gray sweater dress that tied at the waist. Her round face was open, her eyes slanted slightly downward at the edges. She flashed a radiant smile, full of strong white teeth, lighting her whole face. As she leaned back in her backward-tilted, black canvas chair, somewhat like an indoor deck chair, the camera captured her long legs stretched in front of her in nude panty hose. At fifty, Maria still radiated sexuality. She was earthy, as Ruth had noted, not ethereal. She had breasts, she had legs, and she was tall, robust, athletic, energetic. One can imagine her sweating, or lighting a cigarette. White nurse she was not.

Maria arrived at Hanover's Clementinenhaus Hospital, a Red Cross facility, filled with enthusiasm for her work despite the threat of "arduous" training.

Unlike the official Nazi nurses, who wore the Nazi brown, Maria donned a long-sleeved blue dress with a pointy white collar, covered with a full white apron and bib that wrapped around her waist, the outfit topped by a crisp white nurse's cap. Like all Red Cross nurses, she took a loyalty oath not much different from the German schoolchildren's oath, swearing faithfulness to Hitler and obedience to authority.

Maria's days began at 6 AM, when she walked across the garden from her dormitory to the hospital.[10] Training subjected her to a social leveling comparable to the army, where neither her name nor her ability to "count up to three or a bit higher," as she put it, mattered. Work was work. The "ward sisters have an absolute moral responsibility to be dragons," Maria wrote.[11] Her job included dressing the babies in her care and "look[ing]

---

9. Ibid., 126.
10. Bismarck and Kabitz, eds., *Love Letters*, 23.
11. Ibid., 29.

after" a third-class women's ward and two second-class private rooms. She described the "educated, wealthy breed" as "really an awful bunch," but immediately took to the more appreciative women in the third-class ward.[12]

Most significantly, the ethos of nursing in that period reinforced the primary message of Maria's Altenburg experience: "The nurse [was devalued] . . . as an independent person . . . in that only her anonymous and self-sacrificial service to her people was honored. Nurses were still not seen as individual persons with their own wishes and needs; on the contrary, the sacrifice of their own personality was declared to be their contribution."[13]

On April 4, Eberhard and Renate made a whirlwind visit to Eberhard's mother, returning to the Schleicher house either that night or the next Monday morning, April 5.[14] April 5 was a warm day, the morning overcast, but after 11:00 the sun came out.[15] Dietrich worked on the section "The Concrete Commandment and the Divine Mandates" of his *Ethics*.[16] Around noon, Dietrich phoned the von Dohnanyis. A strange voice answered. Dietrich realized the Gestapo was searching the house. He assumed von Dohnanyi had or would soon be arrested. Not wanting to wake his parents, who were napping,[17] Dietrich walked next door to Ursel's to discuss the situation. Ursel fed him a big meal to fortify him for his arrest.

After eating, Dietrich took advantage of the time left to reexamine his attic bedroom and plant his phony diary fragments. Then he returned to Ursel's, waiting, smoking, and talking the afternoon away with Ursel, Renate, and Eberhard. At 4 PM the Gestapo arrived. So many of Dietrich's friends had been imprisoned over the years; now, at long last, his turn had come.

On April 5, Maria confided to her diary: "Has something bad happened? I'm afraid it's something very bad . . . ."

---

12. Ibid.
13. Rafferty, *Nursing History and the Politics of Welfare*, 18.
14. de Gruchy, *Daring, Trusting Spirit*, 64.
15. Dramm, *Dietrich Bonhoeffer and the Resistance*, 226.
16. Ibid., 229.
17. Ibid., 230.

PART VIII
Alone

— 52 —

Locked In

Dietrich found himself herded with a group of new arrivals into Tegel prison, a rambling old building in the northwest corner of Berlin.

Dietrich found a camp cot in his cell, with blankets so filthy he wouldn't use them despite the cold. The only toilets were buckets, collected once a day, and in the close quarters the odors must have been overpowering. In the morning, guards tossed a piece of dry bread to him—he picked it from the ground and ate it.

That morning guards transferred Dietrich to an isolation cell on the top floor, the home of death row prisoners. At this time, he did not know whether he would soon be executed. He experienced, he later wrote to his parents, "a violent mental upheaval."[1]

While we have few details of Dietrich's first prison days, we can turn to Victor Klemperer. Klemperer, a Protestant—and a Confessing Church member—of Jewish descent, served an eight-day prison term in Dresden for failing to properly black out a window in his apartment.

Once locked into his cell—like Dietrich, alone—he recognized that although he had seen many movies about prison, nothing had prepared him for the "banal perception [that] . . . we know nothing at all except what we have experienced ourselves."[2] When the heavy cell door shut behind him and the latch fell, he felt a "nameless fear" and his eight days turned into 192 "empty, caged hours." Time passed with excruciating slowness.

"It was no horrible medieval dungeon," wrote Klemperer, " . . . but . . . a dreary cage with bare gray green walls and whitish ceiling . . . It all emanated an oppressiveness, a rising increasing fear . . . ." He was depressed by "the abstract space of the cell, the naked idea of imprisonment. . . . this idea of emptiness."

---

1. Bonhoeffer, *LPP*, 21.
2. Klemperer, *I Shall Bear Witness*, 394.

He breathed "stuffy and nasty" air as the toilets were flushed—by external control—only twice a day, although flush toilets were no doubt preferable to Tegel's buckets.[3]

But the "torment" was the "absence of activity, the awful emptiness and immobility." Victor felt "despair," "choking emptiness."[4] For the forty-eight hours before his Bible was returned to him, Dietrich might have experienced a similar emptiness, exacerbated by uncertainty about his fate. Scrawled notes to himself not long after his initial days in prison indicate his situation: "dissatisfaction, tension, impatience, longing, boredom, sick—profoundly alone . . . fantasy, distortion of past and future, Suicide . . . because basically I am already dead . . . ."[5]

At night, Klemperer battled bedbugs, scratching for an hour until they had "drunk their fill," and he could sleep in peace. Bonhoeffer coped with long nights that lasted from a lights out at eight until six the next morning on a hard wooden bed.[6] At night, he would later write, "I hear the uneasy creaks of bed, I hear chains . . . the steps and cries of the guards . . . cold, thin strokes of the tower clock."[7] For twelve days Dietrich's cell door only opened a crack to pass in his food and receive his bucket—or to take him to interrogations, which started on the third day and would continue on and off for seven months. For the trip downtown to the Reich War Court for questioning, he endured the humiliation of being handcuffed.[8]

Dietrich established a routine to cope with the dirt, hunger, the shouting guards, the moaning, sobbing prisoners, the cries of inmates taken off for execution and the fearful, empty days. He exercised, meditated, and read and memorized the Bible. For the first time, Dietrich fully experienced the "view from below." He was as faceless and nameless as any other prisoner. He had no recourse if he were treated unfairly or even struck, although prison rules forbade beating.

Dietrich spent his early days not allowed to lie on his cot until night fell. He depended on what little light filtered in through a high, barred window to read his Bible, and managed his food with only a spoon.

On April 14th, nine days after his imprisonment started, pencil and paper transformed Dietrich's life. He almost immediately wrote to his parents. He tried to sound cheerful. He noted that he had access to the prison

---

3. Ibid., 395.
4. Ibid., 399.
5. Bonhoeffer, *LPP*, 35.
6. Ibid., 21.
7. Ibid., 351
8. Bethge, *DB: A Biography*, 799.

library. By Easter, April 25, he'd received at least two letters and a package from his family. He implored them not to worry.

Dietrich made full use of his writing privileges, though his paper often consisted, according to Bethge, of "the most wretched scraps." When his father sent a detailed list of items the family had delivered for Dietrich, Dietrich wrote copious notes around the mentions of matches, tobacco, and malt extract.[9]

In his May 5 letter, Dietrich mentioned pacing his cell: "Our day lasts fourteen hours, of which I spend about three walking up and down the cell—several kilometres a day, besides half an hour in the yard."[10]

After the first days, Dietrich received a steady stream of food—apples and pears, cookies and cakes, hard-boiled eggs and sausage, pork fat and pumpernickel, strawberry jam and aniseed biscuits, tomatoes, grapes, bottled fruit, red wine pudding, cake, cocoa and milk, the occasional chocolate bar. His letters are filled with thanks for the extras that came his way. Karl-Friedrich would later write: "In the last years it wasn't very easy, and aunt Ursel in particular could hardly do enough. She starved herself until she was a skeleton."[11]

Three days after allowing him writing supplies and twelve days after his arrest, the prison got wind of Dietrich's family connections, and he became a Bonhoeffer again. The Commandant of the City of Berlin, with Tegel prison under his command, was a cousin, Paul von Hase. Paul came to prison and pointedly asked after Dietrich.

The staff immediately moved Dietrich to the larger cell and eventually to a cell in a location safer from the bombing raids aimed at the nearby locomotive factory.[12] Another prisoner now cleaned this cell every day. But Dietrich's situation remained grim. The wooden door that closed him in had a slot through which he could be observed, but he could not see through it. As in the first cell, dim light filtered in from a high window. This cell, like the other, contained a wooden bed, a bucket, a stool, and a wooden bench.[13] The floor was "stone" and the walls gray. On one wall a philosophical former inmate had scratched "in a hundred years it will all be over."

Dietrich now began a daily, companionable stroll with the prison's captain. The wardens and staff began to treat him politely, and some even apologized for their former rudeness. Dietrich found the situation

---

9. Ibid., 831.
10. Bonhoeffer, *LPP*, 29.
11. Ibid., 409.
12. Bethge, *DB: A Biography*, 799.
13. Ibid., 828.

"embarrassing," but used his privilege. To help others, he successfully made "energetic protests" against the behavior of some guards.[14]

With his connections known, the prison offered Dietrich larger rations, which he refused, knowing his meals would deprive others. From early on, he looked forward to Wednesday, delivery day for food, books, laundry, tobacco and, other supplies from the outer world.

Supplies not only provided for crucial physical needs but became part of a secret system of communication devised long before any arrests. In a regime reliant on spying and lying, coded language had long been normal, but now messages came on tiny bits of cardboard hidden inside jars of food or bouquets of flowers[15] and something as simple as a request for a toothbrush could communicate whether an interrogation had gone badly or well.

---

14. Ibid., 847.
15. Stern and Sifton, *No Ordinary Men*, 55.

— 53 —

Care and Feeding

FOLLOWING APRIL 5, THE day of Dietrich's arrest, Maria's fears lingered. What had happened to him remained, for her, the unanswered question. On April 18, Maria took a quick holiday from nursing to visit Pätzig. Once home, Maria strolled about with her sister's husband, Klaus von Bismarck, across grounds that showed signs of spring. She forced the family's hand by telling Klaus she was about to visit Dietrich in defiance of the one-year separation. When they returned home, Hans Jurgen admitted what she suspected, that Dietrich was in prison.[1]

We have no record of Maria's initial response to the news. Pätzig cocooned her in an eighteenth-century world and nursing duties kept her busy, if not exhausted. The Bonhoeffers at first did not contact her, perhaps thinking the arrests would be quickly resolved. But as time passed and Dietrich still languished in prison, Maria's visitation rights as his fiancée became important. By May 7, Paula had written to Maria.

It was by and large the women who rallied to care for the prisoners, while both genders worked behind the scenes to get Dietrich and Hans von

---

1. Why did nobody—either her future in-laws or her own family—inform her of an event that might be expected to be of deepest interest to her? Why were they content to leave her in a state of anxiety? If not for the heartfelt letters to Dietrich from Ruth, filled with relief and joy over the betrothal, we might suspect the entire engagement was a ruse. If Dietrich could leave notes on his desk about what he could contribute as a spy for the Abwehr, on paper that had not been produced since 1940, not to mention false diary entries, how difficult could it be for Maria likewise to fabricate journal passages about getting married? Yet the engagement rings true, not only because of Ruth, but because Maria's evasions during the courtship sound like the moves of a relentlessly pursued young woman.

Most likely, it was to "protect" Maria that she was not told about about Dietrich. Also, almost nobody knew of the engagement. Perhaps those few who understood the facts were hopeful that Dietrich would be released quickly and the whole brouhaha would blow over. Yet we can also see it as part of the pattern of the families—both Bonhoeffer and von Kliest—disregarding Maria's needs.

Dohnanyi released. Susi routinely bicycled to Tegel with a suitcase full of food, books, clothes, and odds and ends for Dietrich, hopping off her bike at the outskirts of the prison and wheeling it slowly down the broad lane between the brick walls of the gloomy compound. She passed the fenced courtyards, then glanced up at barred windows. Chaining her bike, she took her shabby suitcase in hand and entered the waiting room, joining the silent row of people on narrow benches along the walls, everybody holding a package or suitcase on their lap.

Eventually, Susi would be called and the contents of her suitcase carefully examined, as were all the items Dietrich returned: books, underwear to be washed, the empty waterproof cartons that had to be used in lieu of glass or tin containers. Susi would read Dietrich's requests for the following week: soap or handkerchiefs or books. Often a request was a coded way to relay information to his family. Susi could copy but not keep his note.

Then came the slow trudge out of the prison, slow in case she should catch a glimpse of Dietrich in the exercise yard, followed by the long bike ride home to Dahlem.[2] On the days or weeks when Susi did not come, it would be Ursel or Christel, Emmi or later Maria, sometimes accompanied by Karl-Friedrich.

Dietrich confided in Eberhard some months later: "I should have to start telling you that, in spite of everything that I've written so far, things here are revolting, that my grim experiences often pursue me into the night and that I can shake them off only by reciting one hymn after another, and that I'm apt to wake up with a sigh rather than with a hymn of praise to God. It's possible to get used to physical hardships, and to live for months out of the body, so to speak—almost too much so—but one doesn't get used to the psychological strain."[3]

Meanwhile, outside the prison walls, Maria waited. Until the end of July, Dietrich only had permission to write to his parents and then only once every ten days. Paula and Karl copied and sent Maria portions of Dietrich's letters.

Initially Dietrich, aware his mail was censored, and knowing it was his investigators, Franz Sonderegger and Manfred Roeder,[4] who censored it,

---

2. Zimmermann and Smith, eds., *I Knew*, 213–20.
3. Bonhoeffer, *LPP*, 162.
4. This is one of the bizarre aspects of the case: friends and family knew that Roeder was reading all their correspondence and Roeder must have known they knew, so one wonders what the censorship accomplished. Of course, on one level it functioned as a de facto channel of communication to Roeder that he didn't have to acknowledge; on another, it drove open communication underground into the series of code words and

tried to use his connection to Maria to his advantage. Roeder, purportedly a frequent guest at Göring's Carinhall, would become the nemesis of both Dietrich and von Dohnanyi.[5]

Dietrich accentuated his status as betrothed lover worried about his young bride-to-be. He played the loyal German, allied with a prominent Prussian family. On April 14, in his first letter, he wrote to his parents with an eye to the censor: "I'm feeling especially sorry for my fiancée at the moment. It's very hard on her, having so recently lost her father and brother in the East. An army officer's daughter . . . ." On April 25, "how courageously she bore the death of her father, her brother and two beloved cousins last year." In the same letter: "Does everybody know of our engagement by now," followed by more reminders of allying himself with a family suffering losses in the war.[6]

Despite the censorship, letters, wrote Bethge, became Bonhoeffer's "elixir of life."[7] Given Dietrich's upbringing, which discouraged emotional displays, along with the need to write in code, emotions were, as Bethge wrote stiffly, "indicated only in the manner of asking about [or commenting on] the wishes and affairs of the other person. One's own needs seemed to be transposed into advice for others."[8] We can see this, in just one example, when, in his first letter to Eberhard, he urges him to eat well for to "get very hungry . . . would be horrid."[9] Yet getting enough to eat was lower on Dietrich's list of worries than another cause of deep anguish and distress.

Despite strict limits on how much he could write, in his first letter from prison on April 14 Dietrich asked his parents if "Renate's wedding preparations are going well." To protect Eberhard, nobody at this point would mention his name. He is "Renate" and his presence springs forth from the

---

double entendres that were such a hallmark of this totalitarian state, so much so that it seems that, as in this case, the regime unconsciously wanted people to produce esoteric speech.

5. Bethge, *DB: A Biography*, 801.

6. Bismarck and Kabitz, eds., *Love Letters*, 21–22. Military connections conferred reliability in Nazi Germany. For example, Bernt Englemann volunteered for the Luftwaffe after graduating from the gymnasium in 1938 because the suspicions of the police and the foreign currency office—his father was planning to emigrate to England—would be quelled if he, "an only son, proved the family's 'national loyalty' by volunteering for military service" (See Engelmann, *In Hitler's Germany*, 140).

7. Bethge, *DB: A Biography*, 838.

8. Ibid., 839.

9. Bonhoeffer, *LPP*, 133.

very beginning of the correspondence, mentioned in the parents' first brief note—"Loving greetings from Mother, Renate and fiancée."[10]

These early letters show Dietrich's preoccupation with Eberhard and Renate's marriage. He insisted in his second letter home, as if assuming he had the power to control their affairs, that nothing must stop Eberhard and Renate's wedding: "I want to make it clear that it is my express wish that Ursel should not postpone the date by a single day, but should let Renate get married as soon and as happily as possible.... Renate knows... how much I share her joy."[11] However, it didn't seem to have crossed anybody's mind but Dietrich's that the wedding might possibly be delayed.[12]

On May 5, Dietrich again mentioned the wedding: "I can see nothing but great good fortune for this marriage, and I'm already looking forward ... to sharing the joys of their home.... I would like to give them the spinet, which already half belongs to them, and also, as I've already said to Ursel, my contribution to the piano, as much as they need.... I would so like it if they in turn could think of me only with happy thoughts, memories, and hopes."[13]

His mother wrote back on the 9th: "On Saturday it's the wedding, and we intend to celebrate it happily in accordance with your express wishes."[14]

Hans-Werner had leave to come home from the front for the nuptials. Paula wrote to Dietrich: "Today Ursel is at [Eberhard and] Renate's home and is getting it ready. She is rather sad that everything cannot be as beautiful as she would like to make it."[15]

On the evening of the 14th cousin Bärbel, Christel's daughter, gave Renate the traditional garland of roses, "a final farewell gift from her days as a maiden."[16] Then, as Sabine and Dietrich had done at Ursel's wedding, and Susi and Dietrich at Sabine's wedding, the much younger Bonhoeffer niece and nephew, Thomas and Cornelie, only eleven and eight, performed "Ring-a-Ring o' Roses, I'm dancing with my wife." Thomas came on the scene again to play a Mozart trio with his parents. Ruth, who had done so much to broker the marriage, sent a "gorgeous bouquet" of lilies of the valley

---

10. Ibid., 21–22.
11. Ibid., 26.
12. Ibid., 26.
13. Ibid., 29–30.
14. Ibid., 37.
15. Ibid., 28.
16. Bonhoeffer, *DBWE 8*, 89.

from her garden, given a place of honor on the table in front of the bride and groom.[17]

The wedding itself took place the next day at 2:30 at the Schleicher's home. Hans-Walter arrived from duty, "tanned and looking well fed." The bride wore the fitted white gown with the long, diaphanous train that Paula and all her daughters had worn in their own weddings and "the simply arranged veil with the round, delicate myrtle garland."[18]

Eberhard's brothers Hans and Christophe attended the event. Rüdiger, Karl, and Hans offered wedding toasts. In their wedding photo, young Renate looks aglow, Eberhard tall, dark, and handsome. The couple left early, while the young people danced. Renate and Eberhard headed for a honeymoon in yet intact Dresden, where they would hear *Carmen*, as Sabine and Dietrich had in Berlin so many years ago, then sightsee, and move on to the Czech Republic, still firmly held in Nazi hands.[19]

Dietrich meanwhile remained either caged in his prison with its unpleasant noises and foul smells or suffered interrogations. Joint stiffness—what he called rheumatism—began to plague him in May.[20] Still preoccupied by the wedding, he used precious paper to compose a multi-page wedding sermon that in veiled ways communicated his ambivalence, and even bitterness, about the nuptials. Did he sit on the bench that now also held his books, pictures, and precious food? Did he pull his stool into the patch of sun let in by his high window, using a book balanced on his knees as a hard surface on which to write? Could he by this time sit on his bed by day? Was his rheumatism a result of sitting on the floor? We don't know, but a bizarre document emerged.[21]

---

17. Ibid., 89.
18. Ibid., 90.
19. Ibid.
20. Bonhoeffer, *LPP*, 124.
21. A good contrast is Bonhoeffer's 1936 wedding sermon in Bonhoeffer, *DBWE 15*, 913–16. Even the titles provide a point of contrast: "Wedding Sermon on 1 Thessalonians 5: 16–18" versus "A Wedding Sermon from a Prison Cell," the prison cell possibly meant to convey the gap between Bethge's charmed life and Dietrich's condition.

54

The Wedding Sermon

THE SERMON BEGINS AS a thinly veiled personal reproach to Eberhard, indicating that Dietrich's acute awareness that the marriage fulfilled Eberhard's ambitions.[1] "What you have done and are doing is not, in the first place, something religious, but something quite secular . . . . The children of the earth are rightly proud of being allowed to take a hand in shaping their own destinies . . . . We ought not," he continued witheringly, "to be in too much of a hurry here to speak piously of God's will and guidance." Dietrich repeats the word *triumph* four times—four out of the six times the word appears in all of the prison letters. He uses it directly in the first sentence: "It is right and proper for a bride and bridegroom [you Eberhard] to welcome and celebrate their [your] wedding day with a unique sense of triumph." In the next sentence: they "[you, Eberhard] have indeed achieved the most important triumph of their [your] lives [life]." Eberhard, who himself called the Bonhoeffer class "a new world" has "conquered a new land to live in." Then, "It is obvious, and it should not be ignored, that it is your own very human wills [will] that are at work here, celebrating their [your] triumph . . . ." The country parson's son who knew nary a soul of any importance was now part of a family on a par with the Kennedys. This was the world's way, not God's: "So you yourselves, and you alone, bear the responsibility for what no one can take from you . . . ."[2]

Dietrich then points to all the blessings of the couple. While addressing both, he speaks directly to Eberhard, enumerating the ways Dietrich, among others, has made his life easy: "The beautiful things and the joys of

1. The couple did not receive the sermon for many months. Karl Bonhoeffer had "mistakenly filed" it with Dietrich's will (Bonhoeffer, *DBWE 8*, footnote to Eberhard's letter of November 30, 1943). Eberhard wrote: "we never received any wedding sermon." Given a world in which missing diary pages could signal conspiracy work and also the care with which the Bonhoeffers usually preserved documents, one might surmise that Karl Bonhoeffer read the sermon, understood its barbed message and decided to "lose" it for a time.

2. Bonhoeffer, *LPP*, 41.

life have been showered on you, you have succeeded in everything, and you have been surrounded by love and friendship. Your ways have, for the most part, been smoothed before you took them, and you have always been able to count on the support of your families and friends. Everyone has wished you well . . . ."[3]

Having sent his barbed message, Bonhoeffer addressed God's—and Christ's—presence in the marriage as redemptive elements, though still using words of the fall—triumph and pride. "God approves of your triumph and rejoicing and pride," Dietrich wrote. Marriage is "God's holy ordinance, through which he wills to perpetuate the human race til the end of time."[4] The newlyweds should work together, each supporting the other to make the marriage a success.

Wistfulness also threads through this section; Dietrich contrasts marriage, a public position—"a status, an office"—as well as "indissoluble," to "love . . . a private possession," one filled with anxiety over loss of the beloved. "Free from all the anxiety that is always a characteristic of love, you can now say to each other with complete and confident assurance: We can never lose each other now; by the will of God we belong to each other till death."

Renate would later write that the sermon, which the couple received well after the marriage, distressed her in its call for wifely subservience. But Dietrich, hoping to be released from his prison any day, needed to believe in Renate's submission so that as little as possible might be changed with Eberhard.

By May, Dietrich wrote to his parents of adjusting to his imprisonment "in a kind of natural and unconscious way." He had in front of him primroses from Maria, and he had hung a print of Albrecht Dürer's *Apocalypse* torn from a newspaper. Very possibly, this was the most famous of the Dürer woodcuts, the third, illustrating Revelation 6:1–8, in which the four horsemen of Revelation trample the earth, while a winged angel watches from on high.

As Dietrich's strict isolation lifted, guards began to talk to him as they delivered meals, brought in the other prisoner to clean his cell, delivered his food parcels, or took him to the prison courtyard for exercise. Dietrich could be charming when he chose and was able to meet people where they were and listen to them attentively. He had as well a commanding presence. More practically, he could dispense food, cigarettes, and money, and function as a de facto chaplain.

3. Ibid., 42.
4. Ibid.

Dietrich soon found his way to the most humane guards, and they to him, sometimes through seeking pastoral counsel. Some understood that the war was lost and, anticipating the new postwar order, tried to position themselves favorably with the Bonhoeffer family, an attitude Dietrich encouraged. Dietrich's well-bred sangfroid in a crisis, especially during a bombing, earned appreciation: like Paula, he could keep his head in an emergency and be of help. He worked in the well-equipped sick bay, and sometimes gained entrance to the chess room to play a few games. In his spare time, he began to study chess moves.

Although he spent most of his day in his cell, he did also get out: trips to downtown Berlin to the Reich Court for interrogation, sick bay treatments, including warm foot baths, to try to relieve his bouts of arthritis, his daily walks, and visits from his parents and his lawyer. He had food, books, tobacco, paper. What he most missed was Eberhard.

In May, the Bonhoeffers invited Maria and Mrs. von Wedemeyer to Berlin. Ruthchen and Maria duly arrived. Paula outdid herself to create a delicious lunch despite the scarcity of food: "a green spring-pea soup, veal cutlets (we saved up during the week) with green beans (the last can!), tomatoes and iced strawberries, which I was just able to get,"[5] Paula wrote to Dietrich. All but the veal cutlets were garden foods. The von Wedemeyer's brought some "good sausage," which Paula divided between Dietrich and Hans, also still in prison.

Tegel prison was still unknown to her, but Maria for the first time sat in Dietrich's attic bedroom and examined his things.

The family responded to Maria warmly on her first visit, apparently, not having noticed her when she attended Hans Walter's going-away party in October. Only father Karl seemed to remember she had visited with them after helping herself to grapes from their garden. She is "a nice, intelligent girl" wrote brother Karl-Friedrich, who chided her for saving her butter ration for Dietrich. She "makes a thoroughly dependable, hard-working, warm-hearted impression," wrote Paula. [6]

Both Paula and Maria wrote Dietrich letters about Maria visiting his room. "I like your parents. . . . Oh, I fell in love with everything. Your house, the garden [both of which she had seen in October], and—most of all—your room," wrote Maria. The parents she "liked"; the setting she "loved." "I don't know what I'd give to be able to sit there again, if only to look at the ink blots on your desk pad." The visit made everything "real and clear to me . . . the

---

5. Bonhoeffer, *DBWE 8*, 92.
6. Bismarck and Kabitz, eds., *Love Letters*, 25.

desk where you write your books[7] and letters to me, your armchair and the ash tray, your shoes on the shelf and your favorite pictures. Those things were all a part of you." After writing, "I never thought I could miss you and long for you more than I do, but I've done so twice as much as yesterday," she stops short and indicates her hesitation: "You're right; one just can't imagine what a wedding means."[8]

In "Writing to the Spouse from Prison," H. Martin Rumscheidt questions whether Maria and Dietrich's correspondence can be rightly called "love" letters. The title of the published letters—*Love Letters from Cell 92*—and the cover photo—strikingly, as Rumscheidt notices, only of Dietrich—trivializes and privatizes the relationship, such that the letters stand in danger of being "gravely misunderstood."[9] Rather than a private "love story," he argues, the relationship was public and theological.[10]

When Rumscheidt spoke with Maria's sister, Ruth Alice von Bismarck, she agreed that terms like *love letters* and *love story* "fail the reality of this couple."[11] As Rumscheidt points out, the relationship was largely, almost wholly, public. The absence of Maria's photo in a book about her indicates strongly her merely symbolic function in the Bonhoeffer discourse; her photograph, documentary evidence that she actually existed and had a definitive shape and form, really doesn't matter, because her reality as a full human being doesn't matter. She is a placeholder, an outer form, "attractive," as Bethge calls one of her essays.

Most of what we know about Maria comes from what she herself tells us, primarily through her autobiographical musings in her prison correspondence and from her essay, "The Other Letters from Prison." Some documentary evidence exists about her after 1945, but to Bonhoeffer's church contemporaries she was a blank. The engagement, of course, remained hidden until Dietrich was in prison, but even among people, most notably Bethge, who interacted with her during the war years and promoted the marriage, we get only the scantiest of information. Bethge offers seemingly the least possible he can get away with in his mammoth biography. He states frankly in the introduction to the expanded edition of *Letters and Papers from Prison* that in the first edition "hardly a single reference to

---

7. Bonhoeffer actually wrote the bulk of his later books at Sabine's home in Göttingen and Ruth's Klein Krössin cottage.
8. Bismarck and Kabitz, eds., *Love Letters*, 26–27.
9. Rumscheidt, "Writing to the Spouse from Prison," 201.
10. Ibid., 207.
11. Ibid., 201.

Bonhoeffer's fiancé [still not giving her name] appeared" (vii). Partly this is what Theweleit understands as the convention of erasure of women from German memoirs of the period,[12] but beyond that it's a mysterious gap, given her role. When the "love" letters later appeared Bethge seemed, more than anything, surprised by the correspondence. He evinces, in the preface to the new edition of *Letters and Papers from Prison*, irritation that "she herself has kept control over the disposal of her letters." However, he notes "the period of Bonhoeffer's engagement is more vivid than it was before," no doubt a relief after questions started to surface about the nature of the Bethge/Bonhoeffer friendship.[13]

The lack of solid information is not so mysterious. Beyond a few biographers who have perceived the relationship as odd, one can hear an almost audible sigh of relief when, at the eleventh hour, the beautiful young fiancée arrives on the scene and saves the day. Maria shows that Bonhoeffer was a man's man. He not only gets a girl, but the kind of beautiful young woman other men would envy. In the standard story, that's all we need to know about Maria. The details can be dismissed, as popular biographer Metaxas does, as a "thunderbolt" of love. The relationship doesn't even need to rise to a cliché—one word suffices.

Maria wrote Dietrich ten letters between May 7 and July 30, 1943, the day he finally could respond directly back to her. She would have been aware censors were reading her words, weighing her words, judging her words. It was indeed a public relationship.

Thus began a courtship through correspondence between two people who scarcely knew each other. Through painting word pictures, Maria tried to fill the largely blank canvas of their relationship. Maria's letters imagine a future with her fiancé as if Germany isn't collapsing. She vividly evokes her love of Pätzig and of nature, her energetic persona, her beloved father and Max, her desire for domestic warmth and security, her love of children. At times she hurtles forth boldly, seemingly heedless of censorious eyes, including Dietrich's. But Maria is performing, fashioning a self to present to Dietrich, sometimes using the hackneyed prose of a romance novel, at other times soaring in her descriptions of life around her, and at her best, witty and wry. The responses she receives back express gratitude for her letters, but Dietrich's guard is often up. He too presents a persona, and sometimes it's hard to know what "you" he is addressing when he seemingly speaks to her. He conflates

---

12. Theweleit, *Male Fantasies*, vol. 1, 26–27.
13. Bonhoeffer, *LPP*, ix.

her with other people—people he feels closer to—and he also keeps her at a distance. She, in turn, exhibits passive aggression.

Mutual loneliness drove the couple together through the early stages of this correspondence, as perhaps it did during that week in October when the keyless Maria had to wait on the stoop of Spes's apartment in blacked-out Berlin, and Dietrich drifted at loose ends, fearing arrest as Eberhard drew ever closer to marriage. In her early prison correspondence, Maria speaks poignantly of her sense of isolation: for instance, she leaves a Bach organ concert early "because the loneliness was too much to bear."[14] In these first prison months, Dietrich also experienced deep loneliness: he didn't dare contact the one he most wanted to hear from, who had married since he was arrested, leaving him in an agony of uncertainty over what the future would hold; Maria likewise dealt with family losses and a collapsing country with no realistic roadmap for her future. Anxieties about Germany's fate, which were illegal to express, drove her to dream of an idyllic domestic life. The couple's letters also often reflect a flurry of responses meant to paper over errors or reassure one another that all is well after their painfully awkward monthly visits.

In her first letter to Dietrich, Maria wrote that Paula had given her eight small photos of Dietrich. Playing the role of the "white nurse," she stated, "I'm determined to be very brave." Her maternal qualities on display, she described telling the four infants in her care about "Uncle Dietrich." She denigrated her ability to help him—"I'm so poorly endowed with all that you possess."[15]

On June 15, Maria transferred to Berlin's Augusta Hospital. She took two weeks of sick leave because of foot problems. Finally, on June 24th, she paid Dietrich a short visit, the first of eighteen she would be allowed. The two had not seen each other since October 26.

---

14. Bismarck and Kabitz, eds., *Love Letters*, 35.
15. Ibid., 23.

55

Don't You Like Being Romantic?

WHEN MARIA APPEARED AT the Reich's Court to see Dietrich, guards ushered her into a room with a red plush sofa. Dietrich had received "practically no forewarning" of her arrival. Dietrich, "visibly shaken," was silent and didn't kiss her. Maria realized she was being used by Roeder.[1] What she meant by that she doesn't explain. Did Roeder doubt the reality of the relationship? When Dietrich regained his composure, he talked normally, but held her hand tightly, a gesture both brotherly and controlling, as if warning her.

For Roeder's eyes, Dietrich described this unsettling experience in a letter to his parents as "an indescribable surprise and joy." He also relayed information: "I knew about it only a minute beforehand," and then, ascribing to Maria thoughts that were probably his own, wrote it "all" must seem to her: "unimaginable, mysterious, terrifying."[2] In fact, he used *unimaginable*, a term that for him conveyed strong emotion, twice, as well as *indescribable*. Paula would write more wryly of Maria's reaction: "Maria was quite thrilled about the reunion and of course she had to tell us all about it . . . ."[3]

In a letter Rutchen wrote to Dietrich, she described Maria's response to the meeting as highly emotional, even mystical: "Maria was initially so shaken that for a long time she could not utter a word and first had to release her strong emotions through tears. Then she told me many things, and in each sentence one could sense a great, brightly burning joy. To my eyes, her expression was totally transformed. Now she lives entirely from this hour and ponders all the words in her heart. How wonderful that there was no strangeness between you, that you were able to be so cheerful with her!"[4]

---

1. Wedemeyer-Weller, "The Other Letters from Prison," 413.
2. Bethge, DB: *A Biography*, 839: "emotions were indicated only in the manner of asking about the wishes and affairs of the other person."
3. Bonhoeffer, *LPP*, 71–72.
4. Bonhoeffer, *DBWE 8*, 119.

How much this relays of what actually occurred and how much was manufactured to explain to Roeder Dietrich's shock, "strangeness," and awkwardness is impossible to determine. Maria herself would write to Dietrich in the language of a romance novel: "It might all be a dream plucked from the midst of other dreams, lovely or haunting or unreal . . . a fragment of my heart has remained clinging to you . . . . Everything at Pätzig seems different."[5]

During the summer of 1943, Maria recovered from her foot problems at Pätzig, amid younger brothers and sisters, dogs and horses, flowers and kitchen gardens, tramping (one hopes carefully) in the cool forests of the estate or visiting the wheelwright, and then going to an aunt's "model farm" in Seefeld, complete with its "school of breathing."[6] "I've always [sic] looked forward so much to showing you Pätzig in August especially," Maria wrote to Dietrich.[7] Another time she imagined "we can . . . go for walks (or pinch raspberries from the kitchen gardens)."[8] In Seefeld, "masses of bright flowers are laughing all around me, the sun is shining and the trees are draped in pure gold,"[9] she wrote as mused over their married life together, followed by disbelief: "I suddenly think I'll have to awaken from this dream and realize that none of it is true."[10] "Oh, if only we were living in a proper apartment!" she complained in one letter. "I've stopped believing that we ever will."[11]

On July 11, 1943 Maria wrote in her diary of "the cornfield rippling, birds singing, flowers laughing, the village girl singing, the blacksmith hammering, horses whinnying." She would contrast that eighteenth-century vista of Pätzig with her own inner turmoil and foreboding: "And the news has just come that British troops have landed in Sicily."[12] After this, according to a note, "Maria sealed her diary and never opened it again."[13] But of course she did—or began a new diary, for she made another entry on July 30th.[14]

Maria imagined herself into married life via furniture: "There's a chest of drawers too and I'll get our carpenter to make a bookshelf. All we'll need

5. Bismarck and Kabitz, eds., *Love Letters*, 39.
6. Ibid., 46–47.
7. Ibid., 33.
8. Ibid., 44.
9. Ibid., 51.
10. Ibid., 33.
11. Ibid., 44.
12. Ibid., 347.
13. Ibid.
14. Ibid., 55.

then are some armchairs . . . . The dining room is a problem. I hate sideboards and really decent cupboards are quite unobtainable . . . . As for a kitchen cupboard, we'll have to be quite nice to Grandmother. The one from Stettin should be available now. We already inherited a small carpet from there . . . ."[15] She sent a drawing Dietrich cherished: "Maria has been writing to me about setting up house; it's made me tremendously happy. I find the sketches of the furniture in her room most attractive."[16]

While Maria, aware of the deteriorating war situation, convalesced amid the beauties of the countryside—her sick leave, due to the efforts of her mother, extending to three months—the air attacks on Germany grew more severe. In late July, Hamburg suffered a series of raids, resulting at one point in a firestorm that killed 40,000 civilians. Berliners knew Hamburg's fate could be theirs.[17] Refugees streaming in from Hamburg to Berlin added to the unease with their graphic descriptions of melting bodies and flaming buildings. Dietrich wrote a tense letter to his parents, worried about their basement shelter and advising them to use more sandbags. The government ordered women, children, and the elderly from Berlin. This would send part of the Bonhoeffer clan to Friedrichsbrunn, though the elder Bonhoeffers refused to leave the city. While Dietrich sat frustrated in prison, words such as "catastrophe" and "panic" swirled in the air. If Dietrich felt trapped in Tegel, other Berliners felt equally trapped, for despite all their former bragging and bluster, the government could do next to nothing to protect them from air attacks, antiflak towers notwithstanding. But after the initial hysteria, life again settled down—Berlin experienced damaging "nuisance" raids, but no devastating bombings for the rest of summer and early fall. England, however, was biding its time.

Hints of dire reality peek out of Maria's letters. On August 9, city evacuees arrived at Pätzig: "Mother has taken in no less that 15 acquaintances from Berlin, who have come to escape the bombing."[18] Since Ruthchen at that time was accompanying Maria's younger sister Christina (Ina) to the Altenburg school, the ever assertive Maria was left in charge: "It's very amusing and instructive, but I sometimes feel quite glad I'll only be running a small household later on and won't have to cross swords with impertinent policemen, bickering maidservants and fussy guests." She suggested too that part of their "honeymoon" be a swing by to see the no-doubt homesick Ina

---

15. Ibid., 41.
16. Ibid., 74.
17. Moorhouse, *Berlin at War*, 317–18.
18. Bismarck and Kabitz, eds., *Love Letters*, 62.

at Altenburg.[19] Bonhoeffer wrote back that he was "trying to picture the milling throng in your house . . . . Could it be that, in the long run, these transplantations will give townsfolk some appreciation of the country, and thus help to pave the way for the return to the land which will, one hopes, comes around someday? . . . I'm sorry for poor little Christine."[20] He liked to imagine Maria not as lover, but as, like his mother, matriarch of a household.

While Berlin dealt with bombs, Eberhard had more personal concerns to cope with. By July 3, it was clear that Renate was pregnant, a worry to the family because of her youth. Dietrich reassured his parents that Goethe's mother was barely eighteen when he was born.[21] He also asked after Sabine, but the family knew little of her situation.[22]

In early August, the Bethge newlyweds resettled into a "beautiful" home in Dahlem, in the Burckhardthaus where Eberhard had been living in conjunction with the Gossner Mission for more than two years. The apartment was made complete with Dietrich's spinet and a piano given to them by Hanna Canna, Dietrich's third cousin, who had two. (Meanwhile, Dietrich's Bechstein grand piano, years ago rescued from Finkenwalde the day before the Gestapo had closed by Ruth's grandson, survived a bombing raid in Stettin, despite fires in houses on either side.)[23] The Bethge apartment was tastefully decorated with "many well known things . . . all blended together" in a way that would have "been a great delight" to Dietrich, according to a letter from Renate, dictated by Eberhard.[24]

On July 30, Maria and Dietrich met again at the Reich's Court, sitting on the same red plush sofa. At first Dietrich seemed a stranger in his well-cut dark suit. Maria almost addressed him with the formal Sie rather than Du, a slip which would have raised suspicions. Dietrich kissed her for the first time[25]—later he would write to Eberhard that "we . . . were obliged to exchange our first kiss under Roeder's gaze," and Maria, in words that could have again been cribbed from a romance novel, wrote of the kiss, "I knew I'd found you again—found you more completely than I'd ever possessed you before." Holding hands, however, actually generated more erotic heat than kissing for

19. Ibid.
20. Ibid., 75.
21. Bonhoeffer, *LPP*, 74.
22. Leibholz, *The Bonhoeffers*, 147.
23. Bonhoeffer, *DBWE 8*, 96.
24. Bonhoeffer, *LPP*, 107.
25. Bismarck and Kabitz, eds., *Love Letters*, 131.

Maria, as she recorded in her diary: "You caught hold of me [my hand] . . . . Although I was inwardly so calm, I was shivering. It felt so good, your warm hand, that I wished you would leave it there . . . . It transmitted a current that filled me up and left no room for thoughts. But you took it away. Don't you like being romantic?" She ended her diary entry with a quote: "Your eyes were with me," a possible reference to Schumann's "Dear friend, thou lookest at me in amazement."

Once again, Dietrich wrote to say, probably projecting his own feelings, that the visits to see him at the Reich Court must "surely be awful" for her.[26] Maria reassured him that she did not mind the visits at all.[27]

Maria's yearning sensuality contrasted so sharply with Dietrich's lack of temperature that she had posed the haunting question in her journal that she dared not express to him openly: "Don't you like being romantic?" He did not, and tried to fashion her into a replacement for Sabine. Sabine had learned English and played the violin—this was also Maria's instrument, so Dietrich pushed her to resume playing it, as well as to study English, apparently going on about these so much during their visits that it stuck in Maria's mind more than twenty years later: "He never tired of urging me to learn better English or to resume practising the violin, although both of these seemed irrelevant to me at the time."[28]

On July 30, the day of the visit, Dietrich received permission to write one letter every four days, instead of every ten, and immediately contacted Maria to say that he would alternate between his parents and her. But on the first opportunity to do so, he drew back, possibly finding the idea of communicating directly so uncomfortable that he wrote instead to his parents. He told them he was afraid it would cause Maria problems if people recognized a postmark from a prison. Maria laughed off this worry.

In August, Eberhard's call for active military duty came, ordering him to Spandau barracks for basic training. However, a bombing run in late August destroyed the Burckhardthaus, displacing the young couple, and delaying Eberhard's departure until September 15. He wrote through Renate of the damage: "Everything is in such a mess and scattered all over the place." The couple moved temporarily into Bärbel's room at the von Dohnanyi home. The senior Bonhoeffers stored the unscathed piano.[29]

---

26. Ibid., 56.

27. Ibid., 61.

28. Wedemeyer-Weller, "The Other Letters from Prison," 415. We remember, too, Dietrich's letters from 1923, urging Sabine to keep practicing her violin.

29. Bonhoeffer, *LPP*, 108.

— 56 —
Writing and Dissatisfaction

By the end of summer, Dietrich left his cell regularly for prison air raid drills.[1] Although his cell was hot, he thought it would be unfair to use his privileged position to request a change. "Please don't worry," he wrote his parents, "I've often had to put up with worse heat . . . almost the worst of all, in New York, in July 1939."[2] He took an interest in his parents' preparations for the expected fall air attacks. He arranged for his Bible to go to Eberhard as a birthday present and a bottle of sweet wine to Susi for her birthday. (Although he mentioned Maria's April 23rd birthday in a letter to his parents, getting her a gift never seemed to have crossed his mind.)

Bethge would write of Dietrich's time in Tegel almost as if it were a country club: unlike the bulk of Berliners, he had enough to eat, primarily through the combined efforts of his mother, sisters, and Maria and Ruth; he was not serving in the army; he did not have to witness the half-starved slave laborers brought into Berlin to work or "the pale faces of careworn women and the serious eyes of undernourished children . . . ." He didn't, like so many Berliners, have to pick up cigarette butts from the street or scavenge ashtrays in restaurants, carefully mixing bits of tobacco with herbs, to smoke in pipes or rerolled cigarettes.[3]

As time went, he would resume a former interest, handwriting analysis, this time for his cohorts in Tegel.

Yet he faced a possible death sentence—and was a prisoner.

Sitting in his cell one day that summer, bothered by flies and heat, Dietrich enjoyed the lilies and other flowers, fresh fruit, and tomatoes sent by his family and friends. He wrote to Maria: "I'd like to drive through the woods with you to the lakeside, go swimming and lie in some shady spot with you, listening to you for ages without saying a word. My desires are quite earthy

1. Bethge, *DB: A Biography,* 847.
2. Bonhoeffer, *LPP,* 87.
3. Lubrich, ed., *Travels in the Reich,* 293.

and concrete as you see."[4] The "as you see" suggests she had questioned him about his desires. He would go on to recall Cuba and rhapsodize about the sensuality of the sun.

Around the August 20 date of this letter, he was also working on a novel, set in part by a lake in a forest reminiscent of Friedrichsbrunn. The person he sits with at the lake is modeled on Eberhard, raising the question of which "Du" he had in mind when writing to Maria of lying together at a spot by a lake: "On a treeless slope rising gently from the pond in full sun, Christoph and Ulrich lay on their backs in the tall grass, their hands cradling their heads, their gaze directed at times to the sky, at times across the pond, each with a gray linen slouch hat on his head. Their tanned and toughened bodies were impervious to the sun. Anyone seeing the two would have thought they were brothers, as in fact often happened."[5]

Later in the same August 20 letter, after asking if the food he received came from Maria or her grandmother, he wrote, "If you can, bake me some more good things, not only because they're tasty, but because I like so much to think of you while eating them." Was it Maria or her grandmother he thought of, as he seemed to imagine the food was from Ruth? He sent regards to Maria's mother and added a postscript of "my love to your grandmother too. I really miss her letters!"[6]

While Maria dreamed of their future times alone together, Dietrich envisioned the relationship in the context of two good families uniting. This helped keep Maria in the "sister" role. The day after her third visit late in the summer, as if in response to any doubts she might have been harboring about him after their meeting (or he about her), he wrote, somewhat stiffly: "I . . . can only point to a number of good friends who know me but have nevertheless remained, and will remain faithful to me, and the fact they include members of your immediate family [such as Ruth] cannot, I suppose, remain wholly unimportant to you."[7] When Maria talked of disagreements with her grandmother, he chided her: "You mustn't do this *to me*, the two of you! I know you've always been on slightly different wavelengths, but I'd so much like you to be attuned to each other. Actually, you can't really be anything else." Then came the burst of longing: "What wonderful times I've had at Krössin! We simply must pay her a visit soon."[8]

---

4. Bismarck and Kabitz, eds., *Love Letters*, 68.
5. Bonhoeffer, *DBWE 7*, 102.
6. Ibid., 70–71.
7. Ibid., 74.
8. Ibid., 74.

Maria, in an August 27 letter in response to a visit, wrote that she had discovered afterwards that he was ill and running a fever throughout her stay. "How will we look back on these visits?" she wrote. "Please don't brood on any aspect of them . . . . It always feels a bit like sitting on a stage, acting out a bad novel . . . tasteless theatricals."[9] When she received his letter of the 27th she reacted strongly against his framing of the relationship in terms of friends and family, clearly understanding its subtext: "If I want to be your best friend, why should I mind about your other friends? . . . And why should I love you because other people are fond of you? I've no wish to find my way to you via other people, not even if they are members of my immediate family and very close to me. I accepted you because I love you." "It can be so hard," she added, "simply believing in this direct relationship without any intermediate or subsidiary aids."[10]

Yet Ruth was deeply embedded within this engagement, even offering the couple her wedding rings, a prospect that made Dietrich "often rejoice. . . . They're so splendidly old-fashioned."[11] Maria was silent on this subject.

In his September 20th letter to Maria, Dietrich managed a remarkable insight as to what in fact joined them. Both of them, he wrote, were wedded to duty: "Neither of us had any fundamental desire for an easy life, much as we can both take pleasure in life's lovely, happy times, and much as we doubtless yearn for such times today. For both of us, I believe, happiness lies elsewhere, in a more remote place that not only passes many people's understanding but will continue to do so. At bottom we both seek tasks to perform. Each of us has hitherto sought them separately, but from now on they will be common tasks in which we shall fully grow together"—but as always with a hesitation—"if God grants us the requisite time."[12]

On September 13, Maria wrote Dietrich that the doctors had advised that she not resume her Red Cross nursing. Still adrift after a summer of loose ends, she wrote of learning to cook, "so that you get no more than one burnt and over-salted meal a week later on. But I could also take up a profession— I could study. It needs discussing though. Anyway, I want to do something sensible at least, and I'm glad Mother agrees."[13]

---

9. Ibid., 72.

10. Ibid., 96. (Of course, we remember from her diary that she accepts Dietrich because of her grandmother without being in love with him.)

11. Ibid., 74.

12. Ibid., 86.

13. Ibid., 84.

Dietrich replied sharply to Maria about this idea of a profession: "I find that [taking up a profession] rather hard to understand." "If only I could advise you what to do," he wrote. "Is your work at home really so unfulfilling? . . . won't you later regret every day you didn't spend at home? . . . Please, if you can, write me a fuller account of your thoughts and reasons." Once again the painful visits come into play. "One can't say everything during a visit and you were so upset by our surroundings last time."[14]

Dietrich poured his desires and discontents into the unfinished novel he'd begun not long before receiving Maria's letter. As he would later write to Eberhard: "Then I started on a bold enterprise that I've had in mind for a long time: I began to write the story of a contemporary middle-class family. The background for this consisted of all our innumerable conversations on the subject, and my own personal experiences; in short, it was to present afresh middle-class life as we know it in our families, and especially in the light of Christianity. . . . You would recognize many familiar features, and you come into it too."[15]

As a counterpart to the discontented Renate von Bremer, the character based on Maria in the novel,[16] Dietrich envisioned the idealized Klara, perfectly satisfied to serve other people's needs in the domestic sphere. Klara is sexless, innocent, and childlike with long braids. She is also physically indistinct, at one point her braids blonde, at another brown.

Christophe, the character Dietrich modeled after himself, wondered: "Would Renate[17] and Klara get along? They seemed completely different. Klara knew nothing but her family's house and her brothers and sisters and didn't want to know anything else. . . . She would hardly comprehend Renate's questions and difficulties and would answer them by the way she lived. . . . untorn by any inner dissatisfaction, and . . . much too proud to pursue short-lived pleasures." In fact, Klara, the perfect "white nurse" desires nothing more than a selfless and sexless life with her family.[18]

---

14. Ibid., 94. Dietrich would later come up with idea of her attending the Rackow language school (*DBWE 8*, 165).

15. Bonhoeffer, *DBWE 7*, 5.

16. Ibid., 5.

17. In his prison fiction, Bonhoeffer always names the girlfriend of the character based on himself "Renate," obviously the name of Bethge's wife, as if he wished to conflate Maria into Renate and himself into Eberhard. Theweleit, *Male Fantasies*, vol. 1, 124, writes: "As for the homoerotic, the brother [friend—though in the novel fragment Bonhoeffer likens the Bethge figure to a brother] is loved through the medium of the sister [niece]. Both men, brother and husband, are united in her."

18. Bonhoeffer, *DBWE 7*, 139. The novel fragment is influenced by Adalbert Stifter's novel *Indian Summer*, which also includes an idealized sister figure.

Klara's day begins at 5:30 AM with tidying her room, preparing her parents' breakfast, served with the herbs Klara has chopped and the bouquet of fresh flowers she has picked, then bringing her grandmother breakfast on an "old fashioned silver service." Klara would knock on her grandmother's door "enter, kiss her grandmother's hand and lean down to receive a kiss on her forehead. She would put the Bible in its place beside the desk, then offer her grandmother her arm and lead her out where she ate breakfast all year round . . . . This time sitting with her grandmother was one of the few times that Klara's hands were not busy with some sort of mending or sewing." From her grandmother Klara "learns to love her everyday tasks." This Victorian angel's relationship to household duties takes on an "inner order and an even rhythm."[19]

Frau von Bremer, Renate's mother, perceives that Klara "wasn't one of those emancipated half men"[20] like her own daughter. "'We must live more intensely,' a worldly young woman had said to Frau von Bremer the other day . . . with Klara would probably have just smiled and shaken her head in surprise. She had no need for all this; she lived more intensely than these extravagant young women." Klara "doesn't share the sort of hunger for experiences, changes, the unknown that makes life so unhappy for so many young girls nowadays."[21] Frau von Bremer hopes that under Klara's influence, Renate can be fixed of her waywardness and dissatisfaction, and as her reformation was the intended trajectory of the novel, so Maria's reform was the intended trajectory in Dietrich's script for her life.

This desire for Maria's stasis reveals the anxieties and aggressions her assertive personality—"half man . . . intense"—aroused in him.

On September 21, Bonhoeffer was formally charged with undermining the morale of the armed forces, a victory of sorts: His family and friends had worked feverishly to avoid more serious treason charges. Yet the lesser charge could still carry the death penalty. Dietrich made a will, leaving everything to Eberhard, as he had in 1939. He did not seem to think of Maria, his future wife. After September 21 his life entered a new phase. He was no longer being interrogated. He no longer had to worry as intensely

---

19. Ibid., 135.

20. Ibid.,137. A footnote in Bonhoeffer, *DBWE* 7, 182, notes, "The Weimar avant-garde ideal of the 'new woman' implied dressing in men's clothing, smoking, and riding motorcycles; critics of the 'emancipated' women often called them 'half-men.'" We know Maria had tried smoking and enjoyed being in motion—and wrote to him of wanting a "profession." The "emancipated half-men" sound close to Theweleit's dangerous, sexual, and castrating "red nurses."

21. Ibid., 139–40.

about Roeder intercepting his mail and using it against him. He had struck up friendships with prison guards. Soon, though he moved cautiously, he would be able to enact his deepest wish.

"I am tormented by my inability to make you happy by my letters and visits," Maria wrote to Dietrich after her October 7th visit. "Shall I tell you that I was utterly desperate when I lost the two people dearest to me, that I felt empty and lonely and crushed by the love I felt within in me but no longer could give? ... And then you came along, and I realized you were coming to me and you'll be my father and brother and more than everyone else put together...."[22] If Dietrich wanted to fashion Maria into a substitute for both Ruth and Sabine, into Klara, into a white nurse, a sexless being who would take care of him, Maria wanted Dietrich to be both her father and Max. Desires clashed between these two lonely souls, especially for Maria, whose ardent sexual longings complicated the relationship.

In this respect, Maria's letters vibrated with her movement, her inherent sexuality, her "half man" attributes. She loved to ride—"Tonight I rode for two hours ... under a clear, starry sky," to ski, to hunt, to dance—she refused to become the cold, chaste angel of the home. She described herself "in the kennels with my sleeves rolled up and my boots covered in mud, attending to Harro [her dog] who is sick."[23] She acknowledged their psychic kinship in her October 19 letter while also alluding to sexual feelings: "Our thoughts and feelings are so close knit ... but I become more and more aware of my longing, and my desire to be alone with you becomes overwhelming." He filled her fantasies: "How poor my life would be now, and how poor it would have been all this past year, if it hadn't been for you. I feel so terribly selfish to have said 'yes' to you."[24] Of course, in the past year, she had spent, as far as we know, small portions of as many as seventeen days with him (we have evidence, however, of only nine encounters), and not even an hour alone, so what has filled her life has largely been imagined.

By mid-October Eberhard was in Lissa, in Poland. The Bonhoeffer connections once again proved invaluable: Justus Delbrück, brother of Klaus's wife Emmi, and Count Karl-Ludwig von Guttenberg would end up arranging for Bethge to be sent to Italy, where his chances of survival were much higher than on the Russian front.[25] He left in January 1944,

---

22. Bismarck and Kabitz, eds., *Love Letters*, 96–97.
23. Ibid., 89.
24. Ibid., 107.
25. Bethge, *Friendship and Resistance*, 39.

Renate's baby due in a month. By July, he had been promoted two ranks to Lance Corporal.[26]

Back in Oxford, the Leibholzes had to leave their Little House by the Railway, where once they had seen a swan serenely floating in the back yard after a flood. Oxford continued to be jammed with the dislocated, and German refugees remained at the bottom of the housing hierarchy. The girls continued to undergo torments at school for being German, because, as Sabine put it, some couldn't distinguish between Nazis and refugees from Nazi persecution. The family also missed their Bluthner grand piano, having to make due with borrowed time on other people's often inadequate instruments. At one point they lived in three attic rooms in a boarding house with an abusive landlady who forced them to speak in whispers, blamed them for Nazi war crimes, and made them enter the house through the back door. Sabine got revenge by bringing Bell, a bishop, in through the back entrance, to the embarrassment of the landlady.

On the other hand, since the Leibholzes, like most Germans, much preferred coffee to tea, they never used their tea ration and could give it away, helping them to win friends. Coffee remained unrationed, so all were happy. And as the war continued to go badly for Germany, the threat of an invasion receded, causing the family to sleep more easily. Their worries now focused on relatives and friends back in Germany.[27]

That fall, Dietrich wrote to his parents cheerfully of his jail routine—up for breakfast at seven, then a day of alternating reading and writing, the walk in the prison yard, brightened by "a few beautiful chestnut and lime trees." October temperatures had dropped to about 50, but Dietrich kept comfortable in his chilly cell with the help of a white sweater and ski suit.[28] By the end of October, the days were warmer and balmy, and Karl Bonhoeffer sent Dietrich some of the tobacco he had grown, with instructions to throw it out if not good. But despite the beautiful fall, Berliners were on edge.[29]

In October, Patizg hosted a hunting party. Maria wrote to Dietrich of its uncanny nature: "a strange occasion in wartime and without father.... Masses of guests have turned up.... They think it's wonderful to de-moth their tails and evening gowns, have a good time, and enjoy making small talk."

26. Ibid., 39
27. Leibholz, *The Bonhoeffers*, 130–31.
28. Bonhoeffer, *LPP*, 119.
29. Ibid., 122.

Watching them gather around the punch bowl with their cigarettes during this last gasp of an old way of life, already almost ghosts in yesteryear's splendor, Maria felt her alienation and clung all the more to her fantasy Dietrich, at the same time collecting spare cigarettes for the real one.[30]

Meanwhile, Dietrich continued encoding his visceral, aching longing for Eberhard in his novel, along with his growing frustrations with Maria—she was not domestic or docile enough, she was too discontented, too much her own person. However, he had as well a larger project in mind—envisioning a postwar world. He looked to the past in this novel fragment, as he had in an earlier play fragment—but abandoned both, perhaps recognizing that the past by itself was a dead end as a template for the future.

---

30. Bismarck and Kabitz, eds., *Love Letters*, 106.

— 57 —

Doubts and Delights

On November 9, Dietrich wrote to his parents: "Maria is to come on a visit tomorrow. I keep encouraging her along from month to month and ask her to be patient, but it's indescribably difficult for her." In other words, using Bethge's formula of Dietrich ascribing to others his own feelings, indescribably difficult for him. Another painful visit ensued, the two side by side on the sofa after Maria had been up all night traveling on the train straight from visiting older sister Ruth Alice and her new baby. Dietrich's letter of the same day poured out gratitude to her, rushing to paper over any defects in the meeting: "How can I thank you for everything? I can't. I can only tell you all is well when you are with me." Maria's reply, written on a "nasty" day, "cold and Novemberish," was filled as well with the usual concern over the uncomfortable visits: "it strikes me that the things I said are sillier than usual . . . things will be very different later on—so different there'll be absolutely no comparison." Then, as with Dietrich, she expressed the hesitations: "We aren't even properly engaged yet, are we? . . . I don't think we'll get married right away. Let's be properly engaged for awhile."[1]

In the world of Nazi Germany, every independent action carried a risk, not only to oneself but to one's associates. Nevertheless since the end of his interrogation period on September 21, Dietrich had angled to begin a smuggled correspondence with Eberhard. Even using trusted guards for delivery was risky: any communication could be intercepted or betrayed and even the most innocent secret letter misconstrued as conspiracy. Yet for Dietrich, the yearning for Eberhard had risen to an overwhelming pitch. Thus, when Corporal Knobloch, part of Dietrich's prison fellowship of "decent" people, agreed to take letters with him and mail them from his home, the opportunity was too tempting to pass up.[2]

1. Bismarck and Kabitz, eds., *Love Letters*, 113.
2. de Gruchy, *Daring, Trusting Spirit*, 69.

On November 18 Dietrich wrote his first prison letter to Eberhard, probably sitting in his white sweater and ski suit, cigarettes at hand. Unlike the letters to his parents or Maria, which were limited to one page and every four days, the illicit channel meant Dietrich could write for as long as he wanted as often as he wanted. The first long letter, dated from November 18–23, streamed out over a series of days.

In it, Dietrich tumbled from topic to topic, unleashing a pent up outpouring that constantly touched on how deeply he missed Eberhard: "I wish I could talk . . . with you every day. Indeed, I miss that more than you think. . . . I long to read you some of what I've written. . . . I shall be thinking of you every day and asking God to protect you and to bring you back . . . ." And then striking the same theme as at Ettal: "We've had some incomparably good years together, and I hope that some more are before us!!"[3] He began with the wedding still foremost on his mind, protesting too much his happiness that the plans hadn't been "shattered" by his arrest. Later, he would write to Eberhard: "Sometimes I've thought that it is really very good for the two of you that I'm not there. At the beginning it's not at all easy to resolve the conflict between marriage and friendship."[4] No doubt Eberhard echoed that thought. But for all of Dietrich's purported joy at the marriage and desire to "report" to both of them, "this letter is for you alone . . . ."[5]

In marked contrast to how he treated Maria, Dietrich urged insistently that his money and goods were Eberhard's—"Please take *everything* you can use from among my things; I am happy *only* to know they are with you! And *please* take from among the groceries that have come to me as much you can possibly use. This would be a very reassuring thought for me"[6] [Bonhoeffer's italics]. And "if you need money, feel free to draw 1000 marks of mine. I can't use it."[7]

He had not reconsidered his September will, though he now asked that Maria be offered a token should he die: "Maria must be allowed to . . . choose . . . a remembrance." Dietrich left "almost everything," including his car, his motorcycle, his books, other physical possessions, and all the money in his checking account to Eberhard. Maria was his fiancée, but he didn't want to make her his heir or wish to divide his estate between her and Eberhard—or even give her a piece of it, even though he had heard from her mother in November1942 of the sorry financial state of Pätzig.

3. Bonhoeffer, *LPP*, 131–32.
4. Ibid., 131.
5. Ibid., 128.
6. Bonhoeffer, *DBWE 8*, 182.
7. Bonhoeffer, *LPP*, 131.

He moved on to discuss Eberhard's conscription and the possibility of his own. At this point, he would no longer try to remain out of combat.

Four times he apologized for his high-handedness over the course of their years together. First, Dietrich wanted to confess "how grateful I was that with so much patience and forbearance your bore my tyrannical and self serving manner, which often made you suffer, and everything with which I sometimes made your life difficult."[8] Later he asked, "What is going on with your sudden attacks of fatigue? (I remember how inconsiderate I often was about that. Terrible! But I know you don't hold that against me.)"[9] Then, the heady early days on his mind, he ruminated on how he pulled Eberhard abruptly from his Saxony circle and into his own orbit: "I ask myself, did I in some way alienate you from your old friends? I don't believe it; rather it was your path that led you in a different direction."[10] The long-ago tensions with Vibrans still on his mind, and still trying to make amends, he wrote, "I think of Gerhard [Vibrans] as my own brother even today."[11] Finally, "I was hardly able to swallow your well-deserved reproaches, a horrible trait that you bore with endless patience."[12]

As usual, Dietrich equivocated on his own wedding, deciding he would marry if he had "at least" a couple of months before call up, but if it was only two or three weeks he would wait until after the war. "Maria is astounding!' he declared, though he wondered if he had been selfish not to delay the engagement.

It was toward Eberhard that Dietrich poured out his caretaking: "I know now that my weak attempts at looking after you are in much better hands with Renate and the best mother-in-law imaginable." Then, "If there is anything at all that you could think of that would please you, it would give me the greatest delight." And, "If there is anything that would help Renate in her present condition, and you need money for it, please simply take as much as you need without saying any more about it."[13]

The responsibility he felt toward Eberhard was absent from the letters he wrote to Maria, all the more striking as he repeated the same information about Advent and table fellowship to both of them—and even more startling given that she had suffered grievous losses in the death of her father and brother while Eberhard had gained a wife.

8. Bonhoeffer, *DBWE 8*, 181.
9. Ibid., 185.
10. Ibid.
11. Ibid., 185–86.
12. Ibid., 190.
13. Bonhoeffer, *LPP*, 132–36.

Dietrich never asked Maria if she needed anything, be it food, money, or goods. He was grateful to her for her letters, for the food, flowers, and gifts she sent, and for her kindness, but he offered her none of the free flow of sharing that one might anticipate in a soon-to-be spouse. Maria, though her nurse's training had been "arduous" enough that she had to be put on sick leave, and though she gave up her butter ration as well as a precious gift of coffee beans for Dietrich, was never once offered a share of his food.

The Allies had been biding their time as they cranked out an endless number of fighter planes. RAF commander Arthus Harris wrote to Churchill, "We can wreck Berlin from end to end. It will cost us 400–500 aircraft. It will cost Germany the war."[14] Churchill gave the go ahead. Just as Dietrich began his correspondence with Eberhard, the Allies attacked Berlin full force.

When the siren sounded at 7:30 the evening of November 22, it was business as usual. The elder Bonhoeffers, their windows nailed shut and sand bags in place, descended into the Schleicher's well-equipped basement next door, a familiar, if wearying, ritual, usually a false alarm.

But that night the Allies struck with a massive 750 planes, saturation bombing the city. The raid targeted the western side of Berlin, including Charlottenburg, where the Bonhoeffers and Schleichers lived. Speer, who liked to watch the "magnificent spectactle" of bombing raids, headed for a downtown flak tower platform to better view the flashes of the exploding bombs, the stiff, crisscrossing headlight beams scanning the skies, perhaps reminding him of the lights he used for the Nuremburg rallies, the drama of planes downed like "flaming torch[es]." This night, however, he was soon forced inside.[15] Eyewitness Theo Findahl recorded the damage when he emerged on the street after the all clear. "Along the sidewalk there are rows of cars engulfed in flames; on the pavement a bus is flaming like a giant torch. Our faces are whipped by black smoke from the storm above the sea of flames. . . . From the plaza it seems like the whole city is burning. Behind the park the entire Hanseatic Quarter is in flames. . . . The Tiergarten is now a jungle . . . Handelallee a sea of fire!"

Findahl, seeing his apartment in flames, made his way to the Adlon Hotel. He witnessed a scene once inconceivable in the grand hotel. The place was jammed. "People covered in soot are packed in everywhere, on chairs and benches, suitcases, bundles, and packages are all over the marble

---

14. Moorhouse, *Berlin at War,* 320.
15. Speer, *Inside the Third Reich,* 288.

floor—like in a refugee camp. . . . A strange and oppressive mood of destruction fills the atmosphere. Indeed, a metropolis is falling right in front of us."[16]

Speer's armaments ministry went up in flames. Even the next day, the smoke made the city "dark as night."[17]

16. Lubrich, ed., *Travels in the Reich* 302–3.
17. Speer, *Inside the Third Reich,* 288.

PART IX
Eberhard and Maria

— 58 —
Joy

The bombing raids that rattled the lives of the Bonhoeffers and Schleichers created a chaos that led to ecstacy for Dietrich. Prison rules relaxed. On November 26 a joyous reunion took place as his parents, Maria and—for the first time since his imprisonment—Eberhard, visited Dietrich.

"So it really came off!" Dietrich wrote to Eberhard that same day. "When I got back to my cell afterwards, I paced up and down for a whole hour, while my dinner stood there and got cold, so that at last I couldn't help laughing at myself when I found myself repeating over and over again, 'That was really great!'"[1]

Sitting in his cell and writing his letter, he breathed the scent of the cigar Karl Barth had sent home for him with Eberhard last July, saw Maria's Advent garland standing on a box, and on his shelf, two giant eggs from Eberhard that he deemed "ostrich" eggs because of their size, "waiting for breakfasts yet to come." He felt his cup runneth over. Best of all, though a fantasy: "I believe that a moment was enough to make clear to both of us that everything that has happened in the last seven and a half months has left both of us essentially unchanged; I never doubted it for a moment, and you certainly didn't either."[2]

Maria was back at home at Pätzig manor the day after the visit, busy "singing, gluing Advent calendars, decorating the pine branches with cards and gingerbread, making Advent roses and hanging wreaths." Finally back alone in her room that evening with two candles to light her desk, the picture of the angel above her bed wreathed in shadows, she wrote to Dietrich, "I'm thinking of those hours in Berlin and how lovely it was." She doesn't say for whom. This time, she offered no apologies or reassurances. Instead, she exhibited sharp quivers of jealousy: "Might they some time grant us a visit alone together?" she asked, and then revealed a flash of a different Maria,

---

1. Bonhoeffer, *LPP*, 145. The contrast to the "unimaginable," "terrifying" and "awful" emotions he attributed to "Maria" during their visits could not be greater.
2. Ibid.

one who perhaps had just recognized who her rival was—"I'm nowhere near as innocent as everyone thinks me on first sight"—quickly buried under "[but] I'm far too stupid to say anything that would be forbidden," an odd statement for someone who knew her letters were read by a censor. What would she say that would be forbidden? Had seeing Dietrich's trembling response to Eberhard led her to understand why Dietrich was so cold to her? Did she realize where his heart lay? She returned to the private visit: "It's just that I'd really like to be alone with you for once. And considering we've been engaged for a year and never have been alone together, I think," she added, "it's an understandable request."[3] The pique continued: "Perhaps my last letters got burnt in Berlin." She was drumming her fingers waiting to hear from him. Meanwhile, he was busily writing to Eberhard.

The evening of the 26th, as Dietrich helped out in the sick bay, "Christmas trees," the red and green flares the Allies dropped to mark a bombing location, fell from the sky, not, as usual, in the distance over central Berlin, but overhead. Soon bombs aimed at the nearby Borsig locomotive factory exploded around Tegel, and the frightened prisoners, still locked in their cells, began screaming and banging on their doors. A landmine detonated, destroying part of the prison and blowing out the windows and the lights of the sick bay. Dietrich dove to the floor as the shock of the blast sent glass bottles and supplies flying out of cupboards to shatter all around him.

Getting up in the darkness, cold blasts of air coming in through the broken windows, he groped his way with guards and orderlies to help the other prisoners, many still shouting and banging, the wounded screaming for help. Moving cautiously through the darkness, opening cell doors carefully lest a prisoner attack them and try to escape, Dietrich and the orderlies tended to the wounded. Dietrich distributed a few cigarettes left from his store to unnerved men. He remained outwardly calm, inwardly unsettled by the open displays of terror around him. Miraculously, nobody died. By 1 AM Dietrich had bandaged the last patient and gone off to bed in a place, which, like the Adlon Hotel, became eerily silent after the pandemonium. "The horrors of war," as Dietrich called them, were coming home. As late as Monday morning, two days later, even the most bullying guards remained shaken and subdued.

The window had not shattered in Dietrich's cell, as in so many others, leaving him protected from the freezing cold. He ate one of his large eggs for breakfast the next day, hung his advent wreath from a nail, added Lippi's picture of the nativity to the middle of it, and, later, during a "pleasant

---

3. Bismarck and Kabitz, eds., *Love Letters*, 124.

conversation" in the sick bay, smoked the cigar from Karl Barth. Back in his cell, he wrote to Eberhard. He discussed the attack, but he also discussed Rilke.

Berlin might be going up in flames in an air war such as the world had never seen, but Dietrich's mind was on literature. "I'm not on the same wavelength as Maria yet in the literary sphere," he wrote conversationally to Eberhard, as if they were sitting together in their attic bedroom after dinner smoking and discussing the day. "She writes me such good, natural letters, but she reads . . . Rilke, Bergengruen, Binding, Wiechert; I regard the last three as being below our level and the first as being decidedly unhealthy. And in fact they don't really suit her at all . . . . We ought to be able to talk to each other about such things, and I don't know whether they are altogether unimportant. I would very much like my wife to be as much of the same mind as possible in such questions. . . . I don't like it when husbands and wives have different opinions. They must stand together like an impregnable bulwark. Don't you think so? Or is that another aspect of my 'tyrannical' nature that you know so well? If so, you must tell me. . . . The more we have come up against the really good things, the more insipid the weak lemonade of more recent productions has become to us, sometimes almost to the point of making us ill."[4]

The distaste for Rilke revealed Dietrich's growing underlying unease about Maria: She was young, in her own words, "unmusical," uninterested in theological questions, and robustly athletic rather than docile. Given Dietrich's own words and Maria's reactions to the visits, it's likely that during their strained monthly meetings he exhibited what Zimmermann had a decade before described as "an impression of coldness, of distance . . . as if he wanted to withdraw from the other person."

Maria would dismiss Dietrich's concerns about Rilke, her "cocky" and defiant self coming to the fore: "Incidentally, don't imagine I am deeply hurt by your dislike of Rilke. Actually I'm shocked at how little I mind it." In fact, she noted, one of her favorite teachers at Altenburg, who radiated "warmth and kindness," no doubt a shot at Dietrich, was "very fond of Rilke!"[5] Behind Dietrich's concerns about Rilke lurked the question about Maria: Was she too a "weak lemonade"? Was she beginning to make him almost "ill"?

Maria also heard criticisms from Ruth—and didn't care. For her response to Rilke also had its subtext. If her liking of the poet stood in for all her character flaws in Dietrich's mind, as well as his visceral distaste for her,

4. Bonhoeffer, *LPP*, 148.
5. Bismarck and Kabitz, eds., *Love Letters*, 154.

her open dismissal of his concerns marked the beginning of the end, her way of signaling to him that she could care less what he thought or didn't think. If tensions had already emerged, after she witnessed his meeting with Bethge, they escalated.

That night another air raid hit Berlin. A bomb fell near the senior Bonhoeffer's house, shattering windows and taking off part of the roof.

Across Berlin the next morning, the magnitude of the air attack stunned people. Whole blocks of buildings had burned out in firestorms, heavy smoke made it difficult to breathe, and through a suffocating fog people navigated wrecked trams, broken water mains, twisted metal and huge piles of rubble where familiar landmarks had stood. Some buildings still burned vigorously; other collapsed suddenly. People walked around dazed. More than 500,000 were left homeless after the attacks; 10,000 were injured, 3,758 killed.[6]

Amid the destruction, the first smuggled letter from Eberhard arrived at Tegel.

"How and with what can I possibly begin to let you know my joy," Eberhard began, joy at the meeting, at the letter he'd received, that Dietrich looked so well. He thanked Dietrich for sending him bacon and a pipe along with the letter—"beautiful, beautiful things."[7] He imagined Dietrich marching "endlessly in formation" at Lissa with him, forced "to bellow out these moronic songs with us," amused at the image.

But then came the hint that they both wouldn't simply pick up again where they'd left off. Renate had wrought a profound change in Eberhard's life: "Briefly: we are more in love than ever. . . . For me, it is a continuous fountain of happiness." Both he and Renate had experienced "utterly" that their marriage was "what is right." "Marriage is what remains stable through all passing relationships,"[8] he wrote.

Dietrich would write back: "You're certainly right in describing marriage as 'what remains stable in all fleeting relationships.' But we should also include a good friendship among these stable things."[9]

The sparring would continue, Eberhard responding in what presages by half a century the concerns of the gay marriage movement: "You write that, apart from our marriage, our friendship should count as one of the things that remain stable. But just this is not so in the consideration of

---

6. Moorhouse, *Berlin at War,* 433.
7. Bonhoeffer, *DBWE 8,* 208.
8. Ibid., 210–11.
9. Bonhoeffer, *LPP,* 164.

others and the consideration that they give it. It is marriage—whether it is the more stable of the two or not—that gets the outward consideration and recognition. Everyone . . . must take it into account and thinks it right that much has to be done, and should be done, on behalf of a married couple. Friendship, even when it's so exclusive and includes all of each other's goods, as it does with us, doesn't have any 'necessitas.'" To underline the way a friendship could be overlooked or dismissed, Eberhard pointed to the difficulty of getting a visitor's pass to see Dietrich, the military's complete nonrecognition of friendship as a reason for a leave, the Bonhoeffer family's lack of "any serious thought" as to how the two might serve in the military together, and the constant reminders he needed to give to be sure Dietrich's letters to Karl and Paula passed to him.[10]

Eberhard experienced the public recognition of marriage as "something very lovely . . . it gives me a sort of calm and makes me feel more manly. . . . [making] being bombed out, being called up, losing my entire security in many ways, less terrible . . . ."[11]

At the end of November, what Dietrich humorously called the "travelling fur" from Maria, the object of a series of mishaps, finally arrived to keep him warm, along with Max's scarf and a suitcase full of canned goods from home.

Thinking that Eberhard had delivered the package, Dietrich had himself rushed downstairs with a guard, longing to catch at least a fleeting glimpse of his friend. But the "young man" who had dropped the parcel off had left.[12]

10. Bonhoeffer, *DBWE 8*, 247–48.
11. Ibid., 248.
12. Bonhoeffer, *LPP*, 204.

— 59 —

Christmas

"There's a thick white layer of snow outside," Maria wrote Dietrich from Klein Krössin where she was visiting Ruth in early December. "The trees are leafless and motionless, and the temperature has dropped. The bare twigs and branches are glistening to their very tips and only the dark firs look warm and motherly."[1]

At Klein Krössin, Maria stayed in Contentment, Dietrich's guest bedroom, remembering the summer of 1942, when the smell of Dietrich's cigarette smoke had been so heavy in the air. Now, during the cold winter days, she walked around the grounds surrounding the rambling Snow White cottage, her mind on Max and her father, hardly able to fathom the war in the untouched quietude of her grandmother's domain.

The two women chatted over needlepoint, took walks or rode together in Ruth's small trap, and made Christmas preparations. Maria knit a sweater for Dietrich.

Ruthchen continued to try to delay Maria and Dietrich's marriage. Maria's letters to Dietrich abound with warnings of her mother's disapproval: "Mother is far from taken with our plan to get married right away, incidentally," she wrote in June. In October: "Mother, of course, is understandably apprehensive" about the marriage.[2]

Ruth, on the other hand, could hardly wait for the wedding. She talked endlessly about Dietrich on this visit. "It's so lovely," Maria wrote. "She keeps telling me the same things, but I enjoy listening to them over and over. Grandmother is a wonderful storyteller."[3]

Ruth had been sending Maria a daily letter, and from hints Maria dropped, worked hard on making her a fit wife for Dietrich. Ruth remained watchful, worried that the marriage had not yet taken place. During one phone call prior to the December visit, Ruth questioned Maria as to whether

1. Bismarck and Kabitz, eds., *Love Letters*, 129.
2. Ibid., 102.
3. Ibid., 130.

she had "confessed" to Dietrich that she'd danced with another man. "Grandmother naturally leapt to the conclusion that I'd taken a fancy to Friedrich Wilhelm [von Diest] . . . I can't imagine your seriously objecting to it," Maria wrote to Dietrich, deadpan.[4]

Maria had already hinted at some rivalry with Ruth over Dietrich—"Grandmother can't bring herself to forgive me" for the "silly things" she, Maria, had done during the odd period of courtship. "I keep sensing it from what she says and writes . . . I think you've recently displaced me a little in her heart and made yourself at home there on your own."[5] Ruth's preference for Dietrich above most others had emerged long ago, but the letters show Maria's evolving awareness of how the relationships around her had always been constituted: she realized now, if fleetingly, that perhaps her charismatic grandmother had Dietrich's welfare in mind more than her own, while Dietrich seemed more interested in Eberhard—and Ruth—than herself.

In early December, Ruth still hoped for a Christmas wedding. She wrote to Dita Koch that "the nearness of the Eastern front, where most of our relatives are fighting, is unsettling . . . in addition, there are worries about Dietrich and these affect me very much. Recently we have been given hope that in the not too distant future we shall see him again."[6]

Meanwhile, Dietrich confided to Eberhard an uncanny occurrence: He'd met an imprisoned medic who was present at Max von Wedemeyer's death and told him that Max had died when he took a patrol out against orders and was shot through the heart. "I can't tell this to Maria yet, since, of course, such conversations are forbidden and I fear further questions in her letters. But it is nevertheless quite remarkable."[7]

Dietrich again expressed his concerns about the relationship with Maria, which was showing so many signs of wear, in a December 15th letter to Eberhard, written in a pool of candle light because the electricity in the prison had failed:

> I could not but talk to you also about Maria. We've now been engaged nearly a year, and still haven't ever had one single hour alone together! Isn't that absurd? We have to consciously repress everything that is usually part of the engagement period—the sensual-erotic dimension [this is stiff wording; in a later letter Dietrich will discuss his lack of heat toward Maria]; our first kiss had to be exchanged right under Roeder's eyes . . . . We

4. Ibid., 113–14.
5. Ibid., 66.
6. Pejsa, *Matriarch of Conspiracy*, 310.
7. Bonhoeffer, *DBWE 8*, 214.

are obliged to talk and write about things that aren't the most important to either of us; Month after month we sit next to each other for an hour, as obediently as schoolchildren on their bench, and then we're torn apart again. We know almost nothing about each other, we have experienced nothing together, for we experience even these months separately.... Only occasionally does a different note sound, for instance in her last visit, when I told her that even Christmas wasn't certain, she sighed and said, "Oh, it's becoming *too* long for me."

Dietrich continued, offering another revelation as to what the relationship meant to him: "But I am quite certain that she won't leave me in the lurch; it is not becoming 'too long' for her conduct but for her heart, and that [her conduct] is much more important."[8]

Dietrich wrote to Eberhard about wronging Maria by expecting too much of her and then about the age difference. Though he had written earlier in the same letter that the future "announces itself for me in Maria," now he "has the feeling . . . my life is more or less behind me and all I have left to do is complete my *Ethics*. But you know, in such moments I am gripped with an incomparable longing to have a child and not to vanish without a trace," a wish he immediately theologizes as more "Old Testament" than New.[9] In this letter, Dietrich attempts to be sensitive to and aware of Maria's needs—not to expect too much of her—and to remain grateful to her, but is unable to perceive her outside of the nexus of his own wants—that she not leave him in the "lurch," that she provide him with a child. Maria, he hopes, will fulfill his own desires, as an object to use, if uneasily, to gain his ends.

Dietrich absorbed Eberhard's assertions of happy marriage. "You already write like an old married man that marriage is the one and only true thing—and I take you at your word, for you have never spoken in clichés." In this context, Dietrich played for sympathy: "despite everything I have written, it is horrible here . . . ."[10]

The map of the world had shifted, and in this new world a Maria might be necessary to amuse a Renate. A few days later he wrote, dreaming of traveling to Palestine with Eberhard after the war, an oft-quoted line: "We'll take our wives to Italy and leave them there to wait for us. What do you think?"[11] He could talk freely to his friend but not his fiancée: "I must spare

---

8. Ibid., 221–22.
9. Ibid., 222.
10. Ibid., 220.
11. Bonhoeffer, *LPP*, 171.

my parents and also Maria, but you I will not deceive in any way, nor must you deceive me. We haven't done that before, and mustn't do it ever."[12]

While Maria enjoyed the freedom and luxuries of a young aristocrat, across Germany, Eastern European slave laborers and prisoners of war worked under inhumane conditions. Anna Rudolf, just a year older than Maria, had a job in film duplication in Berlin during the war, and remembered the Russian forced laborers who arrived "all at once" to work in the department. The overseer in charge of the Russian women forbade the Germans to fraternize with the Russians, but Anna did anyway, sometimes getting into trouble. "Those girls were always hungry. They hardly got anything to eat. Sometimes I would give one of them a slice of bread and butter and they would say over and over again, 'You good girl! You good girl!'"[13] Anna remembered their living conditions: "They all had plank beds to sleep on and they only got food to eat once a day. . . . They had to work like dogs, and they had to carry those heavy reels." Once, Anna saw the overseer kick one of the girls. She said that although many of her coworkers were kindhearted, "they just looked away and said nothing about it as they were all afraid."[14]

When her father suffered a hearing loss, he was put in charge of a Russian work camp. The thirty men lived outside in such "filth" that her father couldn't "bear to look at [them] anymore." He had the prisoners cut trees and build a roof for themselves for shelter but "they still froze and shivered." Her mother, also horrified, handed them cigarettes through the prison fence. For Christmas, she made a plate of cookies for the young prisoner who shined her husband's boots, asking him to share it with the others in the camp. "Tears rolled down his face," Anna remembered. "Then he stammered out 'Comrades too! Comrades too!' I've never seen anything like how they tackled those cookies. Despite everything, they shared with one another . . . [and] said 'You good woman. You good girl.'"[15]

Under National Socialist ideology, such kindnesses were considered a misplaced sentimentality that weakened the state. Even offering a loaf of bread to starving laborers became a death penalty offense.

At Pätzig, slave labor replaced farm workers sent to war. Ruthchen was deeply disturbed by the bullying guards in charge of the Russian prisoners, but could do little, in part because her loathing of those in charge made communication difficult. Her brother-in-law, Ruth's son Hans Jurgen,

12. Ibid.,173.
13. Johnson and Reuband, *What We Knew*, 168.
14. Ibid., 186.
15. Ibid., 169.

insisted that his workers be given two straw pallets rather than one so that they didn't freeze to death, and enough rations not to starve.

Dietrich's trial, originally scheduled for December 17th, faced another delay. He had hoped to be out of Tegel by Christmas, but his family feared either that he'd be convicted of a crime or, worse yet, freed, then picked up like Niemöller and put in a concentration camp. Dietrich expressed his frustration in a letter to Eberhard: "My own view is that I shall be released, or called up into the army, in January or February. If you can do anything —and want to—where you are about my joining you, don't let yourself be dissuaded by the suggestions of others. . . . We must learn to act differently from those who always hesitate, whose failure we know in a wider context. We must be clear about what we want, we must ask whether we're up to it, and then we must do it with unshakable confidence. Then and only then can we also bear the consequences."[16]

He ached to be with Eberhard: "It's truly horrible that they refuse a soldier who wants to visit his closest friend,"[17] he wrote, and used words echoing his Ettal period: "When we are forcibly separated for any considerable time from those whom we love, we simply cannot, as most can, get some cheap substitute through other people—I don't mean because of moral considerations, but just because we are what we are. Substitutes repel us; we simply have to wait and wait; we have to suffer unspeakably from the separation, and feel the longing till it almost makes us ill. That is the only way, although it is a very painful one, in which we can preserve unimpaired our relationship with our loved ones."[18] He would repeat this sentiment as he wrote a Christmas letter from his dim, chilly cell to Renate and Eberhard, ruminating on the upcoming separation and identifying closely with Renate as Eberhard prepared to leave for Italy: "First: nothing can make up for the absence of someone whom we love, and it would be wrong to try to find a substitute; we must simply hold out and see it through . . . ."[19]

Back at Pätzig after her visit with Ruth, Maria continued to throw herself into Christmas preparations. With the war going badly, orders from the Labor Office arrived to offer a Christmas treat to the prisoners doing farm work on the estate. Maria presided over a small party for them, handing out gingerbread and apples. She made the wry statement that a Christmas party

---

16. Bonhoeffer, *LPP*, 174.
17. Ibid., 145–46.
18. Ibid., 167.
19. Ibid., 176.

was "a complete innovation" on the part of the authorities.[20] Otherwise, we don't know how the presence of the suffering prisoners affected her, though we must assume it was disturbing.

Later in the day, the village children each received a little book and some cardboard cut-outs. Maria remembered her father, as village patriarch, in years past tying the bows of the girls' crisp new pinafores, the traditional Christmas gift, though an impossible luxury this year. Maria mused that she was glad simple gifts were bringing delight and "that the plate of gingerbread, instead of being taken for granted, is becoming a real treat."[21] A box of the gingerbread, beautifully packaged, made its way to Dietrich's cell.

Despite austere times, Maria's brothers received hunting horns, skinning knives, and soccer balls, not to mention a fur coat for Hans Walter. Maria's gifts, outlined to Dietrich, included "white-on-white evening dress material—organdie, I think—which is fine, because I shall make some curtains out of it. I've got plenty of evening gowns, and anyway, what else am I to do with it? I also got a tablecloth with our family crest woven into it, a very pretty necklace from mother, lots of books and masses of other things."[22]

As a Christmas gift, Dietrich gave Maria a cross necklace he had once given Paula. If anything spoke chaste sister, it was that. Maria responded to it acerbically, scarcely acknowledging it as a gift from him."What I liked best, I think, was the necklace from Mama [Paula]—the one you chose for her—which I'm already very attached to. It was so kind of Mama to give it to me. She must have found it hard to part with, especially as it came from you."[23]

Ruth's famous smoked goose breast became a subject in letters to Eberhard—Dietrich wanted it split between Eberhard and Renate and his parents—but then asked for a slice for himself.[24] Maria would famously bring Dietrich a Christmas tree that she cut at Pätzig with Hans Walter. It created merriment, as it couldn't hope to fit in Dietrich's cell. Authorities placed it in the guard's room, where Dietrich was taken to see it.

Susi wrote to Dietrich with her characteristic energy of the Christmas she was spending with her children and Karl-Friedrich's family at Friedrichsbrunn to keep the children safe from bombings. The removal from Berlin frustrated her: "I was very happy to spend those awful days in Berlin, in order to help . . . instead of only hearing the airplanes buzzing overhead

20. Bismarck and Kabitz, eds., *Love Letters*, 146.
21. Ibid.
22. Ibid., 147.
23. Ibid.
24. Bonhoeffer, *DBWE 8*, 216 (around December 15).

here and having no possibility of news for days at a time."²⁵ Never having been in the Harz Mountains at Christmas, Susi enjoyed "the enchantingly beautiful landscape. On the bare beeches the hoarfrost is hanging in four-centimeter-long crystals." But two families were crowded, in part due to lack of heating. The house had, in fact, been wired for electricity, probably with the money Sabine gave Dietrich years ago, "otherwise," wrote Susi, "it would be scarcely endurable."²⁶ She and her sons shared one bedroom to conserve fuel. "Christmas preparations have been completely abandoned this year," she wrote, hoping the coal they had would last until spring.²⁷

As well as he could, amid imprisonment, bombings and deprivation, Dietrich infused his family with Christmas cheer. "The Christmas parcel was a great delight," he wrote to his parents, "especially great-grandfather's goblet from 1845, which is now standing on my table with evergreen in it. But the things to eat were also very fine, and will last for a while. I got interesting books and Christmas sweetmeats from the family; do thank them all very much. Maria, who was here on the 22nd, gave me the wristwatch that her father was wearing when he was killed. That pleased me very much."²⁸

On December 23rd, Dietrich received another present, a visit from Eberhard, who would soon be off to Italy as a soldier, albeit one behind the lines: "Just tell your father [Rüdiger Schleicher] that this was the best thing he has done for me in my entire life to date!"²⁹

25. Bonhoeffer, *DBWE 8*, 216.

26. Ibid., 217.

27. Early in December, Albert Speer, now the Nazi minister of armaments, inspected a V-2 rocket facility in underground caves in the Harz mountains, not far from the home that provided refuge for Susi. Whatever Susi's privations, they paled against those of the forced laborers.
"The shocking effect the camp had on us," Speer wrote in *Inside the Third Reich*, 370, "is indicated in the deliberately veiled phraseology of the Office Journal entry for December 10, 1943: 'On the morning of December 10 the minister went to inspect a new plant in the Harz Mountains. Carrying out this tremendous mission drew on the leaders' last reserves of strength. Some of the men were so affected that they had to be forcibly sent off on vacations to restore their nerves.'" One might wonder that such architects of Aryan supremacy were shocked that their ideology should translate into treating "subhuman" groups inhumanely. We don't know what they saw, except that the workers were housed in damp caves without adequate sanitary provision. While we hear that merely seeing such sights threw these leaders into nervous fits requiring restorative vacations, we have no evidence that anything was actually done to help the prisoners. The shock also failed to prevent Speer enjoying Christmas holidays in Lapland less than two weeks later. Nearby Nordhausen—the beautiful town where Dietrich first saw the inside of a Catholic Church—held a notorious concentration camp and would be heavily bombed toward the end of war by the US, but he would never know it.

28. Bonhoeffer, *LPP*, 179.

29. Bonhoeffer, *DBWE 8*, 240.

The season ended with both Dietrich and Maria protesting their love for one another, but Maria's affection was fraught with an awareness of their troubles, beginning with a command: "You must love me very much and keep on doing so. I know it's a lot to ask. I'll only ask it of you for as long as you can do it of your own volition. No one could understand you as well as I could, believe me, even if you couldn't [love me anymore]. Let's always be completely honest with each other," she wrote. She saw her own shortcomings, repeating her understanding that he wasn't entirely satisfied with her, then wrote of her hopes for the new year, adding ominously, "I won't be able to love you anymore than I have done this year, because my love has already reached its peak."[30]

Meanwhile, Dietrich wrote a joint letter to Eberhard and Renate on Christmas Eve: "I still live constantly from your visit, Eberhard."[31]

---

30. Bismarck and Kabitz, eds., *Love Letters*, 148.
31. Bonhoeffer, *DBWE 8*, 240.

60

Berlin Falling

REPEATED WAVES OF BOMBING hit Berlin as December ended and 1944 opened: the Allies struck on December 25, December 29, January 1, January 2. Ruth Andreas-Friedrich wrote "We move rubble. We nail up corrugated board. Here we are without water, transportation, or current. The telephone is dead too, and we learn only by roundabout ways whether our friends . . . are alive. Such a life, she wrote, had become "strangely routine" for Berliners.[1]

"The destruction of Berlin is a catastrophe of historic proportions," wrote Konrad Warner. "It will be spoken of for centuries to come. And who knows what this ruined city will symbolize? We can see the signs of collapse but we cannot yet interpret them. We see the remains of walls in aerial photographs. Black and dead, they stare up like the empty eye sockets of a mutilated corpse. And all the other cities look up, in the same way, into a merciless sky. These wounds cry out for peace and healing in every country. But their cries of despair are not heard. The destruction will go on until the word has bled to death . . . ."[2]

For the Nazi leadership, the year opened, once again, in fantasy. "The departure from reality, which was visibly spreading like a contagion," wrote Speer, "was no peculiarity of the National Socialist regime. But in normal circumstances people who turn their backs on reality are soon set straight by the mockery and criticism of those around them, which makes them aware they have lost credibility. In the Third Reich there were no such correctives, especially for those who belonged to the upper stratum. On the contrary, every self-deception was multiplied as in a hall of distorting mirrors, becoming a

---

1. Moorhouse, *Berlin at War*, 324.
2. Lubrich, ed., *Travels in the Reich*, 299. Clearly, Dresden, Hiroshima, and Nagasaki would soon overwhelm Berlin.

repeatedly confirmed picture of a fantastical dream world which no longer bore any relationship to the grim outside world."[3]

One sign of the unreality was Göring's birthday party on January 12, 1944, which he held at his magnificent Karinhall. Guests came bearing gifts: cigars from Holland, gold bars from the Balkans, artwork and sculptures. If the meal, served by attendants in white livery, was scaled down to reflect the austerity of the times, Göring's ambitions were not, for he unveiled plans at the party to double Karinhall's size. Precious resources were to be squandered on an already palatial home. Meanwhile, troops shivered, ordinary people went hungry, and cities were in ruin.

That same day, January 12, Elisabeth von Thadden, ousted founder of the Wieblingen School that Maria had attended, was arrested by the Gestapo in France. In Berlin, she had established ties with the still imprisoned Martin Niemöller, collected illegal ration cards for people in hiding, helped "community aliens" (non-Aryans) escape Germany, and joined the Solf Circle, a group considered traitorous because its members discussed politics. She had strong ties with the remnant of the Confessing Church. This, along with her friendships with Jews and dissidents, led to her arrest. Von Thadden was sent to Ravensbrück concentration camp, notorious for its sadistic female guards.

As Dietrich's birthday approached, guards and inmates in Tegel continued to seek him out: he was self-assured, personable, comforting, strong, and cheerful. In many ways, prison was an easily navigable, if hardly ideal, world for him: all male, strictly ordered, and hierarchical. By this time, visitors included two clerics, Hans Dannenbaum, an army pastor and Harald Poelchau, a prison chaplain. The flowers brought by Maria and others, the Dürer print on the wall, the shelf of food and cigarettes, books and small gifts made cell 92, in Dannenbaum's words, "almost a cozy retreat" where Dietrich liked to play host to guards and pastor guests.[4] On his birthday, a warden brought him a bouquet of early spring flowers from the prison greenhouse.[5]

On January 23, Dietrich wrote again to Eberhard of friendship, coming as closely as he could to articulating a queer theology, defined as a space for all those pieces of life that didn't fit a rigid grid. Marriage, work, government, and the church might be institutions organized as divine mandates—"the sphere of obedience"—but Dietrich posited a parallel "sphere of freedom" that included culture, education, play, and friendship.

3. Speer, *Inside the Third Reich*, 291.
4. Bethge, *DB: A Biography*, 852.
5. Ibid., 848.

"Precisely because friendship belongs within the scope of this freedom ('of the Christian person'?!), we must defend it confidently against all 'ethical' existences, that may frown upon it—certainly without claiming for it the necessitas of a divine decree, but by claiming the necessitas of freedom! I believe that within this realm of freedom, friendship is by far the rarest . . . and most precious good. It is beyond comparison [i.e., can't be compared] with the benefits we have from the mandates; over against them it is sui generis [i.e., unique]; but belongs together with them as the cornflowers belong to the field of grain."[6] Much later, Eberhard would write that Dietrich, "this experimental thinker in a prison cell," who liked "playing games," believed "his theology of the mandates should not fall captive to a new rigidity . . . but be kept open in fruitful illogic" and "permit responsible freedoms."[7]

Given the many male friends Dietrich had amassed over the years, the "friendship" that "is by far the *rarest*" good was of a different kind. He had the closest of friendships with all his brothers-in-law, including relaxed visits to their homes, jokes, music-making, conspiracy work, and the possibility of constant contact (except, of course, for Gert) with their lives. He could expect to have that sort of relationship with Eberhard, now almost a brother-in-law. Yet he yearned for more. The friendship with Eberhard was of another order, celibate perhaps, but infused with a deeper love.

In early January, Maria arrived at her old boarding school in Altenburg in eastern Germany to substitute teach. Immediately, an air raid alert sent the school's staff and students scrambling to the cellar.[8]

Maria supervised a dorm room of young girls, rousing them from bed at 6:45, overseeing their washing, and helping them to tie the bows of their black pinafores. Maria's next task was to sternly ladle out two scoops of the school's foul-tasting porridge.[9]

During the day, she assisted in the classroom and offered tutoring in math and English. Another job was scolding her charges for misdemeanors, such as, she wrote to Dietrich, whistling, losing a hair ribbon, or letting a pinafore bow trail untied. "These are certain really cardinal sins, you see," she wrote with amusement. She longed to take part in the antics.[10]

Maria had the evenings to herself. She checked on her sister Ina, listened to music on the radio, or curled up on a deep windowsill, either

6. Bonhoeffer, *DBWE 8*, 268–69.
7. Bethge, *Friendship, and Resistance*, 96.
8. Bismarck and Kabitz, eds., *Love Letters*, 153.
9. Ibid., 155–56.
10. Ibid., 156–57.

looking out over the quiet town or gazing up at the sky: "I watched the clouds as I sat on my windowsill this evening," she wrote to Dietrich. "They drew nearer, merged with one another, and then dissolved again. It was as if all the unpredictability and inexorability of events were taking on shape, becoming perceptible and comprehensible." [11]

On the same January 5th that she'd arrived at Altenburg, Maria had traveled into Berlin for one of her awkward prison visits, this one short as her tram had been delayed, no doubt due to the bombings. Then, after writing about how she'd wished she could take Dietrich's hand and walk him out of the prison, she continued: "But I don't really want you just to myself. If you had to go off somewhere on a long trip and I couldn't come with you and you couldn't even write to me, I think I'd be very, very happy and thankful."[12]

"I never want to tell you sad things," she continued. "You know they hurt me as much as you they do you, but I've got to tell you everything, haven't I? . . . And so, having gotten that off my chest," she went on, "I must tell you how wonderful it was to be with you." Later, she thanked him for his Christmas letter: "It's the loveliest letter you've ever written me."[13]

On January 13th, Maria would inform him that it was their first anniversary and "there's really no more to be said on the subject." She advised him that he didn't need "to make up for anything," "We have so few things in common. Don't be angry, but it's true. Do you understand that?" [14]

After letters like that, it's no wonder Dietrich was troubled. Near the end of January he confided in Eberhard about his struggles. Yes, the engagement was a "lucky strike" as he put it, but "What I would call a truly exclusive and great love can only grow from knowing the other person fully . . . . But as long as it has to take place through letters and talking in the presence of other people . . . somehow it all lacks color and life for me."[15]

It went deeper than simply lack of private time together. Even when he'd had the chance, he'd not pursued her—a fact Maria would later notice in asking him why he hadn't followed her to Pätzig in November, 1942—and he had, as recently as January 13, a year past, told Ruth he would drop the reluctant courtship. "Now I'm not the sort of man who gets consciously worked up about things," he wrote to Eberhard, but he was finding Maria wearing thin. She left him cold—"lack[ed] color and life for him"—and he wondered,

11. Ibid., 159.
12. Ibid., 92.
13. Ibid., 154.
14. Ibid., 158–59.
15. Bonhoeffer, *DBWE 8*, 277.

"does it have to do with her sex, or her youth, or the way she gives herself up so wholly to such thoughts? [presumably of passion]." He continued: "In the letters . . . I can't speak the way she does and perhaps that's becoming hard on her." He felt in her "a different intensity, which on the one hand makes me very happy, but which on the other makes me uneasy as to whether I am being fair to her."[16] In a deleted passage in his novel fragment, Klara, the young paragon of femininity who brings her grandmother breakfast on a tray every morning, rejects living "intensely" as a fruitless quest to "always look for new strong impressions, throw yourself into the whirlwind of life, learn to love people and then throw them away again, don't let yourself be tied down or fettered by anything, enjoy everything to the hilt and be independent in all things."[17] In the lore of the actual Bonhoeffer family, an art teacher's exhortation that Sabine live more intensely had been long ridiculed.

What did he mean by "does it have to do with her sex"? Did her gender repel him or was it that she was so ardently a sexual being?[18] The months were passing, he wasn't warming to her, she was growing impatient, unhappy, and hostile, and yet he depended on her visits, her food and her nurture, and the status she lent him as a beautiful young woman. He dreamed of Eberhard and he as married men with young wives, he dreamed of having children. Yet, the hesitations kept rising: "She does have some of her grandmother's [temperamental] blood in her. Do you understand what I am saying?"[19] he asked Eberhard.

---

16. Ibid., 277.

17. Bonhoeffer, *DBWE 7*, 182. Bonhoeffer seems to regard intensity with less distrust in male relationships.

18. Ibid., 167: In the third part of his prison novel fragment, Dietrich tells the story of a schoolboy rivalry that becomes a close friendship. Within this section lies a psychosexual dream sequence, and a focus on male friendship reminiscent of *The Last Puritan*.

The overt moral of the story concerns men finding ways to compromise while maintaining their integrity. The two rivals learn they are not "demigods," but "human beings who must live depending on, and related to, each other."

Here, the character representing Dietrich reveals sexual anxieties. These anxieties focus on a short young schoolmate named "Meyer," which sounds like an abbreviated version of Wedemeyer. This phallic Meyer, who in a dream blows up to huge proportions and then squirts "ink" into the hero's face before shrinking down to almost nothing and being kicked away, and who also plants a broken pole for the pole vault that stabs the Eberhard character in the "thigh," seems to reflect anxieties about Maria's both sexual and castrating presence between the real Dietrich and Eberhard. Notably, in a section of the novel entirely inhabited by men, we move away from the earlier chaste world of sibling relationships and enter into a charged environment that introduces a sexual dimension to male friendship.

19. Bonhoeffer, *DBWE 8*, 277.

Eberhard's response, which arrived weeks later, was nonchalant: "I'm not sure you should focus on this and scrutinize it too consciously."[20] At the same time, Eberhard tried to help by writing Maria some of his charming letters.

As the relationship slowly unraveled, Eberhard also heard from Ruth, who questioned her own zeal as architect of a collapsing engagement, her concerns exclusively for Dietrich's welfare: "I often raise the idle question as to whether it was good that Maria came into his life—whether it sweetens his situation or makes it more difficult. Both are possible. I would also consider another question—whether I pushed my own wish into the foreground and therefore expedited something that had not yet matured. But Eberhard, I say this only to you and it is better that these thoughts not go any further. In fact it is incredible that I even think such thoughts. If only I did not have this feeling of guilt. As old as I am, I have never learned the great art of waiting."[21]

As his relationship with Maria faltered, Dietrich wrote to Eberhard that he was "again . . . busy on the little work [now lost] that I mentioned to you before, about the meeting of two old friends after they had been separated for a long time during the war. I hope to be able to send it to you soon." And then the cryptic statement: "You needn't worry—it will not be a roman à clef . . . ."[22]

---

20. Ibid., 309.
21. Pejsa, *Matriarch of Conspiracy*, 319.
22. Bonhoeffer, *LPP*, 136.

61

Birth and Ruin

ON FEBRUARY 3, MARIA arrived in Berlin—the city "totally destroyed" as she put it[1]—for the prison visit the next day to celebrate Dietrich's thirty-eighth birthday.

That day, Renate unexpectedly went into labor and events progressed rapidly. She gave birth to a boy named Dietrich. Maria helped Paula and Christel with the delivery.

Maria delivered the news to the older Dietrich: "Renate had a little boy, and his name is Dietrich!"[2] The quick labor—only an hour and a half—had meant no time to get to the hospital. Dietrich had already written with his desire that the baby be named, if a girl, Sabine: "Wouldn't Sabine be a nice name? You both have a good relationship with her, find the name itself quite charming, a bit old-fashioned, but maybe because of that."[3]

"I can't tell you how delighted I am! How ecstatic you must be!" Dietrich wrote Eberhard.[4] The birth of the baby became a watershed, especially after Dietrich found he was to be the godfather. He looked forward to his new role: "I hope I can promise you to be a good godfather and 'great-uncle(!),' and I should be insincere if I didn't say that I'm immensely pleased and proud that you've named your first-born after me." Not surprisingly, he was "particularly pleased" at how close the birthday was to his own.[5]

Maria also wrote to Eberhard:

> I must tell you how much I rejoice with you over your little boy. It was a great gift to me that I could be present for the event. He is the dearest little fellow. . . . It was something very special for me, to be the one to bring Dietrich the report of the birth. Yet

1. Pejsa, *Matriarch of Conspiracy,* 321.
2. Bonhoeffer, *DBWE 8,* 289.
3. Ibid., 269.
4. Ibid., 289.
5. Bonhoeffer, *LPP,* 208.

after I told him about it, I thought it was not right for me to be sitting so close to him. You should have been there to hear his joy.... I say thank you for your letter. Parts of it I read aloud to Dietrich... and he rejoiced no less than I. That was dear of you, to write on Dietrich's birthday. Actually, I rejoice in all the dear things you write me....[6]

When Eberhard told Ruth that Dietrich was "too proud ever to be unhappy," words Dietrich had written to him, Ruth found the sentiment "fit in exactly with her memoirs," which she was writing at the time. She continued to fret over the engagement: "I had imagined it would be easier than it has turned out to be."[7]

"Totally destroyed"—two succinct words, but what did Maria see as she traversed Berlin in early 1944, the day of little Dietrich's birth? Bombers had raided on February 1, but the damage she witnessed was cumulative. Rats had become a "dangerous plague," while Nazi propaganda posters were scrawled over with the words "Stalin is winning."[8] No longer were the defaced posters replaced; no longer were vigilant brownshirts on hand to beat the scribblers.

Yet Berlin, at least, with its wide streets and many buildings made of stone, didn't succumb to the firestorms that destroyed Hamburg and Cologne.

At Altenburg, Maria befriended two deaconesses at the school and an aged Russian princess living in a nearby castle. The unnamed princess, of German descent, had left Russia during the revolution and now had the ducal box at the local theatre. Whenever she wanted see a performance, Maria had only to call the princess, who would take her, without charge, to her "softly upholstered" box with the best seats in the house.[9] But by mid-February, Maria's work at Altenburg ended.

Maria headed to the Bundorf village in lower Franconia to become governess to her cousin Hedwig (Hesi) von Truchess's children. She arrived with assurances from the headmistress at Altenburg that should Maria want it, a permanent position awaited her at the school. Maria, who particularly liked Hesi, looked forward to settling happily into her newest situation.

---

6. Pejsa, *Matriarch of Conspiracy*, 321.
7. Ibid., 320.
8. Lubrich, ed., *Travels in the Reich*, 309.
9. Bismarck and Kabitz, eds., *Love Letters*, 167.

On February 20, on her way to Bundorf, Maria visited Dietrich. "It was lovely to see her, but all this is really very hard on her," Dietrich wrote his parents.[10] It's unclear whether Dietrich understood the physical realities of how difficult travel continued to be. One traveler described trains in Germany in 1944 as worse than ever: "The compartments are filthy, the upholstery worn to shreds, the windows covered in soot. There is an undefinably unpleasant odor, a smell of decay.... The corridors are jam packed with passengers and luggage, and it is not uncommon to see someone leave the train by climbing out the window...."[11]

In contrast, Bundorf, Maria wrote Dietrich when she arrived, "is a very small village clustered around a very big church," of "pretty, whitewashed, age old houses." The town sat in the middle of a long valley flanked by wooded hills. Hedwig's home was a castle by the church. It was, wrote Maria, a "regular castle of the type you never see in our part of the world, with thick walls, masses of nooks and crannies, a fat round tower with a corked timeworn wooden staircase, cozy bay windows and heavy oak doors with iron fittings." A low ceilinged main hall was lined with dark wood cabinets and supported by rough hewn columns. In the center of the hall stood a "scrubbed" table, surrounded by "old, carved chairs" and set with brown plates and mugs, where Maria ate with the family. The Truchesses, whose family had lived in the castle for 800 years, followed a simple, Spartan lifestyle. Maria would learn to spin, carrying her spinning wheel with her to join the other ladies, also spinning, in front of the fire.[12]

A big stove took up a quarter of Maria's bedroom. Here, Maria gave lessons, wrote letters, told fairy tales to Cordula, her four-year-old goddaughter, and darned clothes. She roomed next door to the private chapel, where daily prayers were held.[13]

Despite letters to Dietrich that continued to declare her love—"I love you. That says it all.... I'm very happily engaged and no one can deprive me of that"[14]—she complained so much to her mother about the relationship that the alarmed Ruthchen visited Dietrich. And while, according to one of Maria's letters, Hesi's "dearest wish" was that "this wait will soon be over,"[15] in reality, Hedwig disapproved of Maria being engaged to someone twice

---

10. Bonhoeffer, *DBWE 8*, 302.
11. Lubrich, ed., *Travels in the Reich*, 306.
12. Bismarck and Kabitz, eds., *Love Letters*, 187–88.
13. Ibid., 188.
14. Ibid., 193.
15. Ibid., 192.

her age.[16] On March 2, Maria, knowing of her mother's upcoming visit to Tegel, warned Dietrich "not to mention the wedding. It would only prey on her mind at the present and once we're together . . . we'll get our way, no matter what."[17]

On March 11, Maria's mother confronted Dietrich with a host of worries—that Maria suffered from bouts of depression, that she disliked the prison visits, that Maria feared Dietrich found her wanting—prompting Dietrich to smuggle out an alarmed letter to Maria.

Maria's depression, now often accompanied by fainting fits when she returned home from prison visits to Pätzig or Bundorf, alarmed her family. Both Maria's mother and grandmother expressed concern, Ruthchen for her daughter, Ruth for Dietrich. Further, Maria had been questioning Dietrich's desire for her since July, and for all her words and gifts, and all her desire to be loved and in love, the relationship sputtered on the reality of the mismatch. She enjoyed her time with the polished and social Bonhoeffer family, but her doubts about Dietrich had only grown. Dietrich, in turn, confided his worries to Eberhard but projected a different front for Maria, while Maria confided her upset to her mother and poured out love language to Dietrich.

Dietrich, always proud and self-conscious, was deeply embarrassed that troubles in the relationship were conveyed through Maria's mother and in the presence of a guard he called "a prize gossip sitting in on our conversation!" He wrote that wanted to "fold" Maria "in his arms."[18]

"Let us be quite frank with each other, dearest Maria. There are times when we find it hard to believe that we really, truly love each other. We know each other so little. And yet, whenever doubt begins to gnaw at me, I banish it and drive it away. . . . Mother told me you're somehow not entirely satisfied with your visits here."[19]

Ruth's presence cast its long shadow over the relationship. Dietrich vehemently rejected her suggestion for patching up the awkward visits by turning them into prayer meetings.

He included a long postscript, asking Maria to tell him about problems, not relay them through her mother as she had done. He begged that their relationship be kept private and added, "One more thing, to be quite candid: You know how much I respect grandmother, how fond I am of her, and how well I believe I know her. We're both aware how much our future means to her, but after all her troubles of the winter before last I don't think

---

16. Schlingensiepen, *Dietrich Bonhoeffer 1906–1945*, 347.
17. Bismarck and Kabitz, eds., *Love Letters*, 195.
18. Ibid., 199–202.
19. Ibid., 202.

it would be good, either for us, or for Mother or for Grandmother herself, to 'burden' her with problems that are nothing of the kind. It would only cause a lot of needless complications, as it did once before . . . ."[20]

In a letter written before she received Dietrich's, Maria also wrote of receiving advice from her mother and grandmother on improving the uncomfortable situation. "We know we're both depressed by the shortcomings of the visits," she wrote, but like Dietrich, she rejected the idea that they pray together and "talk about profundities."[21]

20. Ibid., 202–4.
21. Ibid., 205.

— 62 —

Seesaw

MARIA'S TRAVELS TO BERLIN continued to confront her with devastation. While her letters, meant to cheer a prisoner, conveyed the beauties of her country settings, she left out Berlin's changes. The once vibrant capital filled with theater and cabaret, fine dining and dancing, where first Sabine and Dietrich, then Eberhard and Dietrich, had thrilled to grand operatic productions, Shakespeare's plays, art museums, and the world's best orchestras, had become a shell. It was, said one observer, by spring of 1944, a place of "dullness, anticipation, fear and continuous bombing.... The flowers had gone, the books had been burnt, the pictures had been removed, the trees had been broken, there were no birds singing, no dogs barking, no children shrieking... there was no laughter and no giggling. No face ever lit up in a warming smile, no friendly kiss or hug. There was still the sky above... but then it was often effaced by the stinking and greasy carpets of voluminous black smoke."[1]

At the end of March, Maria answered Dietrich's smuggled letter, sitting in her Bundorf room late at night near the big fireplace, awake at a time when the castle was silent. She was up and alert because "I dreamt of you so intensely and vividly." "My moods are so erratic they are real burden to me," she wrote. While she was open about her feelings, she said since her father and Max had died, no one had understood her. However, she insisted, "I don't need anyone's help because I have you. I possess far more in you than in all of them put together, and I belong to you more than all of them put together." Yet while the visit from her mother had "deeply distressed" him, she couldn't simply say the words her mother spoke were untrue. "I can't write to you about it—I simply can't.... All I want to do is be with you and cry on your shoulder and say 'Forgive me, Dietrich!'" If Dietrich had been confused, this letter could not have helped.[2]

---

1. Moorhouse, *Berlin at War*, 346–47.
2. Bismarck and Kabitz, eds., *Love Letters*, 207–9.

After the March 30 Tegel visit, Maria wrote Dietrich several more letters professing her love, perhaps trying to please, perhaps to confuse the censors, perhaps confused herself. In the first, penned from Bundorf: "You must write me a letter very soon and tell me you found our reunion as lovely as I did and are feeling happy.... Has it dawned on you that I love you very much?"[3] The second letter, written on April 4th, was a chatty Easter letter: "Think how lovely it will be when we celebrate Easter together.... I love you just the same, and the love I send you is not less heartfelt—more so."[4]

April 5 marked Dietrich's one year anniversary in Tegel. For this man who lived by patterns—especially birthdays and the recurring holidays of the church calendar—a rhythm had emerged, and he could reflect with some satisfaction on how he had adapted to prison life. "This second spring that I am spending in this cell is very different from the first, a year ago," he wrote to his parents. "Since then, what I'd never thought was possible has happened—I've gotten used to it."[5]

Now, Bonhoeffer burst into an unparalleled period of theological creativity, fueled as always by the life around him, as well as by Eberhard's response to his musings.

On April 11, Maria wrote Dietrich a third letter from the Bundorf castle. "Your letter [one that is missing] is so beautiful." When she received a letter from him: "I go dancing and singing across the courtyard, race up the spiral staircase, knocking over buckets and garbage pails, and finally, with a pounding heart, flop down on my bed. (Really, Maria, you ought to be more careful of your bedspread!) . . . Quickly take me in your arms so I can tell you, very softly, how much I love you."[6]

By mid-April, Ursel had arrived at Ruth's, enjoying the garden blooming with "daffodils, squills, violets, crocuses and daphne." Ruth remained as energetic as ever despite eyesight problems and difficulties sleeping.[7]

On April 16, Dietrich wrote Maria a birthday letter for her twentieth birthday on April 23, offering her the little Spanish lamp in his room that he had bought in Barcelona many years ago and telling her: "You enact, know, learn, and fill with real life what I have only dreamed. Perception, volition, action, emotion and suffering don't disintegrate in your case; they're a grand totality . . . . Always remain as you are. Remain so for my sake, because that's what I need, what I've found in you and what I love—the whole undivided

---

3. Ibid., 211–13.
4. Ibid, 214–15. Of course, "I love you just the same" may not mean much.
5. Bonhoeffer, *DBWE 8*, 360.
6. Bismarck and Kabitz, eds., *Love Letters*, 217–19.
7. Bonhoeffer, *DBWE 8*, 354.

object of my longing and desire. You're so young and you'll always remain so for me."[8] She was, in fact, the same age as Sabine had been when she married and left him, and his words echo those in his birthday letter to Sabine written from Manhattan when they both turned twenty-five—Maria, like Sabine, would always be frozen as a twenty-year-old.

When Maria visited Tegel on April 18, Dietrich's alarm rose high enough to smuggle another letter out to her, the primroses she had brought him still blooming before him in the cell: "I want it to reach you quickly. That won't be possible too often." He spoke of their visit as "lovely . . . . But tell me, were you sad about something?" He assumed it was that his release was still delayed. He ended the letter looking through her to other people: "Bring his [Eberhard's] letters with you whenever you can, also Grandmother's, which I always enjoy so much. I sorely miss Eberhard's and Grandmother's letters—I was so accustomed to them and they formed such an integral part of my life." He ended on a note of love: "be tenderly embraced and kissed and loved, more and more . . . ."[9]

On April 25, only a week after her visit, Maria visited again. The letter Maria wrote the next day showed restraint, saying nothing about the visit, though "happy and cheerful . . . and rejoic[ing]" to receive a letter from Dietrich when she returned to Bundorf. She apologized for seeming "sad" at the last meeting, noting it was "thoroughly ungrateful" to do so.[10] Most of the letter described Holy Week at Bundorf and, uncharacteristically for her, the word *love* never appeared.

Not long after, sitting outside in the sun at the Tegel exercise yard, Dietrich smuggled Maria yet another letter, always a sign of distress: After discussing religious issues, he turned to the subject she had broached with him, her desire to skip visits. "If coming to see me is more of an upheaval and an ordeal than a relief and a pleasure—and I could understand that so readily!—then I beg you most sincerely, skip it for a few weeks and rest assured that I shall continue to love you very dearly, even from afar." Their love had "miraculously" come into being and would just as miraculously survive. "If you think it better not to come here for a few weeks, my longing for you will only increase, but I am reassured to think we are being entirely frank and open with each other, and that the peace and quiet you need are not being disrupted."[11]

---

8. Bismarck and Kabitz, eds., *Love Letters*, 220.
9. Ibid., 223–24.
10. Ibid., 225.
11. Ibid., 228–30.

He had praised her faithfulness in visiting as an example of a Christian ethic that displayed itself in action, not words—"the simplest deed is much more than the most extensive proposals and plans and discussions . . . my parents' travelling here every week, and the journeys Maria has made are examples of what I mean,"[12] he wrote to Eberhard—but Maria, lonely and at loose ends, who loved to be helpful, the daughter of the selfless Ruthchen, granddaughter of the indomitable Ruth, continued to pull away, and Dietrich magnanimously granted her space—but only for a few weeks. As she tamped down her love language, he increased in his attempt to cling to the deteriorating situation: "I give you a long, tender kiss and embrace you . . . filled with gratitude for this hour alone with you dear, dear Maria."[13]

Maria managed a cheerful if chillier than usual letter on May 1, one which stated decidedly her preference to remain with Hesi rather than come to Berlin to stay with his parents, a subject Dietrich had raised during her visits. "But please, I beg you don't mention it. It's so lovely here, and I'm really happy to be here. . . . I don't want to leave at all . . . I am happier here than I have been in ages, anywhere."[14] Having made her point, the flower-loving Maria wove domestic fantasies of gardening together with Dietrich, making "borders with delphiniums and tulips and lemon-colored lilies and marguerites and bleeding hearts and sunflowers." The dream, however, was filled with holes, and Maria left Dietrich only with "Kisses!" as a final greeting.

---

12. Bonhoeffer, *DBWE 8*, 324.
13. Bismarck and Kabitz, eds., *Love Letters*, 231.
14. Ibid., 232.

— 63 —
Maria, Eberhard

On May 6, Maria wrote Dietrich from Bundorf that the Altenburg school was closing. "It's enough to make one weep. The school has existed for nearly 250 years . . . and now it can be destroyed, utterly destroyed, with the stroke of a pen! Incomprehensible."[1] It was the place, she told Dietrich pointedly, where she had spent the happiest years of her life.

Maria's incomprehension spoke volumes about the government's success, despite all the rumors that swirled, in hiding how close the enemy had come. The school had to close: the government had to clear the aristocratic young girls from the path of the rapidly advancing Soviet army.

Maria spoke of Ruth, mentioning their mutual jealousy of Dietrich. Both women, Maria stated lightheartedly, secretly thought "Dietrich's on my side." Maria wrote that she would burn all of Ruth's letters to her, for fear that she would be jealous even of the letters themselves should Dietrich read them, a sharp repudiation of Dietrich's request that she bring him her grandmother's "sorely missed" letters. Maria continued to weave marriage fantasies but as if to underscore her discontent—or the mockery their dreams had become—ended this letter with another knife twist, using ellipses in place, apparently, of the word love: "Do you still . . . me a bit? I still . . . you a little, but only a little—hardly at all! I think this is quite a nice letter all the same! Yours, Maria."[2]

By the middle of May, Dietrich's letters to Maria had, perhaps not surprisingly, tapered off, though his outpourings to Eberhard continued unabated. Maria wrote to him, "I haven't heard from you in ages. What on earth has happened?"[3] Two days later, on May 16, she wrote again. She enjoyed the balmy spring weather at Bundorf, relaxing after dinner with her hosts in armchairs, "smoking cigarettes, drinking apple wine, and discussing some

1. Bismarck and Kibitz, eds., *Love Letters*, 234.
2. Ibid., 234–35.
3. Ibid., 236.

burning topic of the day." The "strange mishmash" of the life there amused her—Hesi and her husband, lord and lady of the manor, did manual labor, hauling out rugs themselves and beating them, but the maidservants wore, in old-fashioned style, aprons and lace caps. "I think they're appropriate to novels and great-aunts reminiscences, but not to the modern age," Maria wrote, mentioning as well an eighty-two-year-old aunt of Hesi's husband who "used to be at court and will only touch her shoes with her gloves on . . . . You, being in favor of old-fashioned ways, like that sort of thing!"[4]

Dietrich responded, "I'm sure I'd take to the old aunt with the gloves!"[5] But Maria's criticism of the aunt was a criticism of Dietrich: "I think it's terribly overdone . . . . Not even these old ladies can completely insulate themselves, and I think their preoccupation with such superficial trivia makes it immensely hard for them to live in the modern age and feel in sympathy with it." Yet the letter ended with more warmth than the previous few: "All my fondest love, and remember that my thoughts are with you hourly."[6]

On May 19, while home on leave for the baptism of baby Dietrich, Eberhard visited the older Dietrich in prison. Eberhard brought Renate with him, but that didn't in the least dampen Dietrich's enthusiasm during and after the visit. Although the letter following the visit addresses both Eberhard and Renate, after some perfunctory comments, Dietrich quickly turns to Eberhard alone, as if it only the two of them had met: "It was marvelous to have a conversation with you again. I'd like to know if there are any two people who can tell each other and understand as much as we can, in an hour and a half! That takes practice and we're now in the tenth year of it—that's right, the tenth, and I'm really proud of that." Again, he repeated his longing for their life together to be as it was: "I never doubted you would come back the same person who went away and that there would be no change in understanding between us about everything. Now that this is a reality, I can't describe how happy it makes me."[7]

Dietrich addressed a question Eberhard had raised in another letter, a question at the heart of the changes Dietrich denied: why, asked Eberhard, did all his thoughts center on his love for Renate and not on God? Writing in his cell on a late May day amid the scents of the two lilac bushes and the fat cigar Eberhard had brought him, Dietrich advised his friend to embrace the "polyphony" of life. A polyphonic musical piece has several parts, each with

4. Ibid., 238–39.
5. Ibid., 241.
6. Ibid., 238–40.
7. Bonhoeffer, *DBWE 8*, 390–92.

its own distinct melody but harmonizing with the other parts. All the voices ground themselves in the primary voice, the cantus firmus. In Dietrich's vision, God is the cantus firmus, supporting a life of many voices. Polyphony, like the cornflower, opened the possibility of a place for Dietrich, distinct but harmonic, in Eberhard's life, along with Renate—a place unchanged from what it had been.

Maria came to Berlin to attend baby Dietrich's baptism and also took advantage of the opportunity to visit Dietrich. She brought him food—cakes, meat, and eggnog. He used them for others: "there's always such a run on these treats that they don't last long," Dietrich wrote. "Too many of the inmates here are plain hungry, and it's one of my greatest pleasures to be able to help occasionally."[8]

"I've heard much [about the baptism] yesterday and am very happy about it," Dietrich wrote to Eberhard. "Maria liked the sermon very much; even the brief sketch of it I received made sense to me . . . . You gave what I wrote a very honored place in the proceedings . . . ."[9] Outside his window at Tegel, as the days grew longer and warmer, he heard birds sing and even the cry of a cuckoo in the distance.[10] Although his engagement with Maria was in crisis, he made no mention of this, except to hope that because Maria wasn't planning to come again for six weeks, perhaps Eberhard could arrange another visit.

---

8. Bismarck and Kabitz, eds., *Love Letters*, 247.
9. Bonhoeffer, *DBWE 8*, 398.
10. Ibid., 407.

64

Unravelled

ON THE DAY BEFORE Pentecost, following the prison visit, Maria wrote to Dietrich from Bundorf where she was busy gathering "sprigs of May from the woods to decorate the house and church." Maria had spent the morning happily baking Whitsun cakes for the parish.[1] She once again professed her love for Dietrich, and repeated a story in which two people exchange an eye with each other so that they can see not only what is around them, but what the other person sees as well. "I'd so often like to lend you one of my eyes," Maria wrote, "so you could see and share in all the beauty and joy around me."[2]

This, the last extant letter she wrote to him, mentioned nothing of her increasing distress after her visits, indications of what her sister Ruth Alice would later call "an emotional crisis." Maria had been emotional since her very first visit, but now she appeared "desperate."[3]

While the rest of Maria's letters have disappeared, we can trace the crashing trajectory of the relationship from Dietrich's letters to her. Maria sent him a now lost letter in late May. Dietrich responded in a smuggled missive of May 29, stating that "the very uniqueness of your letter touched me particularly."[4]

Dietrich's letter, defensive and hectoring, makes clear that Maria continued to question Dietrich's passion for her. The plaintive question from her journal—"don't you like to be romantic?"—her worries that another held his heart, had again surfaced. Had Renate and Eberhard discussed their visit to Dietrich or the smuggled letters in front of Maria during the baptism celebrations? Did Maria wonder why Dietrich seemed so much more joyful to see Eberhard than her? Why a smuggled letter to her was a rarity, but to him commonplace? Whether or not Dietrich really cared about her?

1. Bismarck and Kabitz, eds., *Love Letters*, 242.
2. Ibid., 244.
3. Ibid., 253.
4. Ibid., 245.

In her lost letter, she apparently brought up Dietrich not pursuing her to Pätzig in November, 1942, when Ruth had invited him to Max's memorial service. Dietrich responded: how could he come when her mother had forbidden it? Maria in the lost letter had still professed some love for him. Dietrich answered: "You say what your love is, and what is it not, and I thank you for it. If our love was merely agonizing deprivation, we should probably die of unassuaged longing in our separate cages."[5] In the missing letter, she must have asked, where, Dietrich is your sexual desire, the ardor of romantic love? Why are you so cold? Why don't you seem to like me? Have you ever been in love with a girl? He responded that "mutual longing mustn't always connote frenzy and insensate desire . . . . It should surely be like one's longing for a glorious spring morning, when one sees the sky tinged red by the sun's first rays."[6]

He lectured her: "Listen, Maria, I want to tell you something. I am much older than you. I, too, have known that insensate, heady, uncertain desire in my time. . . . Do you understand, Maria, that a man who has undergone such experiences is not what he was at 21? . . . Can you love me even so?"[7] At that point, he put aside the anguished letter, only to finish it the next day on a calmer note, but with a sharp warning to use the smuggled letter channel "only in exceptional circumstances . . . it mustn't be a frequent occurrence." He needed to keep it clear for Eberhard. He ended again with the language of enclosure and domination of Maria—I "fold you tightly in my arms . . . ."[8]

On the afternoon of June 3, Eberhard arrived at Tegel, summoned by a sudden phone call. Here he and Dietrich managed an hour alone together in "a solitary cell."

Among other things, the two men discussed Christel's request that they stop smuggling letters—and decided to continue.[9] Then, two days after the meeting, which Eberhard met with "elation" and Dietrich found "very special,"[10] Dietrich sent Eberhard a poem called "The Past." He initially told Eberhard, but not Maria, about the poem, even though it most, he said, "concerned" Maria.[11] While Dietrich framed the poem within the context

5. Ibid., 245.
6. Ibid., 246.
7. Ibid., 246–47.
8. Ibid., 246–48.
9. Bethge, *Friendship and Resistance*, 44.
10. Bonhoeffer, *DBWE 8*, 411 (Eberhard) and 415 (Dietrich).
11. Ibid., 416.

of women—perhaps, he wrote, Eberhard had similar feelings about leaving Renate—given that Dietrich associated Eberhard with the past and fretted that he and Maria had no past on which to build, one might conclude the poem centers on Eberhard and the oft mentioned incomparable years. It suggests that during the long, private discussion alone in the cell, Eberhard made forcefully clear what he had been saying in his letters from the start of the prison correspondence, that Renate was and would remain first in his heart. If the poem is a response to their meeting, Eberhard had impressed upon him that everything would not be as it was once Dietrich was freed.

"The Past," though written in the anguished day following the visit from Eberhard, *could*, however, be about Maria: after all, their forever shaky relationship had by now entered a death spiral. Further, the clutching imagery in the poem mirrors the imagery of holding and enfolding Dietrich had addressed to her in letters. The poem's images of sunrise and sunsets also mirror imagery in Dietrich's smuggled letters to Maria. The poem *could* be a cry of pain at her leaving him. Or, very possibly, she and Eberhard are both on his mind. Or we circle back to the beginning and the poem—after all titled "The Past"—could be primarily about the Eberhard.

The opening imagery alludes to the loss of a relationship, the past visualized as a person whose footsteps fade away. The poem then records the narrator's frenzied pain, and his dreams of clutching, clawing, and wounding the beloved until blood flows.[12]

The image of the beloved sinks like the sun at dusk while the narrator dreams of growing drunk on the beloved's scent. But such thoughts bring renewed pain, as if hot pincers tear out pieces of his flesh, along with defiance and anger as the beloved leaves.[13] The narrator rejects the substitutes offered as a consolation prize: what he demands is the return of the past. At the end, however, he comes to a place of reproachful peace, saying God will forgive those who left.

Not only the timing of the poem, written all at once in a burst after Eberhard's visit, but the constant repetition of the word *past*—used twelve times—points to Eberhard as the subject. (The past is personified: "my past/ You".) After all, it was Eberhard's November visit that caused Dietrich to pace his cell in restless ecstacy, Eberhard he rushed down with a guard to try to catch a glimpse of leaving the prison, Eberhard's whose visits he "lived" on, Eberhard to whom her poured his heart out, Eberhard with whom he

12. Ibid., 418.
13. Ibid., 420.

had spent the last nine years. In contrast, Maria, by his own confession, left him cold.

Eberhard responded at length, but tactfully, to a poem he was probably uncomfortably aware was about him.

Eberhard made sure to note in a June letter to Dietrich that the family had received a message from Sabine. This message, relayed through Sutz, congratulated Paula on becoming a great grandmother with the birth of baby Dietrich. In his June 8 letter to Eberhard, Dietrich responded with a burst of frustration: "I was very happy about the greetings from Sabine and G. (I hadn't heard about either of them! Why do people always forget to tell me important things? I had asked about them often enough.)"[14]

Dietrich sent Maria another letter in June, undated, and of which only a fragment remains. He asked for a candle and food: "bouillon cubes [for soup] . . . . If there were a bit of bacon left, that's always the best thing. Forgive these material requests, there's no hurry!"[15]

In late June, after a long silence, Maria smuggled Dietrich her "very outspoken letter,"[16] now missing, trying again to break off the engagement and telling him that thoughts of him tormented her. After June, she would no longer visit. Dietrich replied on June 27, following a visit from her, in a letter that flatly refused to let her go, still willfully blind to her needs and full of reproaches towards her. Her wounding letter had, he wrote defiantly, made him "boundlessly happy" because her frank speech meant they "loved each other very much." Nothing she had written had depressed, surprised, or dismayed him: "It was all more or less as I thought." The lack of his passion was a reality she should accept as he did: "If the sun shines on us and warms our innermost selves, should we complain because it doesn't scorch us? I'm quite content with that warmth, and you must be, too."[17]

In a letter to Eberhard just three days later, Dietrich expressed quite different thoughts as he ruminated on his friend roasting in Italy's heat: "I should really like to feel the full force of it again, burning [scorching?] one's skin and gradually making one's whole body glow . . . ." While in late May he had explained the love he and Maria should share like a gentle, mild sunrise, "the sun's first rays," to Eberhard he wrote, "The romantic enthusiasm for the sun, which only gets intoxicated over sunrises and sunsets, has no idea

14. Ibid., 425.
15. Bismarck and Kabitz, eds., *Love Letters*, 252.
16. Ibid., 253.
17. Ibid., 254.

of the power and the reality of the sun but only knows it as a picture."[18] The "sun," alluded to so often in these letters, stands as a metaphor for passion: "making the whole body glow."

Dietrich went on to explain to Maria that she should stay with him because their relationship satisfied his needs:

> My dearest, dearest Maria, isn't it enough for you to know you've made me glad and happy—more so than I ever hoped to be in all my days? Isn't it enough, if you doubt your love for me, that I love you as you are, and I want nothing from you—no sacrifice, just you yourself? The one thing I do not want is that you should be or become unhappy because you feel the lack of something—because I am failing to provide you with what you seek in me. On Whit Monday, you felt you "couldn't go on." So tell me, can you go on without me? And if you feel you can, can you still do so if you know that I can't go on without you? No, it's all quite impossible. . . . I shall hold you tight, so we know we belong together, and I won't let you go; I shall hold you tight, so you know we belong together and must stay together.[19]

In the same letter in which he says, "I want nothing from you—no sacrifice," he does require sacrifices from her, while reproaching her:

> You decline to be medically examined and treated in a sensible way, you suffer from insomnia and headaches, and you don't take care of yourself. Wouldn't it be better to tell your cousin, straight out, that you want to retire to your room at eight . . . and that this will enable you to recoup your energies sufficiently to visit me . . . . You mustn't think I'm saying this out of pure selfishness . . . I'm saying it for both our sakes. . . . Betrothed couples belong together, and never more so than in our present predicament. No one knows better than I, dearest Maria, that I'm subjecting you to unparalleled *sacrifices*, privations and exertions, and no one would more readily spare you them. . . . I have to exact this *sacrifice* from you—without being able to recompense you for it in any way—for the sake of our love. . . . In April you went for Mother's birthday, in May you came to see me and Doris, and this time you are going for the confirmation, so your trips are always prompted by other things *as well*. Why shouldn't you *just* come to see *me* for once?[20]

No reply to this letter exists. Maria did not go to him. In the first six months of his imprisonment, from the time she could start visiting, Maria had poured

18. Bonhoeffer, *DBWE 8*, 448–49.
19. Bismarck and Kabitz, eds., *Love Letters*, 255.
20. Ibid, 256–57.

herself out. She traveled long hours on dirty, crowded, unreliable trains to bring him food, flowers, and her company, only for him to be physically cool to her, seemingly dissatisfied. In those first six months she gave him gifts: an angel, her father's watch, cookies, bouquets of flowers, cakes, sausages, an advent wreath she made herself, a Christmas tree, a fur car coat, a picture of Max, a sweater, and a pair of gloves she knit herself. In return, he offered her the chaste repurposed Christmas gift of a gold cross—more Paula's gift than his—and the offer of a lamp as a birthday present. In between, he gave Maria nothing—never once did he offer to share his money, as he did with Eberhard, never once did he ask his parents to provide him a small gift from his room to give to her during a visit. Never, in the long hours in his cell, did it occur to him to make her a simple present. He asked for favors from her—food for Renate, housing for an acquaintance at Pätzig—but never extended himself to obtain a favor for her, except to ask Eberhard to write to her. He thanked her for all she did, in genuine gratitude, but it never entered his mind to reciprocate in kind.

By 1944, Maria's enthusiasm for pouring herself, body and soul, into Dietrich, had waned. Her only birthday present for him was food— "a fabulous package," as Dietrich described it to Eberhard—but no gift. She continued to visit, though by March the situation had reached such a crisis that her mother and grandmother intervened. She no longer wanted to see him. She wished he were far, far away. She no longer gave him presents beyond the obligatory food and flowers (the flowers sometimes containing messages, so possibly not even from her). How might she have felt when he earned the thanks and credit in prison for distributing food she had gathered, prepared, packaged, and carried to Berlin? Her letters became laced with veiled passive aggressive expressions of her resentment. She had migraines and fainting spells at the thought of seeing him.

If Dietrich was the man for others, Maria was the woman serving his needs—as women always had, their own needs invisible. The tragedy in the relationship was Dietrich's inability to see Maria as more than a "lucky strike" to help him out. She was a high-status woman—an aristocrat and a beauty, Ruth's granddaughter, the means to the baby he wanted, a being he expected would align herself to all his thoughts and desires, a woman whose object in life would be to sacrifice herself for him. To the extent that she struggled to be her own person, he discouraged her. She, not surprisingly, fought back.

Except for a strange twist of fate, by the end of June the ill-fated relationship, based on machinations, manipulations, and mismatch, would have been over. As it was, they remained engaged, in limbo.

PART X
Saints

— 65 —
Catastrophe

AT THE END OF June, cousin Paul von Hase paid Dietrich a visit. "He had four bottles of sparkling wine served up, probably the only time in the annals of this place and behaved in a way more generous and kind than I ever would have expected of him," Dietrich wrote to Eberhard.[1] "He no doubt wanted to make it ostentatiously clear what his attitude is towards me." Von Hase, like the rest of the conspirators, was looking forward to a planned assassination of Hitler on July 20th, followed by a coup. The plan seemed foolproof and von Hase felt expansive. Using "Klaus" as a code word for the assassination, Dietrich wrote cheerfully to Eberhard on the 16th "that Klaus is in such good spirits! . . . I think that all his worries will soon be over; I very much hope so, for his own and the whole family's sake!"[2] Dietrich listened to *Carmina Burana*, which he had never heard before, on the radio and anticipated freedom. But he was anxious for "Grandmother Kleist," with the Russian army advancing ever nearer. He had the books he stored at Pätzig sent west to Friedrichsbrunn.

When Dietrich awoke on his cot in his cell on July 20th, he must have imagined that this day or the next his prison doors would fling open forever—that finally, after years of dithering talk, plans, and misfires, his cohorts would dispose of Hitler. That morning, Claus von Stauffenberg, the strikingly decisive player among the conspirators, a conservative morally outraged over German atrocities on the Russian front, carried a bomb in a briefcase into a meeting with Hitler at Hitler's Wolf's Lair. General Erich Fromm, one of the conspirators, had appointed Stauffenberg his chief of staff precisely so that Stauffenberg could attend military briefings with Hitler. Stauffenberg placed the briefcase with the bomb, its fuse slowly burning, under the oak table in the conference room and left, ostensibly to make a phone call. When he was gone, somebody idly pushed the briefcase behind a heavy leg of the conference table. At 12:42 the bomb exploded, killing four

1. Bonhoeffer, *DBWE 8*, 451.
2. Ibid., 474.

people. However, a table leg absorbed most of the force of the blast. Hitler survived with minor injuries.

Stauffenberg, witnessing the explosion, assumed Hitler was dead and so flew back to Berlin, arriving around 4 PM. By this time rumors of Hitler's survival had surfaced. People key to the conspiracy hesitated, and Fromm, in an effort to save himself, switched sides, executing von Stauffenberg and two other conspirators. Stauffenberg reportedly died shouting "Long live Holy Germany!" What George Bell called "Hitler's spell," both his extraordinary luck and the fear people had of him, had not been broken. By 6 PM the failed coup was over and the round-up began.[3]

In England, Sabine had followed the D-day invasion with hope and joy. "Great excitement," she wrote, "reigned throughout" Oxford. "No one spoke of anything else." Even the arrival of the V-2 rockets a week later on June 13th did nothing to shake the optimism. When Eisenhower, in July, broke through the German border, joy ran over and hopes for peace turned to "plans for peace."[4]

On July 20, "Marianne burst into the room" with the news of the Hitler assassination attempt. The family rushed to the radio. Not having had news from friends or family in a long time, "we were indescribably excited," Sabine wrote. "What was happening?"[5]

The next day Dietrich in his prison cell learned the coup had failed. Eberhard kept the letter Dietrich sent him in response in his wallet until he died.

"I thought," Dietrich wrote, imagining he would soon be executed, "I myself could learn to have faith by trying to live something like a saintly life . . . . Later on I discovered and am still discovering, that one only learns to have faith by living in the full this-worldliness of life. If one has completely renounced making something of oneself . . . then one throws oneself completely into the arms of God, and this is what I call this-worldliness: living fully in the midst of life's tasks, questions, successes and failures, experiences and perplexities—then one takes seriously no longer one's own sufferings but rather God's sufferings in the world. Then one stays awake with Christ in Gethsemane."

---

3. "World War II Resistance."
4. Leibholz, *The Bonhoeffers*, 155.
5. Ibid., 156.

He felt no regrets for the path he had followed since 1939: "I am grateful that I am allowed this insight . . . I am thinking gratefully and with peace of mind about past and present things."[6]

The biblical texts for that day felt providential—trust not in chariots . . . but in God (Ps 20:8) and "The Lord is my shepherd, I shall not want" (Ps 23), and from the Gospels: "I am the good shepherd. I know my own and my own know me" (John 10:14).[7]

---

6. Bonhoeffer, *DBWE 8*, 486.
7. Ibid., 541.

66

Endings

FOR ALL HIS SUCCESSES, the adulation paid him, his power, his palaces, and his palpable triumphs, Hitler had never managed to transcend his lowest compulsions. He felt compelled to carry a whip, beat his dogs, and exact horrendous revenge on his enemies. Lately, the levels of revenge that could satisfy him—1,000 to one, 100 to one, even ten to one—had been impossible to achieve. He could round up every Jew in Germany and the occupied territories, from infants to eighty-year-olds, and kill them all, and yet the figures barely exceeded one-to-one his beloved German soldiers killed on the front. He could launch V-1 rockets against England in revenge for the bombing of Germany's cities, but they hardly came close to inflicting the damage his own people sustained. With the conspiracy, however, he could fully satisfy his lust for revenge: thousands had participated and thousands would pay—some through death by slow torture, which Hitler would have filmed so he could watch—for an attempt on his one life. The people paying were Bonhoeffer's friends, acquaintances, and relatives. They had eaten, drunk, and made merry, fully knowing what Hitler was doing, willing to talk rather than act until the game was almost up, so perhaps they deserved their fate, but it was a grim day of reckoning.

On July 23, 1944, an editorial in the Nazi newspaper *Angriff* revealed Hitler's plans for Bonhoeffer's cohort: "Degenerate to their very bones, blue-blooded to the point of idiocy, nauseatingly corrupt, and cowardly like all nasty creatures—such is the aristocratic clique which the Jew has sicked on National Socialism.... We must exterminate this filth, extirpate it root and branch.... It is not enough simply to seize the offensive.... We must exterminate the entire breed."[1]

The lists of arrests read like a Who's Who of Dietrich's life. Paul von Hase, who only a month prior had elatedly shared the four bottles of sparkling wine with Dietrich, was hanged. Von Haeften, with whom Dietrich had excitedly discussed an assassination at Wolf Zimmermann's house in

---

1. Speer, *Inside the Third Reich*, 390.

November 1942, was shot, and Ruth's son, Maria's uncle, Hans Jurgen, was arrested, as were Hans Oster, Wilhelm Canaris, Helmuth von Moltke, Adam von Trott zu Solz, and Fabian von Schlabrendorff. Ruth would write to Dita Koch of her distress. For the moment, little attention was paid to Dietrich, in prison so long he could hardly be considered part of the plot.

Sabine reacted with frustration and disappointment to the British press, which accepted Hitler's version of the story that the plot was the work of a small clique of power-hungry army officers bent on a coup—a sudden desperate move by a few at the top, who saw defeat coming, to save their own skins. "On the contrary," she wrote, "the opposition had been in existence from the moment Hitler seized power."[2]

On July 25th, following a bombing raid over Berlin, Dietrich again wrote to Eberhard. He'd received a now missing letter from Maria, in which she told him that her time in Bundorf was over. She planned to go to Westphalia with a younger brother and sister to stay with an aunt. Ever thinking of Eberhard, Dietrich wondered if Renate and little Dietrich might not go with her too, for safety. He added, however, "I don't know how she gets along with Maria."[3] This was a remarkable flash of insight for him: for a moment both Renate and Maria became real people who might not get along, not pawns to be deployed at will.

Dietrich continued to theologize the reality of the failed attempt on Hitler. "Not only action but suffering, too, is a way to freedom. In suffering, liberation consists in being allowed to let the matter out of one's own hands into the hands of God. . . . I find this very important and very comforting," he wrote to Eberhard.[4]

On July 28, Susi rode her bicycle across the apocalyptic landscape of Berlin to deliver a package of food and supplies to Dietrich—and to try to catch a glimpse of him, to see how he was holding up under the news of the coup's failure. Loitering by the fence to the prison yard, fiddling with a tire, she waited until finally Dietrich arrived for his daily walk, accompanied by the faithful guard Knobloch. In quiet tones, Dietrich told Susi his prison circumstances were still good, but Susi, scanning him with her round brown eyes, thought "he looks so ill, worse than before." To her, he expressed "hopeful, wishful thinking." He went back to their childhood in a message as much for Sabine as for Susi, alluding to the time when, after he was put in a separate bedroom, he would knock on the wall to alert them when he

2. Leibholz, *The Bonhoeffers*, 156–57.
3. Bonhoeffer, *DBWE 8*, 487.
4. Ibid., 491.

thought of God. Now, he said, "here [there] has never been so much going on with knocking signs at night." God was close.[5]

Susi left slowly. It was the last time she would see her brother.

In August, without consulting or informing Dietrich, Maria made plans to come to Berlin to live with and help his parents. She had always liked his family. Her Munich plans had fallen through. She did not wish to go to Pätzig to be her mother's helper. For a brief time, she thought she would return to the Red Cross. Bethge wrote that she came to Berlin to "avoid being called up for military duty" by registering as an office assistant for Karl Bonhoeffer, "as was permitted because it was a medical office."[6] Maria, however, rationalized her decision differently in a letter to Hesi: "But you know very well I don't want to break off my engagement now, nor can I. I tried to ask him for some time to myself, but failed.... And if Dietrich doesn't grant my request, I can't carp at him or bully him into accepting some extremely selfish viewpoint of my own—under present circumstances least of all. But because I can't go on traveling to Berlin all the time, I'm going to go and be really near him."[7] If nothing else, this letter indicates that even if hurt or confused by his treatment of her, Maria still valued at least the idea of an engagement to him. After all, it had given her, attention starved and at loose ends (she, like Dietrich at her age, sought a ground to stand on), status, place, and importance in the eyes of both her beloved grandmother and the Bonhoeffers. It provided her as well as with the "tasks to perform" that Dietrich so perceptively understood as essential to her nature.

Dietrich knew about her decision by August 10, as he mentioned it in a letter to Eberhard. He must have been nonplussed, but wrote to Maria, "So now, entirely of your own volition . . . you've made the big decision to come here and help my parents. I just can't tell you how happy I am. I couldn't believe it at first, when my parents told me, and I still can't quite grasp how it happened . . . . It's a godsend from my point of view."

After thanking her, he gently advised her to expect a more reserved family life than at Pätzig, especially in terms of religious language, and to be very patient with his mother. "Mama . . . needs an outstanding daughter-in-law at this time . . . ." At the end he added a poignant postscript: "Have my other letters turned up? . . . There must be three or four in the mail . . . I've only had one from you in the last six weeks!"[8]

On August 23, shortly after arriving in Berlin, Maria paid Dietrich a final visit, which he mentioned in a letter to Eberhard: "Maria was here

---

5. Zimmermann and Smith, eds., *I Knew*, 220–21.
6. Bethge, *DB: A Biography*, 838.
7. Bismarck and Kabitz, eds., *Love Letters*, 263.
8. Ibid., 261–63.

today, so fresh and at the same time as steadfast and calm as seldom before." Since July 20, it was Dietrich himself who had become steadfast and calm.

Towards the end of August, Dietrich sent Eberhard a birthday letter. In it, he wished Eberhard "a really great task and responsibility and at the same time sufficient calm to be able to write something very good from time to time." For himself, he wished for the continuation of their "intellectual exchange" and "that we might continue to have in each other the person we can trust unreservedly without limit.... God does not fulfill all our wishes," he wrote, "but does keep all his promises." He ended by asking if he could give Eberhard his icon from Sofia.[9]

"Your letter is a real birthday letter," replied Eberhard, "—detailed, calm, with words of friendship, and therefore a true joy." He struggled briefly to accept the costly icon: "You know that I love your fine possessions.... You ... give even more generously than before, in striving to give great joy ... but I feel a tug of resistance every time you think of us so generously. Of course ... you would love seeing it when you come to visit, being reminded of the rooms in Finkenwalde, Schlonwitiz, Sigurdshof, and Berlin. So you see, I've half accepted it after all ...."[10]

In addition to the icon, Dietrich gave Eberhard another birthday gift, a poem called "The Friend." The mood and imagery couldn't be further from that of the frenzied, angry, clawing anguish of "The Past." The tone of "The Friend," as in the letters after July 20, is gentle and elegiac, reflecting spiritual depth and strength.

In it, Dietrich theologizes again, renewing the image of the cornflower he had used earlier in his letters to represent friendship as that which grows freely between the ordered rows of the mandates, an image that would have included Sabine, evoking as it did their long ago walks together among the cornflowers of Greifswald, dreaming of the future: "No one planted it, no one watered it./Vulnerable, it grows freely." Such is the image of friendship; such is the image of grace. Such is the manifesto of people everywhere, gay, straight, male, female, black, white, who might not quite fit, seeking sacred communion with the other: "each knows in the other/the faithful helper."[11] In these last weeks, Dietrich had transcended tyranny and possessiveness. In these final times came an outpouring of poetry.

9. Bonhoeffer, *DBWE 8*, 510–11.
10. Ibid., 524.
11. Ibid., 527–30.

67

Revenge

NAZI GERMANY MIGHT HAVE been near its end, but as Speer notes in his memoir, Hitler now had both an explanation for the defeat in Russia and a new scapegoat—the upper classes. In his mind, they had betrayed Germany to the enemy, and like the Jews, had to be exterminated in order to win the war. Spending time and resources investigating them was not a diversion, but integral to victory.

On August 8, the trials had begun. Many of accused, who had just weeks before shared dinner tables with the Nazi elite, arrived at court battered from torture. No humiliation, however petty, escaped the regime: not allowed either belts or underwear, defendants faced laughter and ridicule when, forced to stand at attention, their prison pants fell down around their ankles.[1]

On September 8, the Nazi's beheaded Elisabeth von Thadden, now in Berlin's Plotzensee prison, as an enemy of the state. Maria's former headmistress, who had for years fought for human rights, women's rights, and human decency, died thinking of others as well as herself: "Put an end, Lord, to all our sufferings," she said—or sang—from Bach's St. Matthew's chorale in the moments before the guillotine fell and her head rolled into the basket.[2]

On September 22, Inspector Sonderegger, rummaging around the now-dissolved Abwehr's underground bunker in Zossen, south of Berlin, found an armored safe, hidden there by von Dohnanyi. Sonderegger broke it open. He found incriminating documents, naming names and proving the conspiracy against the Reich had been ongoing since 1933.[3]

The Zossen file was a fatal blow to the Bonhoeffer family, exposing them as conspirators, including Dietrich. Those who once would have shielded Dietrich were now dead or in prison. Worried, the family turned

---

1. Sereny, *Albert Speer*, 452.
2. Fox, "An Opera for my Resistance Fighter Aunt."
3. Bethge, *Friendship and Resistance*, 57.

to the "view from below," arranging for prison guard Knobloch to help Dietrich escape. The two would walk out of Tegel and disappear into the chaos of bombed Berlin. Knobloch received workman's overalls for Dietrich from the family, as well as money and ration cards.[4] Yet in early October, when both Klaus and Rüdiger were arrested, Dietrich abandoned his escape plan so as not to endanger them.

In mid-October, Maria made the bike ride to Tegel across the ruined landscape of the city, planning to leave her normal delivery of laundry, food, and supplies for Dietrich. She was surprised to find he was gone. On October 8, the Gestapo had transferred him to a basement cell in the Gestapo's Prinz Albertstrasse prison in central Berlin. Here he met, at least in passing, an old home club of friends and acquaintances, including Oster, Canaris, and Fabian von Schlabrendorff. Though the prison washroom had only a cold-water shower, inmates were glad to go there so they could meet with others.

Dietrich by now knew something of prison life, but he was far worse off here than in Tegel. Here, his cell, number 19, was smaller than before, only five by eight, and cruder. He didn't know the guards and the routine. Rations were a third of what they had been in Tegel, meaning a starvation diet. In the mornings, inmates received a mug of ersatz coffee with two pieces of bread and jam, at lunch soup, no dinner.[5] The prison lacked an exercise yard. Letters and visits were forbidden. Worse yet, Dietrich was subjected to the full force of Gestapo interrogations.

Quaker Leonhart Friedrich of Pyrmont, whose situation somewhat paralleled Dietrich's, was imprisoned by the Gestapo after the start of World War II for helping Jews and having an attitude insufficiently aligned with National Socialist ideology. When his wife, Mary Friedrich, finally saw Leonhart in prison, she described him as "thin and shaken." He had not been able to change clothes for a month, and the laundry he gave her was flea infested. When she saw him again, "his body was shaking. He was still being taken for frequent interrogations and never knew when they would fetch him. He said he read the Bible constantly when he was alone."

Standard practice involved arresting a suspect, then leaving him isolated, then suddenly taking him for questioning in shifts that could last as long as twelve to twenty hours. Interrogators changed periodically, so that they were fresh and lively, while the prisoner, left without food or rest, became increasingly exhausted. Such pressure was mental rather than physical, exacerbated by examiners shouting, bullying, or pretending to lose control, all

---

4. Wind, *A Spoke in the Wheel,* 173.
5. Bethge, *DB: A Biography,* 907.

the while continuing the relentless questioning. Sometimes prisoners would be told they were to be questioned at a certain time, such as 11 PM, only, after waiting several hours, to find that they were not to be questioned after all. This could happen repeatedly, and then, without warning, the interrogation would begin.

Friedrich, like Dietrich, spent weeks in solitary confinement, initially cut off from all contact with family. "What I had to endure," he wrote, "reduced me to an extremely low physical and spiritual condition. The endless stress of repeated interrogations affected me badly. The process stretched on for weeks."[6]

While Dietrich does not seem to have been overtly tortured, he was threatened with torture and treated with "brutality" according to von Schlabrendorff.[7]

Dietrich and the others could receive laundry, books, paper, cigarettes, and food, so the women again went into high gear. Rüdiger Schleicher initially refused food packets, having watched his wife and daughter starve themselves to feed Dietrich and Hans. Dietrich, who had Schlabrendorff in the cell next door, shared his food—Maria delivered a weekly package with bread and apples—and cigarettes with those around him. With his prior prison experience, as well as the calm and assurance he projected, Dietrich was able to exert some influence even in this much harsher prison.[8]

A few months later, Karl-Friedrich wrote of these times: "I've accompanied aunt Ursel and aunt Christel, aunt Emmi and Maria there. They often went daily to bring things or take them away. They often went in vain; they often had to suffer the taunts of supercilious commissars; but sometimes they also found a friendly porter who showed some humanity and passed on a greeting, accepted something outside the prescribed time or gave the prisoners something to eat against the rules."[9] Maria in particular, had good luck: both Sonderegger and a guard named Runge had a "soft spot" for her, appreciating her beauty, energy, and sexuality—but even she could never get permitted a visit inside the prison.

Much of the women's time would have been spent obtaining and preparing food. They had the garden while it lasted into fall, and their rabbits, but otherwise would have waited on line with ration cards for scant supplies, scoured the city for needed items, and searched out black markets, then prepared what they had found so that it could be transported and eaten

---

6. Bailey, "The Integrity of German Friends."
7. Zimmermann and Smith, eds., *I Knew*, 228.
8. Ibid., 229.
9. Bonhoeffer and Bethge, *LPP,* 409.

easily. They washed and mended clothes. The women crossed Berlin, despite the risk of daytime bombings, to try to get information or deliver goods. Paula buried Dietrich's letters, received from Eberhard, in gas mask canisters in her home's backyard.

By this time, the once mighty Anhalter train station, symbol of the long reach of the Reich, had been bombed into shambles, reduced to an open platform under twisted steel girders where trains ran on erratic schedules. Torn posters around the city fluttered on pockmarked walls. Gone were the grand, clean buildings hung with the long red swastika banners: There was no cloth left to spare for displays. Gone were the swelling ranks of healthy, young, well-fed soldiers on parade, followed by seemingly endless rows of tanks, horses, and artillery. The swooping practice planes that had bothered Bonhoeffer's seminarians were silent—there was no gas to spare for flight training and Allied bombing had brought German plane production to a crawl, leaving the skies over Berlin empty and undefended.

— 68 —

Arrest

In Italy, Bethge's unit retreated north against the Allied onslaught, across the swollen river Po, while the relentless American spitfires attacked. His unit took up residence in a grand but already plundered palace. Eberhard had hardly settled there when a cable arrived for his major with orders to send him under heavy guard to the Reich Security Office in Berlin.

According to a confidential October 12, 1944 Gestapo report: "The daughter of Bonhoeffer is married to a pastor named Eberhard Bethge. According to Schleicher's statement, Bethge, a follower of the confessional front, is a lance corporal in Italy. From his very connection to the confessional front he rejects the National Socialist state. During his last leave they discussed plans for the coup again."[1]

Eberhard had been caught in the dragnet around the conspiracy. In his first moments of fear, his impulse was to destroy the message, but he realized that would only increase his problems. Since he was alone, his second impulse, which he followed, was to destroy all the letters and notes he had in Dietrich's handwriting, burning them in a small stove.

His commander, however, made light of the investigation, sure Bethge would be back in a few weeks. Rather than returning him under heavy guard, he sent Eberhard to Germany with two middle-aged soldiers, family men "full of inner decency."[2]

The men, in no hurry, stopped in Munich to visit their families, leaving Bethge on his own. He didn't dare phone Berlin, worried the Schleicher house was under surveillance, but he possibly visited Countess Ninne, whose husband, Dr. Josef Müller, was in prison with Dietrich.

When he and his guards finally boarded the train to Berlin, Eberhard gave them cigarettes and offered them a "fine dinner," no small enticement in these hungry times, if they would stop first at the Schleicher house. The men, still in no hurry, agreed.

1. de Gruchy, *Daring, Trusting Spirit*, 89.
2. Bethge, *Friendship and Resistance*, 51.

On a foggy noon, Bethge and his guard arrived at the Schleicher's. After making sure the house was not being watched, Eberhard rang the doorbell. To his surprise, not only Ursel but Renate answered. Their shock at seeing Eberhard must have immense. He quickly hurried Renate upstairs to fill her in on events and work out a code. She told him the prison guards would deliver and receive short notes if bribed with cigarettes. Meanwhile, Ursel delved into her precious food stores to provide a decent dinner for the men.

Bethge then arrived at the star-shaped Lehrterstrasse prison, not the Prinz Albertstrasse where Dietrich was held. Lehrterstrasse had been especially cleared out for July 20 political prisoners, and here Eberhard too found an old home club that included Klaus Bonhoeffer and Rüdiger along with many other friends and acquaintances. They could greet each other by standing in their doorways as dinner was distributed. Exercise time in the prison yard also provided the "great moment," short as it was, when there was a chance to communicate.[3]

Klaus sent home bloody underwear to indicate he had been tortured. Eberhard was interrogated but not tortured, and managed to keep his connection to Dietrich hidden. He explained his frequent presence at the Schleichers, now known to be a center of conspiracy, as courting Renate—and was believed. Yet as fall became winter, he sat in prison, so far not charged, but also not freed. Renate sent him meals wrapped in many layers of newspapers. Five Bonhoeffers or spouses were in prison now: Dietrich and Eberhard, Hans von Dohnanyi at Sachsenhausen concentration camp, Klaus and Rüdiger.

Towards the end of 1944 and into early 1945, prison rules "relaxed" somewhat, probably because some SS higher-ups wanted to put out "peace feelers" abroad.[4] Because of the relaxed rules, Bonhoeffer was able to send three letters, a Christmas letter to Maria, a birthday letter to his mother, and a second letter to his parents. In the Christmas letter he told Maria he "hadn't for a moment been lonely or forlorn,"[5] which of course meant the opposite. He asked for books, sent love to his family, and encouraged her to keep up her spirits. He enclosed a gentle poem.[6] In his birthday letter to his mother, he thanked her for always living for her family and never having a life of her own. She was his exemplar of womanhood.[7]

---

3. Ibid., 53.
4. Bismarck and Kabitz, eds., *Love Letters*, 267.
5. Ibid., 267–68.
6. Ibid., 270.
7. Bonhoeffer, *DBWE 8*, 551.

His final letter, addressed to his parents, written on January 17, 1945 was allowed because of Goebbels' people's sacrifice, meant as a preparation for the coming Soviet assault on Berlin. Dietrich directed that some of his clothing be given to the cause, asked after Eberhard, sent Maria greetings and thanks—and in this final letter, still relied on her for "favors": books, matches, washclothes, towel, toothpaste, and coffee beans, each word no doubt a code as well. Sonderegger's fondness for Maria allowed Dietrich to receive supplies on days other than Wednesdays—and it was through Sonderegger's appreciation of Maria that Dietrich's last three letters were delivered.[8]

---

8. Ibid., 553.

— 69 —
Escape

On January 26, Maria was back at Pätzig, the blasts of Russian artillery so close that sometimes the manor's windows rattled. It was cold, the temperatures below freezing. On the 27th, Ruthchen decided Maria would lead the three youngest children, the two oldest and frailest of her refugee guests, and the wife of her estate manager and their two children west across the Oder River to safety. A covered wagon was quickly improvised, topped with an Oriental rug and a tarp, loaded with food and hitched to the three strongest horses on the estate. Passengers were strictly limited to one suitcase apiece. Maria took Dietrich's letters, and on impulse, ran back to the manor house, dumping newly washed silver from the dumbwaiter into the floor of the wagon.

Before dawn, the wagon left, driven by a Polish worker. Maria quickly discarded some of the cargo—heavy art books brought by the elderly women. By the 28th, the wagon had joined a huge stream of refugees hoping to make it across the Oder ahead of the Russian army. Nobody had gasoline but wagons, bikes, wheelbarrows, and baby carriages, pushed by a sea of people, surged forward, overcrowding the roads. At times, the roads had to be cleared to allow the retreating German army passage.

Maria decided to avoid the Oder bridges, clogged with the refugees and guarded by SS troops who sometimes turned people back. Instead, she moved north, found a spot where the Oder's ice seemed firm, and ordered everyone out of the wagon to cross the river on foot. When they were safely over, the driver led the horses and wagons, hoping the horses could leap and scramble to safety should the ice break. Everyone got across, and they shared a moment of jubilation.

Ruthchen wrote to Paula, after having sent Maria on the dangerous venture, to explain why the family wasn't coming to Berlin but going instead to relatives in Celle. "I need her help desperately," she wrote of Maria. "It is a task far beyond her strength.... Pray with me that she will be equal to this hard task. If all goes well, the journey will take 14 days. But there has been a lot of snow and the winds are very strong."[1]

By January 29, the Russian army was almost on top of Pätzig. Ruthchen decided her estate workers and the rest of her refugee guests must leave, but the local Nazi group leader forbade it: it would jam the road that was needed for reinforcements coming to the front. What reinforcements? Ruthchen asked. What front? Everyone knew the German army was retreating. Nevertheless, the Nazi group leader insisted that abandoning the estate was betraying the Reich. People were being hanged along the Oder for trying to flee. Ruthchen abandoned her plans.

Instead, Rutchen ordered all the food, blankets, pillows, and other goods the Russian army might need to be gathered and placed in the main hall, hoping to avoid the plundering of her beloved home. At 2 o'clock in the afternoon of January 31, the first Russian tanks appeared on the edge of the village. A column of tanks crossed the Pätzig estate slowly, for the moment ignoring the manor, but stopping to kill the village's Nazi spokesman.

At 5:30, Herr Dopke, the estate manager whose wife and children were in the covered wagon with Maria, appeared at the door and begged Ruthchen to leave immediately. A Russian tank was parked in front of the main entrance to Pätzig and Dopke feared it would demolish the manor with the people still inside. Ruthchen ordered all the women in the manor to slip out through the French doors leading to the back terrace, saying she would follow. As she herself left, having gathered the money from her husband's desk, the Russian tank began to fire on the manor.

Huddled in the gardener's cottage, Ruthchen tried to decide what to do. She and one other woman would attempt to escape; the rest chose to stay. Because the perimeter of the estate had been sealed by Russian troops, Ruthchen and her companion left in the cold, full-mooned night through a gap in the fence behind the gardener's cottage. As they fled they looked back to see the Pätzig manor house going up in flames.

On February 3, the Allies launched their biggest air attack ever over Berlin, in broad daylight. A cold snap had ended, leaving the weather mild and springlike. Waves of American planes came in, swift and smooth, "as if on parade" across a clear blue sky cut with a few soft clouds. Bombs hit the Potzdammer Place and the Anhalter Station in the center of the city. People took shelter in the subway tunnels, listening to the deafening explosions overhead. The lights went out. The tunnels filled with soot and smoke. Injured people called out for doctors and nurses but none came.

1. Pejsa, *Matriarch of Conspiracy*, 346–50.

Bethge would write: "For two whole hours, squadron after squadron sailed through the bright blue winter sky and transformed the urban area east of Tiergarten into a wasteland of smoke and ashes.[2]

During the air raid, Dietrich and other prisoners huddled in a shelter where guards had herded them. To von Schlabrendorff, as the prison was hit, it seemed as if the shelter "were bursting and the ceiling crashing down on top of us." It "rocked like a ship tossing in a storm, but it held." Through the panic, Dietrich remained calm and unmoving.[3]

The elder Bonhoeffers were sitting in a railway car in the Anhalter Station, hoping against hope to pay a birthday visit to Dietrich, when the attack came. The Anhalter Station, already weakened by bombing, collapsed, but the Bonhoeffers came away unscathed, except for a covering of soot.[4]

The aftermath of the bombing was the same as always: smashed streetcars, fires, smoke. "Everyone must trudge on foot through a chaos of rubble, around craters filled with greenish brown water," wrote Theo Findahl. "Nobody is the least bit curious to see more ruins and fires, just exhausted.... Everything looks ugly and horrible." The Esplanade Hotel, once one of the finest in Europe, took a direct hit and became a "flaming ruin."[5]

Findahl wondered if this were, belatedly, the moment the Germans would rise up. Would "the first cry of 'Down with Hitler!' . . . spread like wildfire? It feels like it would. It's in the air like the coming spring.... Where is the church militant? If only it would rise up again and lead a crusade against all the false prophets and seducers of the people, who promise all the power in the world to their supporters if only they follow blindly."[6]

One of the few who had a dozen years ago hoped to be that church militant, Dietrich huddled in the damaged Prinz Albertstrasse prison.[7] Because of the damage, Dietrich and nineteen fellow prisoners were moved south to Buchenwald concentration camp.

At Buchenwald, the "prominent prisoners" that included Dietrich found themselves in cold, dark, and damp basement air raid shelters on the edge of the camp.[8]

2. Bismarck and Kabitz, eds., *Love Letters*, 273.
3. Zimmermann and Smith, eds., *I Knew*, 229.
4. Bonhoeffer, *DBWE 8*, 555.
5. Lubrich, ed., *Travels in the Reich*, 312.
6. Ibid., 311–12.
7. Bethge, *DB: A Biography*, 917.
8. Schlingensiepen, *Dietrich Bonhoeffer 1906–1945*, 368.

The two meals a day were meager, and the enemy troops coming closer disrupted supply lines, but the prisoners could still buy black-market cigarettes from the guards, and in lieu of an exercise yard, were allowed out of their cells to walk the corridors, where they were able to chat.[9] Dietrich made friends with two theologians imprisoned with him: the English Pastor Payne Best and his own cellmate, a general and theologian, Friedrich von Rabenau. Payne gave a chess set to Dietrich and Rabenau, apparently the only two cellmates who got along.[10] Everyone prayed for the war to end.

9. Bethge, *DB: A Biography,* 918–19.
10. Ibid., 920.

— 70 —
Threads

THE BONHOEFFERS HAD NO idea what had happened to Dietrich. In the meantime, Maria, who had successfully shepherded her part of the family to Opperhausen, a village near Celle, was reunited with her mother. On February 12, Maria headed back towards Berlin, while the rest of the family planned to head onward to their relations near Lohne.

In Berlin, Maria found that Dietrich had again been moved. She headed towards Bundorf, checking to see if Dietrich had gone to Dachau and arriving at the gates of nearby Flossenbürg. Frustrated, she wrote to her mother of her inability to find out any news. At this point, of course, he was not at either camp. "I'm feeling utterly miserable, but that's only because I've been on the train two days now, had to walk seven kilometers to get there and, then, without any prospect of hearing anything, had to trudge the same seven kilometers back again." She did this while carrying a knapsack full of warm clothes and food for Dietrich. She decided that rather than return to Berlin and be trapped by the Russian army or drafted into the Flak, a defense unit, she would stay in Bundorf.[1]

In March 1945, Dohnanyi smuggled a letter to Christel in his dirty laundry: "They have everything, absolutely everything, against me, and in my own hand."[2]

Ruth, at Klein Krössin, decided to stay. She was old. She does not appear to have feared rape. If the Russians killed her, so be it: she was half blind, frail, elderly, walking with a cane. She had had a life of suffering and joy and surprises. Who would have expected spiritual renewal in her last decade, with the bursting on the scene of Dietrich and the seminary? Who would have expected Hitler to become chancellor of Germany?

The Russians would come and maybe kill her, but life would go on. The Junker families—von Bismarcks, von Wedemeyers, and von Kleists—would

1. Bonhoeffer, *DBWE 8,* 556.
2. Wind, *A Spoke in the Wheel,* 173.

rebuild their estates, and women like her would continue to broker marriages and help with births, sacrifice for the men and manage in times of war. It had always been that way. Ruth couldn't know it was over.

In mid February, now freed from prison after seven months, Hans Jurgen returned to Kieckow, hitching rides on military vehicles as no civilian train service still existed. Like Ruthchen, he tried to organize a caravan to escape to the West; as it had been at Pätzig the Nazi leader in the area threatened him with hanging if he tried to leave. On February 26 Ruth, her eyesight failing, wrote to Dita of the "mousetrap" they were in, caught between the Russian army and the Baltic, the estate overrun with refugees, so many it was difficult to feed them all.[3]

By March 2, the Russian army had arrived at Gross Tychow, and the von Kleists, including Ruth, finally left Kieckow and Klein Krössin in caravan wagons under the cover of darkness. Soon the road was overrun with Russian troops and the caravan was forced to hide for six days in the forest. Once the road was clear, Hans Jurgen decided it was safe for the family to return to Kieckow, but that was a mistake—the Russians soon arrested them. After interrogation but no mistreatment, Hans Jurgen was sent to Moscow, Ruth and her daughter-in-law Mieze freed. They headed back to Kieckow. The manor had been stripped and turned into a dairy; Klein Krössin was uninhabitable, though Ruth found a hidden stash of paper she had once gathered, and felt a sudden rush of nostalgia for days gone by. She had no idea what had become of Dietrich.

Early in April, with the Allies almost at Buchenwald, the prominent prisoners went in stages to Flossenbürg crowded in the back of a wood-powered truck. En route, Dietrich and the others, who must have been emaciated, stopped with their guards in Regensberg and ate a meal of baked potatoes and potato salad provided by sympathetic villagers.[4] They stayed at a school in Schönberg in the Bavarian Forest, until April 8, a warm, balmy day. The classroom/infirmary where they were held had beautiful views of surrounding countryside and an electrical outlet, so   Pastor Payne plugged in his razor and let them all shave. Bonhoeffer still clutched the *Ethics* manuscript he was working on.

Dietrich had just led a church service, as April 8 was a Sunday, when guards came to take him to Flossenbürg. He left behind his Plutarch book with his name and address in three places, hoping his family would find it.

3. Pejsa, *Matriarch of Conspiracy,* 360–62
4. Schlingensiepen, *Dietrich Bonhoeffer 1906–1945,* 375.

Knowing his time was up, he left a message with Payne for Bell that is often quoted as, "This is the end; for me the beginning of life." This is often used as evidence of Dietrich's faith in the afterlife, but another version is more consistent with Dietrich's determination to find Christ in *this* world and his attitude of his caring for others' salvation more than his own: "This is for me the end, but also the beginning—with him [Bell] I believe in the principle of our Universal brotherhood which rises above all national hatreds and that our victory is certain—tell him too, that I have never forgotten his words at our last meeting."[5] He ended not thinking about an ethereal, Platonic heaven for himself, but of a heaven on earth for others.

Bonhoeffer never wanted to be a pillar saint,
but that literally became his fate.

---

5. Bethge: *DB: A Biography*, 1022.

At Flossenbürg, where he arrived late Sunday evening, he was tried, sentenced, and hanged the next day, April 9, 1945. The guards, already tipsy, received an extra ration of schnapps and blood sausage. Canaris, Oster, and Sack were also hanged in the grayish early morning. The deaths could not have been pleasant, devised hastily, with no time to calculate body weights. It's possible their deaths were dragged out as a form of torture. One remembers Dietrich's words about fallen seminarians on the Russian front: "pierced with horror when we think of the loneliness of their death." The corpses were then cremated and the ashes thrown into the middle of the concentration camp. At Sachsenhausen on April 9, Hans von Dohnanyi was executed.[6]

---

6. Ibid., 374.

— 71 —
Over

On April 22, Rüdiger, Klaus, and a dozen other prisoners learned they would be released after being transferred from Lehrter Street prison to another facility. Instead, guards led them behind the Lehrter railway station and shot them.

Still in prison in April, Eberhard discovered the army had discharged him. He received notice he would stand trial on May 15. On April 25, the first Russian troops entered Berlin. Eberhard and his friends convinced their guards that they, not the prisoners, would be killed when the Russians arrived. At four o'clock that afternoon the guards released the prisoners so that they themselves could escape. After almost six months behind bars, Eberhard was free.

He entered the rubble and chaotic street fighting of Berlin. Eberhard, who as Dietrich often noted, seemed to be born under a lucky star, travelled through the streets with a Russian Jew he had befriended in prison. When Russians tried to shoot Eberhard, the friend saved the day.

At the Schleicher home, Eberhard's emotions overcame him. He could hardly believe he was still alive. The next day, the family tried to get out of Berlin, but had to give up the attempt. On April 27th, a grenade hit the house and the family was "buried alive,"[1] forced to take shelter in the basement. The next day, April 28, the first two Russians arrived at the cellar. On April 29, Russian officers took over the senior Bonhoeffer house and ordered the elderly couple to evacuate.[2]

Hitler committed suicide on April 30th. On May 2, Berlin surrendered. Eberhard and the others tried again to escape the city and failed. Finally, on May 5, they made it to Sackrow, where the von Dohnanyis lived, and Eberhard was reunited with Renate and baby Dietrich, who had gone there to stay. On May 8th, Germany surrendered. The war was over.

---

1. de Gruchy, *Daring, Trusting Spirit,* 92.
2. Ibid.

In Sabine's Oxford, the English celebrated V-E Day. People cried and danced in the streets and thronged into churches while all the bells of the city rang in a joyous cacophony. In London, people waited in lines for hours to attend the around-the-clock church services at St. Paul's and Westminster Abbey. "For all of us," Sabine wrote, "this was the moment of liberation from the scourge of National Socialism, and it brought tears of joy to our eyes."[3]

She contrasted Hitler's suicide to the later actions of the Emperor of Japan, who put himself into the hands of his enemies, but asked that his people be spared. "What a difference in attitude from the German leader, who made sure he would not be called to account in any way for his actions!"[4]

Eberhard spent days bicycling around Berlin, trying to find lost friends and relatives. On May 31, he learned that Klaus and Rüdiger were dead.[5] On the same day, Sabine received the news, along with word of Dietrich's death. "I have not forgotten Gert's face streaming with tears, or the sobbing of the children," Sabine wrote. "Somehow I had been living wholly for the moment when I could be reunited with Dietrich in a new and better Germany . . . . Now I felt as if all the lights had been put out."[6]

But still the family in Germany did not know. "Why isn't he here yet?" Karl-Friedrich asked in the essay he wrote at the end of June. About the time he asked that question, Maria heard the news, but communications had been cut in Germany, leaving her no way to contact his family members. They found out at the end of July, when a neighbor told them there was to be a BBC broadcast of a memorial service for Dietrich. Even at the end of July the family still did not know if von Dohnanyi was alive.[7]

In those grim days after the surrender, the once powerful Bonhoeffers went hungry. Ursel moved in with her parents because of the grenade damage to her home. The Russians took over Hans and Christel's house. Bombs had destroyed Walter and Susi's home.

Eberhard could hardly believe that after twelve years of witnessing the Nazi horror, the church would want to go back to what it had been. "We were hardly able to grasp that things could simply pick up from the time before 1933 . . . as if nothing had happened since 1933. It took awhile before it was clear to us that just that was probably going to happen after all . . . ."[8] It might have been almost the most stunning blow of all.

3. Leibholz, *The Bonhoeffers*, 159
4. Ibid.
5. Schlingensiepen, *Dietrich Bonhoeffer 1906–1945*, 374.
6. Ibid., 161.
7. Ibid., 167.
8. Bethge, *Friendship and Resistance*, 7.

Back at occupied Kieckow, Ruth started a village school and found a pair of glasses, a miracle to her. On September 8, 1945, on the way to her school, she tripped and fell down the stone steps of the forester's cottage where she lived. Her leg was badly broken, and she went to a hospital. In late September, Ruthchen arrived in Berlin, looking for news of her mother. She visited the Bonhoeffers and ran into Eberhard, who had had a letter about Ruth's injury.

Rutchen headed east with a companion, a Polish landowner named Pan Sukalski trying to reclaim his estate, in a train with no glass in the windows. They warmed themselves by a bonfire once off the train, and the former mistress of Patzow slept by her companion in an empty pigsty. The next morning, they entered Stettin, now part of Poland, and agreed not to speak German. Near Stargard, however, hostile Poles identified Ruthchen as German and threw her off the train. She eventually reached Gross Tychow. Ruth had returned to Kieckow. The hospital, lacking even plaster to set her leg, had sent her home. On the morning of October 1, Ruthchen arrived at Ruth's forester's cottage to find her on her deathbed, sick with pneumonia.[9]

Rutchen delivered the news that Fabian von Schlabrendorff was alive, as well as Klaus von Bismarck, Ruth Alice's husband. Ruth then asked about Dietrich. As the story goes, when she heard the answer, she welcomed death with the expectation she would meet him in heaven.[10]

---

9. Pejsa, *Matriarch of Conspiracy,* 379–82.
10. Ibid., 382.

— 72 —

More Threads

BETHGE PUBLISHED BONHOEFFER'S *Ethics* in 1949 to hardly a ripple of interest, and in 1951 edited the German version of *Letters and Papers from Prison*, expecting it to appeal only to a small circle of friends and family. Instead, it became a worldwide best seller, and Bethge would spend the rest of his life as keeper of the Bonhoeffer flame. The son who the Bonhoeffer family thought had thrown his life away in becoming a pastor became their most famous member.

Bethge, like Niemöller, both initially supporters of National Socialism, would turn in later life to Jewish reconciliation. Bethge would finally understand the grave dangers of supercessionism—believing Christianity superior to Judaism or other religions—and come to believe that simply deposing Hitler without eradicating anti-Semitism would have been of little help to the Jews. In Niemöller's and Bethge's paths, we can trace what Bonhoeffer, already so determined to pay for Nazism, might have become. Bonhoeffer, ahead of his times in 1933, would likely have worked to atone for Nazi war crimes and, as an advocate of Gandhi, may have embraced not only ecumenicalism but interfaith dialogue.

Maria's story shows the enormous ground she covered in a life of little more than fifty years. Going from the eighteenth-century Pätzig manor house, with its blacksmith, wheelwright, and pinafored peasants to her subsequent life in America could be likened to a character in a Jane Austen novel stepping through a time machine into the 1970s.

After the war, with the help of Bonhoeffer's Quaker friend Herbert Jehle, who would name his two sons Eberhard and Dietrich, Maria moved to America to study at Bryn Mawr.[1] Described repeatedly as a brilliant, head turning, high-energy beauty, she married a German, Paul Schniewind, and arranged for him to join her in America. The couple had two sons before divorcing in 1955. Maria then remarried a businessman and entrepreneur, Bart Weller, who owned his own company. This marriage ended in divorce

---

1. Bismarck and Kabitz, eds., *Love Letters*, 349.

in 1965, leading Maria, according to her pastor, Scott Paradise, to conclude her life was a failure. Meanwhile, post-war America gave her an opportunity to use her mathematical skills in ways impossible in either Junker Prussia or Nazi Germany, and she ended up working for Honeywell's computer division just as the woman's movement was sweeping America.[2]

For a woman who likely suffered from post-traumatic stress disorder—in a short time she had lost a father, beloved brother, fiancé, and home, and seen the devastation of her country—the remarkable fact about Maria was the life she achieved. She bought her own modern home, complete with a lake. By 1975, she had become the highest-ranked woman manager at Honeywell. In 1976, she bought a house on the ocean.[3]

Friends and coworkers noted her sometimes domineering personality, a Junker trait that never left her. "There was something about Maria that, if you yourself didn't have the same self-assurance, it would be difficult to deal with," friend Lucy Sayre said.[4]

Her relationship with the Bonhoeffer group that arose after the publication of *Letters and Papers in Prison* remained distant. Like other women around Dietrich, she largely maintained a discreet silence. As Ruth Alice worded it "Maria was not close to the 'Bonhoeffer Society.'"[5] Eberhard would have liked, possibly to quell rumors about his relationship with Dietrich, to include some of her letters to Dietrich in his expanded edition of *Letters and Papers from Prison*, published in 1970, but she refused. That there may have been some tension as to who owned the rights to Bonhoeffer's letters to Maria is suggested by the fact that in November 1967 Bethge signed a formal declaration that the letters were Maria's property.[6] Late in her daughter's life, Ruthchen would express remorse that she had not allowed the marriage to Dietrich to move forward. Given the difficulties in the engagement and Ruthchen's accurate perception that the couple was ill-matched, that seems a remarkable sentiment—unless her mother believed that Maria would have had rights as wife to challenge Bethge's control of Bonhoeffer's estate.

In 1967, Maria stepped out of the shadows again when she published an article called "The Other Letters from Prison." This piece obscures the realities of the relationship, maintaining silences that speak volumes to the careful reader while not dismantling the public fantasy.

2. Ibid., 349–53.
3. Ibid., 354–55.
4. Ibid., 352.
5. Ibid., 357.
6. de Gruchy, *Daring, Trusting Spirit*, 124.

Maria sidesteps her own love—or lack thereof—for Dietrich, writing instead that she had "very undeservedly gained his love." The train wreck of their relationship becomes Dietrich's "ability to convert the annoyance at the limitations of our relationship [a reader could be forgiven for assuming she meant only the imprisonment and not the other limitations], and the misunderstandings that resulted from them, into a hopeful and eager expectation and challenge." Her anger, depression, and fainting spells become the "erratic emotions of a young girl."[7]

Like Sabine, Maria remembered what touched her emotionally—the shock of Dietrich taking her to lunch at Alois Hitler's restaurant, his initial support of her interest in mathematics, his rejection of her beloved Rilke. Asking to be invited to Hans Walter's going-away party in October, 1942, where she had to walk home by herself afterwards, turned into Dietrich's desire "to present me to his family." His hesitancy to pursue the relationship and her desire not to see or hear from him after the engagement morphed into "no urgency on his part" and his "great sensitivity . . . to my willingness to receive his attentions."[8]

Maria remembered particularly Dietrich's repeated requests that she perfect her English and practice her violin, hints that he tried to conflate her with Sabine. Maria couched the general dissatisfaction of their visits in "there were some happy times during these visits," but included Dietrich's observation, "that even when we are laughing, we are a bit sad."[9]

Did she know as she quotes his November 21, 1943 letter to her, written just as he is in the midst of his first prison outpourings to Eberhard, that Dietrich is thinking of Eberhard, not her: "the pain of longing, which can be felt even physically, must be there, and we shall not and need not talk it away"? If so, Maria isn't saying. Perhaps her footnote: "no one but Bethge could have produced it [the biography]. He is unique in his knowledge of Bonhoeffer," drily sums up her perceptions.[10] And yet her article, and the letters she allowed to be published after her death, show an insistence on having a voice in the story. Perhaps she even thought people would pay attention.

Her 1974 television interview with Malcolm Muggeridge became her last public word on Bonhoeffer. If her 1967 reappearance after two decades of silence represented her flapping her wings against Bethge, her 1974 reappearance is more mysterious.

7. Bonhoeffer, *LPP*, 412.
8. Ibid., 415–16.
9. Ibid., 412.
10. Ibid., 418–19.

The interview itself is a remarkable document. In it, she sits in her modernist US home with Muggeridge, in front of a fire burning in her big brick hearth. Beneath their feet lies what is possibly the Oriental carpet that made it from Pätzig to the US. In the background, a sliding glass door looks out over a vista of woods, while a blond wood upright piano stands against one wall, a modern sculpture in a corner.

Maria tries, tactfully, to speak the truth that the letters support: "I had times in which I could be actually happy about this engagement and times when it was very hard to take because I was getting somehow or other closer and closer to a man I was not really getting closer to." The film cuts then to her talking about searching for Bonhoeffer at Flossenbürg, where she speaks confidently, flashing a radiant smile as she remembers the guards' warm response to her.

Muggeridge asks her about the effects of Dietrich's death on her. "I had never really been so close to him and had these long periods of not seeing him," she answered. "It [his death] seemed like another big period of not seeing him. It was very hard to come to grips with the fact that this was finished." Not that he was dead, but that "this" was over. And here the telling pauses begin: "I have continued to live my life looking at this as a great, uh," pausing, "gift, a great, uh, uh, uh . . . ." Her head turns from the camera, and she peers into the distance. As she thinks, Muggeridge supplies the words "great addition," which Maria repeats, adding and "a great enrichment of my life." But she does not stop there as she struggles to speak truth: "Yet on the other hand, it had its very hard parts to it. It has been difficult, even to this very day, it is sometimes difficult to accept it that . . . " Here she pauses again and Muggeridge again jumps in to steer the script along its proper path, urging his beautiful prop to say the right words: "that it's no longer there." She repeats his words. "In other words," supplies Muggeridge, "that nothing else has ever really quite replaced it . . . ." "That is absolutely correct," says Maria of his cryptic and ambiguous utterance. And then the camera cuts to a helicopter in 1970s Berlin, patrolling the wall that once divided East from West, and that might as well stand as a metaphor for the divide between the reality of Maria and Dietrich's situation and its facade. Rather than let her grope to tell her own truth, another man has dictated her final public utterances, and Maria has capitulated, miming his words. What would she have supplied in place of the "uhs" if Muggeridge had not rushed in?

In the winter of 1977, she joined a family ski reunion at Klosters. Her beloved Pätzig, now as dissolved as the House of Usher, remained close to her heart. Perhaps sensing the end was near, she had begun recording her memories of this home, down to the furniture and pictures in each room. At Klosters, contributing to the memoir became a family project.[11]

Today, according to Ruth's biographer Jane Pejsa, the site of Pätzig is a forest, the village one of brick homes and a church. Perhaps reversion to a woods is a graceful end for Pätzig, an estate that looked back to the past.

Maria died of cancer late in 1977.

---

11. Bismarck and Kabitz, eds., *Love Letters*, 357.

Epilogue

CLEARLY WOMEN PLAYED A decisive role in Bonhoeffer's life and hence the development of his theology—Paula, Sabine, his grandmother, the Horn sisters, Ruth, Maria, his other sisters—as well as Bertha Schulz and Elisabeth Zinn and so many other women who provided help along the way. Even Harriet Beecher Stowe, touching him across time with her story of suffering slaves, and the seminary housekeeper, Mrs. Struwe, left their mark.

Had through some miracle an advance group of Allies suddenly appeared, chasing away the executioners before they could kill Dietrich at Flossenbürg, would a post-war Bonhoeffer have come to see women as more fully human? Or would women always have been there as they had been before as secretaries, mothers, sisters, cooks, cleaners, helpers, nurturers of men?

Bethge's almost total erasure of women from his biography of Bonhoeffer can be understood in the context of time and place, coming out of genre of German memoir in which ignoring women was commonplace. However, even modern scholarship has devalued the role of women in Bonhoeffer's life.

In Dietrich's prison theology of friendship we see the beginnings of a theology that yearns to legitimize same-sex relationship, be it friendship or more, be it celibate or not. Both Bonhoeffer and Bethge acknowledged struggles due to the lack of formal recognition of their close companionship—Bonhoeffer could receive visits from Maria, a woman who he barely knew, but not from Bethge, whom he longed for with every fiber of his being. And Bethge, his friend of almost a decade, had to remind Bonhoeffer's parents to pass him Bonhoeffer's letters—letters they routinely copied for new fiancée Maria. Both men felt the frustration of the military's indifference to their friendship. These sorts of assertions against invisibility have become the mainstay of the gay marriage movement. In Bonhoeffer's time and place, the idea of same-sex marriage was inconceivable, but insisting on the beauty, necessity, and value of same-sex friendship existing as a cornflower between the rigid rows of more formal social organization offered a beginning vision.

"God does not fulfill all our wishes," Dietrich wrote, "but does keep all his promises." Dietrich, the man who feared loneliness more than death, died as he had dreaded: alone, without the comfort of his "brethren," without Eberhard at his side. For the man who had once dreamed, like Little Eva, of influencing others on his deathbed, surrounded by loved ones, inspiring them by his courage to come closer to God, suffering and dying unmourned in a concentration camp courtyard was not what he had wished. He died too without achieving his deepest hope of participating in the rebuilding of the postwar world.

Yet God did keep promises: Bonhoeffer may have initially died alone, but later his death was honored by millions. In his own lifetime, he only touched a handful—many of them killed in the war—but in his death he influenced the course of twentieth-century theology and made his mark, as he would have loved, in the here and now on people across the political spectrum from evangelicals to liberation theologians.

After the failure of the July 20th plot, Bonhoeffer achieved a sainthood of sorts. While recollections of him in his last months may be tinged with hagiography, a remarkably consistent picture of a soul at rest in God emerges. And even before those final months, he did that perhaps hardest thing, if imperfectly: he maintained decency and courage and goodness in "this world" during a terrible time.

Appendix 1

Maria von Wedemeyer
Timeline: 1935–45

August, 1935: Maria moves to Stettin to live with her grandmother, Ruth von Wedemeyer, along with her older sister Ruth Alice, her older brother Max and three cousins. "I went to Stettin at 11 . . . ."

August, 1936: With Ruth in Stettin. Maria "flunks" Bonhoeffer's entrance quiz for his confirmation class. Bonhoeffer takes on her older brother Max and cousins Hans Friedrich von Kleist and Spes von Bismarck for confirmation instruction. Both Max and Hans Friedrich will die in World War II.

1936: Maria begins attending Magdalenen-Stift boarding school in Altenburg.

c. 1940: Attends Wieblingen Castle School near Heidelberg run by Elisabeth von Thadden.

March 20, 1942: Graduates from Wieblingen Castle School.

June 5–8(?), 1942: Maria and Dietrich meet for one day at Klein-Krössin, Ruth's cottage.

June 24, 1942: Maria leaves for Gross Tychow to begin her service year with her von Kleist cousins.

June 25, 1942: Dietrich writes to Bethge of his meeting with Maria in early June.

July 1942: According to her diary, Maria is being pushed by Ruth to marry.

August 22, 1943: Maria's father is killed on the Russian front. Maria returns to Pätzig.

September 1, 1942: Maria sees Dietrich at Klein-Krössin.

Late September/early October, 1942: Maria moves to her cousin Spes's Berlin apartment in the Brandenburgische Strasse to help Ruth, who is in Berlin for cataract surgery.

October 2, 1942: Maria and Dietrich meet in Ruth's room at the Berlin Franciscan Hospital. Dietrich is there to say goodbye to Ruth, planning to be gone for six weeks in the Balkans and Switzerland on counterespionage business. He leaves for Munich on October 3.

Sometime between October 2–14: Maria visits Renate and Hans-Walter Schleicher. Maria is invited in to meet Bonhoeffer's parents, and sees a photo of Walter.

Tuesday, October 13, 1942: Ruth has cataract surgery.

Wednesday, October 14, 1942: Dietrich returns to Berlin, his trips abroad cancelled for fear he'll be arrested at the border. This is probably the evening he walks Maria home to her aunt's house at the Brandenburgische Strasse.

Thursday, October 15, 1942: Party for Hans Werner Schleicher, leaving for the army the next day. Maria and Dietrich both attend. Maria ends up locked out of her Aunt Spes's apartment.

Sunday, October 18, 1942: Bonhoeffer leads morning devotions at the hospital for Ruth and Maria.

Sometime between October 16–25: Dietrich takes Maria to eat at Hitler's brother's restaurant.

Sunday, October 25, 1942: Another round of devotions, this time apparently at Spes's apartment: "you rang the bell again because you'd forgotten your texts." However, Ruth's hospital room also had doors and a bell so it may have been there.

Monday, October 26, 1942: Maria's brother Max is killed on the Russian front. She leaves Berlin suddenly in response to the news. Dietrich thinks she has gone because of Ruth's matchmaking.

Saturday, October 31, 1942: Dietrich writes Maria a condolence letter. His Abwehr superior Schmidhuber is arrested, putting him in grave danger.

Sometime between October 26 and November 7: Ruth returns home to Klein-Krössin. Without consulting anyone, she invites Dietrich to Max's memorial service.

Before November 8, 1942: Ruthchen von Wedemeyer, Maria's mother, writes to Dietrich, asking him not to attend Max's memorial service, due to gossip Ruth is spreading, presumably of a probable engagement with Maria.

November 8, 1942: Memorial service for Max at Pätzig.

Between November 9–11, 1942: Maria arrives back at Gross Tychow to resume her service year.

November 11, 1942: Maria writes to Dietrich to apologize for the brouhaha over his not coming to the funeral.

November 13 and 15, 1942: Dietrich writes Maria two letters indicating his romantic interest. Maria is startled.

November 19, 1942: Ruthchen von Wedemeyer, at the request of Maria, calls Dietrich and tells him not to contact Maria. Ruthchen also offers to speak with him face-to-face. Dietrich sends Maria a letter of apology.

November 24, 1942: Dietrich goes to Pätzig and confers with Maria's mother. Maria is not there. Rutchen insists on a year of total separation to give Maria "peace," and tries to discourage the relationship by talking about Pätzig's sorry economic state.

November 25–27, 1942: Dietrich informs Ruth of the year-long separation. She is vexed at the delay. "I must calm her lest she cause even more trouble," Dietrich writes to Eberhard on the 27th.

November 27, 1942: Maria confides to her diary that she is "relieved and happy" at the separation.

November 29, 1942: Ruth, highly annoyed at the delay, is "causing a good deal of trouble with her endless telephoning," Dietrich writes to Eberhard.

December 19, 1942: Maria returns to Pätzig from a visit to her grandmother. During the visit, Ruth talks her into marrying Dietrich.

December 20, 1942: Bethge and Bonhoeffer's niece Renate become officially engaged.

January 8 or 9, 1943: Engagement party for Bethge and Renate. Ruth attends it. She decides to go straight to Pätzig from Berlin to talk to Ruthchen about Dietrich.

January 10, 1943: Maria's mother and her uncle Hans Jurgen agree to the engagement, with the stipulation of a one-year postponement and no announcement.

January 13, 1943: Maria writes to Dietrich, agreeing to marry him. She travels to Stettin that day to visit her grandmother and finds Dietrich has told Ruth he's going to stop pursuing Maria. Maria and Ruth most likely quarrel. Maria does not tell Ruth of her acceptance.

January 24, 1943: The "mistress of Gross Tychow," Baroness von Kleist, certifies that Maria had been "employed in the house and kitchen as a Pflichtjahrmadel [girl doing one year's compulsory service] until December 31, 1942." Maria repeats to Dietrich that she does not want to hear from him for a year, but that her "yes" is sincere.

February 4, 1943: On his thirty-eighth birthday, Dietrich tells Ruth and his parents of his engagement.

February 5, 1943: Ruth writes to Dietrich with great approval and joy, informing him that his engagement is "probably the greatest act of your life."

March 9, 1943: Maria breaks her vow of silence and calls Dietrich, upset over her grandmother's repeated hints that he will soon be arrested.

c. March 26, 1943: Maria arrives at the Clementinenhaus Hospital in Hanover for nursing training, where she will work until the middle of June.

April 5, 1943: Bonhoeffer is arrested and put in Tegel prison.

April 18, 1943: Maria at Pätzig confirms Ruth's hints that Dietrich is in prison.

April 23, 1943: Maria's nineteenth birthday.

May 23, 1943: Maria and her mother visit the Bonhoeffers in Berlin.

June 15, 1943: Maria transfers to Augusta Hospital in Berlin, with two weeks sick leave due to foot problems.

June 24, 1943: Maria visits Dietrich in prison (at the Reich court).

June 25 1943: Maria visits her grandmother at Klein-Krössin.

June 26, 1943: Maria goes to Pätzig. She has been granted three months sick leave due to foot problems.

July 13–c. July 29: Maria visits her aunt, Maria Grafi von Bredow, who runs a model farm and school of breathing at Seefeld.

July 30, 1943: Maria visits Dietrich again in prison at the Reich court in Berlin.

c. July 31–August 8 1943: Maria visits Seefeld.

August 9–14: Maria is at Pätzig.

August 15–c. 22: Maria is at Seefeld.

August 23–25: Maria is at Pätzig.

August 26, 1943: Maria visits Bonhoeffer in prison.

August 27–c. September 11, 1943: Maria is at Pätzig.

September 12, 1943: Maria is in Schönrade, her father's ancestral home, for a memorial service for a cousin killed at the front.

September 13–c. 20, 1943: Maria is at Stargard.

September 21–October 5/6: Maria is at Pätzig.

October 7, 1943: Maria visits Bonhoeffer in prison.

c. October 11, 1943: Maria takes younger sister Christine to the Magdalenen-Stift boarding school in Altenburg.

October 12, 1943: Maria is in Berlin, visiting the Bonhoeffers, and writes to Dietrich from his desk.

c. October 14–c. 22, 1943: Maria is at Pätzig.

October 23–November 9, 1943: At Kniephof Maria visits her sister Ruth-Alice; she stays longer than she intended because Ruth-Alice is sick.

November 10, 1943: Maria visits Bonhoeffer in prison.

November 12, 1943: Maria is at Jarchlin.

November 18–c. 25, 1943: Maria is at Pätzig.

November 26, 1943: Maria visits Bonhoeffer in prison.

November 27–c. 30: Maria is at Pätzig.

c. December 1–9, 1943: Maria is at Klein-Krössin with Ruth.

December 10, 1943: Maria visits Bonhoeffer in prison.

c. December 11–15 to January 4: Maria is at Pätzig.

December 22, 1943: Maria visits Bonhoeffer in prison.

January 1, 1944: Maria "pops over" to Wartenburg to visit the Tresckows.

January 5, 1944: Maria visits Bonhoeffer in prison. Maria arrives at Magdalenen-Stift school in Altenburg "to stand-in for a teacher in charge of the juniors" (ten–thirteen-year-olds). "I'm very much looking forward to it. They're so sweet...."

February 3, 1944: Maria helps deliver Dietrich Bethge: the labor goes too quickly for Renate to go to the hospital.

February 4, 1944: Maria visits Bonhoeffer in prison and delivers news of Dietrich Bethge's birth.

February 10, 1944: "I'm actually leaving [Magdalenen-Stift] the day after tomorrow.... Tomorrow there's to be a farewell skit of which I, of course, know nothing...."

February 16, 1944: Maria, at Pätzig, writes of her "rootless existence."

February 20, 1944: Maria visits Bonhoeffer in prison.

February 23–March 27, 1944: Maria stays in Bundorf, near Hassfort in lower Franconia, to help out Hedwig von Truchess. She will be based in Bundorf for five months.

March 28–29, 1944: Maria is at Pätzig. Bonhoeffer's parents visit and Maria helps host them.

March 30, 1944: Maria visits Bonhoeffer in prison.

March 31–April 17, 1944: Maria is based in Bundorf.

April 18, 1944: Maria visits Dietrich in prison.

April 23, 1944: Maria's twentieth birthday.

April 25, 1944: Maria visits Dietrich in prison.

April 26–May 21, 1944: Maria is in Bundorf.

May 22, 1944: Maria visits Bonhoeffer in prison.

May 25–June 26, 1944: Maria is in Bundorf.

June 27, 1944: Maria visits Bonhoeffer in prison.

June 28–c. August 20, 1944: Maria remains based in Bundorf.

August 20, 1944: Maria arrives in Berlin to stay for at least six weeks with the Bonhoeffers until early October. She seems to have stayed until about January 12, 1945, when she returned to Pätzig because of the collapse of the Eastern front.

August 23, 1944: Maria visits Dietrich in prison.

January 29, 1945: Maria leaves Pätzig. She brings Dietrich's letters with her.

January 31, 1945: Russians enter Pätzig.

Early February, 1945: Maria arrives with younger siblings in Opperhausen, a village near Celle, and is reunited with her mother.

February 12, 1945: Maria returns to Berlin and learns Bonhoeffer is missing.

c. February 13–19, 1945: Maria travels "in vain" to Flossenbürg looking for Dietrich. He is not to be found because he is not yet there.

Appendix 2

Orientation and Celibacy Questions

Orientation, celibacy, and sex

WHY NOT SIMPLY ACCEPT Dietrich's relationship with Eberhard as an especially close friendship, now sometimes called a "bromance," in which loving and hugging between men are part of the relationship, but the males in question define themselves as heterosexual? I will go over the evidence below, and then move into a discussion of Bonhoeffer's possible celibacy. As I do so, I will bring in a Bethge essay, written late in his life, called "Bonhoeffer's Theology of Friendship."[1]

Dietrich had many male friends and many men seemed to respond to him instinctively, to like him, admire him, and see him as a man's man. We can understand his relationship with Bethge as different by comparing it to some of his other friendships.

Dietrich was exceptionally close all his life with all his brothers-in-laws, a fact Bethge notes. Dietrich befriended most of them prior to their marriages to his sisters, corresponded with them, traveled and visited with them, talked theology, made music, and plotted conspiracies with them. Although close to each of them, with none did Dietrich experience the intensity of relationship or palpable longing that he did for Eberhard. He had every conceivable reason to expect he would have a similarly close relationship with Eberhard after his marriage to his niece, but in prison he worried incessantly about their relationship changing. While he could have expected with the married, almost-brother-in-law Eberhard the kind of close, congenial, welcoming relationship he had with his other brothers-in-law, his prison letters indicate him yearning for more.

---

1. Bethge, "Friendship," 80–103.

Famously, he wanted he and Eberhard to leave their wives behind to go to Israel, something he never asked or seemed to want or expect from any of his brothers-in-law, despite their friendship.

Gerhard Vibrans, who, as part of the first Finkenwalde contingent, lived in close quarters with Bonhoeffer and Bethge and was in earlier years Bethge's closest friend, likened Dietrich's friendship with Bethge to Vibrans's own desire for a woman—and he ribbed Dietrich about it in a letter: "But what happens if Eberhard must leave? Then your name will once again stand in heaven [as] a lonely star. . . . Endless elegies could demonstrate to you how I view my *womanless* existence as an equally joyless one"[2] (emphasis Vibrans).

After an unfortunate threesome vacation, Vibrans signaled in "a few revealing sentences, his acceptance of the very special relationship" between his two friends."[3] He called it a "unique relationship," not just a normal close friendship, such as the one he had enjoyed with Bethge. Vibrans stepped aside and accepted "what is present and always will be." These statements suggest that at least one close friend of Eberhard's understood the Dietrich/Eberhard relationship to be more than a good friendship.

If we had any real indication of interest in a woman, we might frame Dietrich's relationship with Bethge as bromance, but the suggestion that Dietrich might pursue a romance with Elisabeth Zinn distressed him, and instead he broke off the relationship. His relationship with Maria was reluctant, especially notable in a man who seldom hesitated when he found what he wanted. Further, Dietrich never married, an especially unusual circumstance given that he valorized his family, and the Bonhoeffer way of living—and all his siblings married family friends relatively close in age at a relatively young age. Dietrich had no lack of opportunity to marry within the family paradigm: Elisabeth Zinn was a neighbor from the same social class and brother-in-law Walter Dress had a suitable sister.

When he went to Manhattan in 1939, it was Eberhard alone Dietrich wanted to bring to the US. It was lack of letters from Eberhard while he was in Manhattan that drove him into a frenzy. It was to Eberhard he wrote "do you still want me?" We also have unexplained ellipses in at least one the letters to Eberhard, a censoring of texts deemed too "intimate" to share. All of this suggests more than mere close friendship.

Bethge distinguishes between the many friends Dietrich had and what he calls the four "singular" friendships. Dietrich, says Eberhard, had a singular friendship with his cousin, Hans Christopher von Hase, one with

2. *DBWE* 14, 195
3. De Gruchy, *Daring, Trusting Spirit*, 29–32.

his brother-in-law Walter Dress, one with Franz Hildebrandt, and one with Bethge himself. I would place only Franz and Eberhard in the "singular" category.

As Bethge notes, by the late 1930s, Eberhard and Dietrich had intertwined lives. They shared money, what Eberhard called "our" room in Dietrich's parent's home, clothing, and travel. Even after he had his apartment in the Burckhardthaus, Bethge writes in the friendship essay that "I lived with him [Dietrich] in the Marienburger Allee almost more than my own place."[4] Dietrich also repeatedly made Eberhard—and not Maria (nor Hildebrandt, von Hase or Dress) his sole heir.

In addition, a running subtext of his engagement is Maria questioning his warmth toward her. Maria wonders about his sexual temperature. She asks, "Don't you like being romantic?" She writes after the meeting that included both her and Bethge that she isn't as innocent as she might seem and wonders why she and Dietrich never get any time alone together. In at least one missing letter Maria seems to have questioned Bonhoeffer's interest in women point blank, causing him to write defensively about having had a relationship with Zinn, though by his own testimony and corroborated by Zinn, it was one that never got off the ground. Maria also appears to have questioned his enthusiasm towards her in a missing letter, asking why he didn't pursue her more ardently during their courtship.

The sun is a potent metaphor for Bonhoeffer. He writes to Bethge about wanting to experience the full force of the sun, to feel its heat, to "have it awaken my animal existence," to make him "purer and happier." He contrasts this to a "romantic enthusiasm," which only "gets intoxicated over sunrises and sunsets," which "sips at it [the sun] a little," which knows it "only as a picture."

In his May 29, 1944 letter to Maria, however, he describes their love as like "a glorious spring morning, when one sees the sky already tinged red by the sun's first rays . . . . That's what our love is like . . . ." But to Eberhard he writes on June 30, 1944, that "I should like to feel the full force of it [the sun] again, burning on one's skin and gradually making one's whole body glow."

Given that Maria was a beautiful and sexual woman, it's telling that Dietrich never revealed much, if any, physical temperature toward her. At times, he gestures warmth on paper towards Maria, but in reality, he seems to have been tepid towards her, withdrawing his hand, giving her the feeling she displeased him. In contrast, his prison letters to Bethge reveal a man physically atremble at the presence of his friend after their November meeting and on another occasion having a guard rush him down stairs in an

---

4. Bethge, "Friendship," 87.

attempt to catch a glimpse of Bethge. He told his brother-in-law Rüdiger that arranging the Christmas prison visit with Bethge was the best thing he had ever done for him.

Did they have a physical relationship?

Evidence indicates that Bonhoeffer may have been celibate. Marsh cites a prison letter in which Bonhoeffer notes that he has had more experience than Bethge, except for "one thing." This Marsh understands as sex, and he decides Bonhoeffer was celibate. Yet the context of the letter indicates that Bonhoeffer meant marriage. It is other evidence that points towards celibacy.

In *Creation and Fall*, Bonhoeffer writes, "sexuality is a *passionate hatred* of any limit" (Bonhoeffer's italics). Sexuality "lays violent hands on the other person" and "hates grace." "Sexuality," Bonhoeffer summarizes, "[is] a perversion of the relation of one human being to another."[5]

Could Dietrich, a young man coming of age in the open sexual circus of Weimar Berlin, have remained a puritan? Possibly. The sexual exploitation he would have been of aware from men and women selling their bodies on the Berlin streets could have reinforced a violent rejection of sex. Throughout his writing, he rejects coercing the other. If *Creation and Fall* was a cry of pain from a man sundered from his beloved sister due to her marriage and fall into sexuality, did this view change after Dietrich met the man who completed him? His shocked letter in 1936 to Eberhard about his seminarians' behavior indicates it may not have.

The context of this 1936 letter is a beach holiday with a set of seminarians, where Dietrich learned that five seminarians had gone out after dinner and been, in his words, "overwhelmed by temptation . . . indeed by an unbearable desire for pleasure, dancing, girls, etc. Two then went off with girls with whom they had spoken. Nothing else happened. But a terrible onslaught of nature against the word emerged." He wrote to Eberhard of the confrontation with him: "There were wild outbursts of sexual desire against the word of God. They spoke in completely frank language. . . . The five stood against me and themselves . . . . It was clear how serious things had become. I was overwhelmed. All I could do was pray to myself and ask the Lord Jesus to step in . . . . I have to be there with the brothers every moment; after yesterday you can understand why!"[6]

---

5. Bonhoeffer, *Creation and Fall*, 123
6. Bonhoeffer, *DBWE 14*, 229–30.

We have testimony too from friend Helmut Gollwitzer who remembered that Dietrich "again and again in his conversations evoked the vision of a religious order living in voluntary celibacy."[7]

And if the handsome, dark-haired, pleasant Bethge functioned as another Sabine, his role as socially "lesser" replicating Sabine's as the "lesser" gender, that would support a chaste relationship. In his prison fiction, Bonhoeffer notes that the characters Christophe (Bonhoeffer) and Ulrich (Bethge) look alike and are often mistaken for brothers, suggesting that Bethge became the twin replacing Sabine, a sign of a chaste relationship.

Bonhoeffer's possible celibacy doesn't mean he wasn't same-sex attracted. Many people, gay Christian blogger Jason Lee writes, "mistakenly think that being gay is about sex. It's not ... being gay isn't what I like in bed. Being gay, like being straight, has to do with much more: how my brain is wired, how I relate to men and to women, and who I will or won't fall in love with." It is, he emphasizes, an issue of experience. "Even if I never go on a single date, just being *gay* means I'm wired differently and my experience of the world is going to be different than if I were straight. Keeping that secret would be like trying to hide my masculinity from you. You would never really know me."[8]

Was he celibate?

A questions remains: did Dietrich's willingness to embrace sexuality increase as he got older? Although gay marriage would likely not have occurred to him as part of a divine mandate, and he seems to have kept marriage and friendship entirely separate, his theology of marriage, as Dahill notes, opens the institution up beyond German mid-century patriarchal norms.

Hints that he may have changed his views towards sex emerge in statements Zimmermann remembered in *I Knew Dietrich Bonhoeffer*. Dietrich resisted the idea that "marriage began with being together in the flesh," telling Zimmermann "that aspect was not decisive," which supports celibacy, but then Dietrich wondered if monogamy was truly a Christian demand, since the patriarchs "had lived in a different way." Dietrich asked: "[Since] in marriage everything is permitted; what else is permitted over and above that?"[9]

Zimmermann also remembered that the homoerotic *The Last Puritan* by Santayana was a book that occupied Bonhoeffer's mind for some time. "He seemed to feel some affinity there." The juxtaposition of *The Last*

7. Zimmermann and Smith, eds., "The Ways of Obedience," *I Knew*, 143.
8. Lee, "Questions from Christians #4."
9. Zimmermann and Smith, eds., *I Knew*, 190.

Puritan with the biblical patriarchs' willingness to stretch the boundaries of monogamy suggests that the unarticulated background of Eberhard's relentless push towards marrying Renate during this period led to Dietrich's attempt to construct a theology that would allow him to maintain an undiminished relationship with Eberhard (something more than the very strong friendships among male in-laws that Dietrich already enjoyed with his brothers-in-law) alongside Eberhard's marriage.

The *Ethics*, written later than *Creation and Fall*, celebrates the sexual in a way the earlier work does not, using language towards sexuality that suggests a growing appreciation. Bonhoeffer writes that sexual pleasure could not be designed solely for procreation. "For if the body is an end itself, then there is a right to bodily joys, without having to subordinate them to a further, higher purpose. . . . The joys of the body are a sign of the eternal joy that is promised human beings in the presence of God." He also writes, contradicting his rejection of sex in *Creation and Fall*: "Sexuality is not only a means of procreation, but . . . embodies joy." He quoted Ecclesiastes 11:9: "Rejoice young man while you are young. . . . Follow the inclination of your heart and the desire of your eyes, and know that for all these things God will bring you into judgment."[10]

His statement to Zimmermann that sex was not decisive thing in a marriage can be connected too to his remarks about polyphony to Bethge in the context of the erotic.

A long, private meeting coinciding with Bethge being home for the baptism of his son provides the context for the letter about polyphony. Apparently, Bethge confided in Bonhoeffer how overwhelmingly he loved Renate, perhaps even to the point of being diverted from God (and certainly, by implication, from Dietrich). Bonhoeffer responds by writing, in what has become a famous passage, of the "danger, in any passionate erotic love, that through it you may lose what I'd like to call the polyphony of life."

The polyphony rumination opens a way to make room for more than marriage as part of life's song. Dietrich writes that, "where the cantus firmus is clear and distinct, a counterpoint can develop as mightily as it wants."[11] The whole tenor of the polyphony metaphor implies, perhaps demands, the possibility of close relationships, of whatever sort, alongside marriage.

The letter breaks off midstream and one wonders what Bonhoeffer went on to say about polyphony. While letters can go missing, what is striking about the prison correspondence, both in terms of Eberhard and Maria, is the pattern of missing letters and pieces of letters just at moments where

10. Bonhoeffer, *DBWE 6*, 186–87.
11. Bonhoeffer, *DBWE 8*, 394.

there's apparently an uncomfortable discussion of love or sexuality. It could be accidental, but the pattern doesn't *seem* accidental.

Bethge uses Maria as a placeholder in his friendship essay, stating more than once that Bonhoeffer had a fiancée, and putting her letters to Bonhoeffer in an "entirely different third category, the wonderful correspondence to his fiancée from Tegel Prison."[12]

He never, however, explains what this category is or what makes it "entirely different." Apparently, we are meant to understand these as "love letters," of a deeper, more passionate nature, but this is disingenuous: the reality of the situation is that more passion runs through Dietrich's correspondence to Eberhard than his to Maria.

Finally, Bethge reveals the openness of the theology of friendship Bonhoeffer was developing. He writes of a joyful, playful Dietrich, "this experimenting thinker in the prison cell" who liked "playing games" including experimenting with the idea of a fifth mandate, a "sphere of freedom" that would include friendship, along with art, education, and play. Bonhoeffer conceived of this friendship entirely in male terms, despite his close friendships with Ruth and Sabine, and felt this kind of male friendship made him "fully human." According to Bethge, Dietrich believed "his theology of the mandates should not fall captive to a new rigidity . . . but should be kept open in fruitful illogic" and "permit responsible freedoms."[13]

Whether sexual pleasure flowed into Dietrich's life, we don't know, but we do know the theological was the personal for him and the personal the theological. Certainly we have no smoking gun, but we do have hints of a "responsible freedom" and an embodied physical joy "above" monogamy that make it impossible to unequivocally conclude Dietrich was celibate. Yet he may have been.

Whatever the exact nature of the relationship, Dietrich's love for Eberhard dominated his last ten years. Theologically, his quest for a way to navigate around the rigid social structure of heterosexual marriage led him to begin to establish the idea of relationships located in a "sphere of freedom" rooted in the Bible rather than the culture.

---

12. Bethge, *Friendship and Resistance*, 90.
13. Ibid., 96.

Bibliography

A Third Testament: A Modern Pilgrim Explores the Spiritual Wanderings of Augustine, Blake, Pascal, Tolstoy, Bonhoeffer, Kierkegaard, and Dostoevsky. DVD. Directed by Malcolm Muggeridge. 1974. Worcester, PA: Vision Video.

Anonyma. *A Woman in Berlin: Eight Weeks in a Conquered City: A Biography*. Translated by Philip Boehm. New York Metropolitan, 2006.

Aycoberry, Pierre. *The Social History of the Third Reich, 1933–1945*. Translated by Janet Lloyd. New York: New Press, 1999.

Bailey, Brenda. "The Integrity of German Friends During Twelve Years of Nazi Rule: Mary's Troubles in Pyrmont." http://criticalconcern.com/integrity_of_german_friends_duri.htm.

Barnes, James J., and Patience P. Barnes. *Nazis in Pre-War London, 1930–1939: The Fate and Role of German Party Members and British Sympathizers*. Brighton: Sussex Academic Press, 2010.

Barnett, Victoria. "The Church and the Jewish Question." http://www.ushmm.org/information/exhibitions/online-features/special-focus/dietrich-bonhoeffer/opposition.

———. "Dietrich Bonhoeffer: Opposition." http://www.ushmm.org/information/exhibitions/online-features/special-focus/dietrich-bonhoeffer/opposition.

———. *For the Soul of the People: Protestant Protest Against Hitler*. New York: Oxford University Press, 1992.

Beachy, Robert. *Gay Berlin: Birthplace of a Modern Identity*. New York: Knopf, 2014.

Bernstein, Robin. "Children's Books, Dolls, and the Performance of Race; Or, the Possibility of Children's Literature." *PMLA* 126, no. 1 (2011) 160–69.

Bethge, Eberhard. *Dietrich Bonhoeffer: A Biography*. Translated by Eric Mosbahcer, Peter Ross, Betty Ross, Frank Clarke, and William Glen-Doepel. Edited by Edwin Robertson and Victoria Barnett. Minneapolis: Fortress, 2000.

———. *Dietrich Bonhoeffer: Man of Vision, Man of Courage*. New York: Harper and Row, 1970.

———. "Friendship." In *Friendship and Resistance: Essays on Dietrich Bonhoeffer*, 80–103. Grand Rapids: World Council of Churches, 1995.

———. *Friendship and Resistance: Essays on Dietrich Bonhoeffer*. Grand Rapids: World Council of Churches, 1995.

———. *In Zitz gab es keine Juden: Erinnerungen aus meinen ersten vierzig Jahren*. Munich: Chr. Kaiser, 1989.

Bethge, Eberhard, ed. *Last Letters of Resistance: Farewells from the Bonhoeffer Family*. Translated by Dennis Slabaugh. Edited with Renate Bethge. Philadelphia: Fortress,

1986.Bethge, Renate. "Bonhoeffer and the Role of Women." *Church and Society*, August 1995, 34–52.

Bethge, Renate, and Christian Gremmels. *Dietrich Bonhoeffer: A Life in Pictures*. Translated by Brian McNeil. Minneapolis: Fortress, 1987.

Bismarck, Ruth-Alice, and Ulrich Kabitz, eds. *Love Letters from Cell 92: The Correspondence Between Dietrich Bonhoeffer and Maria Von Wedemeyer, 1943–45*. Translated by John Brownjohn. Nashville: Abingdon, 1995.

Blackbourn, David. *History of Germany, 1780–1918: The Long Nineteenth Century*. Malden, MA: Wiley-Blackwell, 2002.

Bonhoeffer, Dietrich. *Act and Being: Transcendental Philosophy and Ontology in Systematic Theology*. DBWE 2. Translated by Martin Rumscheidt. Edited by Hans Richard Reuter and Martin H. Rumscheidt. Minneapolis: Fortress, 2009.

———. *Barcelona, Berlin, New York: 1928–1931*. DBWE 10. Translated by Douglas W. Stott. Edited by Clifford J. Green. Minneapolis: Fortress, 2008.

———. *Berlin: 1932–1933*. DBWE 12. Translated by Isabel Best, David Higgins, and Douglas W. Stott. Edited by Larry Rasmussen. Minneapolis, MN: Fortress, 2009.

———. *Conspiracy and Imprisonment, 1940–1945*. DBWE 16. Translated by Lisa E. Dahill. Edited by Mark Brocker. Minneapolis: Fortress, 2006.

———. *Creation and Fall*. DBWE 3. Translated by Douglas Stephen Bax. Edited by John de Gruchy. Minneapolis: Fortress, 1997.

———. *Discipleship*. DBWE 4. Translated by Barbara Green and Reinhard Krause. Edited by Geffrey B. Kelly and John D. Godsey. Minneapolis: Fortress, 2003.

———. *Ecumenical, Academic, and Pastoral Work, 1931–1932*. DBWE 11. Translated by Isabel Best, Nicholas S. Humphrey, Marion Pauck, Anne Schmidt-Lange, and Douglas W. Stott. Edited by Victoria J. Barnett, Mark Brocker, and Michael B. Lukens. Minneapolis: Fortress, 2012.

———. *Ethics*. DBWE 6. Translated by Reinhard Krause and Charles West, with Douglas W. Stott. Edited by Clifford J. Green. Minneapolis: Fortress, 2005.

———. *Fiction from Tegel Prison*. DBWE 7. Translated by Nancy Lukens. Edited by Renate Bethge. Minneapolis: Fortress, 2005.

———. *Letters and Papers from Prison*. DBWE 8. Translated by Isabel Best, Lisa E. Dahill, Reinhard Krause, and Mancy Lukens. Edited by John de Gruchy. Minneapolis: Fortress, 2010.

———. *Life Together: The Classic Exploration of Faith in Community*. New York: HarperOne, 2009.

———. *Life Together and Prayerbook of the Bible*. DBWE 5. Translated by Daniel W. Bloesch and James H. Burtness. Edited by Geffrey B. Kelly. Minneapolis: Fortress, 1995.

———. *Sanctorum Communio: A Theological Study of the Sociology of the Church*. DBWE 1. Translated by Reinhard Krause and Nancy Lukens. Edited by Clifford J. Green. Minneapolis: Fortress, 2009.

———. *Theological Education at Finkenwalde: 1935–1937*. DBWE 14. Translated by Douglas W. Stott. Edited by H. Gaylon Barker and Mark Brocker. Minneapolis: Fortress, 2013.

———. *Theological Education Underground, 1937–1940*. DBWE 15. Translated by Claudia D. Bergmann, Peter Frick, and Scott A. Moore. Edited by Victoria Barnett. Minneapolis: Fortress, 2011.

———. *The Young Bonhoeffer: 1918–1927. DBWE 9*. Translated by Mary Nebelsick with Douglas W. Stott. Edited by Paul Matheny, Clifford J. Green, and Marshall Johnson. Minneapolis: Fortress, 2002.

Bonhoeffer, Dietrich, and Eberhard Bethge. *Letters and Papers From Prison*. New York: Macmillan, 1972.

Bosanquet, Mary. *The Life and Death of Dietrich Bonhoeffer*. London: Hodder & Stoughton, 1968.

Butler, Judith. *Gender Trouble: Feminism and the Subversion of Identity*. New York: Routledge, 2006.

Clausen, Jeannette. "Culture is What You Experience: An Interview with Christa Wolf." *New German Critique* 27 (Autumn 1982) 89–100.

Clements, Keith. *Bonhoeffer and Britain*. London: Churches Together in Britain and Ireland, 2006.

Cox, Chris. "Career." http://www.antonwalbrook.co.uk.

Crouthamel, Jason. "'Comradeship' and 'Friendship': Masculinity and Militarisation in Germany's Homosexual Emancipation Movement after the First World War." *Gender & History* 23, no. 1 (April 1, 2011) 111–29.

Dahill, Lisa E. *Reading from the Underside of Selfhood: Bonhoeffer and Spiritual Formation*. Eugene, OR: Wipf and Stock, 2009.

———."Reading from the Underside of Selfhood: Dietrich Bonhoeffer and Spiritual Formation." *Spiritus* 1 (2001) 186–203.

———. "'There's Some Contradiction Here': Gender and the Relation of Above and Below in Bonhoeffer." In *Interpreting Bonhoeffer: Essays on Method and Approaches*, edited by Peter Frick, 53–82. New York: Peter Lang, 2013.

Damrosch, Leo. *Jonathan Swift: His Life and His World*. New Haven, CT: Yale University Press, 2013.

Dawidowicz, Lucy S. *The War Against the Jews: 1933–1945*. New York: Bantam, 1986.

De Gruchy, John W. *Daring, Trusting Spirit: Bonhoeffer's Friend Eberhard Bethge*. Minneapolis: Fortress, 2005.

Dramm, Sabine. *Dietrich Bonhoeffer and the Resistance*. Translated by Margaret Kohl. Minneapolis: Fortress, 2009.

Durkin, Neil. "Our Century's Great Achievement." BBC News, December 9, 1998. http://news.bbc.co.uk/2/hi/special_report/1998/12/98/50th_anniversary_declaration_of_human_rights/231204.stm.

Engelmann, Bernt. *In Hitler's Germany: Daily Life in the Third Reich*. New York: Pantheon, 1986.

Fallada, Hans. *Every Man Dies Alone*. Translated by Michael Hofmann. Brooklyn, NY: Melville House, 2010.

Fowler, James W., and Robin W. Lovin. *Trajectories in Faith: Five Life Stories*. Nashville: Abingdon, 1980.

Fox, Christopher. "An Opera for My Resistance Fighter Aunt." *The Guardian*, November 21, 2012. http://www.theguardian.com/music/2012/nov21/opera-for-my-resistance-fighter-aunt.

French, Paul. "London's Chinese Restaurant Scene in the 1930s (one of three posts)." *China Rhyming*. http://www.chinarhyming.com/2012/12/28/londons-chinese-restaurant-scene-in-the-1930s-one-of-three-posts/.

Frevert, Ute. *Women in German History: From Bourgeois Emancipation to Sexual Liberation*. Translated by Stuart McKinnon-Evans, Barbara Norden, and Terry Bond. New York: Bloomsbury Academic, 1990.

Frick, Peter, ed. *Bonhoeffer's Intellectual Formation: Theology and Philosophy in His Thought*. Tübingen: Mohr Siebeck, 2008.

Friedrich, Otto. *Before the Deluge: A Portrait of Berlin*. New York: Harper & Row, 1972.

Fritzsche, Peter. *Life and Death in the Third Reich*. Cambridge, MA: Belknap, 2009.

Gay, Peter. *Weimar Culture: The Outsider as Insider*. Westport, CT: Praeger, 1981.

"George Santayana: A Biography." *Stanford Encyclopedia of Philosophy*, October 6, 2014. http://plato.stanford.edu/entries/santayana/.

Gole, Henry G. *Exposing the Third Reich: Colonel Truman Smith in Hitler's Germany*. Lexington, KY: The University Press of Kentucky, 2013.

Green, Barbara. "Poore Foolische Friend: Bonhoeffer, Bethge, Vibrans and a Theology of Friendship." In *Reflections on Bonhoeffer: Essays in Honor of F. Burton Nelson*, edited by Geffrey B. Kelly and C. John Weborg, 185–98. Chicago: Covenant, 1999.

Green, Cifford. *Bonhoeffer: A Theology of Sociality*. Grand Rapids: Eerdmans, 1999.

Griswold, A. Whitney. "The Junkers: Hostages to the Past." *The Virginia Quarterly Review* 19, no. 3. http://www.vqronline.org/issues/19/3/summer-1943#toc.

Grunberger, Richard. *A Social History of the Third Reich*. London: Weidenfeld and Nicolson, 1971.

Haynes, Stephen R. *The Bonhoeffer Phenomenon: Portraits of a Protestant Saint*. Minneapolis: Fortress, 2004.

Haynes, Stephen R., and Lori Brandt Hale. *Bonhoeffer for Armchair Theologians*. Louisville: Westminster John Knox, 2009.

Holland, Scott. "First We Take Manhattan, Then We Take Berlin: Bonhoeffer's New York." *Cross Currents* 50, no. 3 (Fall 2000). http://www.crosscurrents.org/hollandf20.htm.

Huchthausen, Peter. "The SS Bremen Article: Shadow Voyabe—Escape of German Liner SS Bremen." *The Maritime Network*. http://web.archive.org/web/20120615085339/http://www.freewebs.com/tmnarticles/bremen.htm.

"Jack the Ripper." *BBC Online*, 2014. http://www.bbc.co.uk/history/historic_figures/ripper_jack_the.shtml.

Johnson, Eric A., and Karl-Heinz Reuband. *What We Knew: Terror, Mass Murder, and Everyday Life in Nazi Germany*. Cambridge, MA: Basic Books, 2006.

Kelly, Richard M. *Thomas Kelly: A Biography*. New York: Harper & Row, 1966.

Klan, J. S. "Luther's Resistance Teaching and the German Church Struggle under Hitler." *Journal of Church History* 14, no. 4 (1987) 432–43.

Klemperer, Victor. *I Shall Bear Witness: The Diaries of Victor Klemperer 1933–41*. London: Trafalgar Square, 1998.

Kyung, Chang Hyun. "Dear Dietrich Bonhoeffer: A Letter." In *Bonhoeffer for a New Day: Theology in a Time of Transition*, edited by John de Gruchy, 9–19. Grand Rapids: Eerdmans, 1997.

Larson, Erik. *In the Garden of Beasts: Love, Terror, and an American Family in Hitler's Berlin*. New York: Crown, 2011.

Lee, Jason. "Questions from Christians #4: 'Why Do You Have to Tell People You're Gay? Can't You Keep It in the Bedroom?'" *Crumbs from the Communion Table*. http://gcnjustin.tumblr.com/post/54922915606/questions-from-christians-4-why-do-you-have-to.

Leibholz-Bonhoeffer, Sabine. *The Bonhoeffers: Portrait of a Family*. Translated by F. Burton Nelson. Chicago: Covenant, 1994.

Lovin, Robin, and Jonathan P. Gosser. "Dietrich Bonhoeffer: Witness in an Ambiguous World." In *Trajectories in Faith: Five Life Stories*, edited by James W. Fowler and Robin W. Lovin, 145–97. Nashville: Abingdon, 1980.

Lubrich, Oliver, ed. *Travels in the Reich, 1933–1945: Foreign Authors Report from Germany*. Translated by Kenneth J. Northcott, Sonia Wichmann, and Dean Krouk. Chicago: University of Chicago Press, 2010.

Magid, Robin. "Lublin, Poland: Stettin (Szczecin) Jewish Deportation into the Lublin Area." http://www.jewishgen.org/databases/holocaust/0188_Lublin_Stettin.html.

Manning, Olivia. *Fortunes of War: The Balkan Trilogy*. New York: NYRB Classics, 2010.

Marsh, Charles. *Strange Glory: A Life of Dietrich Bonhoeffer*. New York: Alfred A. Knopf, 2014.

Marty, Martin E. *Dietrich Bonhoeffer's "Letters and Papers from Prison": A Biography*. Princeton, NJ: Princeton University Press, 2011.

Metaxas, Eric. *Bonhoeffer: Pastor, Martyr, Prophet, Spy*. Nashville: Thomas Nelson, 2010.

Miller, Alice. *For Your Own Good: Hidden Cruelty in Child-Rearing and the Roots of Violence*. New York: Farrar, Straus and Giroux, 1984.

Moorhouse, Roger. *Berlin at War*. New York: Basic, 2010.

Nafisi, Azar. *Reading Lolita in Tehran: A Memoir in Books*. New York: Random House, 2003

Nagorski, Andrew. *Hitlerland: American Eyewitnesses to the Nazi Rise to Power*. New York: Simon & Schuster, 2013.

Nicholas, Lynn H. *Cruel World: The Children of Europe in the Nazi Web*. New York: Vintage, 2006.

Pachter, H. M. *The Weimar Etudes*. New York: Columbia University Press, 1982.

Paldiel, Mordecai. "The Poisonous Well of Anti-Jewish Rhetoric." *Haaretz*, November 6, 2009. http://www.haaretz.com/print-edition/opinion/the-poisonous-well-of-anti-jewish-rhetoric-1.4664.

Paradise, Scott. "Eulogy for Maria Friedricka von Wedemeyer Weller." *International Bonhoeffer Society Newsletter*, no. 82 (Summer 2003). http://dietrichbonhoeffer.org/Newsletters/IBSNewsletter82.pdf.

Paterson, Tony. "How the Nazis Stole Christmas." *The Independent*, October 22, 2011. http://www.independent.co.uk/news/world/europe/how-the-nazis-stole-christmas-1846365.html.

Peck, William Jay. "The Significance of Bonhoeffer's Interest in India." *Harvard Theological Review* 61 (1968) 431–50.

Pejsa, Jane. *Matriarch of Conspiracy: Ruth Von Kleist, 1867–1945*. Minneapolis: Kenwood, 1991.

Peukert, Detlev J. K. *Inside Nazi Germany: Conformity, Opposition, and Racism in Everyday Life*. Translated by Richard Deveson. New Haven, CT: Yale University Press, 1989.

Radford, Rosemary. "A Query to Daniel Sullivan: Bonhoeffer on Sexuality." *Continuum* 4, no. 3 (Autumn 1966) 457–60.

Root, Andrew. *Bonhoeffer as Youth Worker: A Theological Vision for Discipleship and Life Together*. Grand Rapids: Baker Academic, 2014.

Rosenbaum, Ron. *Explaining Hitler: The Search for the Origins of His Evil*. New York: HarperCollins, 1999.

Rowe, Dorothy. "Desiring Berlin: Gender and Modernity in Weimar Germany." In *Visions of the "Neue Frau": Women and the Visual Arts in Weimar Germany*, edited by Marsha Meskimmon and Shearer West, 143–64. Menston, England: Scolar, 1995.

Rubenstein, Richard L. "Was Dietrich Bonhoeffer a Righteous Gentile?" *Newenglishreview.org*, April 2011. http://www.newenglishreview.org/custpage.cfm/frm/29721/sec_id/86357.

Rumscheidt, H. Martin. "Harnack, Seeberg, and Bonhoeffer." In *Bonhoeffer's Intellectual Formation: Theology and Philosophy in His Thought*, edited by Peter Frick, 211. Tübingen: Mohr Siebeck, 2008.

———. "Writing to the Spouse from Prison: Dietrich Bonhoeffer and Vaclav Havel." In *Reflections on Bonhoeffer: Essays in Honor of F. Burton Nelson*, edited by Geffrey B. Kelly and C. John Weborg, 199–209. Chicago: Covenant, 1999.

Said, Edward W. *Orientalism*. New York: Vintage, 1979.

Santayana, George. *The Last Puritan: A Memoir in the Form of a Novel*. New York: Charles Scribner, 1940.

Schlingensiepen, Ferdinand. *Dietrich Bonhoeffer 1906–1945*. Translated by Isabel Best. London: T & T Clark, International, 2010.

Sereny, Gitta. *Albert Speer: His Battle for Truth*. New York: Vintage, 1996.

Sherratt, Yvonne. *Hitler's Philosophers*. New Haven, CT: Yale University Press, 2013.

Shirer, William L. *Berlin Diary*. New York: Alfred Knopf, 1941.

———. *The Rise and Fall of the Third Reich: A History of Nazi Germany*. New York: Simon and Schuster, 1960.

Sider, Ronald J. *Nonviolent Action: What Christian Ethics Demands But Most Christians Have Never Really Tried*. Grand Rapids: Brazos, 2015.

Smith, Robert. "Bonhoeffer and Musical Metaphor." *Word & World* 26, no. 2, Spring 2006. Online: http://wordandworld.luthersem.edu/content/pdfs/26-2_renewing_worship/26-2_smith.pdf.

Smith, Roberta. "A New Exhibit Highlights Cultural Decadence of Weimar Germany—Culture—International Herald Tribune." *The New York Times*, October 24, 2006. http://www.nytimes.com/2006/11/24/arts/24iht-germart.3653712.html.

Speer, Albert. *Inside the Third Reich*. New York: Simon & Schuster, 1997.

"Starvation and Disease." http://www.nationalarchives.gov.uk/pathways/firstworldwar/spotlights/blockade.htm.

Stephenson, Jill. *Women in Nazi Society*. London: Routledge, 2001.

Steppe, Hilde. "Nursing Under Totalitarian Regimes." In *Nursing History and the Politics of Welfare*, edited by Anne Marie Rafferty, Jane Robinson, and Ruth Elkan, 11–28. London: Routledge, 1997.

Stern, Fritz, and Elisabeth Sifton. *No Ordinary Men: Dietrich Bonhoeffer and Hans von Dohnanyi, Resisters Against Hitler in Church and State*. New York: New York Review Books, 2013.

Stifter, Adalbert. *Indian Summer*. Translated by Wendell Frye. New York: Peter Lang, 2006.

Stowe, Harriet Beecher. *Uncle Tom's Cabin or Life Among the Lowly*. http://www.saylor.org/site/wp-content/uploads/2011/11/saylor-Engl405-7.3-uncletom.pdf.

Theweleit, Klaus. *Male Fantasies, Vol. 1: Women, Floods, Bodies, History*. Translated by Chris Turner, Stephen Conway, and Erica Carter. Minneapolis: University of Minnesota Press, 1987.

Vat, Dan Van Der. *The Good Nazi: The Life and Lies of Albert Speer.* Boston: Houghton Mifflin Harcourt, 1997.
Wedemeyer-Weller, Maria von. "The Other Letters from Prison." In *Letters and Papers From Prison,* by Dietrich Bonhoeffer and Eberhard Bethge, 412–19. New York: Macmillan, 1972.
Wind, Renate. *Dietrich Bonhoeffer: A Spoke in the Wheel.* Translated by John Bowden. Grand Rapids: Eerdmans, 1992.
"Winter 1940/41 a climatic research delight." *Seaclimate.com.* http://www.seaclimate.com/d/d.html.
Wolfe, Thomas. *You Can't Go Home Again.* New York: Sun Dial, 1942.
"World War II Resistance: Operation Valkyrie: The 'July Plot' to Assassinate Hitler." *Jewish Virtual Library.* http://www.jewishvirtuallibrary.org/jsource/Holocaust/julyplot.html.
Young, Josiah Ulysses. *No Difference in the Fare.* Grand Rapids: Eerdmans, 1998.
Zerner, Ruth. "Dietrich Bonhoeffer's Prison Fiction: A Commentary." In *Fiction from Prison: Gathering up the Past,* edited by Renate and Eberhard Bethge, 139–67. Philadelphia: Fortress, 1978.
Zimmermann, Wolf-Dieter, and Ronald Gregor Smith, eds. *I Knew Dietrich Bonhoeffer.* Translated by Käthe Gregor Smith. New York: Harper and Row, 1966.

Index

Abyssinian Baptist Church, 66, 134, 186
Act and Being, 63
After Ten Years, 294–95
Altenburg, *See* Magdalenen-Stift boarding school
Andreas-Friedrich, Ruth, 303, 362

Bai, Mira, 88
Barcelona, 53, 61–62, 71, 117, 132, 275, 374
Barmen Declaration, 85, 111
Barnett, Victoria, 153
Barth, Karl, 73n22, 76, 77, 85, 87, 99, 117, 119, 137, 218, 349, 351
Beck, Ludwig, 271
Bell, George, Bishop of Chichester, 21, 81–82, 87, 112, 146, 150, 152, 173, 176, 177, 181, 184, 216, 245, 251, 258, 280–81, 303, 339, 390, 409
Bell, Henrietta, 82
Berggrav, Eivind, 273
Berneuchens, 277
Best, Payne, 406, 408, 409
Bethel, 128–29
Bethge, Christophe, 321
Bethge, Eberhard, 97–100, 104–05, 109, 119–21, 125–27, 129, 132, 135, 138, 139–42, 150, 152, 153–54, 159, 160–64, 166–67, 168, 169, 175, 177, 179–82, 183–97, 201–04, 208–09, 210, 211–214, 218, 219, 221, 223–25, 226, 230, 231–35, 237–44, 247, 248–49, 252, 254–55, 257, 263–65, 270, 273, 278, 283, 285, 291–93, 296, 298, 299, 300–01, 304, 305, 308, 310, 318, 319–24, 327, 331, 332, 333, 334, 336–339, 340, 341, 342–44, 349–61, 363–367, 368–69, 371, 373–76, 377–83, 385, 389, 390, 393, 394, 395, 399, 400–02, 411–13, 415, 416, 420, 428–31, 433–34
Bethge, Elisabeth, 189, 234, 235, 237, 310
Bethge, Hans, 321
Bethge, Renate, 42n18, 100, 203, 212, 241–43, 252, 271, 286, 287, 292, 296, 299, 301, 305, 308, 310, 319–21, 323, 331, 332, 336, 339, 343, 352, 356, 358, 359, 361, 368, 378, 379, 380, 382, 385, 393, 401, 411, 433
Beveridge, William, 181, 181n17
Bismarck, Hedwig von, 115
Bismarck, Herbert von, 115
Bismarck, Klaus von, 197, 317, 413
Bismarck, Ruth Alice von, 110, 119, 197–98, 229, 272, 276, 325, 341, 380, 413, 415
Blaskowitz, Johannes, 207
Block, Eduard, 159
Bluher, Ernst, 141
Bonhoeffer, Cristel, *See* Dohnanyi, Christine Bonhoeffer

Bonhoeffer, Dietrich,
  Buchenwald, 405–08, 410
  Childhood and teen years, 21–45
  Collective pastorates, 159–160,
    161–62, 163–64, 176, 182–83,
    203, 204, 208–09, 211–213
  Ettal, 229–44
  Flossenbürg, 408–10 New York,
    1939, 183–193
  Königsberg retreat, 222–23
  Maria, 282–03, 305, 324–329,
    331–2, 333–36, 339–40, 343–44,
    349–50, 351–52, 354–59, 361,
    365–69, 370–78, 379–81, 382,
    383–85, 393–95, 397, 407,
    415–17
  Prinz Albertstrasse prison, 397–99,
    401–02, 405
  Prison fiction, 336–37, 338,
    340, 366n18, 367   Prison
    sermon-321–23
  Seminaries, 94–111, 119–121, 131–
    32, 135–38, 152–53, 155
  Sexuality, 140–144, 233–34, 428–35
  Tafel, 28, 32, 35, 36–37, 39, 40, 44,
    49, 56n22, 62, 65, 66, 87, 88, 89,
    127–129
  Tegel prison, 310–21, 323–24, 333,
    337, 339, 341, 349–53, 357–58,
    360, 363, 374–75, 378, 381,
    389–90, 393, 397
  Theology, 53–54, 72–73, 134, 134n2,
    154n30, 169, 172, 178, 254–57,
    363–64, 378–79, 393, 395,
    419–20, 433
  Thoughts on death, 194–97, 222,
    409
  Trip with Vibrans, 139–140
  Visiting Sabine in London, 1939,
    179–182, 194, 197, 198
  Young adulthood, 46–53, 55–63,
    65–93
Bonhoeffer, Emmi Delbrück, 36, 47, 55,
  79, 227–28, 318, 338, 398
Bonhoeffer, Julie Tafel, 21, 28, 29, 32, 35,
  36–37, 39, 40, 44, 56n22, 49, 57,
  62, 65, 66, 69, 87, 88, 89, 126,
  127–129, 131

Bonhoeffer, Karl, 21, 25, 35, 42, 44, 49,
  55, 56, 71, 126, 127, 154, 182,
  183, 191, 192, 202, 204, 215,
  286, 292, 304, 305, 306, 318,
  321, 322n1, 324, 339, 353, 394
Bonhoeffer, Karl-Friedrich, 30, 33, 42,
  54, 67, 89, 127, 184, 185, 191,
  193, 197, 208, 308, 315, 318,
  324, 359, 398, 412
Bonhoeffer, Klaus, 30, 33, 36, 40, 42, 49,
  50, 51, 55, 73, 84, 206, 304, 306,
  397, 401, 411, 412
Bonhoeffer, Paula, 21, 26–27, 28, 31,
  33, 34, 37, 41, 43, 44, 52, 69, 70,
  78, 81, 89, 21, 94, 104, 105, 112,
  126, 127, 150, 160, 161, 163,
  164, 172, 174, 175, 177, 179,
  182, 191, 192, 202, 203, 207,
  210, 211, 223, 230, 265, 292,
  295, 317, 318, 320, 321, 324,
  327, 328, 353, 359, 368, 383,
  385, 399, 403, 419
Bonhoeffer, Sabine. *See* Leibholz, Sabine
  Bonhoeffer
Bonhoeffer, Susanne. *See* Dress, Susi
  Bonhoeffer
Bonhoeffer, Ursula. *See* Schleicher, Ursel
  Bonhoeffer
Bonhoeffer, Walter, 30, 33, 34, 35, 37,
  44, 194, 195, 258, 286
Book burning, 73
Bormann, Martin, 151, 161,
Bornkamm, Gunther, 133
Brand, Adolf, 141
Brauchitsch, Walther von, 271
Braun, Bertha, 307
Breslau, 21, 25, 34, 53, 112
Buchenwald concentration camp, 405,
  408
Bundorf, 369–70, 373, 375, 377
Butler, Judith, 143

Canaris, Wilhelm, 211, 271, 393, 397,
  410
Chamberlain, Neville, 206,
Chardonne, Jacques, 263
Cheap grace, 134, 134n2, 154n30, 169,
  178

The Church and the Jewish Question, 72, 72n21
Churchill, Winston, 163, 217, 251, 280, 344
Confessing Church, 82n38, 85, 89, 94, 95, 99, 100, 108, 111, 119, 120, 131, 133, 135, 136, 137, 138, 142, 147, 149, 150, 152, 153, 159, 160, 161, 162, 173, 176, 182, 191, 206, 218, 222, 223, 227, 228, 229, 230, 238, 248, 261, 271, 274, 308, 313, 363
Creation and Fall, 53–54, 255, 258, 431, 433
Communion of Saints, 56
Coffin, Henry Sloane, 186
Cuba, 28, 67–68, 275, 334
Czechoslovakia, 149, 163, 167, 168, 169–70, 180, 205, 227, 256

Dahill, Lisa, 255, 256, 432
Dannenbaum, Hans, 363
Denmark, 86, 135, 275
Delbrück, Emmi, *See* Bonhoeffer, Emmi.
Discipleship, 134n2, 135, 136, 154, 169, 231, 248, 264–65
Dinesen, Isak, 214
Dodd, Martha, 204
Dohnanyi, Bärbel von, 218, 320
Dohnanyi, Christine von (Christel) Bonhoeffer, 30, 39, 46, 49, 53, 54, 55, 81, 87, 125, 130, 220, 232, 234, 245, 298, 305, 318, 320, 368, 381, 398, 407, 412
Dohnanyi, Grete von, 51, 54, 55n21, 74, 120, 308
Dohnanyi, Hans von, 55, 74, 81, 107, 120, 125, 154, 165, 168, 211, 223, 224, 230, 234, 261, 271, 273, 288, 289, 291, 295, 303, 304–05, 308, 310, 318, 319, 333, 396, 401, 407, 410, 411, 412
Dohnanyi, Klaus von, 218
Dramm, Sabine, 305
Dress, Susi Bonhoeffer, 25, 26, 27, 30, 33, 34–35, 36, 39, 52, 53, 55, 62, 63, 81, 107n2, 131, 308, 318, 320, 333, 359–60, 393–94, 412

Dress, Walter, 55, 62, 81, 107, 144, 161, 308, 412, 429, 430
Droste-Hülshoff, Annette, 105
Dürer, Albrecht, 104, 212, 323, 363

Ethics, 224, 229, 230, 250, 251, 255, 256n9, 257, 282, 282, 301, 310, 356, 408, 414, 433
Eden, Anthony, 280
Ettal, 53, 230–43, 301, 342, 358

Fahle, Doris, 273, 384
Fallada, Hans, 196–97
Findahl, Theo, 344–45, 405
Finkenwalde, 53, 101–09, 110–11, 119–120, 127–28, 129, 132, 136, 138, 139, 142, 152, 153, 154, 159, 160, 168, 169, 183, 218, 236, 240, 258, 264, 308, 331, 395, 429,
Fisher, Frank, 66, 186
Flossenbürg concentraton camp, 407, 408–10, 417, 419
Friedenthal, Charlotte, 271
Friedrichsbrunn, 29–31, 36, 40, 49, 52, 65, 177, 163, 235, 239, 243, 248–49, 250, 330, 334, 359–60
Freudenberg, Adolf, 258–59
Friedrich, Leonhart, 397–98

Gandhi, 82, 87–89, 154n30, 414
Gay, Peter, 83
Gersdorff, Henriette Catharina, von, 145
Goebbels, Joseph, 73, 118, 190, 248, 262, 306, 402
Goethe, Johann, 73, 125, 207, 296, 331
Gollwitzer, Helmut, 138, 432
Göring, Hermann, 74, 167, 247, 302, 319, 363
Göttingen, 68, 69, 72, 82, 83, 86, 126, 153, 163, 166, 167–68, 171, 172, 174, 325n7
Green, Clifford, 143–44
Gross-Schlönwitz, 160, 240
Gruber, Heinrich, 212
Guttenberg. Karl-Ludwig von, 338

INDEX

Haeften, Hans Bernd von, 274
Haeften, Werner von, 291, 392
Haensel, Carl, 210
Harnack, Adolf von, 79–80, 132
Hase, Elisabeth von, 127, 174
Hase, Hans von, 34,
Hase, Hans-Christoph von, 34, 429, 430
Hase, Karl Alfred von, 43
Hase, Paul von, 315, 389, 392
Hildebrandt, Franz, 78–81, 87, 95, 100, 104, 119, 120, 150, 152, 180, 430
Himmler, Heinrich, 135, 223, 271
Hirschfeld, Magnus, 141
Hitler, Adolf, 25, 36n14, 38, 42, 64, 69, 71–75, 78, 78n10, 80, 83, 84–86, 94, 97, 99–100, 108, 112, 115, 117, 118, 126, 127, 129, 130, 134, 136–37, 150–51, 153, 154, 161–62, 163, 164, 168, 169, 181, 182, 185, 198, 201–02, 203, 204–05, 206–07, 210, 211, 216, 221, 226–28, 229, 236, 245, 248, 250–51, 257, 261, 262, 271, 272, 291, 295–96, 302, 306, 307, 309, 405, 407, 411, 412, 414
Hitler, Alois, 288, 416
Hitler, conspiracy against, 159, 163, 168–69, 210–11, 223, 224, 226, 227–28, 246, 271–72, 274, 280–81, 304–05, 389–96
Hitler Youth, 75, 82, 190, 221, 232
Hohenzollern, Prince Louis Ferdinand, 127, 280, 304
Horn, Käthe, 27, 28, 29, 30, 35, 67, 419
Horn, Maria, 27, 28, 29, 34–35, 67, 419
Hyperinflation, 49

India, 65, 87–89, 127–28

Jacobi, Gerhard, 87n15, 89
Jehle, Herbert, 108, 414
Jensen, Hans-Werner, 105
Judaism, Jews, 25, 42, 43, 52, 53, 63, 69, 70, 72, 72n21, 73, 74, 74n31, 75, 76n2, 78, 80, 82, 82n38, 83, 84, 105, 114, 118, 119, 120, 128, 130, 132, 135, 136, 137, 138, 146, 147, 151, 152, 153, 165, 168, 172, 180, 181n17, 185, 202, 203, 212, 214, 216, 219, 229, 237, 245, 250, 261–62, 271, 274, 290, 295, 302, 307, 363, 392, 396, 397, 411, 414

Kelly, Thomas, 196
Kleist, Dieter von, 183
Kleist, Ewald von, 163, 224, 304
Kleist, Hans Jurgen von, 118, 149, 237, 264, 265, 277, 299, 317, 357–8, 393, 408
Kleist, Jurgen von, 112–14, 116
Klein Krössin, 135–36, 152, 161, 169, 211, 218, 224–25, 250, 251–53, 265, 270, 271, 278, 282–83, 283n18, 284n25, 284n26, 285, 290, 325n7, 354, 407, 408
Kleist-Retzow, Ruth von, 109, 110–111, 112–119, 121, 127–28, 129, 131, 132, 135–36, 146, 148, 149, 150, 152, 153, 154, 161, 162, 163, 164, 168, 169, 173, 174, 179, 182, 183–84, 190, 192, 193, 211, 212, 217–18, 221, 223, 224, 226, 229, 231, 233, 234, 237, 239, 240, 241–43, 250, 251, 252–53, 254, 257, 263–64, 265–66, 270, 271, 272, 273, 275, 277–79, 282–83, 284, 285, 286–89, 290–91, 292, 293, 294, 296, 297, 298–99, 300, 302, 303, 305, 309, 317n1, 320, 325n7, 331, 333, 334, 335, 338, 351, 354, 355, 358, 359, 367, 369, 371, 374, 376, 377, 381, 385, 393, 407–08, 413, 419, 434
Kleist-Schmenzin. Ewald von, 118, 163, 224, 304
Klemperer, Victor, 83, 313–14
Klinger, Max, 195,
Kerrl, Hanns, 120, 131, 149
Kieckow, 114, 115, 116, 119, 136, 161, 193, 236, 252, 257, 264, 265, 270, 271, 273, 282, 408, 413
Klapproth, Erich, 269–70
Knobloch, Corporal, 341, 393, 397

Koch, Walter, 101–02, 111, 119, 137, 146–48, 173–74
Koch, Dita, 152, 164, 355, 393
Koenigs-Kalckreuth, Mucki, 174
Königsberg, 220, 222, 223, 224
Koschorke, Manfred, 222
Köslin, 114, 159, 172, 179, 204
Kristallnacht, 29, 172
Kupfer, Angelus, 231

Lasserre, Jean, 66, 186
Lee, Jason, 432
Lehel, Ferenc, 70
Lehman, Paul, 22n1, 73, 22n1, 70
Lehne, Gerhard, 160
Letters and Papers from Prison, 325, 326, 414, 415
Leiper, Henry, 187, 189
Liehholz, Christiane, 66, 82, 166, 176, 216, 217, 260,
Liebholz, Gerhard (Gert), 44n26, 50, 52, 53, 55, 63, 66, 68, 69–70, 72, 74, 77, 82–83, 86, 89, 94, 120, 126, 130, 132, 165–75, 176–81, 186, 189n4, 193, 212, 215–217, 220–21, 224, 235, 245, 258, 260–61, 280–81, 306, 364, 412
Liebholz, Hans, 130, 217
Liebholz, Marianne, 56, 63, 82, 166–67, 217, 272, 390
Liebholz, Peter, 172
Leibholz, Sabine Bonhoeffer. 25–28, 30–36, 38, 39, 42–57, 62–64, 66–69, 72, 77–78, 82–83, 84, 86, 87, 89, 94, 107, 109, 120, 126, 128, 129,130–32, 133, 136, 142, 144, 148, 153, 154, 161, 163, 164–175, 176–181, 183, 184, 186, 189, 190, 191, 193–94, 197–198, 202, 203–04, 206, 211, 212, 213, 215–217, 220–21, 224–25, 228, 235, 237, 243, 245, 251, 257, 258, 260–61, 265, 273–74, 275, 279, 280–81, 283, 284, 296, 300, 306, 320, 321, 325n7, 331, 332, 338, 339, 360, 366, 368, 373, 375, 383, 390, 393, 395, 412, 416, 419, 432, 434

Leibholz, William, 63, 72, 77–78
Life Together, 168, 192, 231, 248
London, 53, 75, 76–89, 93, 130, 132, 137, 149, 150, 152, 168, 171–73, 175, 177, 178, 179–182, 184, 193–94, 197, 198, 206, 213, 215, 217, 275, 302, 412
Lublin transport, 212
Lutheran, Martin, 98, 99, 227

Mackensen, Stefanie von, 109, 119, 153, 162
Macy, Paul, 186
Magdalenen-Stift boarding school, 145–46, 152, 208, 310, 330, 331, 351, 364–65, 369, 377
Manhattan, 63, 65–67, 68, 78, 88, 108, 130, 184–192, 231, 275, 375, 429
Manning, Olivia, 219
Marsh, Charles, 431
Mayer, Rupert, 231
Metaxas, Eric, 132, 326
Mein Kampf, 117, 149
Meusel, Marga, 120
Moltke, Helmuth von, 273, 274, 393
Muggeridge, Malcolm, 309, 417, 419
Müller, Josef, 400
Munich, 21, 78n9, 230–31, 234, 237, 284n26, 285, 286, 300–01, 302, 304, 394, 400

Niebuhr, Reinhold, 71, 182
Niemöller, Else, 150
Niemöller, Martin, 119, 149–52, 154, 161, 173, 211, 251, 264, 358, 363, 414
Niesel, Wilhelm, 87n15, 107
Ninow, Klara, 285
Norway, 135, 273
Nursing, Nazi Germany, 307–08, Maria, 301, 309–10, 317, 327, 335, 344 white nurse, 308–09, 327, 336–37, 338

Oetinger, Friedrich Christoph, 57
Olbricht, Fritz, 61
Onnasch, Fritz, 211, 308

Onnasch, Margret Bethge, 211, 234, 264, 270

Papen, Franz von, 85–86, 146
Paradise, Scott, 415
Pastors' Emergency League, 75, 248
Pätzig, 116, 146, 197–98, 201, 275–78, 284, 290, 291, 296–97, 301, 317, 326, 329, 330, 342, 349, 357, 358, 359, 365, 371, 381, 385, 389, 394, 403–04, 408, 414, 417–18
Perels, Friedrich, 261–62
Poelchau, Harald, 363
Polyphony, 378–79, 433
Powell, Clayton, Sr., 66, 134, 154n30

Quakers, 105, 108, 196, 397, 414

Rabenau, Friedrich von, 406
Rau, Arthur, 264
Ravensbrück concentration camp, 363
The Responsibility of Landed Property in the Social Crisis, 117
Reinhardt, Max, 73, 180
Rieger, Julius, 79, 84, 150, 152, 175, 197
Rilke, Rainer Maria, 351, 416
Ritter, Karl Bernhard, 277
Roeder, Manfred, 291, 318–19, 328–29, 331, 338, 355
Rome, 50–51, 61, 142, 283
Rosenberg, Alfred, 149, 244
Rott, Wilhelm, 153, 228
Rougemont, Denis de, 134, 137
Rudolf, Anna, 357
Rumscheidt, Martin H., 325
Russia, 43, 76n2, 187, 198, 204, 223, 250, 254, 257, 262, 264, 265, 266, 269–70, 271, 279, 284, 286, 289, 298, 338, 357, 369, 389, 396, 403,-04, 407–08, 410, 411, 412

Sachsenhausen concentration camp, 146–48, 154, 161, 173, 211, 401, 410
Salomon, Otto, 280
Sander, Erwin, 269

Santayana, George, *The Last Puritan*, 233, 301, 366n18, 432–33
Sayre, Lucy, 415
Schlabrendorff, Fabian von, 304, 393, 397, 398, 405, 413
Schlawe, 159, 179, 183
Schleicher, Hans-Werner, 287, 320, 321, 324aaaff
Schleicher, Rüdiger, 55, 74, 252–53, 264, 292, 304, 305, 321, 360, 397, 398, 401, 411, 412, 431
Schleicher, Ursel Bonhoeffer, 30, 53, 126, 171, 192, 203, 238, 252, 292, 305, 310, 315, 318, 320, 343, 374, 398, 401, 412
Schmidhuber, Wilhelm, 272, 289, 290, 291
Schniewind, Paul, 414
Scholl, Hans and Sophie, 302
Schulze, Berta, 79–81
Schnurmann, Anneliese, 69, 245
Shirach, Baldur von, 263,
Shirer, William, 83, 151, 154, 180, 190n5, 204, 211, 215, 251
Sigurdshof, 181, 183, 190, 203, 204, 208, 210, 211, 213, 240, 243, 271, 395
Slave labor, forced labor, 250, 274, 306, 333, 357–59, 360n27
Smith, Howard, 262–63
Smith, Kay, 41, 94
Solf Circle, 363
Sonderegger, Franz, 318, 398, 402
Speer, Albert, 36n14, 38, 41n10, 150n11, 151, 201, 261, 270, 344, 345, 360n27, 362, 396
Stahlberg, Alexander (Alla), 153, 218, 264
Stahlberg, Raba, 118,
Stahlberg, Spes, 114–15, 118, 149, 285, 286, 287, 289, 327
Stahlberg, Walter, 114–15, 118
Stalin, Joseph, 203, 204, 369
Stauffenberg, Claus Schenk, von, 251, 389–90
Staritz, Katharina, 262
Stockmann, Dita, *See* Koch, Dita.
Struwe, Erna, 107, 153, 160, 182, 192, 193, 419

INDEX

Sussbach, Willy, 136
Sutz, Erwin, 67, 69, 85, 88, 169, 186, 251, 279, 306, 383
Sweden, 132, 135, 273–74, 275, 280–81, 282, 303
Switzerland, 67, 130, 139, 167, 186, 194, 211, 212, 237, 238, 245, 248, 251, 257, 258, 261, 262, 271, 279, 280, 285, 301, 306

Thadden, Elisabeth von, 228–29, 250, 272, 294, 363, 396
Theweleit, Klaus, 308–09, 326, 336n17, 337n20
Thimme, Hans, 108
Tillich, Ernst, 137, 146–48
Traub, Helmut, 138, 183, 203
Tresckow, Henning von, 198, 304
Trott zu Solz, Adam von, 393
Truchess, Hediwig (Hesi) von, 369, 370–71, 376, 378, 394
Tübingen, 28–29, 43, 44, 46–49, 53, 56n22

Uncle Tom's Cabin, 30, 66, 195
Union Theological Seminary, 22n1, 63, 65–66, 73, 186, 279,

Vibrans, Gerhard, 99, 105, 139–42, 232, 239, 270, 343, 429
Visser t'Hooft, Wilhelm, 248

Warner, Konrad, 362
Wedemeyer, Christine (Ina) von, 221, 330–31, 364
Wedemeyer, Hans von, 85, 115, 116, 118, 146, 169
Wedemeyer, Hans Werner von, 221, 278
Wedemeyer, Maria von, 110, 111, 119, 133, 144, 145–46, 152–53, 164, 197–98, 208, 221, 228–29, 250, 257, 272–73, 275–83, 284–94, 296–99, 300, 301–02, 303, 304, 305, 307–10, 317, 318, 319, 323, 324–27, 328–32, 333–37, 338–40, 341–44, 349–50, 351–52, 353, 354–57, 358–59, 360, 361, 363, 364–67, 368–72, 373–79, 380–85, 393, 394–95, 396, 397, 398, 401, 402, 403–04, 407, 412, 414–18, 419, 429, 430, 433, 434
Wedemeyer, Max von, 119, 161, 257, 272, 275, 279, 284, 286, 289, 290, 297, 305, 326, 338, 353, 354, 355, 373, 381, 385
Wedemeyer, Ruth von (Ruthchen), 115–16, 272, 276, 284, 290, 291, 292, 293, 296, 299, 300, 324, 330, 354, 357, 370–71, 376, 403–04, 408, 413, 415
Weissler, Friedrich, 146–48
Weller, Bart, 414–15
White Rose Letters, 302
Why Should One Read the Bible?, 164
Wind, Renate, 133
Wise, Stephen, 73
Wohlbruck, Adolf, 180
Wolfe, Thomas, 196

Zimmermann, Wolf-Dieter, 70–71, 72, 78–79, 138, 233, 254, 291, 351, 392, 432, 433
Zingst, 95–102, 104, 109, 120, 137, 163, 164, 243
Zinn, Elisabeth, 56–57, 86, 89n26, 132–33, 142, 144, 419, 429, 430
Zinzendorf, Count, 27, 28, 145
Zossen file, 396
Zurich, 142, 168, 169, 186, 216, 245, 258, 279